Holy Scripture

and the Quest

for Authority

at the End of the

Middle Ages

READING THE SCRIPTURES

Gary A. Anderson, Matthew Levering, and Robert Louis Wilken

series editors

Holy Scripture and the Quest for Authority at the End of the Middle Ages

IAN CHRISTOPHER LEVY

University of Notre Dame Press
Notre Dame, Indiana

Copyrght © 2012 by University of Notre Dame
Notre Dame, Indiana 46556
www.undpress.nd.edu
All Rights Reserved

Manufactured in the United States of America

Library of Congress Cataloging-in-Publication Data

Levy, Ian Christopher.
  Holy Scripture and the quest for authority at the end of the Middle Ages / Ian Christopher Levy.
      p.   cm. — (Reading the Scriptures)
  Includes bibliographical references and index.
  ISBN-13: 978-0-268-03414-6 (pbk. : alk. paper)
  ISBN-10: 0-268-03414-1 (pbk. : alk. paper)
  E-ISBN: 978-0-268-08581-0
  1. Bible—Evidences, authority, etc.—History of doctrines—Middle Ages, 600–1500.   2. Church history—Middle Ages, 600–1500.   I. Title.
  BS480.L48   2012
  220.109'02—dc23

2012006673

∞ *The paper in this book meets the guidelines for permanence and durability of the Committee on Production Guidelines for Book Longevity of the Council on Library Resources.*

For my colleagues in the Theology Department at Providence College

Tu es ergo regula veritatis?
Quicquid contra te fuerit, non est verum?
—Augustine, *Contra Faustum* 11.2

Contents

List of Abbreviations	ix
Preface	xi
Acknowledgments	xv
1. Facets of Authority in the Late Medieval Church	1
2. The Indignant Master: John Wyclif	54
3. The Ambivalent Friar: William Woodford	92
4. *Ad Fontes* (?): Thomas Netter	117
5. A Falling Out: Hussites and Their Czech Opponents	150
6. Approaching Final Authority: Gerson and the Conciliarists	189
7. The Enduring Dilemma	222
Notes	236
Bibliography	288
Index	302

Abbreviations

CCCM	*Corpus Christianorum. Continuatio Medieavalis.* Turnhout, 1971– .
CCSL	*Corpus Christianorum. Series Latina.* Turnhout, 1953– .
CSEL	*Corpus Scriptorum Ecclesiasticorum Latinorum.* Vienna, 1866– .
Denzinger	*Enchiridion Symbolorum.* 36th ed. Ed. Henry Denzinger and Adolf Schönmetzer. Rome, 1976.
Friedberg	*Corpus iuris canonici.* 2 vols. Ed. Emil Friedberg. Leipzig, 1879; reprint Graz, 1960.
PG	*Patrologia Cursus Completus. Series Graeca.* Ed. J. P. Migne. Paris, 1857– .
PL	*Patrologia Latina Cursus Completus. Series Latina.* Ed. J. P. Migne. Paris, 1844– .

Preface

Holy Scripture was accepted as the principal foundation of authority in the late medieval church. Everyone—popes, theologians, and lawyers— was bound by the divine truth it conveyed. No teaching or practice could stand if it were proven to contradict Holy Scripture. But if the principal authority of scripture was itself universally accepted, the interpretation and subsequent application of its inspired meaning remained fiercely contested. All sides of the many debates that persisted throughout the Middle Ages were in search of an authoritative determination of the biblical text. This study focuses on the quest for such authority that occurred roughly between the years 1370 and 1430, from John Wyclif to Thomas Netter, thereby encompassing the struggle over Holy Scripture waged between Wycliffites and Hussites on the one side and their British and Continental opponents on the other. No matter the precise subject at issue—be it the sacraments or the papacy—the discussions were dominated by the same fundamental questions: By what means does one arrive at an authoritative reading of Holy Scripture that will decide the matter at hand; and who is in a position to determine whether that reading is correct and therefore authoritative? In short, if Holy Scripture is the principal criterion of doctrinal truth, then these questions pertain directly to the determination of orthodoxy and heresy in the late medieval church.

Without questioning the sincerity of such theologians as William Woodford, Thomas Netter, or Jean Gerson, the fact remains that they were intent on constructing a narrative in which their Wycliffite and Hussite opponents were dangerous heretics with scant regard for the inherent authority of catholic tradition. Having severed themselves from the larger tradition, these "heretics" had broken loose from the accepted standards and channels of orthodoxy. More specifically—in light of the authoritative status of Holy Scripture—there was a concerted effort to de-legitimize Wycliffite and Hussite biblical exegesis, presenting it as specious and tendentious, beyond the bounds of the generally accepted norms sanctioned by the greater tradition. This may have been an effective polemical move, but it was in fact a massive distortion of their opponents' exegetical principles and methodology. As one analyzes these debates it becomes clear that the effort to construct the prevailing narrative of Wycliffite and Hussite "heresy" was largely driven by the deep-seated realization that the Oxford and Prague dissenters were too firmly entrenched in the long-established tradition of medieval exegesis and academic debate to be decisively defeated. John Wyclif and Jan Hus adhered to, and argued on the basis of, the same sources of authority as their adversaries. Indeed, all sides of the debate shared the same fundamental catholic assumptions and aspirations.

One should never lose sight of the context in which these debates most often took place: these were sophisticated disputes conducted among university masters. Wyclif and Hus, along with their opponents, were all very much part of the establishment. Indeed, one could not be much more deeply embedded in the power structure of medieval society than to hold a magisterial position at Oxford or Prague. Again, one is struck by the tremendous amount of common ground that all sides shared. They all held recognized licenses of expertise, venerated the catholic tradition, esteemed the church fathers, and embraced Holy Scripture as the principal authority in Christendom. What is more, they all shared the same hermeneutical strategies with regard to authorial intention, the literal sense, and appeal to the fathers and holy doctors in order to open up the text. What separated Jan Hus from Jean Gerson—the man who went to the stake and the man who sent him there—was almost nothing in comparison to what these two had in common. And it is precisely this commonality that rendered the situation virtually intractable. Hence the effort to frame the whole narrative in such bold strokes so as to relegate the Oxford and Prague "Wycliffites" to the margins. Only when presented as extreme outriders could their positions be effectively proscribed. The lamentable irony is not that the Netter/Gerson narrative prevailed in its own day, however, but rather that it has since taken hold among many modern scholars, who readily accept the categories of orthodoxy and heresy as defined by one set of fifteenth-century protagonists. Indeed, it is commonplace to assume that Netter and Gerson spoke for "the church," whereas Wyclif and Hus were ultimately destructive forces who would tear down this institution. Yet the boundaries between heresy and orthodoxy were never so neatly drawn.

None of this is to say that Woodford, Netter, and Gerson did not generate serious arguments to counter their adept adversaries. But a close reading of those arguments exposes an underlying ambivalence in their own conceptualization of authority. They are not certain themselves where the most authoritative line of argument rests when attempting to establish the correct interpretation of scripture. No doubt they were placed in a difficult position by their opponents, but they had no fully coherent system of authority at their disposal that could meet the sophisticated parries of their reform-minded adversaries. Hence we often find the same writer torn between appeals to the authority of antiquity and that of the present hierarchy of the church. Even appeals to the universal and apostolic church are often vague upon reflection, especially given the fact that their opponents believe just as deeply in the very same church. The truth is that even as Holy Scripture was recognized by all sides as the principal authority in matters of doctrine, Catholicism in the early fifteenth century possessed no absolute means of determining the final authoritative meaning of the biblical text—hence the range of appeals to antiquity, to the papacy, and to councils, none of which were conclusive. In this pre-Tridentine era no one had yet determined the sort of absolutely fixed boundaries of authority that were adopted in the wake of the Protestant Reformation. Thus even as Gerson (unlike Woodford and Netter) believed general councils to be infallible and ultimately superior to the pope, this was itself a contested principle of authority in its own time, which was formally condemned just a few decades later by papal decree. Hence despite what we might call a "rhetoric of finality," which was displayed in an attempt to present these contentious matters as "settled" and thus no longer open for discussion, there was precious little foundation for such assertions.

None of the foregoing should be taken to imply that orthodoxy itself is a relative concept with no objective referent; or worse yet, that it is merely a "power construct" designed to achieve political ends. That is not the case: orthodoxy is objectively real, and it does matter. And orthodoxy certainly did matter to those involved in the late medieval debates that we will examine throughout this book. All the theologians involved sincerely believed that they could locate orthodox doctrine within Holy Scripture as it had been explicated over the centuries by the sacred tradition. Wyclif and Hus were deeply committed to Jesus Christ and the Catholic Church. It is precisely for that reason that they pressed for reform, indeed the very reform of the church in head and members that their opponents also sought. Even if one were to argue that Netter proposed a more reasonable path than Wyclif, that does not amount to proving the former orthodox and the latter heretical. Nor would that determination settle the larger issue as to who has the final authority to bring these debates to a close. Authority in the late medieval church was such a vexing matter precisely because it had not been fully resolved. We should resist, therefore, an anachronistic recasting of these events. The church at the turn of the fifteenth century was still marked by a good deal of flexibility, even fluidity, which could at once be exhilarating and exasperating. This church looked quite different, therefore, than it would some 150 years later in the aftermath of the Council of Trent. And it was even further from the church of Pius IX and the First Vatican Council. Whether one sees this as reason for regret or confidence is a separate matter. Yet from the perspective of a historical study—which this book is—such differences need to be borne in mind.

Acknowledgments

This book has been quite a few years in the making and has undergone numerous changes along the way, both in content and in perspective. It is a work of historical theology, which may help in small ways to inform contemporary theological discussions, although it was not written specifically for that purpose. I hope that this book provides a clear and judicious account of an especially difficult problem that faced the late medieval church—the determination of genuine authority. The task of the historical theologian is modest, perhaps, but important, insofar as one can provide a fair hearing in the present for voices of the past. If one believes in the communion of saints that extends across the ages, then it is only just to allow previous generations a place at the table today. For they are never really absent and thus should not be excluded.

Many colleagues and friends have encouraged and assisted me throughout the writing of this book. Alastair Minnis helped me immensely in focusing this project and in refining my arguments. I am indebted to his generosity. Anne Hudson has been consistently helpful in answering my questions and in lending me scarce and important primary materials. I am grateful to those whom I have known and worked with since the inception of my scholarly career: Stephen Lahey, Mishtooni Bose, Fiona Somerset, Andrew Larsen, and Takashi Shogimen. I would also add to this list the late Mary Dove, who is surely missed by many. Reading the works of these scholars, listening to their conference papers, and conversing with them over the years has been extremely beneficial. They have taught me a great deal. Everyone with whom I have worked at the University of Notre Dame Press has been responsive and supportive throughout the entire publication process. The two anonymous readers provided perceptive analysis that I took to heart. Any failings that remain are entirely my own responsibility. Finally, I thank my colleagues in the Theology Department at Providence College, from whom I have been learning much, and for whose friendship I am truly grateful.

Providence, Rhode Island
Nativity of the Blessed Virgin Mary, 2011

Chapter 1

Facets of Authority in the Late Medieval Church

This introductory chapter addresses the authoritative status that Holy Scripture enjoyed in the late medieval church. More specifically, though, it provides a look at the ways in which scripture was understood in itself, interpreted, and then applied to meet the needs of the church. It will become apparent that there were some very substantial tensions within the late medieval church that the mere recognition of scriptural authority could not resolve. For the problem was not the authority of scripture itself but rather its authoritative determination. If the later debates that form the focus of this book are to be seen in their fullest light, therefore, one need first remember that such debates fit into a long and fractious continuum — one that involves theologians, canonists, and popes. Thus, even as Wycliffism served in large measure to bring the crisis of authority to a boil, the crisis itself had much deeper roots. What is more, though, this chapter helps bring into clearer focus the fundamentally traditional nature of Wycliffite biblical exegesis and conceptions of authority, which will be examined in subsequent chapters. Hence it can serve to dispel much of the misinformation spread by the opponents of John Wyclif and Jan Hus in the midst of these magisterial disputes.

That Holy Scripture stood at the heart of all discussions of heresy and orthodoxy in the Middle Ages is made clear within the pages of canon law. Gratian's *Decretum* offers a definition of heresy taken right from Saint Jerome. The canon *Haeresis* (C. 24, q. 3, c. 27) begins with the saint's observation that heresy, itself a Greek word meaning "choice," refers to a person choosing to follow a teaching that he believes to be better than the church's dogma. And the canon continues: "Anyone who understands scripture in some other sense than that which the Holy Spirit demands—by whom scripture itself was written—although that person does not break away from the Church—he can still be called a heretic."[1] This canon is either directly cited or alluded to on countless occasions throughout the Middle Ages. Indeed, it is simply taken for granted that scripture is the principal standard of Catholic orthodoxy such that anyone who opposes it is by definition a heretic. Thus in his comprehensive *Summa de haeresibus* the fourteenth-century Carmelite theologian Guido Terreni could write: "An opinion is heretical which expressly and evidently stands opposed to Holy Scripture, such that it runs contrary to the express text of the Old or New Testament. For this canonical and Catholic scripture is of the most eminent authority. . . . Hence the canonical scripture contains nothing but the truth."[2] So it was then that medieval theologians and canonists followed the lead—and often the very words—of Saint Augustine, who drew a strict distinction between the theological works of later generations and the unique status of Holy Scripture. No one should be so audacious, says the saint, as to say that the biblical authors might not have grasped the truth. As such, any apparent error must be chalked up to a faulty manuscript, or a poor translation, or misunderstanding on the part of the reader. And even were one to find the same truth among the countless books of later authors they will never come close to achieving the authority and holiness of scripture.[3] The only books to which Augustine could render unequivocal respect and honor were "the books of the scriptures which are now called canonical . . . since I most firmly believe that none of their authors erred when writing whatever is contained therein." Hence no matter the erudition and sanctity of later doctors, none can achieve the authority of these books.[4]

The Book of Life and Eternal Mirror

For the late medieval theologians the authority of Holy Scripture was ultimately grounded in its divine origin such that it served as an eternal and perfect expression of all truth. We will see that this was certainly the case for John Wyclif and that this conception of scripture played a major role in his reform agenda. Thus one does well to remember that much of what Wyclif will have to say on the topic of scripture's ontologically superlative and authoritative status had been voiced by earlier generations of orthodox university masters. In his *Lectura Ordinaria super sacram scripturam*, the secular master Henry of Ghent broke down scripture according to the four Aristotelian causes. The efficient cause refers to scripture's sublime authority, since it is the book of God's commandments. The material cause corresponds to the depth of its truth, inasmuch as it is the law that abides for eternity. The final cause is scripture's fruitful use, which leads to eternal life. And last there is the formal cause, pertaining to the variety of its means.[5] What is more, says Henry, scripture is worthy of greater credence than any human authority, since it surpasses all human reason; its authority is rooted in its Eternal Author.[6] When addressing the truth of Holy Scripture, Henry appeals to what was a classic text in the Middle Ages, Wisdom 7:26: "For she is a radiance of eternal light, a spotless mirror of the working of God, and an image of his goodness." Generations of medieval theologians embraced scripture as the *speculum sine macula*—the eternal standard of all truth. Henry describes scripture as untainted by any falsehood, certain and thus without doubt, and free from all error. As this divine radiance, scripture contains the eternal truths that have been transcribed by the rules of eternal light. It is the truth of divine law and thus of eternal righteousness. Scripture is clear enough to refute all error. By its irrefragable truth, it stands in judgment of, and reigns over, every other doctrine and discipline.[7]

It is the Divine Author who guarantees the veracity, and thus the authority, of Holy Scripture. Following Aristotle's *Metaphysics* (981b), Henry states that the one who possesses an inherent knowledge of the principles and the rules of the art should be called the principal author of the science and not the one to whom he describes these principles and rules. When it comes to scripture, therefore, it is God alone who knows by his very nature the rules of this science. These are the rules which the creature cannot attain by his own natural faculties *(ex puris naturalibus)* but can only know when inspired by God. Hence God alone is properly called the author of this science. Yet Henry does take seriously the role of human beings in the transmission of divine truth. The scriptures are mediated by men who have conscribed them and have contemplated this wisdom to the extent that is possible for the human heart. They were genuine, albeit secondary, authors who described what was infused into them from the great treasury of this art.⁸ Yet Henry insists that this science is principally believed on account of the authority of God and no one else, except to the extent that God's refulgence surrounds his mediator. We must not think that God is the author of this science simply because men offer human testimony, therefore, but rather because the divine power shines forth all around them. Hence God is bearing witness to himself through these men.⁹

Having secured the uniquely authoritative status of scripture, Henry proceeded to consider a perennial medieval question, and one that would stand at the center of the Wycliffite debates a century later: "Whether one ought to believe in the authority of scripture rather than the church, or vice versa." Even as this matter came to a head by the late fourteenth century, this was not an otiose speculative question in thirteenth-century Paris. After all, Parisian masters of theology such as Henry of Ghent and Godfrey of Fontaines did confront ecclesiastical authorities precisely in their role as Masters of the Sacred Page and thus guardians of scriptural truth. And then, in a separate context, the rise of sectarian groups such as the Spiritual Franciscans meant that questions of a true and false church would have clear ramifications.

Now, according to Henry, when it comes to matters of faith, the church and scripture agree in all things and testify together to the true faith. And in that sense it is rational to believe in them both. We believe in scripture on account of the authority of Christ; and we believe in the church on account of the truth that men see therein. Yet Henry then asks a momentous question that goes right to the heart of the church herself: when one compares scripture to the church, are we speaking of what is truly and rightly reckoned to be the church or merely what is considered the church by reputation alone? If the first, then one must believe in both scripture and the church equally, since there is no way in which they can disagree. Taken in the second way, however, one must simply and absolutely believe in scripture rather than the church, precisely because the truth itself is preserved forever within scripture immutably, to which no one is permitted to add, subtract, or change anything (Rv 21:18–19). The people of the church are subject to change, however, such that it is possible for a multitude to dissent from the faith and—through either error or malice—apostatize. Yet in the face of this horrendous possibility Henry retains the traditional confidence that the church will always abide at least among a righteous remnant.¹⁰

Henry has not, however, lost sight of the important role that the church plays in the life of faith. With regard to the generation and acceptance of the faith, the authority of the church does avail more than scripture. When someone first accedes to the faith it is rational for him to believe more in the church than in scripture. Yet with regard to confirming and strengthening the faith that one already possesses the authority of scripture prevails. It is to scripture that the faithful person adheres, even were he to see those through whom he had first accepted the faith fall away from that faith, indeed even if *per impossibile* the whole church were to abandon the faith.[11] For Henry, confidence in scripture is ultimately rooted in the Person of Christ. The believer, having understood scripture and having found Christ within it, trusts more in the words of Christ that he found in scripture than in any preacher, more even than the testimony of the church. This is because it is on account of scripture that he now believes the church. This means that if the church were to say anything contrary to scripture he would not believe it. Hence the strength of such faith consists most perfectly in the divine authority manifested in Holy Scripture. Here then Henry has recourse to Augustine's oft-cited remark that the faith would totter if the authority of scripture were to waver (*De doc. chr.* 1.37.41). Holy Scripture is the last and most steadfast standard of Catholic truth.[12]

The Carmelite theologian Gerard of Bologna had been a student at the University of Paris when Henry of Ghent taught there.[13] And he tackles some of the very same questions in his own *Summa* as did his predecessor, often offering similar answers.[14] Of central concern here is the way that Gerard handles the question of scriptural and ecclesiastical authority. First of all he affirms that the authority of scripture is the very authority of God, and we should believe in nothing more than God. To the extent that one might wish to compare scripture and the church, however, Gerard notes that comparison is only applicable among diverse things. Where the church and scripture agree completely and are one, therefore, we should not make a comparison as to which is to be believed more. They agree that what is written in the canonical books is from the Divine Author. This is what scripture hands down and what the church holds without wavering. In that case, then, it is a moot point.[15] If, however, it turned out that some congregation wished to alter this scripture and hold the opposite, this very act would prove that it is not the church of God. And in that case scripture would have to be believed rather than this so-called church. Yet Gerard is confident that this could not happen to the Catholic Church, precisely because Christ has prayed that her faith would not fail (Lk 22:32). Drawing upon this traditional principle of the Church's indefectibility, therefore, Gerard concludes that it is not a matter of believing one over the other—scripture or the church—since they both hold the same thing in the same way, and do so on the authority of God.[16]

Gerard notes here that there are some (Henry of Ghent, *Summa*, a. 10, q. 1) who distinguish between the faith on the part of the believer with respect to the generation of faith on the one hand and its conservation and strengthening on the other. They say that with regard to the generation of faith, the authority of the church is highest, as when Cornelius came to understand the faith through Peter rather than scripture (Acts 10:25–33). Yet when it comes to confirming and strengthening the faith, it is the authority of scripture that prevails, for it is that to which the faithful adhere.[17] Gerard does not accept this distinction, however, since it appears to create a false choice. This is because the person who believes rightly, believes scripture or the church only on the authority of God. The two may not be juxtaposed, therefore, since the source of their authority is the same. And if it is said that one is led to believe more on account of the preaching of the church than the inspection of scripture, it must be remembered that the church herself preaches nothing except Holy Scripture.[18] Peter went to Cornelius because the latter was in need of a teacher as he could not understand scripture on his own. This does not, however, grant Peter or the church greater authority than scripture. For the teacher does not induce the student to trust in his own authority but rather in the authority and reason of the author of the science that he teaches. Hence the church induces one to believe, not on the basis of her own authority, but on the basis of God's authority. For Gerard, this is ideally a symbiotic relationship: the authority of the church and scripture are to be believed in equally, since they are both governed by the same Holy Spirit.[19]

Gerard will then address the oft-cited remark of Augustine, drawn from his debate with the Manichees: "I would not have believed the Gospel unless the authority of the Catholic Church moved me."[20] Gerard takes this to mean simply that one comes to believe the gospel of God by means of the church's preaching. The authority of the church as preacher and teacher was an exterior occasion for Augustine to believe—not in the authority of the church, however, but in the authority of Christ. Here Gerard weighs in on the crucial question of ecclesiastical authority relative to the creation of law, and he does allow for some flexibility and development. The church does have the authority to establish some positive laws that she can periodically change. Nevertheless, she has no authority over divine law or the law of nature. In fact, the church presupposes those laws precisely because they are wholly immutable. With respect to the biblical canon, that the church receives the Four Gospels is because she believes in God who is the author of all that is contained therein.[21]

Henry and Gerard have brought to light a dilemma that will bedevil Christendom throughout the late Middle Ages. Holy Scripture and the Catholic Church should indeed abide in perfect harmony, each in its unique and authoritative way proclaiming the divine truth that has been revealed in Jesus Christ and subsequently preached by the apostles. Yet if it is admitted that Holy Scripture—which is by definition not subject to error—can be misinterpreted by a false church that proves itself devoid of authority by reason of its apostasy from the truth of scripture, where will the light of divine truth be found? It will be found in the true church, of course, the one that remains faithful to the Word of God revealed in Holy Scripture. It is the primary mark of the true church that it will always interpret Holy Scripture according to the intended meaning of the Divine Author. Yet, as it is agreed that Holy Scripture—this eternal and radiant mirror of truth—stands above all merely human authority in light of its divine authorship, how will anyone be able to grasp its sublime meaning? This is the question that remains at the very heart of the crisis: ascertaining precisely what the Divine Author intends to convey through this sacred text.

The medieval theologians by no means rejected the ways of reason or the benefits of the liberal arts, but the quest for the eternal truth of scripture could not support itself by the efforts of the human intellect alone. There was, to be sure, some lively discussion in the thirteenth century regarding the moral requisites of the theologian and the need for divine illumination.[22] But for all that it was basically taken for granted that divine truth was revealed to those who were spiritually disposed to receive it. Most if not all theologians readily embraced Augustine's belief that genuine comprehension of Holy Scripture comes only to the reader who is humble of heart, rooted in charity, and subjected easily to Christ.[23] In fact, according to this saint, Christ is the true teacher who must illuminate our minds if we are to grasp the truth.[24] The believer must be conformed to

Christ in order to grasp the deepest meanings of the biblical text. One will have to foster the Christian virtues of faith, hope, and love if one hopes to comprehend the scriptures.[25] The nexus between personal sanctity and exegetical acumen loomed over the entire Wycliffite debate as it stretched from Oxford to Prague.

In one form or another, therefore, the reader would have to commit himself to the Person of Christ the Word. For Saint Bonaventure, Franciscan poverty *(summa paupertas)* was the means to Christian perfection inasmuch as it followed the perfect example of Christ *(exemplum Christi)* found within the record of Holy Scripture.[26] Devotion to Christ as it is expressed in one's manner of life will, in turn, prove to be the hermeneutical key that opens up the scriptures — the very scriptures that point toward the Word who abides at their center. The Word is the root of all understanding, the very gate apart from whom it is impossible to enter into knowledge of the highest truths. Indeed, that is why this gate remains closed for the philosophers. The Word is the truth of all created things, which find their cause in him. The Word, therefore, is the principle of all true understanding, the most noble key for the soul that has been purified by faith.[27] Holy Scripture, says Bonaventure, is the work of the most perfect author *(auctor perfectissimus)* who teaches only what is true and useful. And we can be confident that God has provided scripture with certitude of authority *(certitudinem auctoritatis)* such that it can never deceive or be deceived. Handed down through divine revelation, rather than by human investigation, scripture is authentic *(authentica)* and of perfect authority *(perfectae auctoritatis)*.[28] The origin of scripture is the Holy Trinity, which cannot be made the subject of human investigation but is instead the product of divine revelation, beginning with the Father, through the Son, and then completed in the Holy Spirit by whom we receive the gift of faith through which Christ dwells in our hearts. This is the knowledge of Jesus Christ by which one understands Holy Scripture. Indeed, it is impossible, Bonaventure insists, that anyone might ascend to knowledge of Holy Scripture unless he first has the faith of Christ infused in him. This faith is the foundation of all supernatural illumination, and it is by way of faith that we gain understanding of Holy Scripture. Faith, therefore, is the foundation, the light, and the door to knowledge of scripture — all of which begins with the work of the Holy Trinity. To understand scripture one must be rooted in the knowledge and love of Christ.[29]

The Franciscan Peter John Olivi found that in its charity scripture surpasses all other laws and mandates. Scripture is the queen that sits at the right hand of Christ wearing the vestments of charity (Ps 44:10). She stands above all other laws such that every human judgment must submit to her.[30] So it is that Holy Scripture presents herself as the mirror of divine truth: "She is the dazzling brightness of eternal light and an unblemished mirror of God's majesty" (Wis 7:26).[31] To seek Christ at the center of scripture one must proceed more by way of affection *(affectualiter)* than intellect, more through sensual taste *(sensualem gustum)* than visual apprehension. Only in the excess of love *(in solo excessu amoris)* can this way be discerned.[32] And for Peter Auriol, the final end of the whole Divine Scripture is *caritas*, which is rooted in Christ. Glowing with such pure truth, scripture surpasses all the human sciences, since Christ himself is the doctor of this unique and sacred science.[33]

Perhaps the most influential exegete of the late Middle Ages was the fourteenth-century Franciscan Nicholas of Lyra—esteemed by the Wycliffites and their adversaries. Not only did Lyra describe Holy Scripture itself in ways echoed by John Wyclif some fifty years later, but Wyclif would hew closely to Lyra's exegetical methodology. Lyra adopted Sirach 24:32 as his guide: "Haec omnia liber vitae." Scripture, for Lyra, was the very Book of Life—*Liber Vitae*—the key to true life for all who believe. Lyra extolled Holy Scripture as a unique book that is ordered toward happiness in the life to come and thereby surpasses the human sciences of the philosophers: "The book containing Holy Scripture—although divided into many partial books and yet contained under one book—which is designated under the general name of the Bible, is properly called the Book of Life." In comparison to the books of Holy Scripture, therefore, those of the philosophers are more fittingly designated books of death. Holy Scripture can itself be identified with the science of theology, according to Lyra, since it is the sole text of this science and excels all others. It has God for its subject matter, the most noble subject of all. Indeed, it may be equated with *theo-logy* because it is in some sense a discourse about God *(sermo de Deo)*.[34] As Holy Scripture has God for its subject, who is himself the first cause of all things, so it must be designated as Wisdom. This is the wisdom of the saints, the very Wisdom that is Holy Scripture. Although it is true that philosophers have some knowledge of God, it is confined to the properties that can be known by reason through the observation of created things. On the other hand, the prophets and apostles, who have handed down Holy Scripture through the revelation of the Holy Spirit, have a knowledge of transcendent divine properties that exceeds the investigations of human reason.

The Trinity is a prime example of a truth that could not be reached by the efforts of unaided human reason. And if the Trinity is the goal of all human longing, then the study of Holy Scripture can be no mere academic exercise. The person contemplating Holy Scripture, says Lyra, is borne along into the love of the very object of his cognition—who is God himself—and comes to love him above all else.[35] More than wisdom *(sapientia)*, however, scripture is also understanding *(intellectus)*, since understanding is the unerring grasp of principles. And it is on account of such principles that one can render judgment as to the truth or falsity of things. So it is, then, that whatever is found to be in accord with scripture is deemed true and whatever contradicts it must be false.[36]

Looking to Wisdom 1:7, "Hoc quod continet omnia scientiam habet vocis," Lyra finds that Holy Scripture contains all things, precisely because it is a science that brings all things under its consideration. Here one encounters the Christological dimension of scripture as Lyra notes that the phrase *"scientiam habet vocis"* pertains to that which is proper to the word *(vocis)*, to what it signifies. Now what is proper to Holy Scripture is that which is expressed by the Divine Word himself. For it is through the Word that all things were made (Jn 1:1), which means that all things must fall under the consideration of this science, that is, under the consideration of scripture. Lyra notes that this does not apply to knowledge of all particular things that may be found by way of human reason but rather all the created things by which we are led up into the knowledge and love of God through a true faith that has been informed by charity.[37] As Lyra continues he compares the book *(liber)* of scripture to a mirror *(speculum)*, thereby drawing on the classic text of Wisdom 7:26. For just as sensible forms are apparent in a mirror, so in this book the intelligible truths shine forth. It is in this vein that he turns to Robert Grosseteste's comment that "the Word of the Father is [for the angels] the Book of Life and the mirror of eternity in which they intelligibly read—and in clarity gaze upon—the immense power of the Father through which they worship; the inestimable wisdom of the Son by which they are illuminated; and the sweetest goodness of the Spirit which they embrace."[38]

Here we have seen among a number of medieval theologians that the search for the truth of scripture could be an almost mystical quest for Divine Wisdom, for the Living Word of God, Jesus Christ. The sanctity of the exegete was, therefore, an integral factor in this endeavor to reach the intended sense of Holy Scripture, precisely because locating this sense meant coming into personal contact with the Divine Author. This bears emphasizing lest we imagine that any group in the late medieval quest for authority would have been able to set aside the subjectiveness of biblical exegesis. Amid the applications of literary and logical categories (as I discuss below) the late medieval theologians never lost sight of the affective component necessary to bring to light the divinely intended sense of the biblical text. Ironically, though, it was the very recognition of this fact that made matters all the more contentious as each side charged that the other lacked the requisite sanctity to perceive the intention of the Divine Author.

The Literal Sense of Scripture

Because the debate over just what constitutes the literal sense of scripture, and how one locates it, played such an important role in the Wycliffite debates we need to examine some developments in late medieval exegetical methodology, much of which turns on the very concept of the literal sense. Yet it first bears mentioning that the parameters of the biblical canon were not rigidly defined at this time. In his prologue to the Book of Kings, also known as the *Prologus Galeatus,* Saint Jerome specifically denied full canonical status to the Wisdom of Solomon, Sirach, First and Second Maccabees, Judith, and Tobit, which he deemed apocryphal even if nonetheless edifying.[39] Yet the *Decretum Damasi* issued by a Roman council in 382—declaring the Divine Scriptures to be "the foundation upon which the Catholic Church throughout the world has been founded"—included the very books that Jerome had left out of his canon.[40] This document was later incorporated into the *Decretum Gelasianum* (c. 495) and entered into the medieval canon law collections.[41] So it was that these two accounts of the biblical canon—*Prologus Galeatus* and *Decretum Gelasianum*—peacefully coexisted throughout the Middle Ages. Thus, for instance, as Thomas Aquinas appealed to the Book of Sirach in the course of an argument, he admitted that such proof would not be accepted by colleagues who rejected this book's canonical status.[42] Recall too that Hugh of Saint Victor was willing to include the church fathers in a third section of the New Testament, although he qualified their presence, noting they really add nothing new but rather explain obscure passages in the other sections.[43]

Perhaps a more pressing question, however, was the state of the physical codex itself. Roger Bacon complained that the Paris text was "horribly corrupt for the most part" and that the so-called correctors only made it worse.⁴⁴ And, as Gilbert Dahan points out, the textual critical work undertaken at Paris in the thirteenth century did not constitute an effort to create a new edition of the Latin Bible; it was simply a revision of the text. Hence at Saint-Jacques the categories *falsa littera, vera littera,* and *littera verior* all presupposed that there was a "true" text there to begin with. These Dominican correctors did indeed look to the Greek and Hebrew, but they were not attempting to create a new Vulgate; they were only trying to restore the version of Jerome that had since been corrupted.⁴⁵ Yet knowledge of the original biblical languages was still fairly rudimentary, and this had consequences not only for textual correction but also then for exegesis. Bacon argued that it is essential to understand the principles of a language if one is to grasp the literal sense of the text, since this allows one to elicit the genuine spiritual sense. But if the text *(litera)* is false both the literal and the spiritual sense are bound to be false as well.⁴⁶

In fact, the literal sense of scripture was expanding in its range and complexity by the latter part of the thirteenth century. The late medieval theologians still accepted the traditional four senses: literal, allegorical, tropological, and anagogical. Yet their grander vision permitted them to accommodate the mystical senses within the orbit of the literal sense precisely because the theologians had developed theories of authorship that could equate the literal sense of the text with the intended meaning of the author. In the case of Holy Scripture, therefore, when discerning the literal sense one had to contend with both a divine and a human author.⁴⁷ It was the Divine Author, however, who ultimately ratified the genuine meaning of the biblical text. And inasmuch as Holy Scripture formed the basis for all orthodox doctrine in the Middle Ages, determining the divinely intended meaning of scripture was tantamount to arriving at the truth of the Catholic faith itself. Such efforts were fraught with difficulties, though, given the many concomitant factors brought into play: patristic sources, canon law, papal decrees, and even the sanctity of the exegete himself, as well as questions regarding the textual integrity of the biblical codex. Thus even as all sides turned to Holy Scripture as the principal norm in the determination of Catholic truth, they depended upon a host of extra-scriptural factors to render a decisive reading of the biblical text.

Although Thomas Aquinas acknowledged the traditional four senses of scripture, he insisted that the spiritual senses rest firmly upon the literal sense. In his *Summa Theologiae* he stated, "The primary signification, by which words signify things, pertains to the first sense, which is the historical or literal sense. Yet that signification by which things are signified by words and again signify other things is called the spiritual sense, which is founded upon the literal and presupposes it."[48] This would seem relatively straightforward were it not for the fact that beyond the inspired human author there stands the Divine Author, the Holy Spirit. If the Divine Author has many meanings in mind—all of which must be true—does that mean there could be more than one literal sense in any given passage of scripture? After all, Thomas went on to say the following: "The literal sense is that which the author intends. Now the author of Holy Scripture is God, who comprehends all things within the divine intellect simultaneously. Thus it is not unfitting, as Augustine says in Book Twelve of his *Confessions,* if in keeping with the literal sense there would be many senses in one letter of Scripture."[49] Given these parameters Thomas could also state in another work: "Even if the expositors adapt some truths to Holy Scripture that the [human] author does not understand, there is no doubt but that the Holy Spirit, who is the principal author of Divine Scripture, did understand. Thus every truth that, without violating the circumstance of the letter, can be adapted to the Divine Scripture, is the sense of Scripture."[50] These statements have created some confusion—and indeed some controversy—over whether Aquinas believed that Holy Scripture contains multiple literal senses.[51] Mark Johnson has argued convincingly that Aquinas did believe in the plurality of the literal sense, such that the Holy Spirit, as well as the human author, may have intended to convey multiple meanings through the same words. The human author of a given biblical text need not understand all the meanings contained in the letter, but under the inspiration of the Holy Spirit it is possible. Either way, however, the Holy Spirit will have intended all the true readings of the text.[52]

In this vein Nicholas of Lyra found that in Holy Scripture one letter *(littera)* may contain many senses precisely because God is the principal author *(principalis auctor).*[53] Although Lyra accepted the possibility of four senses, he admits that there are times when no mystical sense is required, as with the command to love God with one's whole heart (Dt 6:5). Yet there are other times when there is no literal sense, as with the parable of the talking trees (Jgs 9:8–15) or Christ's advice that we cut off our hand if it scandalizes us (Mt 5:29–30). If the literal sense is restricted to that which properly signifies, then there can be no such sense in these cases. In fact, that sense of scripture would be false if one had to read these texts literally. As such, these passages must be understood by the mystical sense alone. Lyra admits that the doctors say the parabolic sense belongs to the literal, but here, he says, one must realize that they are speaking broadly. For in those cases where there is no literal sense signified by the words, the parabolic sense serves as the primary sense, and in that way can be called the literal, inasmuch as the literal sense is the first when no other sense is present. In fact, Lyra admits that he too has called the parabolic sense the literal in his own commentaries.[54]

Then there are those instances when scripture has both a literal and a mystical sense, as in the account of Abraham and his two sons, Isaac and Ishmael (Gn 21:1–14). While this is true according to the literal sense, it is also true by the mystical, as evinced by the Apostle Paul's allegorical reading whereby they signify the two testaments (Gal 4:24). Even here, though, they are not limited to the allegorical but can signify on the moral and anagogical level as well.[55] Lyra had actually developed an ingenious method of balancing the literal and spiritual senses, which then became standard practice in the late Middle Ages. For he contended that there may in fact be both a mystical and a historical sense under the same letter—hence the "double literal sense" *(duplex sensus litteralis)*. In these instances the truth of the history recorded in the text must be maintained even as it refers to a spiritual understanding. The example he gives in his prologue is taken from 1 Chronicles 22:10, where the Lord is portrayed as a father to Solomon. Read literally *(ad litteram)* Solomon was indeed God's son by adoption, and thus by grace. Yet the apostle Paul had cited this text in Hebrews 1:5 when speaking of Christ, and he also did so *ad litteram* so that he might prove that Christ was higher than the angels. Paul's point of doctrine, however, cannot be based upon the mystical sense. That would violate Augustine's rule that the literal sense alone is the foundation of all doctrine. Here, then, the same text is speaking literally about Solomon, God's son by grace, even as it is also speaking about Christ, God's Son by nature. The same text is fulfilled by both Solomon and Christ, although less perfectly by the former and more perfectly by the latter.[56]

Determining the literal sense of the biblical text became an even more urgent concern as the century wore on. Indeed, it had direct ramifications for the defense of Catholic doctrine. During a stay at the papal court in Avignon, Richard FitzRalph, at the request of Pope Clement VI, composed his *Summa de questionibus Armenorum* in which he addressed a list of errors attributed to the Armenian church by a papal commission in 1341–42. Because the Armenians would not necessarily accept the authority of the Western fathers and traditions, however, FitzRalph decided to base his arguments solely upon Holy Scripture—or, more specifcally, the literal sense of Holy Scripture.[57] The first order of business, therefore, was to determine which senses of scripture should be called the literal *(litteralis)*. This is very important, since the entire *Summa*, and thus the case for the Western church, will be based upon the literal sense of scripture. Were the literal sense found to be false in any way, FitzRalph's arguments would obviously not get very far. Yet if one abides by the common manner of speaking, the words of scripture seem to yield many falsehoods according to the letter *(ad litteram)*. For instance, it is said in Habakkuk 2:11 that "the stones will cry out from the wall." Clearly, then, the literal sense *(sensus litteralis)* cannot always be equated with the common meaning of words *(vulgaris)*. Here, though, FitzRalph offers a rather curt admonition: it does not really matter which sense should properly be called the literal sense of a given passage just so long as you know the intention of the author *(mentem auctoris)*. FitzRalph will accept as the literal sense what the fashioner, or author, of scripture *(conditor sive auctor scripturae)* understands by what he says. This does not necessarily apply to what the scribe *(scriptor)* has in mind, however, for the author may not have personally written the work. He could have instructed another who did not know all that the author or editor *(auctor sive editor)* had in mind. We see this when Baruch took dictation from the mouth of the prophet Jeremiah. Here is an instance where the literal sense was not always the common meaning *(sensus litteralis non semper est vulgaris)*. Instead, the literal sense is the sense of the author *(sensus auctoris)*, which may be expressed figuratively through whatever words he chooses to employ.[58] FitzRalph then went on to lay out a sophisticated theory of authorship and editorship that preserved the biblical writers from the charge of mendacity as they recounted the lies and frauds perpetrated by central actors in the narratives. The point is that scripture is always trustworthy even if the people whose stories it tells are not.[59]

FitzRalph's most pressing concern was convincing the Armenian Christians that Western doctrines could be proven by the clear and plain *(clara et plana)* testimony of New Testaments texts. For instance, FitzRalph is certain that the double procession of the Holy Spirit follows clearly from scripture and manifest reason *(evidenter ex Sacra Scriptura et manifesta ratione)*.⁶⁰ If we carefully consider scripture, he says, we will see that those passages which point to the Spirit's procession from the Father can also be applied to the Son.⁶¹ In fact, FitzRalph believes that the *filioque* doctrine must follow evidently and expressly from Holy Scripture *(sequitur evidenter et expresse ex Sacra Scriptura)*. For if it did not, one could not demand that the faithful hold this doctrine or censure as heretics those who deny it. The admitted fact that many learned Greek doctors have seen no such evidence does not prevent FitzRalph from insisting upon the doctrine's express scriptural warrant and its unshakable rational basis—*haec processio Spiritus Sancti expresse et evidenter ac infrangibili ratione sequitur ex Scriptura*. In the end, therefore, he is left to conclude that the Greeks reject this article due either to pertinacious blindness or a refusal to admit what they actually know to be true. They seem to be driven by pride, he says, exulting in the intellectual superiority they used to enjoy over the Latins.⁶² And papal primacy, obviously a point of much contention, is also clearly spelled out in Holy Scripture. Appealing to such classic texts such as Luke 22:32, Matthew 16:18–19, and John 21:15–17, FitzRalph is confident that scripture clearly proclaims *(scriptura plane praenunciat)* Peter to have held primacy among the apostles and throughout the whole church.⁶³

Across the *Summa*, however, what FitzRalph takes to be the "plain" and "clear," and thus "literal," readings of the biblical text depend upon certain theological presuppositions. When proving the divinity of Christ, for example, FitzRalph quotes from the apostle Paul: "[Christ] who is above all, God blessed forever" (Rom 9:5). He does not even think this requires any explanation, since it could not be said more plainly *(planius dici non posset)* that Christ is God who is himself blessed above all.⁶⁴ And again the Apostle writes, "God sent his Son . . . to redeem those who were under the Law" (Gal 4:5). Of course, says FitzRalph, God alone can redeem from mortal sin; hence this too counts as express testimony *(expressum testimonium)* that Christ is God. As far as he is concerned such passages speak expressly *(expresse)* and leave "no doubt" as to their meaning.⁶⁵ Here, then, FitzRalph's literal sense must be broad enough to accommodate a process of reasoned deduction. There is some assembly required when attempting to determine the clear and plain sense of Holy Scripture. This is important to remember, because it highlights the difficulties attendant upon locating the literal—or clear—sense of scripture. Even so able and influential an exegete as Fitz-

Ralph has to force the issue at times. Having committed himself to arguing from the text of scripture, the biblical text is going to have to bear a substantial doctrinal load if it is to convey the Catholic—and thus divinely intended—meaning.

Inasmuch as FitzRalph has staked so much on this clear and plain meaning of scripture, he needs to address the possibility that the veracity of scripture might be compromised by textual corruptions and mistranslations. For the various Latin translations of the Old Testament contradict one another in many places, and that, in turn, would seem to undercut the principle that the text should bear the one sense of the primary author. Indeed, there appear to be innumerable instances in both the Old and the New Testament where our Latin text *(nostra littera latina)* creates serious doctrinal problems.[66] Yet FitzRalph diffuses the textual dilemma when he contends that authenticity rests not so much with the words *(verba)* as with the meaning *(sensus)*. One can be sure, therefore, that the Latin translation does reflect the meaning of the Hebrew text even where there may be verbal discrepancies. One must never lose sight of the fact, says FitzRalph, that the Holy Spirit is the author of scripture. That the Spirit has spoken through the prophets and apostles means there will be no contradictions among them, since they all asserted the true faith under divine inspiration. No matter the contradictions and falsehoods that may seem to emerge in the text *(littera)*, therefore, no problems will be found in the primary sense *(in sensu primario)*. In fact, FitzRalph admits that he too, in his negligence, often believed that he had located falsehoods and contradictions where the clear truth was actually expressed *(clara veritas fuerat expressa)*.[67] Such an expansive view of scriptural truth—one that is not tied to every comma and dash but rather the overarching sacred sense—is indicative of a general confidence in the Catholic truth itself exhibited by the medieval masters.

FitzRalph has chosen to take a broad view that expresses confidence in the fact that the church has approved Latin translations read according to their primary meaning *(ad primum sensum)* that the translators expressed. The church's approval does not extend to the individual codex that may have been distorted by an ignorant or careless scribe. One must trust, therefore, that the truth rests within the primary scripture *(in primaria nostra scriptura)*. One should likewise trust in those things found in every translation that has been approved by the church's general councils. For these councils were composed of Latin, Greek, and Hebrew prelates who were quite capable of certifying the ancient codices upon which the primordial scripture *(primordialis scriptura)* is based. Hence one should never be so presumptuous as to assume that the particular manuscript one is looking at provides a superior reading to this Ur-text created by such diligent and learned scholars. The fault will always lie with the corrupted hard copy in one's hands. Thus one must compare the text with other versions in the quest for the primary truth *(veritatem primariam)*. If one still runs up against problems when examining the principal translations *(primariis translationibus)*, then it is likely owing to one's own lack of skill in interpreting scripture's myriad forms of expression, idioms, and terminological equivocations, as well as the idiosyncrasies that arise when translating one language into another. Although there are bound to be small verbal discrepancies on the level of the physical text no falsity results, since such things will never contradict the truth that has been approved by the Catholic Church.[68] FitzRalph has not only staked a lot on Holy Scripture as the source of Catholic doctrine, but he is attempting to carry on a debate with Christians who read the scriptures in other languages—often the originals—which he does not really know. If his confidence in Western manuscripts and Latin translations seems excessive at times, it was not out of keeping with the majority of his colleagues in the Latin West. Moreover, one will find Wyclif arguing in much the same way as he struggles to defend the inherent veracity of scripture even while admitting—as everyone must—that the individual manuscripts are often corrupt.

The secular theologian Henry Totting de Oyta tackled many of these same issues some forty years later. Totting, who was praised by Jean Gerson for his exegetical skill, taught in Prague and Paris before moving to the University of Vienna.[69] In 1385 Henry addressed a set of questions concerning the authority and interpretation of Holy Scripture, a number of which are strikingly similar to those Wyclif had tackled at Oxford just a few years earlier. Driving some of the most difficult questions is a genuine concern with the problem of falsehood: can we really trust Holy Scripture? This is no mere speculative matter when one considers that Scripture lay at the heart of Catholic doctrine and was the principal source of all theological inquiry. We find, then, that one question asks "whether all the books of our Bible, and specifically all their assertions, are divine in the literal sense *(in sensu literali)* and were composed by divine revelation."[70] Henry begins by offering the argument of those who say they are not. Here one sees the intersection of the literal sense of scripture and the question of the biblical canon. For Henry's opponents contend that not all the books of our Bible *(libri nostre biblie)* belong to the canon of divine books *(de canone librorum divinorum)*. Saint Jerome's *Prologus Galeatus* is induced as proof for this assertion as the saint had argued that books such as Sirach, Judith, and Tobit are apocryphal and thus not part of the canon.[71]

From there the case is made against the physical text, that is, the codices as we have them. It is said that many assertions in the present biblical text are at variance in the literal sense *(in sensu literali)* with the Hebrew Truth from which the Latin texts were translated. Of course, truth cannot be opposed to truth, and yet there seem to be many discrepancies between the Christian translations and the Hebrew original. What is more, many Christian texts are at variance with each other. Jerome is also to blame here, it seems, since he took it upon himself to correct the Septuagint, whereas Augustine maintained that this text was inspired by the Holy Spirit. Jerome should not have corrected this text, therefore, especially when one realizes that the very Hebrew text he used had already been corrupted by Jews and heretics, thereby rendering his own translation untrustworthy.[72]

Henry offers a response that proceeds first of all from the person of Christ as the guarantor of the tradition. Christ—who cannot lie—testified that he came to open up the scriptures fully and thus disclosed all the senses within the Old Testament that had been intended by the Holy Spirit. Christ removed the veil of the Old Testament and cleared up all its difficulties. This only stands to reason since Christ and many other Jews who then became Christians were experts in the Hebrew language and were also filled with the Spirit. They elicited from these scriptures all the revealed truths that would form the foundation of the faith. Likewise, in the primitive church *(ecclesia primitiva)* there were prophets and teachers who explicated these scriptures through the gifts of wisdom and knowledge.[73] Indeed, it is in light of Christ and the Holy Spirit that Christians know the true meaning of the Old Testament. Thus the fact that the Christian translation of the Old Testament is at variance with the expositions of the Jews is not a problem. Nor was it necessary that the holy fathers make the Christian canon conform to the Jewish version, since the fathers were better able to render such canonical judgments based upon their knowledge of the two testaments.[74] All the books of the Bible that the church has received into the canon, therefore, were written by divine revelation. The fact that Sirach, Judith, and Tobit are not in the Hebrew canon does not mean that they are apocryphal; rather they should be counted among the Sacred Writings. The church in her wisdom has certified their authenticity.[75] Central for Henry in all of this is the unfailing judgment of the church under the guidance of Christ and the Holy Spirit. The church's reception of these books is the most meaningful criterion by which to determine their authoritative status.

With regard to exegetical methodology, Henry had followed Lyra on the *duplex sensus litteralis*,[76] and also adopted FitzRalph's theories of authorship.[77] Appealing as well to Thomas Aquinas (*Summa Theologiae* 1.1.10) and Alexander of Hales (*Summa Halensis* 1.1.4.5), Henry noted that it is not necessary that the literal sense always be taken according to the precise grammatical signification of the words but rather according to the context of the letter. Anyone who truly understands the scriptures will be able to spot a parable and interpret it accordingly, although it is still counted as the literal sense even if not read strictly grammatically.[78] When one attempts to determine the literal sense as conveyed by a parable or metaphor one must first compare the relationship of the things signified as they are presented in different passages. Then, on the basis of some correspondence, one must argue that a particular reading be accepted as the literal sense. One must also study common usage and the signification of terms belonging to that idiom as found in scripture. And finally, one must examine the sorts of human customary idiom to which the literal sense would conform. Careful analysis, therefore, will show how metaphors and figures, as well as hidden senses, still belong to the literal sense. The mystical sense, however, is reserved for those senses that cannot be elicited from the letter *(ex litera)*—hence the allegorical, tropological, and anagogical.[79]

Turning to Paul of Burgos, a fifteenth-century bishop and convert from Judaism who published a comprehensive critique of Lyra's exegesis in the form of the *Additiones ad Postillas Nicolai Lyrani*,[80] we see that the connection between orthodoxy and the literal sense remained a matter of great concern. In his prologue, Paul noted that if the literal sense *(sensus litteralis)* is taken to be the first signification of the letter by which the words signify things there would seem to be many falsehoods in scripture.[81] Now, there is no doubt that when scripture employs parables there will be apparent falsehoods of this sort. But, says Paul, the aforementioned definition of the literal sense is clearly too narrow. Rather, it should be understood to refer to the sense intended by the author of Holy Scripture, who is God. Paul's reasoning is as follows:

> The literal sense of any writing is that which the author intends, since the words which are in his mind are signs of his feelings, as we read in Aristotle's first book of *On Interpretation* (16a). Yet it is certain that the author of Holy Scripture is God, and so it is clear that the literal sense of the text under discussion is that sense which is intended by God. And it is through the words *(voces)* contained in the letter that his intention is signified. It follows from this that one should not call it the literal sense of Holy Scripture if it in some way contradicts the authority or determination of the church, however much that sense might be in conformity with the signification of the letter. For such a sense is not intended by the author, but rather is heretical.

And here Paul has recourse to the classic definition of heresy as an interpretation of scripture that runs contrary to what the Holy Spirit requires (cf. *Decretum* C. 24, q. 3, c. 27).[82] Nor, says Paul, can the literal sense ever be contrary to reason, since nothing irrational could be intended by the Divine Author, who is himself the First Truth from which all truth is derived.[83]

Paul notes that all the mysteries of Christ are clearly set forth *(expressa)* in the Old Testament and are completed in Christ. When Christ spoke of searching the scriptures, which bear witness to him (Jn 5:39), this refers to the literal sense, which is to say, the intended sense—*ad sensum litteralem, quod est intentum*.[84] Hence the literal sense—understood as the divinely intended sense—is ultimately discernible only to those who are predisposed by grace to recognize the truth. For it had been objected that the literal sense has no need of all this intense scrutiny because it is taken from what is signified through words—that which presents itself immediately to the intellect. In response to this claim, however, Paul points out that many people still manage to err in determining the literal sense of both the Old and New Testaments. "The ways of the Lord are right and the just walk in them, but transgressors stumble in them" (Hos 14:9). For Paul, therefore, the spiritual disposition of the exegete is essential if one is to discern the true sense of the text. For he says that although the literal sense is always right, it will be clearer to the just who have the light of faith. Those who walk in the ways of the Lord adhere to what was intended through the literal sense of faith, whereas transgressors lack that very light of faith *(lumen fidei)* and consequently stumble. Hence the blindness for which Christ rebukes the Jews is their false understanding of the literal sense. "To search the scriptures" is to attend to the "true literal sense that is contained within them." The key here is the *verus sensus litteralis*, since a false conception of the literal sense opens up the door to heresy. If Arius had possessed the true literal sense, he would have seen that "The Father and I are one" (Jn 10:30) speaks to the unity of the divine nature, while the genuine understanding of "The Father is greater than I" (Jn 14:28) refers to the Father's superiority with respect to Christ's assumed human nature. Heresy inevitably results when texts are understood *ad literam*, apart from the light of the Holy Spirit. Thus one must abide by the true literal understanding of the Gospel—*verum intellectum litteralem Evangelii*.[85] Here, then, even as Paul does not advert to the Wycliffite disputes, the central exegetical tenets are evident: the Divine Author's meaning—itself the literal sense—is accessible only to those who have been illumined by Christ the Truth.

Finally, it should be remembered that questions pertaining to the literal sense were also taken up in larger discussions of academic discourse. As logic and theology increasingly intersected in the late medieval schools tension between the two disciplines became apparent. Of specific interest for biblical exegesis and theological discussion is the term *virtus sermonis*, that is, the "force of a word." Most basically it denotes proper speech according to strict grammatical signification as opposed to the broader parameters of common parlance *(usus loquendi)* that allow for metaphors and tropes. Thus an author might attempt to get his point across by employing words in an improper sense. As seen above, the late medieval theologians were willing to include metaphorical speech within the literal sense, precisely because they equated the literal sense with the intended sense of the author. Yet if one were confined to the strict rules of grammar and logic it would seem that biblical passages employing metaphors and tropes would actually be false *de virtute sermonis* no matter what the author had in mind. And this would imply that Holy Scripture itself could be proven false on some level. On 29 December 1340 the Faculty of Arts at the University of Paris took up the matter and issued a statute specifically condemning anyone who would claim that patristic and biblical texts were false according to the rules of proper supposition *(virtus sermonis)*, even while they knew such sayings were true when read according to their intended sense. The statute declared that discourse in this case derives its force *(virtus)* from the imposition and common usage of the authors. The author's intended meaning constitutes the literal sense, therefore, and gives the word its true force *(virtus sermonis)*.[86] In fact, as Zénon Kaluza points out, the Paris statute actually offers two definitions of *virtus sermonis:* the first was employed by the Parisian Ockhamists and limited to proper speech, and the second allowed for broader figurative language. Hence it is according to this second, broader definition that the "literal sense" of a text depends upon the common usage of words; and the *virtus sermonis* is ultimately defined by the subject matter. This means, in turn, that a given proposition might be true when taken in its proper grammatical sense and yet false with respect to the subject matter *(secundum materiam subiectam)*. The statute recognizes, therefore, that different branches of knowledge have their own distinct languages proper to their subject matter. Because there was no universal discipline there could be no universal language, and hence no universal literal sense applicable to them all.[87] As we shall see, the matter of the *virtus sermonis* as applied not only to biblical exegesis, but theological discourse generally, figures prominently in the later debates regarding heresy and orthodoxy.

Authority and Inspiration

Holy Scripture may have been regarded as the principal authority in all matters of Catholic doctrine, but there were certainly other authorities that were respected by all sides during the Wycliffite debates. Even as scripture was recognized as the supreme doctrinal standard, everyone acknowledged the need for recognized authoritative guidance in its interpretation and application. The very term "authority" *(auctoritas)* had signified first of all the quality by which a person is worthy of trust. Then the term came to apply to the person himself, and then again to the writing that expresses the will of its author. And so it was that the text finally came to be regarded as an *auctoritas* in its own right. Within ecclesiastical circles, therefore, there arose the notion of an authoritative text that can be called upon when making a theological argument. When, over time, the *magistri* as a whole came to a consensus in defining a point of doctrine that opinion would be considered "received" wisdom and henceforth achieve the status of the *sententia magistralis*. In that sense, the masters' teaching came to carry some weight, but their definitions and glosses could not match the authority of the saints. Indeed, even the relative authority of the masters could be called into question. Roger Bacon famously complained of masters who are cited as though they were authorities *(sicut auctores)* despite the fact that some of their writings are filled with mistakes. Even as it became clear to everyone that certain *auctoritates* should be accepted it was not always clear what they actually meant or how they should be applied. The fathers might appear to contradict one another or speak of theological matters in ways that were no longer acceptable. Hence the practice of "reverent exposition" *(exponere reverenter)* was fostered. University masters would claim to be "piously explaining" *(pie exponendes)* the sayings of the saints in order to preserve their truth.[88]

It was widely accepted that the church fathers were inspired by the Holy Spirit and thus possessed a level of insight that later masters could not attain. This does not mean, however, that the fathers were understood to have received "extra data" that had not been revealed to the apostles. Rather, they had a deeper understanding of that unique apostolic deposit. For when the medieval theologians spoke of revelation *(revelatio, revelare)* they were following Augustine's understanding of it as an immediate illumination of the intellect.[89] Because the fathers were treated as inspired, patristic commentary was sacred and could even be considered canonical. Hence medieval exegetes were limited to authorized commentaries and the standard *Gloss* was itself treated at authoritative.[90] One should recall that studying theology in the thirteenth century meant reading the glossed Bible.[91] The *Glossa Ordinaria* remained the primary textbook for the lectures conducted by the biblical bachelors. In fact, a University of Paris statute issued in 1366 insisted that students bring their glossed Bibles to the lectures.[92]

Some theologians provided a ranking of authorities. Saint Bonaventure cautioned that no one may press beyond the literal sense of the biblical text and reach the spiritual meaning without the assistance of those to whom God has revealed it. This can be found in the primary texts of the saints *(originalia sanctorum)*. Bonaventure admits that the writings of the saints can be abstruse, however, and so it is necessary to seek guidance in the *summae* of the masters where these difficulties can be explained. Even here, though, one must proceed with caution, since many of these writers have drawn upon the works of the philosophers. Actually, Bonaventure thinks it is dangerous to descend to the original writings of the saints, given their ornate language that is not found in Holy Scripture. And one should certainly not neglect the study of scripture for the sake of reading Augustine, inasmuch as scripture is always owed the highest reverence. It is even more dangerous to descend to the *summae* of the masters, for they can err on occasion. Sometimes they think that they understand the original works of the saints and yet end up contradicting them. The greatest danger, however, is reserved for the descent into the philosophers. Bonaventure cautions against mixing the water of philosophy with the wine of Holy Scripture lest one is left in the end with water alone. The faith will not be proven through reason, he cautions, but through scripture and miracles.[93]

Peter John Olivi found that right order begins with "faith and the font of Holy Scripture, and thereafter through the books of the saints which, like rivers, flow immediately from the principal font." Compared with these the works of the worldly philosophers are no more than a stagnant bog.[94] The Gospel writers excelled in tasting the most blessed Trinity, in the worship of the highest divine majesty, and in the vision of the highest splendor and truth. From them alone, therefore, was it possible and fitting that the gospel of Christ be handed down to the universal church of Christ.[95]

For Thomas Aquinas, the proper authorities employed by sacred teaching *(sacra doctrina)* are the canonical scriptures. No other authority can match them. One argues from the canonical scriptures of necessity *(ex necessitate)*, whereas arguments based on the doctors of the church—valuable as they are—carry only probable force *(probabiliter)*. In fact, the Christian faith depends upon the revelation made to the apostles and the prophets, which they then wrote down in the canonical books. Aquinas makes it clear that the faith does not depend upon any revelation made to the doctors of the church. Here he has recourse to Augustine's aforementioned remark that he only honors those books of the canonical scriptures since none other can match their status.[96] Certainly, for Aquinas, the fathers cannot stand on the level of the apostles who had possessed a fuller *(plenius)* knowledge of the mysteries of the faith owing to their proximity to Christ.[97] The apostles hold a unique place in the church and are to be preferred above all other saints, since they possessed the Holy Spirit in greater abundance than all the rest. They received immediately from Christ himself those things that pertain to salvation and then handed them down to others. It is in this sense, therefore, that the church can be said to be founded upon the apostles.[98]

In fact, the relative weight of biblical and patristic authority had ramifications for the battle against heresy. Thus Guido Terreni wrote:

> Although the writings of the holy doctors which fall outside of the canon of the Bible should be examined and read, and received with due reverence, they are nevertheless not of such firm authority and

inviolability that one would not be permitted to contradict them or raise doubts concerning them. Such is the case with those statements which are not proven expressly and evidently through Holy Scripture, nor confirmed, nor authorized through the church, and so determined to contain the steadfast and certain truth. Hence the opinion of heretics cannot positively be refuted through the statements of the saints which remain outside of the biblical canon. For where there is no infallible truth, there can be no steadfast and certain faith, since a steadfast faith depends upon the infallible truth. Yet there is no infallible assent with regard to these writings, nor any certain and steadfast adherence. And so, because there is no certain and infallible truth, there is no steadfast and certain faith, which means that assent in these instances will always be coupled with doubt and the fear of falsehood.[99]

In other words, for Terreni, only arguments based upon the biblical text can claim binding authority in disputes with heretics—such as the Spiritual Franciscans in his case—because scripture is inerrant and thus forms the basis for an infallible determination.

Extra-Scriptural Tradition and Doctrinal Development

However great the authority of scripture remained for the theologians there was surely more to the life of the church than what had been precisely recorded in the Old and New Testaments. Everyone knew, of course, that there were all sorts of "extra-scriptural traditions" that had been observed for centuries. The question that remained was how to determine both their nature and their status relative to Holy Scripture. This would prove an especially volatile matter in the Wycliffite disputes as the different sides traded barbs over so-called human traditions. Back in the fourth century Basil of Caesarea (d. 379) commented on the relationship between written and unwritten traditions in the midst of a tract on the Holy Spirit. His comments were later incorporated into Gratian's *Decretum* (*Ecclesiasticarum*, D. 11, c. 5) and often cited throughout the Middle Ages. Here Basil noted that among the ordinances (δογμάτων) that the church receives, some come in the form of written teachings (ἐκ τῆς ἐγγράφου διδασκαλίας), while others are received from the tradition of the apostles, handed down "in a mystery" (ἐν μυστηρίῳ). Both sorts are to be held in equal esteem. Indeed, Basil says it would be most unwise to reject every custom that cannot claim written authority. For instance, there is no written warrant for making the sign of the cross or facing east during prayer. All this comes from unwritten teachings (ἐκ τῆς ἀγράφου διδασκαλίας). Practices such as the blessing of the water and oil at baptism also belong to the authority of a "silent and mystical tradition." From the very beginning, says Basil, the apostles and fathers, who established laws for the church, sought to safeguard the awesome dignity of the mysteries in secrecy and silence. Basil's remarks led Heiko Oberman to suppose that Basil was advocating a "two-sources" theory whereby scripture was deemed an insufficient source of revelation that had to be supplemented by a separate line of unwritten tradition. But that is to overlook the fact that Basil makes a clear distinction between liturgical rites and articles of faith, that is, between what he calls "dogma" (δόγμα) and "proclamation" (κήρυγμα). The first is observed in silence; the latter is preached to the whole world.[100] This proclamation comes down in the written form of Holy Scripture, which is the basis of the orthodox faith, although it may also be expressed in the many rites of the church. There is no question, however, of the unwritten traditions supplementing an otherwise defective biblical text as though scripture lacked the fullness of Christian doctrine. As the Eastern Orthodox theologian George Florovsky remarks with respect to Basil: "Thus the unwritten tradition in rites and symbols does not actually add anything to the content of the scriptural faith; it only puts this faith into focus."[101]

If it is agreed that scripture is perfectly complete and thus in no need of addition, what does one make of the great creeds of the church? Thomas Aquinas set himself to answer the objection that articles of the faith should not be arranged in the Creed for the very fact that "Holy Scripture is the rule of faith to which it is impermissible to either add or subtract." In reply, Thomas at once defends the sufficiency and authority of scripture while extolling the infallibility of the church: "The universal church cannot err, because she is governed by the Holy Spirit, who is the Spirit of truth.... Yet the creed was published by the authority of the universal church. Therefore, it contains nothing inappropriate." Then proceeding to connect the authority of the church with the authority of scripture, Thomas notes that the truth of the faith is contained in Holy Scripture diffusively and in various ways, some of which are obscure. Hence it often requires dedicated and prolonged study to draw out *(eliciendum)* the truth of the faith from scripture. The teachings of Holy Scripture needed to be summarily collected and put forth in a clear manner so that all the people might believe them. Indeed, says Thomas, "[The creed] is not added to Holy Scripture, but rather is taken up *(sumptum)* from Holy Scripture."[102] In fact, Thomas will insist that the truth of the faith had already been explicated sufficiently in the teaching of Christ and the apostles. Yet because there are wicked men who still seek to pervert apostolic teaching and the rest of the scriptures, it is necessary from time to time to issue an explanation of the faith in order to counter these errors. For this reason a future general council would have the power to formulate a new version of the creed. Of course, that does not mean this later council would alter the very faith of the previous creed, only that it would state the same thing more clearly *(magis expositam)*.[103]

The Franciscan Saint Bonaventure offers a more nuanced view than his Dominican colleague. First of all he made it clear against the more radical elements in the Franciscan order—the so-called Spiritual Franciscans—that after the New Testament there will be no other. Nor can any of the sacraments of the New Law be withdrawn, precisely because this law is itself the Eternal Testament.[104] This does not amount to a static situation, however, for even as Bonaventure believed that the final and perfect revelation was present in the New Testament, he thought there remained an infinite number of multiform theories *(multiformes theorias)* that can still be elicited from the scriptures. As from plants come new seeds, so from the scriptures arise new theories and new meanings.[105] The Holy Spirit is providing hitherto unknown insights into the riches of Christ, which leads to a renewed flourishing of the gospel manifested most perfectly in the Franciscan life of highest poverty. Indeed, it is precisely as a member of the Franciscan order that Bonaventure retained an openness to development that allowed for changes to suit new circumstances *(pro loco et tempore)*.[106] Such openness to the ongoing work of God in the church also meant that the sacraments of Confirmation and Extreme Unction need not have been explicitly instituted by Christ in the New Testament. Instead, Bonaventure believed that that they had been first insinuated by Christ and then later instituted by the Holy Spirit.[107] By distinguishing between insinuation and institution, Bonaventure could at once connect all the sacraments to Christ even as he allows for a measure of genuine development. The Holy Spirit supplied to the church the precise details of these sacraments, thereby in keeping with Christ's promise that the Paraclete would later reveal what the apostles were not yet ready to bear (Jn 16:12). Either way, though, God alone is the author *(auctor)* of the sacraments, which the apostles and their successors merely promulgate.[108]

An even more expansive view of extra-scriptural tradition was offered by another Franciscan theologian at the outset of the fourteenth century. Yet the manner in which Duns Scotus deals with the matter is not entirely clear. Indeed, modern scholars offer a range of opinions as to what Scotus actually believed, and the truth is that he himself may not have completely settled the matter in his own mind.[109] Such an ambiguity with respect to extra-scriptural development does seem to have been a particularly Franciscan trait. Hence we should not be suprised that it was the Franciscan among Wyclif's opponents, William Woodford, who made pointed appeals to extra-scriptural traditions amid an argument that still remained firmly anchored in antiquity.

In the prologue to his *Ordinatio* Duns Scotus addressed the question as to "whether the supernatural knowledge necessary to the wayfarer is sufficiently handed down in Holy Scripture." His response indicates that, even as such knowledge may be contained within scripture implicitly, and therefore remains in need of careful explication, scripture does indeed contain all that the wayfarer needs. One will note, however, that the question does not ask whether such salvific knowledge may also be handed down by other means—only whether scripture is itself sufficient. Scotus begins by observing that there are many heresies that condemn Holy Scripture whether in whole or in part.[110] Scotus goes on to list the various ways in which the heretics may be defeated, all of which rest on affirming the authority and sufficiency of Holy Scripture. First of all, Scotus notes the fulfillment of scriptural prophecies: something that one would have to credit to God's perfect foreknowledge manifested through the prophets.[111] Then there is the general agreement of the scriptures, which must be attributable to a single guiding intellect. This seems to be the only plausible explanation for how the various writers of the canonical books, separated by time and distance, could so thoroughly agree.[112] The authority of these writers is confirmed by the fact that they consistently condemn mendacity, and thus would be unlikely to lie when speaking on God's behalf. What is more, it must be concluded that they are operating under the direction of a supernatural agent when they assented to what lay beyond the natural power of their intellect.[113]

Having thereby demonstrated the inherent virtues that generate trust in scripture, Scotus will then turn to the exterior factors that are necessary to cement one's confidence in scripture's credibility. And that takes us to the church herself. For Scotus contends that the precise books that make up the canon of Holy Scripture are also worthy of confidence by virtue of the community that collected them. Scotus notes that if you wish to believe something pertaining to a contingency that was not, and is not, evident to you, then you should trust in the community or in those things that the community approves. If the community itself is of good reputation and honest that is all the more reason to trust its judgments. Such is the case with the biblical canon. The Jews, like the Christians, were very careful about which books they admitted into their canon when determining their authenticity. What is more, these communities took care to preserve such books, precisely because their contents were regarded as necessary for salvation.[114] We see the symbiotic relationship between scripture and the church. Holy Scripture may indeed convey salvific truth sufficiently, lacking nothing that the wayfarer needs to know, but it cannot be separated from the church, which verifies, or authorizes, its salvific content.

The church's testimony is essential for recognizing not only scripture's trustworthiness but also its capacity to convey divine truth in its fullness. As Scotus notes the different objections to the thesis of scriptural sufficiency, he appeals to Origen's advice that it will sometimes be necessary to rely upon reason to infer the full import of an issue that scripture does not explicitly describe. Scotus follows up on this point when he makes the following statement: "There are many necessary truths which are not clearly described *(exprimuntur)* in Holy Scripture, although they are there in an implicit state *(virtualiter)*, in the same way that conclusions rest within principles. And the effort made by doctors and expositors to investigate such things has proved to be helpful."[115] Hence, whether contained therein implicitly or explicitly, the truths necessary for salvation can be found in Holy Scripture. Yet it is the church, in her sacred tradition, that will draw out the implicit truths embedded in the biblical text. The church that verifies the text will also be the one to bring forth the fullness of its meaning. One might say, therefore, that although scripture lacks nothing in terms of material content, it is the church that furnishes the substantial form. The church—as manifested here in the doctors and expositors—plays an effective role in actualizing the potent matter of scriptural content. The church is unfolding *(explicare)* what otherwise remains folded up *(implicare)* within Holy Scripture.

As noted above, Scotus contends that there are many necessary truths that are not expressly stated in scripture but rather are contained therein implicitly *(virtualiter)* like conclusions within principles.[116] It was a matter of explicating content that was otherwise implicit within Holy Scripture. But is it possible that the church might also hand down salvific knowledge that is not contained within scripture even in an implicit form? Christ's descent into hell is a good test case. Scotus concedes that the descent into hell is not taught in the Gospels, but he says that it must still be held as an article of faith because it is posited in the Apostles' Creed. In fact, he says, there are many others things concerning the sacraments of the church that are not clearly described *(expressa)* in the Gospel but that are still held by the church as having been handed down with certitude from the apostles. And it would be dangerous to err not only in those things that came down from the apostles through writing but also in those that must be held through the custom of the universal church.[117] After all, says Scotus, Christ did not teach within the Gospel narratives all things pertinent to the administration of the sacraments. And here Scotus has recourse to the classic verse when dealing with such issues: Jesus' admonition to the apostles, "I still have many things to say to you, but you cannot bear them now. When the Spirit of truth comes, he will guide you into all truth" (Jn 16:12). On that basis Scotus concludes that the Holy Spirit taught the apostles many things that are not written *(scripta)* in the Gospel, some of which come through writing and some through the custom of the church that the apostles have handed down.[118]

There is some ambiguity in these remarks. For Scotus speaks of things concerning the sacraments that on the one hand are not "clearly described" *(expressa)* in the Gospel and on the other things that are not "written" *(scripta)* in the Gospel. The first phrase leads one to conclude that these things may nevertheless be present in the Gospel in an implicit form, whereas the second gives the impression that they are not found there in any form. What is more, though, it is not clear that Scotus is speaking consistently throughout about Catholic truths necessary for salvation. For he shifts seamlessly from a specific article of faith, that is, Christ's descent into hell, to "many other things concerning the sacraments," which may simply refer to peripheral customs surrounding sacramental administration rather than the institution of the sacraments themselves. In that sense, then, what comes down from the apostles in unwritten form would be elaborative but not constitutive. Indeed, in that vein it must be remembered that when Scotus begins his specific treatment of the sacraments in the fourth book of his *Ordinatio* (4.2.1) he presents multiple passages from the New

Testament in support of each one. He actually finds clear evidence in Holy Scripture that all seven sacraments were instituted by Jesus Christ himself. Hence he does not advert to an unwritten apostolic tradition to verify the sacraments.

The various definitions surrounding the sacraments often proved difficult for Scotus. When the church sanctioned what Scotus took to be a more complicated definition of Christ's eucharistic presence (transubstantiation rather than consubstantiation) he deferred to the guidance of the Holy Spirit. One may well wonder why the church chose the more difficult understanding of this article, when the words of scripture could be preserved according to the easier and truer understanding based upon appearance.[119] We should be clear, though, that only the explanation of real presence was at issue. Scotus regarded the fact of real presence to be thoroughly scriptural. Nor did Scotus ever imply that transubstantiation was itself unscriptural. Actually, Scotus proceeded to make it very clear that the church is not standing over scripture here as though its judge. For he points out that the scriptures are explicated by the very Holy Spirit who fashioned them. The church chose this particular eucharistic teaching for the very fact that it is already true, since it is not in the church's power to make something true or untrue. That is left to God who establishes the truth.[120] Scotus can trust such decisions to be true because he believes in the indefectibility of the church as a whole. In keeping with the classic reading of Luke 22:32, where Christ prayed that Peter's faith would not fail, Scotus affirms that the church cannot err in faith or morals.[121] Again, therefore, the church remains an authority distinct from scripture, since she alone is competent to offer an authoritative interpretation of the text, but there is no sense in which she is in competition with it. The very fact that Scotus never presents a definitive position on the authority of scripture relative to the church may be emblematic of the fact that he did not see this as a problem in need of resolution. Scotus was at ease with a certain amount of tension inherent to the balancing of authoritative sources. Rather than view scripture, tradition, and the church in some sort of contest with one another, they could all—under the guidance of the one Holy Spirit—serve as interlocking witnesses to the truth.

A few decades later Scotus's Franciscan confrère William of Ockham took matters a little further, although he too neglected to offer a definitive position on the relationship between scriptural and extra-scriptural truth. It was in his massive *Dialogus* that Ockham presented a list of five sorts of truth *(genera veritatum)* that might be considered authoritative in the determination of Catholic doctrine. The problem that we encounter in trying to assess Ockham's commitment to the following theory is that Ockham never clearly claims it as his own. He attributes it to "some people" *(quidam)*; he never says that he himself embraces the extra-scriptural material on the list. Now the use of *"quidam"* among the medieval masters was often (purposely) ambiguous; it might signal their own position, although not necessarily. In fact, the term's ambiguity provided cover for a master who presented controversial ideas: reciting the ideas of others rather than asserting such ideas as his own.

At any rate, the first position reflects the more traditional medieval view. Some say that those truths that are Catholic and necessary for salvation are found only in the canon of the Bible, whether explicitly or implicitly *(explicite vel implicite)* asserted. Thus, even as the proposition "Christ is true God and true man" cannot be found in those exact words within scripture, nonetheless it is still Catholic and necessary for salvation inasmuch as it is a necessary and formal inference drawn from the things that are contained in scripture. All other truths, apart from those that are located in scripture or inferred as necessary inferences—even if contained in the writings of the saints or definitions of the highest pontiffs—must not be counted as Catholic or necessary for salvation. On this point Ockham turned to Gratian's *Decretum* in order to bolster the case for the superiority of Holy Scripture. Here he found canons drawn from the works of Saint Augustine that affirmed the perfection of scripture (*Ego solis*, D. 9, c. 5). Not only may nothing be subtracted from scripture, therefore, but nothing may be added as though essential for salvation. Only the canonical books contained in the Bible are worthy of full adherence as necessary for salvation, thereby surpassing the writings of the bishops (*Noli frater*, D. 9, c. 9). As such, one is free to doubt and discuss all that has been written after the confirmation of the canon, whether by councils or popes, until such time as they have been shown to be in keeping with Holy Scripture. And to these texts Ockham also added Augustine's declaration in *De doctrina christiana* that everything useful to the Christian is already contained in scripture (*De doc. chr.* 2.42.63).[122] The argument put forward here in favor of Holy Scripture as the principal source of the Catholic faith bears a marked similarity to Ockham's own argument supporting the superiority of theologians over canonists (as we shall see below).

Ockham then proceeds to lay out the case for Catholic truths that are not found in scripture, whether implicitly or explicitly, and yet are still necessary for salvation. Some people claim that there are truths preserved outside of the biblical canon that have come to be known by Catholics through divine revelation or by means of the apostles, since Christ taught the apostles many things that are not contained in the Bible. What is more, the apostles were taught many things by the Holy Spirit that they then taught to Catholics, and yet such teachings are not found in the Bible. Hence all these truths, along with the necessary inferences that can drawn from them, must be held as Catholic.[123] Advocates of this position appeal to Augustine's remarks against the Manichees—in matters of doubt regarding the faith one must have recourse to the authority of the Catholic Church—as recorded in the *Decretum* (*Palam est*, D.11, c. 9). Hence they argue that the authority of the church suffices for the establishment of the faith apart from Holy Scripture. For if one were really bound to scripture alone it would be permissible to deny that the apostles wrote the Creed, or that Peter was bishop of Rome. But the universal church has taught these truths up until the present day, which would mean that she had erred—itself an unfitting idea. Moreover, Catholics are bound to obey the Roman pontiff when he decrees something that is not contrary to the orthodox faith, and yet there are many truths that popes determine that cannot be confirmed by the biblical canon alone.[124] It seems unlikely that this would have been Ockham's position, however, since it is the very argument made by the canonists that he devotes so much effort to refuting.

Now according to this broad opinion that moves beyond the implicit and explicit truths contained in scripture, there are five genera of truths from which a Christian may not dissent. The first certainly does include all the truths handed down in scripture or what can be necessarily inferred from them; the second category includes those truths that come down from the apostles even if not contained within scripture; the third contains chronicles and histories or accounts of believers that are worthy of trust; the fourth looks to truths that can be inferred from the first and second category alone, or from one of them along with the third category; and fifth and finally there are the truths, apart from those revealed to the apostles, that God revealed to others or would even newly reveal. This would entail a revelation that has come, or would come, and then be accepted by the universal church without any doubt. All the truths that the church defines are included, therefore, in these five kinds.¹²⁵ What is noteworthy in the last category is the possibility that some further truth might be revealed to the church. Ockham offers no example of such a truth, and there need not be one; it could remain merely a possibility. Though it should also be said that this truth would have to pass an extremely high bar before it could be counted as genuine revelation: it must receive the unanimous consent of every Christian. By that standard even one person could block its acceptance, since this person might be the last remaining faithful Catholic in the midst of a mass apostasy.

Later in the fourteenth century, however, Henry Totting de Oyta proved firmly committed to the notion that there is more to the church's faith than what is contained in Holy Scripture. Many other truths have come down from the apostles by way of their successors, he says, or have come to the church through the writings of the faithful. They must be preserved and believed as Catholic, even though they are not contained in the biblical canon or follow formally from its contents. As an example Henry cites Pope Innocent III's 1202 decretal *Cum Marthae* from which he gathers that the formula of eucharistic consecration is not found in its entirety within the Gospels or in any other book of the New Testament. And yet, says Henry, one must believe that Christ handed it down in that form. Henry rejects any attempt to prove that this formula formally follows from some other formula contained in the biblical books.¹²⁶ In other words, it cannot merely be the explication of implicit material. But the fact is that Henry has completely misread the decretal when he regards it as an endorsement of extra-scriptural revelation. Far from looking outside of scripture, Innocent III merely said that in cases such as this the church relies upon the Pauline Epistles or the Book of Acts to supply information about Christ that is not recorded in the Four Gospels. The pope never appealed to any source outside of the New Testament itself.¹²⁷

At all events, Henry then takes up the question "whether only those truths are to be counted as Catholic, and believed as necessary for salvation, which are asserted either explicitly in the biblical canon, or can be inferred from them by necessary and formal consequence." In response, he adopts the five categories of truth that Ockham had presented some forty years earlier, and provides arguments to make his case for the authority of an extra-scriptural tradition.¹²⁸ Henry defends this expansive list, arguing that if one could dissent from these five categories this would mean that the

Catholic Church is not securely grounded in the very things that are necessary for salvation. Hence the church receives and hands down to Catholics not only the first sort of truths (the purely scriptural) but the other four as well—all of which must be observed by the faithful. To dissent from some of these truths is to imply that the authority of the church would vacillate in some part, with the result that the whole of its authority would be rendered suspect. Henry regards this as a threat to the church's authority that could end up casting doubt even upon the purely scriptural truths in light of Augustine's well-worn dictum that he would not have believed the gospel if not for the authority of the church.[129] In other words, one would have no reason for confidence in the Holy Scriptures if the church did not have the authority to verify them. The universal church would not determine something as a matter of Catholic truth unless it is founded upon these five sorts of truth. And the assurance of her rectitude is rooted in the Holy Spirit's continual governance of the church. Thus Henry relies upon Christ's promise to Peter (Lk 22:32), thereby securing the infallibility of the universal church. And it is here that Henry offers the classic proviso that renders the whole debate over authority so difficult: he notes that although prelates and ecclesiastical officials may err in their judgments, this does not mean that the church herself errs in matters of the Christian faith. Prelates are indeed human beings who can deceive and be deceived, but the church pronounces nothing in matters of the faith unless founded upon the five aforementioned truths.[130] No medieval theologian had the slightest doubt that the church would always abide in the true faith, but—whether it be Henry Totting or Gerard of Bologna—they allow for the fact that people in even the highest offices of the church might fall away from that faith. So long as this is admitted in principle, stemming dissent will be all but impossible—as the Wycliffite disputes bear witness.

One of the main problems when talking of scriptural and extra-scriptural truths is determining exactly which are necessary for salvation and which are not so essential. Henry concedes that not all Catholic truths have equal weight in directing believers to salvation. There are the basic Trinitarian and Christological truths outlined in the Creed that one must believe explicitly. Yet there are other truths that need not be believed explicitly in order to attain salvation. Nevertheless, it is still fitting that one hold them with a firm faith, even if only implicitly, since they are divinely revealed and approved. Hence no Catholic should dissent even from these lesser truths inasmuch as they have come down to the orthodox church.[131] Yet no precise list of such truths is forthcoming. Indeed, no such list could really be compiled inasmuch as no single list would be exhaustive and any two would most likely vary.

Yet just when it seems that Henry might consider scripture an insufficient source of salvific truth, he then claims that all Catholic truths are founded upon the canon of the Bible, even if they are not explicitly contained therein, or even formally inferred solely from its contents.[132] This all hinges on the fact that the church's authority is itself sufficiently founded upon scripture. Catholic truths that should be held upon the authority of the church are thus grounded at least indirectly in Holy Scripture. The authority of the church belongs to the first category of truth—those that are purely scriptural—such that scripture becomes the ultimate basis for all the church's teaching. And that is why Henry can once again conclude that beyond those truths explicitly contained in scripture or inferred from its contents alone there are many other truths that it is fitting to hold with a sure faith.[133] In this sense scripture is the principal standard by which to test all nonscriptural assertions. For when it is objected that one must add nothing to scripture (Rv 21:18) Henry counters that this only means one may not add something that proves to be dissonant with the true sense of scripture.[134]

Marsilius of Inghen, who lectured on Peter Lombard's *Sentences* at Heidelberg from 1392 to 1394, was likely familiar with the works of Henry Totting. And, like Totting, he seems to endorse a rather expansive range of authoritative theological sources. Marsilius does not present the matter in the same level of detail, however, and thus leaves us with a rather sketchy appraisal.[135] As is to be expected at the outset of a late medieval *Sentences* commentary, Marsilius tackled the basic question as to whether theology can be considered a science. It is in this context that he distinguished between things that can be known by the light of natural reason *(in lumine naturali)* and those that are founded upon divine revelation *(in revelationibus fundatae)*. The latter category is then divided between the science of canon law and sacred theology. Now, the science of canon law, according to Marsilius, has the Catholic man for its subject insofar as he can be directed to eternal life through the statutes of the church. Its principal material, therefore, are the truths expressed in the canon law books. Sacred theology, on the other hand, has God for its subject inasmuch as God is the end that the Catholic wayfarer hopes to attain by way of a formed faith. And theology, according to Marsilius, is handed down in the books of the Bible whether in itself or in its principles.[136]

So far this seems rather straightforward: the science of canon law draws it material from the legal collections, and theology takes its material from Holy Scripture. Yet Marsilius then inquires into the nature of a theological truth *(veritas theologica)*. And it is here that things get more complicated. Taken in the strict sense *(stricte)*, according to Marsilius, a theological truth is clearly stated *(expressa)* either in the articles of faith or in the canon of the Bible, or at least it can be inferred from these sources. Nor is there any intimation here that the articles of faith and the biblical canon are competing principles; the articles themselves—as presented in the Creed—can be regarded as concise formulations of scriptural material (although Marsilius does not state this explicitly). Yet if taken in the broad sense *(large)*, Marsilius finds that the theologian is bound to confess, or at least not pertinaciously disobey, a wider range of theological truths. There are four categories, the first two of which we have already encountered: an article of faith clearly stated in the Apostles' Creed; and a proposition assertively posited in the canon of the Bible. But the next two categories expand the spectrum. The third includes truths found in the authentic chronicles received by the church and those that have come down to us from the apostles, as well as what has been revealed to the holy fathers, although such truths might not be clearly stated *(expresse)* in the canon of the Bible. And fourth there are the pronouncements of all the sanctioned councils and even all the decretals that have not been repealed.[137]

Unfortunately, Marsilius does not provide a substantial rationale for his list. So it remains unclear how the different categories relate to one another or whether there might be a gradation of authority among them. Nor can we be sure to what extent Marsilius himself is committed to this latter, admittedly "broad," list of truths. Notwithstanding these reservations, Philipp Rosemann may be right—taking as an example Marsilius's appeal to the Clementine Decretals to affirm the necessity of created charity in the wayfarer—that Marsilius came to regard canon law as an authoritative bulwark against the vicissitudes of theological speculation in the late medieval church.[138] What does seem clear, however, is that Henry Totting and Marsilius of Inghen were tapping into a more generally shared sense of unease with the indeterminacy of authoritative sources in this age—an age that was, after all, marked by papal schism. Thus, even if many of their fellow theologians at the turn of the fifteenth century would not follow them down this path of extra-scriptural sources of Catholic truth, they remained equally cognizant of the problem of ecclesiastical authority that had to be solved.

Masters of the Sacred Page

Everyone we have looked at to this point has been a theologian who carried out much of his work within the confines of the late medieval university. Thus it is important to get a better sense of just what it meant to be a university master in the Middle Ages. For many of the debates I will examine were fueled by a strong sense of magisterial identity, central to which was the right to advise and consent. Recognized for having attained a mastery of their topic, *magistri* were accorded social status that allowed them to move among the upper echelons of society. They took their place within medieval society as a distinct social class with their own private law.[139] Medieval theologians ranked at the top of the magisterial ladder and were assigned the task of defending the truth, even as they had no hierarchical standing in the ecclesiastical sense. Some might have been ordained before or after taking the doctoral degree, but the doctorate as such was not intrinsically connected with the priesthood and was thus separate from the ecclesiastical hierarchy. All that linked them to the ecclesiastical hierarchy was the oath that the licentiate took before the university chancellor. Hence the statements of the doctors could be called "scholastic" and "magisterial" but never "authentic," a term reserved for papal and conciliar doctrinal pronouncements.[140]

While it is true that theologians did not therefore have the power of the prelates, they were not their subordinates either. The doctor of theology had an authorization *(auctorizatio)* that granted him the authority to teach. Theologians and bishops had different spheres of authority: to the first teaching and the second governance. Yet the two groups were not necessarily at odds with one another; bishops often handed down their decisions after having consulted with the theologians *(de consilio magistrorum theologiae)*.[141] Indeed, the university theologians saw themselves as the protectors of orthodoxy and expected to be consulted. Paris was especially looked to by popes and kings in need of expert opinion. So it was that in

1331 King Philip VI wrote to Pope John XXII that "our doctors know what ought to be believed in matters of faith better than the jurists and other clerks who inhabit your court and know little or nothing of theology."[142]

The question of magisterial rights and authority came to the fore in the strife between mendicants and seculars dating back to the middle of the thirteenth century. For the debate over privileges turned not only on the legitimacy of new religious orders but also and even more acutely on papal authority to sanction these orders. Many among the secular clergy charged that the papacy was overstepping its duly allotted role of preserving the ancient state of the church *(status ecclesiae)*. Secular theologians often turned to canon law to make the case that papal authority was itself bound by Holy Scripture and the tradition of the apostolic church. Yet even as all would agree that this is true in principle, there was no consensus as to just how much freedom the pope had when attempting to act for the good of the church. It is well worth bearing in mind, therefore, that when Wyclif and Hus asserted their right to dissent from papal directives that they reckoned contrary to scripture, and thereby unjust, they were part of a long-standing magisterial tradition. Indeed, we shall see that their opponent Jean Gerson was also quick to assert the master's right to contest the decisions of an erring pope.

Railing against the newly formed mendicant orders that had descended upon the University of Paris in the middle of the thirteenth century, the secular theologian William of Saint-Amour contended that only two orders had been established to govern the church: the bishops who succeeded the Twelve Apostles and the parish priests who succeeded the seventy-two disciples; there was no third order. The basis for William's claim was actually quite solid, grounded as it was in a Pseudo-Isidorian decretal attributed to the first-century pope Anacletus. Incorporated into Gratian's *Decretum*, this chapter (*In novo testamento*, D. 21, c.2) would appear to be of unimpeachable authority. For William, it assures that the care and governance of souls has been granted solely to the bishops and parochial clergy. Hence William took issue with the papacy's decision to sanction this new type of religious life. He had no desire to dispute papal authority as such, but he could not accept such overextended claims. One overextension was the granting of a license to preach wherever the friars chose even if not invited by the diocesan clergy. As far as William was concerned the pope is thereby violating principles laid down by the apostle Paul himself (2 Cor 10:13) that one not infringe on another's territory. To this end William appealed to the canon *Sunt quidam dicentes* (C. 25, q. 1, c. 6), which stated in very stark language that papal decisions have no authority if they violate the teachings of the apostles and prophets. The order of bishops and priests to which William appealed was, he believed, ratified by its imitation of the celestial hierarchy depicted by Pseudo-Dionysius in his *De ecclesiastica hierarchia*. The *ordo perficientium* comprises bishop, priest, and deacon, whereas the religious orders, or monks, belong to the inferior *ordo perficiendorum*. No inferior order may exercise the office of its superior—as the mendicants are attempting to do when they claim the right to teach, preach, and administer sacraments. Such duties are off-limits to all but the *ordo perficientium*. Hence, as it is not within the rights of any mortal man to change this "divinely ordained and most sacred hierarchy," so no pope may tear it down.[143] In sum, the creation of the mendicant orders is an illegitimate novelty that is upsetting the divinely established order of the church.

Mendicant theologians were acutely aware of the vital role the papacy played in securing their privileges. Saint Bonaventure extolled papal authority as the legal backbone of the Franciscan order, noting that Pope Honorius III had officially approved their rule. To claim that the Franciscans cannot be sent out to preach by papal authority, says Bonaventure, is to deny the pope his rightful plenitude of power.[144] Yet the secular theologians stuck to their basic line. Gerard of Abbeville contends that the *status ecclesiae*—which the pope was attempting to undermine—had been established by Christ himself. The papacy does indeed enjoy a special place in the church as a principle of unity, but the power of the keys has been bestowed upon all the apostles and their successors. Hence the pope's attempt to usurp the jurisdiction of the bishops is without foundation. Gerard is adamant that all power in the church descends from Christ, the head of the whole church. It is not diffused from the papacy among inferior prelates. As such, the supreme pontiff cannot destroy the state of the church that has been instituted by the Lord among the prelates and priests and ordained by the apostles. Gerard also had recourse to *Sunt quidam dicentes* (C. 25, q. 1, c. 6) in order to secure the ancient constitution of the church.[145]

The secular masters Henry of Ghent and Godfrey of Fontaines insisted that—*ab institutione ecclesiae primitivae*—there had been only two grades established for the care of souls and that these grades had been instituted by no one less than Christ himself *(ab ipso Christo)*. Like Gerard before them, Henry and Godfrey appealed to the historical record enshrined in Gratian's *Decretum*. The bishops were the successors of the apostles and the priests those of the disciples; there was no room for mendicants.[146] At the heart of the questions concerning papal power relative to the rest of the episcopacy, and the preservation of the *status ecclesiae*, was the fundamental responsibility of the ruler (in this case the pope) to act for the common good. Godfrey of Fontaines, for his part, held that a superior who acted against the good of the community should not be tolerated if he refuses to correct his error. Because the pope must never act against the common good, Godfrey not only allowed for opposing the pope, but even deposing him.[147] In a series of Quodlibetal questions, Godfrey vehemently objected to prelates unilaterally deciding what is orthodox and heretical. He made it clear that even the decisions handed down by popes are open to scrutiny and that it is precisely for the theologian to inquire into those decisions and determine their validity.[148] Godfrey would not be intimidated in his quest for the truth no matter that he might offend the powerful. When dealing with questions pertinent to the faith the theologian was obliged to speak the truth and would sin if he refused. Indeed, it belongs to the very nature of his public office that he teach the truth.[149] As Ian Wei points out, the Paris theologians claimed for themselves an "immediate authority" that could be at odds with the jurisdictional structure of the church as a whole. That is precisely what troubled the canon lawyers who had earned their degrees at the universities and then left to implement their power within the very juridical structure that the theologians seemed to be undermining.[150]

Theologians were not the only masters in the university, of course, but they were the only ones whose profession was defined by an inherently perfect and sacred text. In the medieval schools each faculty had its own text that served as its foundation. The canonists read the *Decretum*, and the theologians read Holy Scripture. At the beginning of the thirteenth century masters of theology were being called *magistri sacrae paginae* or *magistri sacrae scripturae* because scripture was the text that they read. As Henry Denifle remarked, "The theologian of the Middle Ages lived by Holy Scripture; each *principium*, each book of the *Sentences*, each treatise, each argument began with a text from Holy Scripture." Hence Pierre d'Ailly could proclaim in 1388: *Ad doctores theologos pertinet sacram scripturam docere*.[151] For, as Thomas Prügl has recently observed, "the development of 'systematic' theology during the scholastic period was never separated from its biblical, i.e., textual foundation."[152]

In the *Prooemium* to his commentary on Peter Lombard's *Sentences* the Franciscan theologian Peter Auriol set forth a basic schema of authoritative texts. Here he contends that theology is a science of consequences *(scientia consequentiarum)*. Theological principles are articles of faith and belong ultimately to Holy Scripture. Therefore, what it means "to know" in theology is nothing other than to know how to deduce what follows from the articles and from scripture. Auriol contends, moreover, that theological knowledge pertains only to those things that are written in the Bible: what was understood by the prophets and the apostles and other composers of the divine books. The divine books, therefore, are of greater authority than civil and canon law. Auriol follows the classic medieval principle that texts are the *auctoritates* that form the foundation of a given discipline. He notes that there are authoritative texts in every field, which, if properly understood, yield true knowledge of that discipline. Jurists study the law books of popes and emperors and thereby gain knowledge *(scientia)* of the law. Philosophers study Aristotle's *Physics* to attain true knowledge of their discipline. And those who read Livy will find knowledge of history and can then pass it on to others. But, says Auriol, divine histories are of greater authority. To know what is written in the divine histories pertains to that habit of knowledge which is called divine and theological. Those who know what is written in the divine books, and grasp what the biblical writers understood, will attain the true knowledge *(scientia)* of theology.[153]

So it was, then, that theologians claimed to base their teachings upon the unimpeachable authority of Holy Scripture and thus compared themselves favorably with the canon lawyers who had to be content with the merely human authorities of their own glosses. The Parisian master Francis Caraccioli, for example, upheld the superiority of theology on the grounds that it operates under the inspiration of the Holy Spirit and is concerned not only with matters of faith, but with the whole moral life of the Christian. For it is theology (not canon law) that hands down the very life of Christ, which is the standard of all moral rectitude. Not only was theology about faith, said Francis, but it could even be called faith itself.[154]

When William of Ockham determined that it was for theologians rather than canonists to decide what constitutes heresy, his argument on behalf of the theologians was rooted firmly in their position as *magistri sacrae paginae*. Ockham's case would hinge on the fact that Holy Scripture forms the authoritative foundation for the superior science of theology. First of all, said Ockham, an assertion is only Catholic if it agrees with theology *(consona theologiae)* and only heretical if it is opposed to theology *(theologiae adversari)*. Thus, even if a position were shown to disagree with the pope and the general council, if it did not oppose theology it would not be heretical, even though it may be false, erroneous, or unjust. Most of the following reasons will turn on the superiority of theology as a science, thereby marking out the science of the canonists as inferior and derivative. Thus the second reason given is that theologians treat the science in which the Catholic faith is explicitly and completely handed down. There is nothing pertaining to the rule of faith that is found in the science of the canonists that they did not receive from theology. Third, then, theology is the superior science, and it belongs to the superior science to make judgments about the material that a superior and inferior science both investigate. Fourth, in their different investigations the theologians treat a larger number of Catholic truths under their explicit form than do the canonists. Fifth, the science of theology is not only superior on account of its subject matter, but it is actually prior to the science of the canonists. True and faithful Catholics from apostolic times were already preaching and approving the Catholic faith, and likewise condemning heresy, long before the science of canon law had even been created. Sixth, theologians treat that science to which all other sciences yield in matters of faith. And it is here that Ockham now has explicit recourse to the theologian's unique position as Master of the Sacred Page as he equates the science of Holy Scripture with theology itself *(scientia scripturae diuinae quae theologia vocatur)*. In fact, Ockham stakes much of his case on scripture's divine authorship. For, as the seventh reason states, the theologians treat the science whose immediate author is God, from whom comes the whole of the Catholic faith. The biblical writers wrote nothing from mere human wit but by divine inspiration alone. And finally, again because Holy Scripture is the source of the science of theology, Ockham notes that this is the only science in which one is not permitted to add or subtract anything—based upon the admonitions in Deuteronomy 4:2, Proverbs 30:6, and Revelation 22:18. Only Holy Scripture remains immutable, therefore, whereas the books of canon law are subject to constant revision.[155]

Each discipline has its own authoritative texts *(auctoritates)* that form the basis of its inquiry. Ockham shows to devastating effect that the canonists possess nothing that can compete with the theologians. In a world governed by *auctoritates* Holy Scripture—and thus the science that is based upon it—stands above them all. That does not necessarily make scripture the sole source of Catholic truth, but—given its divine authorship and unique perfection—it is the principal foundation. Thus if Wyclif and Hus—as well as d'Ailly and Gerson—would affirm the principal authority of scripture in the determination of Catholic doctrine they were following along a well-trod path.

Canon Law and Papal Authority

While it is certainly true that theologians were the recognized experts in scripture, whereas canonists had their law books, that does not mean that the canonists did not also recognize the principal authority of Holy Scripture. They surely did, but then they had to find a way to integrate that authority into the life of the church, which was itself a vast corporation held together by laws and customs. Gratian of Bologna began his *Decretum* (c. 1140) with a wide-ranging discussion of law and authority in the church. In the ninth distinction he presented a series of passages drawn from Augustine that firmly established the authority of Holy Scripture. In fact, many of these canons were then cited by Ockham two hundred years later (as noted above): the scriptures take precedence over the writings of the fathers; no lies are to be found in the canonical scriptures; Holy Scripture is to be preferred over the letters of the bishops; and the commentaries on the scriptures must not be given reverence equal to the scriptures themselves.[156] What is more, the *Decretum* itself is drenched in scripture. Gratian cites scripture about five hundred times in his *dicta* and includes some 350 fragments of patristic biblical exegesis. He insisted, moreover, that bishops achieve expertise in the scriptures and said that priests should be reprimanded for reading comedies rather than the Gospels.[157]

Having established the authority of Holy Scripture, Gratian then considered the limits of the biblical canon and the place of the general councils. The canon *Sancta Romana* contains the *Decretum Gelasianum*—thus the longer version of the biblical canon—and begins with an affirmation of the first four ecumenical councils: "The Holy Roman Church does not prohibit—after those scriptures of the Old and New Testament which we accept as normative—the reception [of the following councils]."[158] The authoritative status of these ancient councils is immense, of course, and they will serve as a norm by which future popes and prelates must abide.

Yet the canonists also knew that councils could err as, for example, Rimini (359) and the so-called robber council of Ephesus (449). In the establishment of authoritative texts and decrees, therefore, the church's reception rather than simple antiquity or authorship was a central criterion.[159]

Writing at a time when the Gregorian Reforms were gaining ground and power was increasingly centralized in the papacy, Gratian sought to bolster the authority of papal decrees.[160] Nevertheless, he made it clear that they must always be in accord with the decrees of the earlier fathers or the evangelical precepts.[161] Thus even as the great canonist Huguccio of Pisa accorded the pope the right to revoke the statutes of his predecessors for good cause, he made it clear that the pope may not touch the precepts of the Old and New Testaments, or the articles of faith, or those things that are necessary for salvation, nor those that pertain to the general state of the church.[162] Rufinus of Bologna likewise declared that papal decretals are authoritative only insofar as they do not oppose the precepts of the Gospel or the decrees of the holy fathers.[163]

As seen above, the secular theologians often appealed to the canon *Sunt quidam dicentes* (C. 25, q. 1, c. 6) when attempting to check what they regarded as papal overreach. This important canon begins by affirming that the pope is entitled to make new laws. It then states, however, that in those instances where Christ, the apostles, or the holy fathers have already clearly defined something, the pope cannot pass any new law but rather must defend these precedents. And, what is more, were the pope to attempt to undermine apostolic doctrine, his error would deprive his judgment of any force. In this vein, then, the apostolic see has no authority to concede or change anything against the statutes of the saints. Nothing is permitted to stand against evangelical and prophetic doctrine or custom. Salvation consists in not deviating from the statutes of the fathers and preserving the rule of faith.[164] In this vein, Rufinus of Bologna maintained that the statutes of the ancient and venerable fathers preserve the state of all the churches. They are promulgated with full authority and attain reverence throughout the world. Not even papal authority can abrogate them.[165] Indeed, the authority conceded to Holy Scripture and apostolic teaching in the canon *Sunt quidam dicentes* was regarded as so inviolable that Johannes Teutonicus's *Glossa Ordinaria* on the *Decretum*—which every late medieval canonist and theologian would have read—commented here that if a pope wished to issue a statute that contravened the Gospels, Apostles, or Prophets he would stand convicted as a heretic.[166]

As sacrosanct as the scriptures and ancient councils were, however, the pope needed some leeway in promulgating laws for the good of the church, which is, after all, a living entity that continually faces new challenges. Thus the author of the *Summa Parisiensis* found that the pope retains the right to abrogate the law in particular cases depending upon the circumstances. Decrees that say that the pope cannot abrogate the statutes of his predecessors apply only to matters specifically pertinent to the faith—those central doctrines apart from which there is no salvation. The pope can, however, change those that had once been indifferent prior to their being prohibited.[167] Determining precisely which questions fell into which categories was not always so easily solved. After all, what the pope may believe to be a simple organizational matter could be regarded by others as a much graver issue touching upon the very *status ecclesiae*. The creation and protection of the mendicant orders was just one example of how contentious these questions could become. In this vein, a key term emerges, "dispensation" *(dispensatio)*, and the verb "to dispense" *(dispensare)*, as in "to dispense against" this or that law. A dispensation was a special exemption from some legal obligation—a momentary relaxation of strict canonical discipline that the canonists insisted could only be granted for just cause.[168]

Theologians were often uneasy with the amount of latitude that the canonists gave the pope in matters of dispensation. They could only be alarmed when Tancred and Hostiensis might declare that the pope was the only man capable, like God, of changing the very nature of a thing *(mutando etiam rei naturam)* and creating something out of nothing *(de nihilo aliquid facit)*. Pope Innocent IV claimed that the pope could dispense from the obligations of the Gospels, though only according to the letter, not the spirit *(et dispensat contra verba evangelii, licet non contra mentem)*. Along these lines, Guido de Baysio said that the pope could dispense from the evangelical counsels, although not the evangelical precepts and prohibitions. Even here, though, the canonists did agree that the pope would need good reason to dispense in such instances. Moderate canonists, however, admitted that the pope as successor of Peter was not really free to dispense against all the statements of the apostles—although he could dispense against apostolic ordinances so long as they were not articles of faith. Articles of faith had to be exempt since they were deemed essential for salvation. It was for this reason that the pope could not dispense against the first four ecumenical councils, which contained articles of faith. Nor could the pope dispense against the Ten Commandments, for they too were essential for salvation. It is important to point out that the canonists did not grant the pope a license to run amok; his power of dispensation was grounded in necessity and usefulness *(necessitas vel utilitas)*.[169] Commenting on the *Decretals*, Bernard of Parma argued that the pope could dispense in all matters, although, again, so long as he is not acting against the articles of faith and the general state of the church—*Quoniam Papa in omnibus dispensare potest quae non sunt contra articulos fidei, vel generalem statum ecclesiae*. Innocent IV may have gone a bit further when he declared that the pope can even dispense against the general state of the church, albeit for a great cause. This remark is qualified, however, by the admonition that the pope must not be obeyed were he to act without just cause.[170]

The key to much of this revolves around the concept of the fullness of power *(plenitudo potestatis)*. By the thirteenth century the phrase *"plenitudo potestatis"* was extended to cover the pope's supreme legislative authority and his supreme appellate jurisdiction. Following the lead of Innocent III and Innocent IV, Hostiensis rooted the *plenitudo potestatis* in the pope's position as *Vicarius Christi*. God is at work in whatever the pope does *(quicquid facit papa deus facere creditur)*; the acts and dispensations of the pope are not of man but of God *(non sunt hominis, sed dei)*; with the exception of sin, the pope can do all things by right as God *(omnia de iure potest ut deus)*. Under this schema the pope held both an ordered power *(potestas ordinata)*, as he acted according to established law, and an absolute power *(potestas absoluta)*, when he transcended existing law by way of his fullness of power *(plenitudo potestatis)*. Thus all talk of his absolute power was based upon the fact that the pope was bound by no law *(solutus a legibus)*. As the sovereign, the pope was free to act outside of the law when he determined it was best. Of course, Hostiensis did not regard this as an invitation to capricious or self-serving action, since the pope had received this power for the good of the church. Once more, though, the key factor here is the *status ecclesiae;* the pope could not dispense against the general state of the church, for that would amount to a subversion of the Catholic faith itself—*Non potest tamen contra universalem statum ecclesiae dispensare . . . quod intelligo in fidei subversionem*.[171] Hostiensis also coined the phrase *"suppletio defectuum,"* which allowed the pope to correct a deficiency in the law as part of his fullness of power. In this sense the pope was above the law *(supra ius)*. Having said all this, though, the pope must always act *ex causa*, or *pro ulititate*, or *pro necessitate*. In other words, he must act with good cause for the sake of the common good and without damaging the state of the church.[172]

None of the above should obscure the fact that Holy Scripture remained the principal authority for the canonists. Thomas Izbicki points out that even though there are some changes in the way the canonists arranged their authorities by the end of the thirteenth century, Holy Scripture was always accorded first place. What did change, however, is that conciliar decisions and papal decretals steadily achieved greater authority than patristic texts in matters of scriptural interpretation. Yet it was still scripture that formed the foundation of the faith. The papacy recognized that doctrinal determinations were ultimately subject to Holy Scripture, which was regarded as the sole source of divine revelation. No matter the occasional overreaching, therefore, the canonists consistently saw their role as certifying rites and practices but never setting up tradition as a new source of revelation. Thus no matter how much the rhetoric might be ratcheted up, the canonists consistently maintained the supremacy of Holy Scripture.[173] This attitude persists into the fifteenth century. The papalist Juan de Torquemada declared Holy Scripture the absolute standard—the *lumen et regula*—by which all teachings of the holy doctors are to be judged. Councils and fathers are likewise subordinated to scripture. The reason for later explications of the faith, therefore, is to make sure that the church's teaching remains in keeping with scripture. In fact, Juan believed that pope and council must yield to a theologian who makes a better scriptural argument, though he concedes that once the supreme magisterium—that is the pope and plenary council acting in concert—renders a decision in matters of faith that is infallible. Along these same lines, the canonist Nicholas de Tudeschis (d. 1455), also known as Panormitanus, said: "In matters of faith anyone armed with better reasons and authorities of the New and Old Testament is to be preferred even to the pope."[174]

Even as there was general agreement that the pope is bound by the teaching of Holy Scripture—if not in letter then in spirit—the canonists also had to contend with the possibility that he might err in his interpretation of scripture and even lapse into heresy. As Rufinus of Bologna pointed out, there is precedent for sin in high places: Lucifer sinned in heaven and Adam in paradise. Indeed, there is no one whose position is so secure that he might imagine the office of priesthood provides him with a license to sin.[175] Needless to say, the possibility of an errant or heretical pope was hugely important not only throughout the Wycliffite crisis but also in the resolution of the papal schism that lasted almost forty years (1378–1417). In fact, by the late fourteenth century the leading canonists agreed that a general council could judge a sitting pope who had been accused of heresy, and some even said that he could be held accountable for any grave crime that had scandalized the church.[176]

The *Decretum* provided the locus classicus for future discussions of a heretical pope when the canon *Si papa* (D. 40, c. 6) stated that the pope may be judged by no one, "*unless* he is found to have deviated from the faith."[177] Brian Tierney points out that while the decretists believed that the pope was the supreme judge in questions of faith, this was conditional upon him not straying from the true faith. If he persisted in error he was to be deposed. Christ's prayer that Peter's faith would not fail (Lk 22:32) was not read so as to imply that the pope could not err but rather that the church's faith would always endure.[178]

I noted above that when the canonist Johannes Teutonicus commented on the canon *Sunt quidam dicentes* (C. 25, q. 1, c. 6) he said that a pope who attempted to contravene Holy Scripture would thereby prove himself a heretic. In fact, Johannes makes it clear elsewhere in his *Gloss* that the pope could err and cited *Si papa*, among other canons, to that very effect. The church is not defined by the papacy, he says, but by the *congregatio fidelium*, and it is this church that can never cease to exist.[179] Already in the twelfth century Huguccio had gone so far as to say that not only heresy but other notorious crimes such as fornication and simony were grounds for deposition inasmuch as they too brought grave scandal upon the church. Hence the statutes that claimed the pope was immune from judgment were never meant to cover cases where the pope was causing harm to the church.[180] The problem is that the *Decretum* also said that an inferior cannot bring charges against a superior, so the question remained as to who could actually accuse a sitting pope. For Huguccio, a pope could be accused only if he publicly announced his willful adherence to a known heresy and refused to renounce that heresy after he has been admonished. Moreover, he could only be judged for public heresy and notorious crime, not for secret crimes and heresies. In a notorious case there was no need for a trial, however, and thus the whole problem of judging the pope was not at issue, precisely because he stood condemned already by adhering to a heresy that had been previously condemned. Indeed, the pope who adhered to such a heresy was ipso facto inferior to any Catholic.[181] Johannes Teutonicus concluded that the pope can be accused if he is involved in a notorious crime that scandalizes the church, and is incorrigible. The pope may also be accused for secret heresy, though not for some other secret crime. And finally, the pope may not pass a law that would immunize him from accusation, since that would endanger the whole church.[182]

There was also solid biblical precedent for the correction of an erring pope. In his Epistle to the Galatians, Saint Paul had recounted his confrontation of Saint Peter at Antioch when he "resisted Cephas to his face, because he was reprehensible" (Gal 2:11). Saint Augustine and Saint Jerome had quarreled over whether Paul actually rebuked Peter, the former saying that he did, while the latter chalked the whole incident up to instructive playacting. Saint Augustine carried the day, though, and his reading of the incident set the tone for the next thousand years of Western biblical commentary on this passage. Augustine made it clear that Paul did rebuke Peter, and he had to do so in front of everyone so as to set them all right. For it would not have been useful to rebuke a public error in private. Nevertheless, Augustine also follows Cyprian in extolling Peter's willingness to endure the rebuke of a junior shepherd for the sake of the flock's salvation and the greater unity of the church.[183] All the medieval theologians would have then read the *Glossa Ordinaria*, which had followed Augustine's line. The *Gloss* notes in the interlinear portion that Paul had rebuked Peter in front of all those whom he was harming, while the marginal gloss extols Peter's humility as he provided an example for prelates.[184] In fact, by the twelfth century this passage already served as a major proof text that subordinates could rebuke wicked prelates. And in the late Middle Ages the university masters would develop a theory of authoritative teaching succession that descended from Saint Paul.[185]

Given at least the possibility of papal heresy, some theologians—not canonists—began to consider a doctrine of papal infallibility.[186] Peter John Olivi envisioned a scenario of papal apostasy and in so doing developed a theory of infallibility. He began with the traditional premise that the church herself could never err, for such a possibility would deprive her of any legitimate claim to authority such that she could not be believed.[187] Yet Olivi went further than simply insisting on the inerrancy of the universal church. He proceeded to argue that God would never have given someone (i.e., the pope) full authority to decide matters of faith and divine law while yet permitting that same person to err. And, according to Olivi, God has in fact given this power to the Roman pontiff as shown in the New Testament (Mt 16:18–19; Lk 22:32). Were the antichrist to take control of the papacy, therefore, one would then have to distinguish between the Roman see in appearance and in reality; and likewise between those who hold the see in name only rather than reality. For the true church will never be united to an errant head. Hence any pope who errs in general matters of the faith—as opposed to erring personally *(quoad se)*—could not be the true pope or head of the church.[188]

A few decades later Guido Terreni—who was certainly no friend to Olivi—wrote a small work specifically devoted to the question of papal infallibility. For Terreni, the notion of papal infallibility was seen as a bulwark established for the security of the Catholic faith and thus always considered in a larger ecclesial context. Indeed, Terreni contends that Christ's prayer that Peter's faith not fail (Lk 22:32) was for the faith of the church, which never errs when rendering a determination concerning the Catholic faith since the church in these instances is guided by the Holy Spirit.[189] As discussed above, Terreni was absolutely steadfast in his adherence to scripture as the principal authority in all matters of doctrine. The infallibility of ecclesiastical decrees is most vital in questions that scripture does not address explicitly. For while these decrees are thoroughly scriptural, they are not immediately evident, and thus stand in need of explication. It is to the church that one looks for such clarification. And Terreni insists that the church cannot err when she renders determinations on those matters of belief that are not evidently *(evidenter)* grasped from scripture. For if the church could err that would leave the faithful wondering whether the church has erred in any given instance.[190] Terreni is by no means claiming that the church functions as a separate source of revelation; she merely fulfills her age-old role as interpreter of Holy Scripture. There must be one final arbiter of scriptural truth. Yet, says Terreni, if determinations concerning matters of faith that are not evidently *(evidenter)* grasped from scripture were themselves mutable and revocable, then such determinations would not depend upon the infallible truth but rather upon fallible human judgment. But that would destroy any certain and stable adhesion to articles of faith, since it would leave Catholics in a constant state of doubt. No stability and concord could remain in the church. For if the first determination could be revoked as contrary to the faith by the next determination, then one could reasonably doubt the following determination, and so forth.[191]

So it was that Terreni concluded that Christ, himself the inerrant Truth, is present whenever the pope meets with the college of cardinals, or with a general council gathered in the Lord's name for the sake of his faith. At such moments one can be sure that the pope will be directed by the Holy Spirit who will be speaking through him.[192] Terreni insisted on making a distinction between the man and the office, however, as he must given the reality of human foibles. Even if there were a heretical pope, says Terreni, God would never permit him to determine a heresy, or anything contrary to the faith, since the truth of God must always remain immutable within the church. God would prohibit such a lapse in some way, whether through the pope's death, the resistance of the faithful, instruction from others, or internal inspiration.[193] Hence even as the pope could err personally *(in se)* the Holy Spirit would not permit him to determine anything contrary to the faith.[194]

That Terreni can balance a theory of papal infallibility with his unwavering commitment to the absolute doctrinal authority of Holy Scripture is not problematic, precisely because the pope is understood to be the final arbiter of scriptural truth. When defining a matter of faith based upon Holy Scripture, therefore, the Holy Spirit will preserve the pope from error. Scripture, however, not the pope, remains the source of that truth so defined. Having said that, the fact is that the doctrine of papal infallibility did not gain very much traction at the time. It is still instructive, though, because Terreni has located the central problem in the endless medieval debates over authority. There seemed to be no final authority here on earth that could resolve these matters. Terreni was deeply involved in the struggle against heretical movements in the fourteenth century, so he knew firsthand that battles over scripture—to which all sides appealed—were protracted without end. This is not to say that Terreni hit upon the right answer necessarily, but the answer that he did give shows at least that he was acutely aware of the fundamental problem. Can anyone provide the church with the *verus sensus scripturae;* and if so, how can this be known with absolute certainty?

Chapter 2

The Indignant Master

John Wyclif

John Wyclif was above all else a medieval theologian, which is to say that he was thoroughly steeped in the long-held assumptions and practices of the university masters. Having earned his doctorate by about 1372, Wyclif was fiercely protective of the rights and responsibilities that went along with his position as a Master of the Sacred Page.[1] Integral to Wyclif's vision of reform within the church—one that entailed a vast reduction in ecclesiastical wealth and temporal power—was his emphasis on the authority of Holy Scripture and the consequent authority of the theologian as its interpreter. This chapter offers an analysis of John Wyclif's conception of Holy Scripture as the primary authority in Christendom, examining the means by which he defends its veracity and applies its principles. Wyclif's biblical exegesis and his conceptions of ecclesiastical authority generated both loyal adherence and bitter opposition in his own lifetime and in the decades following his death in 1384 as Wycliffism spread to Prague in the early fifteenth century.

In recent times such notable scholars as Kantik Ghosh and Alastair Minnis have characterized Wyclif as a capricious biblical exegete who precipitated a crisis of authority by insisting upon his own set of subjective criteria for the determination of doctrine.[2] This rather negative assessment can be traced back to the middle of the twentieth century, evinced in the work of Beryl Smalley and the especially critical tones of Michael Hurley.[3] And although a few scholars have objected to this characterization, the perception of Wyclif as a radical proponent of a *sola scriptura* agenda confronting more moderate late medieval theorists still predominates. It is regrettable that the defense of Wyclif presented so ably by Paul de Vooght in 1954 (of which more in the next chapter) has largely been erased from modern scholarly memory.[4] The prevailing picture of Wyclif seems so difficult to dislodge because it has been etched into the minds of modern readers by Wyclif's medieval opponents, most prominently William Woodford and Thomas Netter. These apparently moderate theologians have created a distorted image of Wyclif that holds sway down to the present day. Here I want to dispel the image of Wyclif the dangerous radical and replace it with one of Wyclif the traditional medieval university master whose views on biblical exegesis, patristic tradition, and papal authority were thoroughly in keeping with his contemporaries.

Throughout this chapter Wyclif will emerge as a conservative theologian committed to the mutual coherence of Holy Scripture and the Holy Catholic Church. Even as he dissented from certain prevailing opinions, Wyclif never questioned the church's authoritative role in determining the meaning of the biblical text. Yet he also asserted the principle that theologians had, by virtue of their office, the authority to correct erring prelates. The correction of prelates did not signal an end to hierarchy as such, only its reform. And the means to reform would be found in scripture, which if correctly understood will lead the way to a purer if poorer church. In the end, though, it is Christ who remains the ultimate authority in the church. The will of this Eternal Person is manifested in Holy Scripture to those who follow him in humility and charity. If Wyclif does have a dominant exegetical strategy it is to seek the Christological sense of the text: Christ forms the hermeneutical key to Holy Scripture. This was no mere ideology but contact with a Living Person, and thus a way of being-in-relation. Yet even as Wyclif sought the final authority of Christ within scripture he relied upon a long line of sacred authorities, the fathers and holy doctors, to illuminate this path to truth.

The Biblical Canon

Some valuable insights into John Wyclif's overall understanding of scripture, and thus its authority, can be gained by examining his views on the biblical canon itself. By 1379 Wyclif had produced a commentary on the entire Bible: the *Postilla super totam bibliam*.[5] Here, in his prologue to the Gospel of John, he commented on the symmetry of the biblical canon (*scriptura canonica*). As it starts from an incorruptible beginning with the opening words of Genesis, so it is fitting that the final book, the Apocalypse, should have been written by an uncorrupted virgin (the apostle John).[6] In keeping with this consonance we find that the relationship between the Old and New Testaments is also in perfect accord. Wyclif writes in his Gospel Prologue that the two are of equal authority, usefulness, and reverence, since they really form a coherent whole that can ultimately be traced to the unity of the church herself.[7] Wyclif's insistence on the unity of the scriptures — both the Old and New Testaments — is in keeping with his Augustinian view of the church as comprising all the elect from the time of Abel, thereby spanning the epochs of the two testaments. This notion also serves to reinforce the fundamental coherence of church and scripture, which are bound together by a mutual foundation in the Eternal Word.

Wyclif does, of course, recognize some distinction between the two testaments. They may be in perfect harmony, but they still retain specific characteristics. When commenting on John 13:34, "A new commandment I give to you, that you love one another," Wyclif notes that this commandment of love is called new because it renews the soul and also points to the difference between the two Testaments. He follows the traditional view that although there is mention of love in the Old Testament the observance of the law operated principally on fear, whereas the New Testament induces observance primarily through love. Hence the Old Testament is known as the *lex timoris* and the New as the *lex amoris*. The point is that Christ's love for the human race proves to be the true form of love that all people are called upon to imitate. Christ loved us gratuitously, effectively, and rightly: loving us first, laying down his life for us, and leading us by love to eternal beatitude.[8] Throughout his many writings Wyclif will appeal to the evangelical law that he regards as wholly sufficient for the needs of the church. In the prologue to the Gospels he writes: "The *lex evangelica* is infallible because it has been handed down immediately by God, and is useful because it leads to eternal life, compendious because it is included in two commandments, both good and honorable because it is the end of all other laws."[9] Commenting on various passages in the Epistles, Wyclif will equate the *lex evangelii* with the *lex amoris*, since it casts out servile fear and infuses charity (Rom 6:15); Christ is the *auctor* of the *lex amoris* (Gal 3:19); the *lex Christi* is the *lex caritatis* (Gal 6:2); it is in the *lex evangelii* that one finds the filial law of love and thus perfect liberty (Jas 1:25).[10] For Wyclif, this gospel law—because it is a law of love—is also a guarantee of Christian freedom. This freedom manifested in the love of Christ as set forth in Holy Scripture proves to be an inalienable right of the Christian that cannot be infringed by any human law. Indeed, this principle of Christian freedom grounded in evangelical law formed the backbone of his objections to excessive papal legislation.

In the years 1377–78 Wyclif published his massive *De veritate sacrae scripturae* in which he set out to defend the inherent veracity, logic, and trustworthiness of Holy Scripture in the face of a series of scholastic objections. Not only did he have to defend the unique grammar of scripture, but he had to respond to questions raised concerning the construction of the biblical canon and the state of the biblical texts. Indeed, we must not lose sight of the fact that whatever Wyclif has to say on these matters is offered in direct response to pointed scholastic questions that, if not effectively refuted, cast serious doubt upon the ability of Holy Scripture to serve as the foundation of Catholic doctrine. In other words, Wyclif proves very much "the conservative" in these debates as he defends the substantial veracity of the Catholic tradition in the face of potentially destructive criticism.

Actually, many of the issues that Wyclif tackles in chapter 11 of the *De veritate* bear a striking similarity to those discussed by Henry Totting de Oyta at roughly the same time. Wyclif devotes this chapter to a threefold objection that moves from the contents of the canon to the veracity of Jerome's translation and finally to the accuracy of the manuscripts. There are some people who contend that the authorities of the New Testament confirm particular sayings of the Old Testament books and authors but not all of them. Hence there is no evidence that all of our Old Testament manuscripts are authentic. Even the Jews themselves, as Jerome points out, do not accept the authenticity of all the Old Testament books that Christians include in their canon. What is more, there is no good reason to believe that Ezra had correctly restored the Hebrew scriptures following the Babylonian captivity, even were one to suppose that it had been flawlessly conferred in the first place. And then, prescinding from the status of the original text, some people doubt that Jerome's translation of this text is itself free from error, since his work is at odds with that of other translators. And finally, moving on to the Latin texts that the church currently possesses, it is said that many of these manuscripts are corrupt and thus in need of correction.[11]

Wyclif initiates his response with an appeal to Christ's promise that he would remain with the church until the end of the age (Mt 28:20). He regards this as tantamount to a pledge that Christ would preserve his own law within the church. As such, one should trust that the manuscripts have been duly corrected under the authority of the church who receives her comprehension of the text from the very head of the church—Christ himself.[12] Again and again we find that Wyclif establishes a Christological core that holds together church and scripture and thereby preserves them both. For Wyclif, the questions of canon, translation, and manuscripts all come down to the preservation of scriptural veracity and authority. In that sense it is all of a piece with his defense of sacred grammar and the inherent logic of Christ. Veracity and authority are inseparable; the latter cannot be established without the former. Wyclif argues that the authors of the Old Testament could not be considered authentic if any falsehood were located in their writings. Their veracity is secured, however, by the fact that the New Testament writers cite them, which is sufficient for accepting their entire testimony. Yet their acceptance goes further than this. Not only Christians but also Jews and Moslems accept the authenticity of the twenty-two books of the Old Testament recounted by Jerome in his *Prologus Galeatus*. What is more, the Jews remain as living witnesses to the veracity of the Old Testament books, having taken their Hebrew manuscripts with them into the Diaspora. This, in turn, allows Christians recourse to the original language that will prove the accuracy of the Latin text.[13] As for Jerome's translation, Wyclif finds reason to trust it based upon the sanctity of this saint's life, his expertise in the Hebrew language, and the complete agreement of his translation with the Hebrew and Greek manuscripts.[14]

It must be remembered here that Wyclif does not contest the fact that some manuscripts are corrupt and thus in need of correction. It is precisely because he recognizes that codices can be corrupted that his appeal to an enduring truth that transcends the vicissitudes of textual transmission is perfectly reasonable. He finds consolation in the traditional assurance that the Catholic faith will always endure within Holy Mother Church in keeping with Christ's prayer that Peter's faith would not fail (Lk 22:32). The church can live without her manuscripts but not without the faith that is the very law of scripture. This faith must always exist, whether in the manuscripts or in the hearts of believers.¹⁵ Indeed, when it comes to the substance of the faith, individual manuscripts are of no greater value than the beasts from which they were made. Their real worth rests in the truth that they signify. For if this were not the case, then were the codices destroyed, the Catholic faith itself would perish.¹⁶ This is a very straightforward and conservative response: the faith of the church ultimately rests with Christ the Eternal Word and thus could withstand the destruction of phsyical conduits of that faith if it ever came to that.

It is in this vein that Wyclif remarks that "the mental intellection [of scriptural truth] is more truly scripture than the line upon the parchment, since the latter is only counted as scripture on account of its relationship to [the mental intellection]. Yet the scripture existing in the mind is not sacred except on account of its relationship to that objective scripture which [the mind] perceives. That [scripture] by which all Catholics communicate is primarily sacred, since it is the one common faith of the whole church."¹⁷ Citing only the first section of this passage, Jeremy Catto concluded, "Wyclif's scripture, then, was an idea in the mind, and its authority subjective, being the individual conscience and judgement; all visible standards, including the biblical manuscript itself, were contingent."¹⁸ But surely the full passage makes it clear that the comprehension of scriptural truth in the mind of the believer must be grounded in the objective standard of the Eternal Scripture—the Book of Life—from which the entire church as one body receives her faith. Hence there really is nothing subjective about Wyclif's position.

Wyclif's discussion of the relative value of the material codex has led Alastair Minnis to comment on Wyclif's "dismissive attitude to the Bible as a physical book."¹⁹ And Kantik Ghosh has also reached similar conclusions,²⁰ although Mary Dove to her credit has offered a more sympathetic account.²¹ Throughout this discussion, however, Wyclif is not denying the practical importance of the material codex in the life of the church. It seems that Catto, Minnis, and Ghosh have not fully considered the context of Wyclif's remarks. Wyclif is involved in an academic disputation; he is presenting a magisterial response to a set of scholastic objections. Here, then, Wyclif is endeavoring to respond to arguments that would link the very truth of evangelical law to the manner in which it has been imprinted on a given section of parchment. Corrected manuscripts are valuable, he says, but their status must not be inflated to the point that codicological defects could detract from the very substance of the Catholic faith. Their worth as physical objects must be kept in perspective; they are, after all, merely outward signs of an eternal truth. This is true, of course, and he correctly maintains that the manuscripts derive their value from their capacity to signify the Eternal Scripture—which is itself the ground of all truth.[22] Wyclif's point is really quite straightforward: divine truth transcends any material means of communication. The law of Christ, the evangelical law, is something that may indeed be conveyed by written words but ultimately rests with the faith of the church. Richard FitzRalph and Henry Totting argued along very similar lines (see chapter 1). Actually, in one way or another, all medieval theologians placed their confidence in the faith of the church that cannot fail (Lk 22:32). None of them believed that the Catholic faith itself could ever be imperiled by the corruption or loss of biblical manuscripts. For the truth of Holy Scripture that these manuscripts convey is identical with the faith that abides indefectibly and forever within the church herself. So it is, then, that Wyclif can be seen here to take a rather conservative line as he places his confidence in the greater Catholic tradition that can be counted on to preserve the very same faith that is handed down in Holy Scripture.

Holy Scripture is clearly the most authoritative text, but Wyclif is perfectly willing to concede that many evangelical truths of scripture can also be found among the ancient poets such as Homer, Virgil, and Ovid. In fact, he says, if the authors of the Old Testament are authenticated in the main because some portions of their works are cited as authoritative Catholic sources, this may apply to the poets as well. If Saint Paul sees fit to cite one verse from Eumenides (Ti 1:12), then it seems that this poet's entire book can be reckoned authentic. Beyond the ancient poets, however, there are also the gospels written by the likes of the Pharisee Nicodemus (Jn 3:1–10). Wyclif thinks it is reasonable to accept his account as authoritative on the grounds that he was a faithful and holy man who was present when the events recorded took place. Hence the Gospel of Nicodemus is in an even better place than Enoch whose works were not accepted on account of their dubious authorship.[23] Actually, Wyclif finds it fitting that the truths of the faith would be declared by the poets and even by the Moslems. These truths do not constitute the faith because such people uttered them, however, but rather because they had been spoken by God.[24] Poets, infidels, and even demons can speak the hidden truths of the faith. That is not to say, however, that such sources ought to be cited as full-fledged authors *(auctores)*. That would only be possible were one to discover that they had been inspired by the Holy Spirit and thus were speaking as his scribes. Nevertheless, there are occasions when it is advantageous to draw upon these writers as witnesses because the spirit of prophecy can sometimes shine even among the infidels.[25] Truth itself is the issue here, and all truth must ultimately cohere given its unique divine source.

Wyclif does trust that the Old Testament authors were divinely inspired, not only due to the sanctity of their lives and the authentication they received from the entire church, but because their books resonate with love and their minds were conformed to celestial affections. It is their pure proclamation of the Word of God that secures their authenticity.[26] And yet Wyclif finds that the Gospel of Nicodemus also meets these criteria, even as he admits the work is itself apocryphal. Despite the fact that this book's precise status remained murky, Wyclif was not alone in valuing the Gospel of Nicodemus; it can be found in some late medieval biblical codices. At all events, this conclusion prompts Wyclif to examine the nature of apocryphal books generally. He appeals to Jerome's *Prologus Galeatus* to make the point that we need not disbelieve these books as if they were false; but neither should the church militant explicitly believe in them as if they were authentic. Wyclif then applies this principle to the Gospel of Nicodemus as well as other books that the church has decided neither to condemn explicitly nor to canonize explicitly. Thus even as Wyclif finds value in such books he adopts a rather sensible and realistic position that the current number of biblical books is sufficient since canonizing any more may well prove burdensome for the church. Having said that, however, Wyclif still thinks it likely that many apocryphal books can qualify as Holy Scripture, inasmuch as they are inscribed in the Book of Life — the *Liber Vitae*. And this means that Christians should trust in them, whether explicitly or implicitly, just as one trusts the canonical scripture. Indeed, says Wyclif, many of these apocryphal books do convey sacred truths that are contained in the Book of Life.[27]

Wyclif seems to be drawing a distinction here between what can broadly be classified as sacred writings on the one hand and the biblical canon on the other. The first category comprises texts that contain some divine truth and for that reason are edifying; the second is limited strictly to what the church has received as uniquely authoritative. It remains clear, however, that there is no question of the apocryphal books containing some part of revelation otherwise missing from the canonical scriptures.

The canonical scriptures contain all truth, but fragments of that truth may also be located in other texts, whether the Gospel of Nicodemus or the works of Virgil. Hence Wyclif can say with complete confidence that "if other codices contain the truth let us believe it, for it also abides in our own codices."[28] Although Wyclif makes his case with bold strokes, this is simply an application of the classic Augustinian principle that anything useful found within the books of the pagans will also be found in Holy Scripture (*De doc. chr.* 2.42.63). For Wyclif, the Book of Life is the repository of all truth; it can even be equated with Christ the Truth. Thus any fragment of truth found in pagan or apocryphal material must by definition participate in the source of truth. Whatever individual truths are committed to writing, whether within the biblical canon or without, are extrapolated from this cosmic fund that is the Word of God.

Jesus Christ and Holy Scripture

As noted above, Wyclif draws together into one basic principle the law of love, the evangelical law, and the law of Christ. What is more, Wyclif equates the law of Christ with Holy Scripture inasmuch as scripture principally signifies Jesus Christ who is himself the Book of Life — the one in whom all truth is eternally inscribed. The authority of scripture is derived from the personal authority of Christ whose will and truth it embodies. Because Christ is the author most responsible for scripture *(proximus auctor)* and since he infinitely surpasses every other man, so his book — which is his law — must likewise exceed all other writings to the same degree. It is supremely authentic *(autentica)* and thus most trustworthy. This means, in turn, that the writings of the great church doctors are true only to the extent that they are in conformity with scripture. As for the gospel writers themselves, they are Christ's scribes ordained to print the law of Christ and the Catholic faith. And it is on account of this relationship that the biblical codices, bearing as they do this sacred meaning, can be implicitly reckoned as the faith of scripture. Holy Scripture must be true in all its parts, says Wyclif, precisely because it perfectly conveys what Christ himself intends.[29]

This exalted view of Christ's relationship to scripture has direct ramifications for the biblical canon. The intention of Christ *(sententia Christi)* is itself the source of the biblical canon. It is the font from which the Old

Law receives its authority because Christ cites—whether generally or in particular—all the books of the Old Law that a Catholic must accept. Hence all the codices of the Old and New Law bear a similar authority, inasmuch as they have all received their meaning from the Holy Spirit. And because the Holy Spirit wanted Christians to remain focused on what is necessary, he willed that they study the codices of the Old and New Laws rather than be preoccupied with the other writings. As noted earlier, Wyclif acknowledged that extra-scriptural writings are sometimes true and thus implicitly contain the faith of scripture. This is not to say, however, that God wished for Christians to place their trust in such works explicitly. Whatever authority these extra-scriptural books may have is always derivative, since Holy Scripture is the culmination of all truth. Wyclif's principal concern in this instance is not so much the biblical canon as the need to confirm that the ecclesiastical decrees and the writings of the doctors must always be consonant with Holy Scripture. Hence his perpetual lament that papal bulls are now exalted far beyond their proper limits—hardly a unique complaint in the late Middle Ages.[30]

Wyclif was certainly not alone in his belief that Holy Scripture possessed a unique brand of logic that need not bow to human conventions. He goes as far as to say that failure to recognize this central fact is tantamount to siding with Antichrist. In fact, Antichrist would argue the following: I understand scripture in this way; and it ought to be understood according to my logic; but the sense of scripture is impossible; therefore Holy Scripture—and consequently its author—must be most false and thus unworthy of belief. Of course, given the inextricable relationship between a text and its author, if scripture is supremely false, then its author, Jesus Christ, is the greatest heretic. When such falsehoods are heaped upon scripture it is morphed into the writing of the devil. Wyclif came to the defense of scripture with recourse to the classic patristic comments recorded in Gratian's *Decretum*. He lines up the most traditional authoritative sources. Hence he follows Augustine's remark that perceived errors in scripture stem from either faulty codices or the reader's mistakes—never from scripture itself. And together with Jerome, Wyclif concludes that the heretic imposes an alien sense upon scripture that runs contrary to the demands of the Holy Spirit (cf. *Haeresis*, C. 24, q. 3, c. 27). Through it all, though, Wyclif is confident that antichrist and his disciples will never succeed in impugning any part of scripture according to its divinely intended meaning—*de virtute sermonis*.[31]

As we have seen, Wyclif anchors scripture's veracity in the person of Jesus Christ. And because Christ is himself the Second Person of the Trinity, the Word of God and source of all truth, so it is that scripture attains a level of absolute metaphysical certitude. Indeed, for Wyclif, Holy Scripture reveals the very metaphysical structure of the universe. On the highest level, "What was made, in him was life" (Jn 1:3–4); this speaks to the subsistence within God of the eternal exemplars by which the universe was created. In "God said, 'Let there be light'; and light came to be" (Gen 1:3), Wyclif finds great meaning. "To say" refers to the Word of God (through whom all things are created); "Let there be," to the exemplar principle that subsists within the Word; and "it came to be," to the existence of the creature made according to the pattern of the exemplar.[32] For Wyclif, all discourse must ultimately cohere in the Divine Person of the Word who is the source of all truth. It is not simply that genuine discourse discloses the truth of being but that being itself is a form of discourse that begins in the eternal speech of the Word as it is uttered by the Father within the Godhead. And it is this eternal discourse that goes forth from the recesses of a perfect communion to form the basis of all created existence. This is borne out in Wyclif's theory of pan-propositionalism, whereby whatever exists is itself, in some manner, a proposition.[33] Reality can be said, therefore, to be structured like the very language that we use to describe it, thus with subjects and predicates. Everything that exists, with the exception of God, is a real proposition because it forms some sort of compound. This is grounded in Wyclif's understanding—following in the line of Grosseteste—that the truth of a proposition is ultimately determined by conformity to the eternal exemplars in the divine intellect.[34] All genuine human discourse will serve only to illustrate the eternal discourse of the Word in which the exemplars subsist. Thus when Wyclif demands that all human speech conform to the parameters set by Holy Scripture—itself a manifestation of the Eternal Word—he asks only that men adopt the ways of the cosmic language that is Truth itself.

It is along similar lines that Wyclif will speak of Holy Scripture comprising five different levels. The first is the Book of Life. The second level pertains to the truths inscribed in the Book of Life according to their intelligible being. Both levels of these scriptures are absolutely necessary, says Wyclif, although they are not essentially distinct. On the third level scripture is understood in terms of the truths as they exist in their proper genus.

The fourth refers to the truths as they are inscribed in the human mind; these may even be said to have been abstracted from the truths of the third level. And on the fifth level Holy Scripture pertains to the manuscripts and other artificial signs designed to evoke the highest level of truth.[35] Wyclif could also condense this into a tripartite system while keeping the Christological theme in place. On the highest level Holy Scripture signifies Jesus Christ, the Book of Life, in whom every truth is inscribed. On the second level Scripture signifies the eternal and temporal truths inscribed in the Book of Life. Finally, scripture signifies the aggregate formed from the manuscripts of God's Law and the truth that God imposes upon them. Here again, the material text should not be called Holy Scripture strictly speaking, since these manuscripts are only sacred to the extent that the sacred meaning accompanies them.[36] Both the earlier fivefold version and this later condensed version coincide with Wyclif's grander metaphysical system of universals. Scripture on its highest level is Christ the Word who is himself the repository of the eternal exemplar reasons. The second level of scripture must therefore be equated with those exemplar reasons. For just as the exemplar reasons subsisting in the divine intellect are only formally—not essentially—distinct from the divine essence, so the truths inscribed in the Book of Life are not essentially distinct from the Book of Life itself.

Christ is at the center of Wyclif's descriptions of scripture, therefore, but not merely Christ as transcendent Word. Wyclif is also careful to find a place for the Incarnation, thereby presenting a complete Christology relative to scripture. He was deeply affected by the image of the poor and lowly Christ presented by the apostle Paul in the Epistle to the Philippians (2:7–8). It proves to be a key soteriological text for Wyclif as he emphasizes Christ's humble act of self-emptying for the sake of the human race; only the greatest act of humility could undo the prideful act of Adam. Reversing the pride of the first Adam, this second Adam humbled himself even unto death on the cross. Christ, though God, descended to mankind and made himself small. This was a deeply personal act on God's part. The great sin committed out of ignorance was abolished by Personal Wisdom, which is uniquely the Word of God.[37] This line of thought also bears great significance for Wyclif's whole program of biblical exegesis. Christ becomes the standard of sanctity borne out in humble service that is the essential disposition needed for properly grasping the meaning of scripture. No saint is worthy of praise except to the extent that he or she has followed Christ. This personal and

Christocentric piety is at the root of Wyclif's conception of the Catholic faith. Again, in keeping with his conception of the church as predating the Incarnation, Wyclif finds that the Person of Christ has always been the means to salvation; he was present during the age of the Old Law and thus was followed by the ancient saints.[38]

Jesus Christ, understood as the self-emptying Word of God, figures prominently in Wyclif's reading of the Latin version of John 10:35–36, "The scripture cannot be destroyed, whom *(quem)* the Father sanctified and sent into the world." Wyclif was sure that this cemented the identification of scripture with Christ himself, the Word of God, Second Person of the Trinity. The Word in his divinity sent himself into the world, having assumed a human nature, like the nobleman who went off to a distant country to receive his kingship and then return (Lk 19:12). The book sent into the world is Christ whose divinity and humanity are insolubly united in a single person and thus cannot be destroyed. As Christ is fully human, born of a woman, and yet fully divine, begotten and not made, so God "made" the manuscripts sacred in regard to Christ's humanity, while he "begot" scripture and "caused" it to be sacred with respect to his divinity. Scripture, like the Incarnate Christ, possesses a divine nature that renders it supremely authentic and thereby greater than all created and sensible signs.[39] Given its eternal origin and divine nature, scripture as found in its manuscript form may be counted as Holy Scripture in an equivocal sense, like the painted portrait that represents its human subject. Only this physical manifestation of scripture is liable to destruction in the jaws of dogs and contamination at the hands of fools and heretics.[40] Holy Scripture, therefore, is the result of a hypostatic union. Just as the Eternal Word assumed human nature unto itself such that this nature found its subject, its personhood, in the Eternal Person of the Word, so too is the material codex united to this same Person. And just as the Person of the Word assumed perishable flesh that suffered the calumny of sinners, so now the Word that is united to animal pelts endures the prospect of scribal error and the false interpretations of heretics. As both God and man united in One Person, Jesus Christ was not subject to suffering in his impassible divine nature. And so it is with scripture that the Eternal Word—the *Liber Vitae*—will never suffer in its Eternal Truth. This does not render the physical codices meaningless (as we have seen above), but they are not ultimately definitive.[41]

The Senses of Scripture

Despite the learned criticism of some modern scholars, including Minnis, that Wyclif is so caught up in the idea of an eternal scripture that he eschews the subtle literary classifications that late medieval exegetes employed to differentiate the various senses of the text, one will find that Wyclif actually tacks quite closely to predecessors and contemporaries such as Nicholas of Lyra and Henry Totting.[42] Indeed, Wyclif proves to be a very traditional exegete when it comes to such matters as discerning the literal sense of scripture. There is no doubt, of course, that Wyclif accepted the basic medieval division of scripture into the four senses. Yet he also contended that any sense that the letter possesses might fittingly be called the literal sense if it is in keeping with the author's intention—*de virtute sermonis*. We have seen that for most late medieval theologians the literal sense of Holy Scripture is equated with the intended sense of the Divine Author and thereby constitutes the orthodox meaning of the biblical text. Wyclif too adopted this position. In fact, in words that will be echoed almost verbatim by Jean Gerson some forty years later (discussed below), Wyclif concluded that the literal sense is best understood as the sense that the Holy Spirit primarily imposed for the sake of leading the faithful soul upwards into God.[43] Thus even as Ghosh is quite critical of Wyclif's equation of the literal sense and the divinely intended sense,[44] there really is no difference on this point between Wyclif and his contemporaries.

At all events, there are times, according to Wyclif, when the literal sense might be allegorical as when the apostle recounts that the Israelites were baptized into Christ (1 Cor 10:2). Wyclif wishes to preserve the distinction between the four senses of scripture but cautions that such distinctions must not be overemphasized lest they appear to be in opposition to one another. There are times when scripture moves beyond the history that is literally recounted *(ad literam)* in one passage in order to convey the allegorical meaning. To illustrate this point, Wyclif turns to the apostle Paul's use of Genesis 17 in the Epistle to the Galatians 4:22–24. Here, moving beyond the historical sense, Abraham signifies that God the Father and his sons are the two testaments. Now, someone reading scripture according to the most basic meaning of the letter understands only the historical sense, whereas the person who adds a second level of interpretation will then grasp the allegorical sense by means of the very same letter. Actually, Wyclif thinks that a faithful reader could understand the mystical sense alone through the original text of Genesis 17—even while not discounting the history—with the result that the allegorical sense would be for him the literal. This hinges on the fact that the literal sense of scripture is the meaning the Holy Spirit has appointed it to signify. In those cases when a biblical passage lacks a historical sense the allegorical sense will itself be the literal sense, precisely because it is the intended sense. In saying this, Wyclif believes that he is merely affirming Thomas Aquinas's point that the parabolic sense, or symbolized sense, is the literal one.[45]

Wyclif's rather traditional exegetical methodology needs to be emphasized given the later attacks launched by Woodford and Netter (covered in the next two chapters). In tones reminiscent of Nicholas of Lyra—to whom he owed much—Wyclif contends that when one searches for the mystical sense within the historical the former is mediated by the latter. Yet when the mystical sense is the only intended sense it is perceived by the reader immediately. Hence Wyclif notes that there are times when the moral sense can be the literal sense that is immediately elicited from scripture, since any sense of scripture will constitute the moral sense to the extent that it immediately draws one to the virtues. And likewise with the anagogical to the extent that it teaches the truth that should be expected in the church triumphant. So it is, says Wyclif, that the three mystical senses teach, whether immediately or in a mediated fashion, what must be believed, hoped for, and accomplished meritoriously. In this way they correspond to the three theological virtues of faith, hope, and love. The literal sense is the Catholic sense, therefore, if it is immediately elicited from scripture. If the three mystical senses are immediately derived from scripture they constitute the literal sense. If, however, they are elicited in a mediated fashion by way of the historical, then they are rightly called the allegorical, tropological, or anagogical but not the literal sense.[46]

The schema recounted above did not come easily to Wyclif. In fact, he admits to having once been quite perplexed by the distinction of the senses. It is possible that he had in mind the problem of adaptation relative to multiple literal senses that Aquinas discussed in *De potentia* 4.1. Without mentioning Aquinas here, Wyclif recounts that there was a time when he believed that the truth was a combination of the sense asserted by the author and those senses within the mind of the readers. Thus the true sense of the text would emerge from what the author had intended and from what the readers then adapted.⁴⁷ He eventually left this position behind. In his *Postilla* Wyclif wrote, "It is no problem if Scripture has many literal senses of which one is the principal [sense] and another the more principal [sense], as the Apostle makes clear in Hebrews 1 when he cites the text of Chronicles 22 where what is said of Solomon is spoken literally *(ad litteram)* with regard to Christ."⁴⁸ And when he commented on Galatians 4:24 in his *Postilla* he also noted that the same passage can have a multiple literal sense. Wyclif uses the classic example that Lyra had employed to demonstrate the *duplex sensus litteralis*. In 1 Chronicles 22:10, "I will be as a father to him," was spoken literally *(ad litteram)* about Christ, though also about Solomon inasmuch as he symbolizes Christ. It is precisely this fact that provides the apostle Paul with the authoritative text to prove that Christ surpasses the angels (Heb 1:5). Wyclif concludes from this that any sense of the author that is produced by the letter can be called the literal sense. This rests on the fact that the Author of scripture would know whatever sense he more chiefly *(primarius)* intended, thereby rendering the mystical sense just as authentic as the literal sense.⁴⁹ The author of Hebrews was drawing a theological conclusion based upon the mystical reading of another biblical text. He was speaking literally about Christ, but his statement is based upon a spiritual reading of words directed to Solomon. This leads Wyclif to claim that whenever a biblical writer assigns a mystical sense to another biblical passage it is no less authoritative than the literal-historical sense, precisely because all the senses of scripture are equally authoritative. The apostle Paul knows the full sense of the Old Testament just as authentically as Moses and Solomon, which means that his mystical reading of their words is as authoritative as their literal-historical expression.⁵⁰

Apart from the three mystical senses, medieval biblical exegetes also had to contend with the question of metaphor and figurative language relative to the literal sense of the biblical text. Along lines very similar to what was enunciated in the Paris statute of 1340 (examined in the previous chapter) Wyclif equated the proper sense of the biblical text with the Divine Author's intended meaning, which is very often conveyed through the use of metaphors and tropes. For Wyclif, the *virtus sermonis*—the force of discourse—depends upon authorial intention and, as such, is not governed by the strict rules of the logic and grammar practiced by the Arts faculty. Indeed, he railed against those who regard biblical propositions false in their literal sense *(de virtute sermonis)* when they involve figurative or mystical expressions. Wyclif's decisive response is that every part of scripture must be true in its literal sense *(de virtute sermonis)*, since every expression set in place by the Divine Author of scripture is there for the sake of conveying some sacred mystery. Keeping this in mind, says Wyclif, will help clear up the various ways in which Christ speaks of his relationship to God the Father—sometimes with respect to his human nature and sometimes the divine.[51] There are instances when Christ can say, "The Father is greater than I" (Jn 14:28), and others when he says, "I and the Father are one" (Jn 10:30). There is no contradiction here so long as one keeps Christ's two natures in mind. And it is just such a Christological presupposition that will yield the intended sense of the biblical text. Contradictions arise only when each passage is read according to its strict grammatical signification. Yet Wyclif—like the 1340 Paris statute—locates the force/meaning of the word *(virtus sermonis)* not in the simple grammar but in the author's intention. Christ, of course, never intended to contradict himself.[52]

Everything turns on the matter of authorial intention. All the signs within scripture have been carefully selected by the Divine Author for the sake of signifying the truth in its entirety. One is not permitted to distort scripture, therefore, by pulling out words and phrases to suit one's agenda. Rather one must always abide by the Divine Author's intended meaning.[53] Only when the reader grasps scripture in its entirety according to the sense of its Divine Author will its truth emerge. Because the whole of Sacred Scripture is the one Word of God every part must be read thoroughly in light of the entire Word, the Eternal Person of the Word, who comprises all the truths that the blessed gaze upon in heaven.[54] Once again, for Wyclif, biblical exegesis is drawn back into the orbit of Christology. Christ is the reason that every part of scripture is true *de virtute sermonis*, since he is both the author and the subject matter of scripture. Every part of scripture is literally true according to the Eternal Word. The power of discourse *(virtus sermonis)* is derived from the power of the Word *(virtus Verbi)* who is the source of all truthful discourse. For, in fact, every true proposition subsists within the Divine Person of the Word from all eternity. There is no meaningful discourse that is not ultimately an expression of this eternal speech. Holy Scripture reaches its natural conclusion, therefore, in the Person of Christ the Word who is the very source of truth itself.[55]

As noted above, Wyclif met with resistance to his exegetical methods in his own lifetime and beyond. I devote entire chapters to his posthumous critics, but here let us look briefly at criticisms leveled by two friars in his own day. Both of them were especially worried about Wyclif's understanding of the literal sense. In his debates with Wyclif around 1372–74 the Carmelite John Kynyngham maintained in rather conventional fashion that scripture always asserts the truth, whether according to the literal sense *(ad sensum literalem)* or according to some mystical sense. Yet in those instances where the meaning is not clear it is best to trust in "the common glosses and expositions of the doctors."[56] The two theologians differed on just what is meant by the literal sense. For Wyclif, the literal sense—when designated by the phrase *de virtute sermonis*—can be quite expansive so long as it conveys the intention of the author. For Kynyngham, however, this phrase refers to the literal sense understood as the strict grammatical conventions that exclude figurative constructions. The reader will sometimes have to move beyond the literal sense in order to grasp what the biblical author really means. The intention of scripture may be quite clear, therefore, even as what the bare words signify is erroneous.[57]

It is along these lines that Kynyngham took issue with Wyclif's apparent fixation on the precise wording of the text, which he believed led his Oxford colleague into a maze of contradictions. Kynyngham contends that no one is bound to follow scripture in its precise manner of speaking *(modus loquendi)*. The fact is, says Kynyngham, that "the configuration of the words *(figura verborum)* contributes little or nothing to the truth of things and essences."[58] The point is not to imitate the language of scripture slavishly, therefore, but to speak the truth of things as they are meant to be conveyed by various signs, such that the interpreter adapts to different literary genres, from poetry to prose. Wyclif had just received his doctorate at this time and Kynyngham fears that he is not attuned to all the responsibility that entails. The doctor of theology—*magister sacrae paginae*—has an obligation to his pious listeners to treat figures of speech with care, lest he lead his audience into error by emphasizing the sign at the expense of the truth. In fact, Kynyngham finds that the practice of reading scripture *de virtute sermonis* is at the root of many heresies. He employed the classic examples taken from the Arian heresy whereby "The Father is greater than I" (Jn 14:28) was used to undercut the divinity of the Son. Rather than rely on the strict signification of the terms, therefore, Kynyngham will pursue the true meaning of the discourse *(proprietati sermonis)*.[59] This Johannine passage reveals the fundamental difference between Wyclif and Kynyngham. Wyclif had specifically secured its truth *de virtute sermonis* by taking the theological context into consideration—in this case Christ's two natures—which thereby reveals the intended sense of the author. Kynyngham's restrictive take on the *virtus sermonis*, however, limits the logical validity of propositions to the way they stand, apart from any further contextualization. At any rate, the question of contextualization proves to be of central importance not only in matters of biblical exegesis but also in the determination of orthodox and heterodox statements.

Another opponent, and onetime friend, the Austin friar Thomas Winterton recounted Wyclif's reputation for claiming that every manner of speaking in scripture is proper and true according to the exterior, or grammatical, sense. Yet such a method, says Winterton, will only destroy the distinction of meaning within the biblical propositions and thereby miss the sense of the author. Much like Kynyngham, therefore, Winterton contends that many texts of scripture will be false if read according to their strict grammatical sense, that is, when the terms are considered solely according to their exterior meaning.[60] Yet it should be noted that for Winterton, while it is true that the literal sense of scripture cannot always be identified with the exterior sense of the letter, this is precisely because there are times when the moral or allegorical sense is itself the literal sense.[61] Of course, this last statement could have been spoken by Wyclif himself.[62] It is clear from the reactions of both Kynyngham and Winterton that Wyclif's exegetical theories were not well understood by his contemporaries. Wyclif will later be attacked by William Woodford and Thomas Netter for being a crude literalist, and yet (as discussed below) much of what Wyclif had to say about the literal sense in the last quarter of the fourteenth century would be echoed by Jean Gerson in the first quarter of the fifteenth century.

Theologians and Canonists

As noted at the outset, Wyclif's conception of the nature of Holy Scripture had immediate ramifications for his entire reform program. Holy Scripture serves as the principal authority by which laws and decrees are judged, and to which they are all obligated to conform. There is no genuine authority exercised here on earth, whether royal or papal, that is not ultimately derived from Holy Scripture since it is the font of truth upon which all true authority must rest. Actually, when extolling the unique juridical role of scripture Wyclif could speak in terms very close to what we have already encountered with theologians such as Henry of Ghent and Nicholas of Lyra. They had appealed to Wisdom 7:26 when describing scripture as the brightness of the eternal light and the mirror without taint that is capable of refuting all error. Wyclif would also cite this text as he portrayed scripture as eternal and indelible, the very radiance of eternal light, that flawless mirror of divine majesty. It is "the foundation of every Catholic opinion, the exemplar and mirror designed to examine and extinguish all manner of error and heretical evil."[63] It is in keeping with this notion of scripture as the eternal and perfect mirror that Wyclif contended that nothing could be deemed heretical unless proven to contradict scripture. And if scripture is the absolute standard by which to judge heresy, then it falls to the theologian — precisely in his role as *magister sacrae paginae* — to determine what is orthodox and what heretical.[64] Theologians are the best guides for the very reason that they understand Holy Scripture's unique *modus loquendi* and thus will be able to judge which laws are in keeping with the testimony of the saints and which are merely human inventions.[65]

In his discussions regarding the authority of canon law and the role of the canonists in the church Wyclif emerges as the typical medieval theologian involved in a time-honored professional dispute with a rival faculty. True to his vocation, Wyclif defended the primacy of theology, praising it as the highest of the sciences for the unfailing way in which it proceeds, the nobility of its subject matter, and the principle of its ultimate goal. Only theology begets and rejuvenates the members of the body of Christ. Thus, given its uniquely sublime status, any science that would oppose theology must be diabolical.[66] Such an exaltation of theology is meant to serve the goal of reform. Having mastered this science, theologians are the ones best equipped to reveal the true faith to the people; they will rescue the church from sin and heresy. Hence it is the theologian, not the canonist, who should be advanced to the prelacy.[67] Wyclif was certainly not the first theologian to express his dismay at all the best jobs going to the lawyers! At all events, these theologians will then cleanse the church of heresy based upon the sacred canons of Holy Scripture, itself the foundation of all ecclesiastical law. For scripture surpasses all human canons in usefulness, authority, and subtlety. This is not to disparage canon law as such, for Wyclif allows that much of canon law is really an abbreviated form of divine law. Unfortunately, though, what ought to have remained purely evangelical began to be corrupted with the Donation of Constantine, which ushered in an age of venal pursuits.[68]

In order to restore the integrity of canon law—so that it might again function as an expression of the divine law found in Scripture—there must be a return to the lawgiver. The *auctoritas* of any law depends upon the *auctor* of that law. And, as we have seen, Wyclif based all authority in a person—the Divine Person of Christ the Word. The law of Christ, as conveyed principally in scripture, is infinitely more authoritative than any human tradition, precisely because it finds its source in the divine lawgiver. The law that has been handed down to human beings by uncreated Wisdom proves to be the best means to peace in the world—hence Wyclif's dismay at its being corrupted by human traditions, that is, the proliferation of papal decretals.[69] Now he can only lament that human law is leading people to forsake the wholly sufficient law of Christ that has been handed down in scripture.[70]

Wyclif does not lay the blame solely upon the heads of the canonists, however; much of the responsibility rests with his fellow theologians. Actually, Wyclif admits that some canon and civil lawyers are good theologians at times and are actually better acquainted with the substance of theology and its attendant virtues than many doctors of theology. This, he says, can be traced to the negligence of theologians as well as the attention lawyers give to theology, which is the very lifeblood of their science.[71] There may be a few noble canonists out there, but most, according to Wyclif, treat the theological faculty as a superfluous bunch of troublemakers. Although it must be admitted that Wyclif caricatured the position of the canonists when he claimed that they consider papal decretals to be of equal authority with the gospel and of even greater authority than the letters of Paul, inasmuch as they claim (according to Wyclif) that the pope is entitled to dispense against the Apostle and correct the gospel. Indeed, says Wyclif, any theologian who would dare confine the pope's authority to a scriptural foundation is labeled a heretic.[72] As noted in the previous chapter, the extent of the pope's authority to grant dispensations from evangelical counsels and apostolic ordinances did not extend to articles of faith and would always have to preserve the spirit of Holy Scripture if not the letter. Notwithstanding, Wyclif was certainly not the only theologian to be troubled by some of the more ostentatious proposals of the decretalists.

Wyclif did concede, however, that the pope has the right to pass laws for the good of the church provided that these statutes are in accord with

Holy Scripture. He only objected to the notion that papal decretals were of equal authority with scripture by virtue of their papal sanction.[73] Again, though, much of this revolved around the question of authorship and its attendant authority. Presenting a standard argument of the theologians (as discussed in the previous chapter), Wyclif contends that Holy Scripture is of infinitely greater authority than any papal decretal, since a decretal is merely a human creation, whereas the entirety of scripture is directly authorized by God.[74] Wyclif concedes that the pope is permitted to interpret Holy Scripture but only insofar as he adheres to the divinely intended sense of the text as explicated by the sacred doctors. He must never exalt himself above the sacred text itself. In fact, it is precisely because the pope does not have the right to compose Holy Scripture—as though he were superior to the very writers of scripture—that he must abide by such strict lines of interpretation.[75] Exceeding all human traditions in both authority and subtlety, therefore, the sacred canons of scripture will be the absolute standard so that whatever rules do not conform must be reckoned detestable to both God and the church.[76]

Wyclif was perfectly within his rights, therefore, when he appealed to Gratian's *Decretum* to make his case that all laws passed by the papacy were subject to apostolic and patristic teaching. Like so many before him, Wyclif made much use of the famous canon *Sunt quidam dicentes* (C. 25, q. 1, c. 6). The pope may only establish new laws where scripture is silent (i.e., customs and practices). Otherwise, he is obliged to defend the apostolic and patristic doctrines.[77] Wyclif insists, therefore, on the right of theologians to assess the actions of the papacy. For if the theologian is permitted to examine the most sacred and infinite power of God it stands to reason that he can scrutinize the power of the pope. In fact, it is essential that theologians discuss papal power, says Wyclif, inasmuch as the church is in danger of being led astray by the disguised power of a pseudo-vicar. If the pope is quick to prove from Holy Scripture that he possesses the preeminence of power it stands to reason that he will allow theologians to examine these claims. For as Holy Scripture is true in its entirety, so it should be examined in its entirety by a Catholic doctor. Wyclif recoils at the notion that the pope can at once stake his claim to power on scripture and decree that no theologian can venture beyond the strict limits set by the pope for the study of scripture—which is the very function of the theologian. In truth, though, the license to discuss such matters has been granted by God. Even as the pope attempts to muzzle dissent, the law of scripture obliges the theologian "to provide a reason for everyone asking about the faith" (1 Pt 3:15).[78] Thus Wyclif viewed exalted papal claims as an assault on the Christian freedom that the theologian is duty-bound to defend. For the merit of Jesus Christ has established the perfect law of liberty, which has been revealed most perfectly in the New Testament.[79]

Wyclif never worked out a comprehensive position on papal infallibility—which was only a fledgling theory at the time anyway. All we really have on the subject are scattered remarks, as when he specifically referred to the idea of papal infallibility as both heretical and impossible.[80] He notes that if Saint Peter himself had sinned on numerous occasions after having been chosen as an apostle, it is all the more likely that his vicar will also lapse into sin. Merely being elected pope does not ensure that that person has been confirmed in grace. The only wayfarer who could not sin was Christ the God-man. Wyclif, therefore, dismisses as a "sophistical gloss" the notion that the pope cannot err insofar as he is the pope *(quod papa, sub racione qua papa, nec peccare poterit nec errare)*. In other words, Wyclif does not accept Guido Terreni's distinction whereby the pope might err personally but never when defining a matter of faith for the church. Wyclif follows a long line of canon lawyers, therefore, when he contends that the pope can err both in moral issues and in the judgment of truth. Wyclif makes the traditional case neatly when he remarks that simply because the faith of the Catholic Church cannot fail (Lk 22:32) does not mean that the faith of the curia cannot. Even in the days after the sending of the Holy Spirit, the apostles recognized their own fragility and confessed that they too were liable to sin (1 Jn 1:18).[81]

Wyclif was hardly alone in his belief that the pope is subject to error, and he was likewise in good company in maintaining that councils too could err. In fact, we will see that both Woodford and Netter admitted that even general councils were not infallible. And if these two entities—pope and council—cannot ultimately serve as unimpeachable authorities given their liability to error, then one is left to ask who is going to deliver the final authoritative verdict. Writing in the wake of the Blackfriars Synod that had condemned a number of his positions in 1382, Wyclif addressed the authority of councils. The context must be borne in mind, therefore, since he is clearly reacting to what he reckoned to be an unjust sentence handed down by his enemies. At all events, Wyclif remarks in a sermon that no council should be accepted unless it is believed that the Holy Spirit has confirmed its determination. He laments, however, that many of his contemporaries who hasten to summon councils are themselves ignorant apostates. What is more, they apply a standard of validity that Wyclif finds thoroughly untenable, namely, that the council's findings may be accepted as authoritative on the basis of a simple majority decision *(iudicio pluris partis)*. He considers this principle of the greater part *(maior pars)* to be nothing short of blasphemous since it implies that the majority opinion must always be correct, when in fact the corrupt members generally end up infecting the proceedings. Indeed, says Wyclif, the greater part of a council composed of apostates is bound to be heretical. Thus it is no more an article of faith to believe that such people could not err within a council than that they could also live without error. In other words, Wyclif attaches no automatic gift of infallibility to the council itself; its reception will be based on its content.[82] In fact, reception had always been considered integral to establishing the authority of a conciliar decree. Everyone agreed about that; the problem, of course, was determining when a given decree could be considered sufficiently received and thus authoritative.

The Right to Dissent

Wyclif was not forced out of Oxford University because he praised scripture and protested against the influence of canon lawyers. It was because of the theological conclusions he reached. To Wyclif's enemies—many of whom were theologians themselves—Wyclif was a prime example of the proud master run amok. Already in the days before Wyclif was suspected of heresy John Kynyngham warned him that a theologian must not speak in ways that "ring of error to the common understanding and customary discourse." It is not enough when teaching publicly that one's words be true according to one's own sensibilities. "The truth that the words convey must conform to reality *(a parte rei)* in keeping with the common manner of understanding." Even as Kynyngham would admit that there may be some truth to what Wyclif is saying, he found that it diverged from the plain truth *(plana veritate)* as grasped by the common understanding *(communem intellectum)*, not only of the schools, but of the whole church as well.[83] Kynyngham makes an important point here—one that we will see again with Jean Gerson. Theologians not only have an obligation to speak the truth; they must articulate it in ways that are edifying for the whole community of believers. Wyclif would surely embrace this principle himself. He had, after all, attacked those masters who made sport of scripture as they dismantled its propositions.[84] Yet Wyclif the theologian believed that he was speaking the truth in ways that people needed to hear it. What looked reckless to Kynyngham seemed to Wyclif like the due exercise of his own authority—the very authority conferred upon him with the reception of his doctoral degree.

Wyclif's relentless criticism of the ecclesiastical hierarchy had left him remarkably unscathed through the 1370s, largely due to the support he received from the English Crown. His luck began to run out in 1380, when a commission of Wyclif's fellow Oxford masters censured him for his views on the Eucharist and ended his career at the university.[85] Throughout it all, however, no one questioned the orthodoxy of his sources—only their interpretation. Wyclif had mined traditional materials to make his case; his works are replete with quotations drawn from the fathers and large samples of canon law. And we must also be very clear that Wyclif was by no means opposed to glossing these authoritative texts; there was a venerable tradition not only of biblical but also of legal commentary that he continually evoked.[86] Hence I simply cannot agree with Ghosh, who maintains that Wyclif had wished to set aside all human mediation in the form of glosses.[87]

What Wyclif does object to, however, is the very thing that he is charged with by his adversaries as he upbraids modern postilators for seeking to impose their own logic upon the sacred text. He marvels at their arrogance as they set aside this faithful tradition in favor of their personal interpretations. Having lost sight of the inherent authority of the tradition, they are destroying the very text they were meant to defend. Yet genuine exposition, like a dutiful handmaid, seeks only to explain and disclose her lady's intentions. When done correctly, therefore, glossing exposes the truth embedded in the text; it does not disguise it. Wyclif is struck by the irony that one is forbidden to gloss papal decretals, except to confirm the tenor of the words and clarify them in keeping with their intended literal sense *(de virtute sermonis)*. That being the case, then one is surely obliged to observe the logic of scripture—itself the form of Christ's words—which is more perfectly composed and more duly authorized than a mere decretal. The Holy Spirit has presented the law of scripture in the form the church was meant to observe, thereby surpassing all created authority. Hence Wyclif's refrain that the Catholic theologian is obligated to study scripture's manner of speaking so that he can correctly grasp its meaning, which is possible only when one becomes acquainted with its logic.[88] The words of scripture need not be repeated verbatim by commentators, but the sacred sense they convey must be preserved. Reverence for the *modus loquendi scripturae* will facilitate the disclosure of the *sensus scripturae*.

Wyclif allows for faithful exposition, therefore, but it must proceed within the basic parameters that scripture itself has established. And the work of exegeting scripture in all its subtleties belongs to the master *(opus magistrale)*. Only the *professor scripturae* is qualified to discern the *modus loquendi scripturae*. It is not for the boorish grammarians who know nothing of biblical metaphysics but for the "most high theologians" upon whose minds scripture has impressed the deepest truth.[89] Many of his fellow theologians had faithfully conveyed the logic of scripture. Not only did Wyclif praise the likes of Robert Grosseteste and Richard FitzRalph, but he often pointed to the pious interpretation set out by Thomas Aquinas and Nicholas of Lyra.[90]

Wyclif had no quarrel with commenting on—or glossing—the biblical text. He knew as well as anyone else that pious exposition is needed to reveal the truth of scripture, and that one relied upon the learned comments of the holy doctors who together form the larger exegetical tradition. The problem as Wyclif sees it is that his opponents are no longer controlled by that tradition. If they can gloss texts to support whatever meaning they like—for example, that eucharistic accidents exist without subjects—then they could go on to gloss away the entire history of Christ's life. It must be stressed that it was not the act of glossing itself that so disturbs Wyclif, therefore, but rather the unbridled power that the glossators arrogate for themselves when they are no longer bound by the tradition.[91] The issue was not whether one is entitled to gloss the biblical text—of course one can. The dispute was not over that fact but over the conclusions reached in the act of glossing. Some glosses are right and others wrong, because some serve to explicate the text and others to distort it.

It all boiled down to the authoritative interpretation of scripture, the decrees, and the holy doctors. For his part, Wyclif protests that he has no desire to scandalize the Roman church: "I understand my sayings on this matter [the Eucharist] to be in accordance with the logic of scripture, and also in accord with the logic of the holy doctors and the decree of the Roman church, which I suppose to have spoken prudently." All the trouble can be traced to the recent glossators who have distorted the sacred witnesses to serve their own ends.[92] Throughout his tribulations, whether concerning civil dominion or eucharistic presence, Wyclif made it clear that he would retract his remarks if they could be proven heretical by way of scripture and the saints.[93]

The problem, of course, was that Wyclif did not believe that his opponents had made their case, which meant that he was free to continue in his protests. He asserted the authority inherent to the magisterial position he held; he was an expert and would not back down. Like Godfrey of Fontaines, Wyclif believed that the theologian has a sworn obligation to speak the truth no matter the disruption it may cause. More evil, says Wyclif, can be traced to keeping silent than promulgating the truth. When one knows the truth it would be a sin of omission to remain quiet. In fact, one is never culpable for speaking the truth even if it results in some punishable indiscretion. More people prefer to remain silent, though, rather than join Wyclif in his noble endeavor for fear of losing their temporal possessions and for a servile fear of their superiors.[94]

If Wyclif viewed himself as a true Catholic rooted firmly in the tradition, he also embraced another age-old Catholic principle—that the mysteries of scripture are revealed only to those who conform themselves to Christ. This has troubled some modern scholars, such as Hurley, Minnis, and Ghosh, who believe that Wyclif lapsed into a radical subjectivism whereby the biblical text could be understood only by the pure and humble.[95] Yet this does not seem to be a fair assessment. After all, the principle that humility and sanctity are indispensable to accurate exegesis is as old as the Christian faith itself (cf. 1 Cor 2:6–13). This principle was frequently expressed by Saint Augustine and Saint Bonaventure who both found that genuine comprehension of scripture comes only to those who seek out Christ the Word. Indebted to this same Christological tradition of exegesis, Wyclif contends that if anyone hopes to discern the logic of scripture he must draw close to Christ, who is the subtlest logician of all. This, in turn, demands that the reader purify his heart, since scripture's mysteries are hidden from the proud and the vain. The true disciple of scripture must begin with a virtuous disposition, but he is not embarking on a solitary journey. For even as he humbly accepts the authority of scripture he also adheres to the witness of the holy doctors.[96] Still, the truth will only become clear with the assistance of the one illuminating *Magister*—Christ the Light and the Principle of all knowledge.

The exegete must be conformed to Wisdom himself, all the while believing in order to understand.[97] "The Christian should conform his own sense to the sense of Christ if he is going to understand scripture . . . and conform his own logic to the logic of Christ."[98] In fact, the Christian must be so assimilated to Christ that he can be said to become Christ himself.[99] Conformity to Christ begins with the reading of scripture for it is there that one encounters the love of God made manifest in the poor Christ.[100] And fulfilling Christ's word of love will lead to final perfection and eventual deification.[101] It is not enough simply to have received a university degree or be counted among the regent masters. The true theological expert is a model of Christian piety who has gained a deeper comprehension of scripture's subtleties precisely by conforming himself to the Divine Person who stands at the heart of scripture. Wyclif was not proposing to measure the worth of a master by some set of arcane criteria; he was extolling a long-standing ideal. Nevertheless, when this principle is cemented to the other broadly accepted tenet that no prelate or synod is immune from error, there will be no way to extract any concessions from Wyclif.

The Authority and Nature of the Church

As should be evident by now, an exegetical crisis had developed precisely because Wyclif would not necessarily accept that the decisions of his adversaries — at Blackfriars for instance — are authoritative. Exegetical authority clearly goes hand in hand with ecclesiastical authority. Thus it will be instructive to look briefly at Wyclif's conception of the church. For, as we shall see, Thomas Netter would contend that Wyclif had broken away from the moorings of the visible institutional church so as to exalt an invisible body accountable to no earthly authority. The result of this — so Netter and others charged — was that Wyclif felt free to interpret scripture as he alone saw fit, answering as he did to a purely celestial tribunal. At the outset of his *De ecclesia* Wyclif observes that Holy Scripture speaks of the church in many ways: she is the bride of Christ, the strong woman, the mystical body of Christ, Jerusalem, our mother, the temple of the Lord, the kingdom of heaven, and the city of the great king. Yet Wyclif will focus on one description above the rest: the church as the congregation of all the predestined.[102] Wyclif insisted that, not only in her triumphant state, but even in her pilgrim state, the church contains no part of those foreknown to eternal damnation. In this regard Wyclif notes that he is only following Augustine who had rejected the notion of a bipartite body proposed by Tyconius. As far as Wyclif is concerned those who are merely faithful for a time, and yet remain foreknown to damnation, constitute a fake church *(ecclesiam similatam)*.[103] For all this dramatic language, however, Wyclif did not envision the breakdown down of all earthly authority; he only wanted to see it properly exercised.

Given this basic framework, Wyclif sometimes addressed the topic of papal authority in seemingly extreme tones. It should be remembered, though, that he was writing in the time of papal schism when the two sides hurled intemperate remarks back and forth, each claimant labeling the other Antichrist. In fact, Wyclif's remarks do not look much different from those of the perfectly orthodox conciliarist Dietrich of Niem. Nor should it be forgotten that Wyclif did indeed allow the pope to function as supreme legislator on earth just so long as he abided by the guidelines established by scripture and the fathers—itself a commonplace position. Hence when Wyclif brings the concept of predestination to bear on papal authority he is merely wielding a broad sword designed to limit papal overreach. The fact is, by the way, that all of Wyclif's colleagues believed in predestination and also believed that—short of a special revelation—no one could know who was counted among the predestined. With that in mind Wyclif will argue that if genuine membership in the Holy Catholic Church consists of being predestined, then no pope should presume to assert that he is the head of the church. And, barring special revelation, he should not even assert that he is a member.[104] On more mundane terms, however, the pope is merely the visible head of the Roman church with no claim to sovereignty over all the faithful, for the very fact that the Catholic Church cannot be limited to Rome. The church is diffused throughout the earth, and Christ is her sole head.[105] As there is only one head, so only one Holy Mother Church—the universal body comprising the elect. Like a metaphysical universal, she is whole and perfect, lacking nothing.[106] This is not to say that Wyclif abolishes the notion of a Roman Church, but it is just one particular church within the universal whole. Since Christ alone is the head of the whole church human claims to universal authority are automatically ruled out. Even here, though, the pope's claim to genuine sovereignty in the Roman Church would also require special revelation, since this would imply eternal incorporation into the body of Christ. Membership, let alone headship, of a particular church implies that one is part of Holy Mother Church and thus numbered among the predestined. What, then, is a prelate to do? Wyclif counsels a return to the example of the apostles: they counted themselves mere servants of the head, humble ministers of Christ's bride, never presuming to be the head or the bridegroom themselves.[107]

At this point it would seem that any claims to earthly authority would collapse and chaos ensue. Indeed, this is just what opponents of the Wycliffites and Hussites charged. Yet, as discussed above, Wyclif did in fact permit the pope to exercise genuine authority within the parameters set by canon law itself. Here, then, Wyclif will tone down his inflammatory rhetoric and offer more prudent advice. If the pope governs the whole church militant chiefly according to the law of Christ, then he can indeed be considered the captain placed beneath the arch-head Jesus Christ. Wyclif will give the pope the benefit of the doubt, therefore, pointing out that we ought to suppose the pope is the head unless he does something to prove the opposite.[108] In fact, Wyclif contended that the laity are not called to scrutinize the eternal status of their prelates, but neither are they required to believe anything about their superiors unless it is true. No one is bound to believe anything unless God moves him to believe such, and God does not move people to believe anything false. The pastor is obligated to lead his people by the example of sound instruction and virtuous works. If the laity see no evidence of fruitful works on the part of their superiors they are not bound to reckon them worthy clerics.[109] Hence if an ecclesiastic is so enthralled with earthly things that he bypasses the heavenly, one may take this as a sign. It is by works that the true affections of the mind may be judged.[110] Not unlike the eleventh-century Gregorian reformers, therefore, Wyclif calls upon the laity to consider the evident moral status of the clergy.

The situation as it stands is one in which the elect and the damned mingle within the visible institution. In this vein, Wyclif drew a distinction between being "in the church" *(in ecclesia)* and being "of the church" *(de ecclesia);* only those in the latter category are truly members of the body of Christ. As for those who are merely in, but not of, the church they fall into two categories. Some remain in their perpetual infidelity, having never received charity or grace. Others are like superfluous foods received into the stomach of Holy Mother Church through the grace of present righteousness but on account of their hypocrisy or heresy are never digested. These are the clerics and laity who pretend to be working on behalf of the church but prove to be hypocrites interested only in temporal gain.[111] The fact is, however, that there are some among the predestined who are themselves not in a present state of grace, and conversely, some among the damned who are currently righteous. Yet even while the predestined man is in a state of mortal sin he does not cease to be a member of the true church, although he might be presently excommunicated within the earthly church.[112] This is because the grace of predestination can exist alongside mortal sin.[113] By limiting the church, properly speaking, to the predestined, Wyclif was clearly at odds with some of his contemporaries. Well aware of this fact, he recounts the position of his opponents that even the foreknown who are reborn through baptism are members of the Catholic Church. And, conversely, none of the predestined can be counted within the church when straying from the faith. It is right faith, they say, that makes one a member of the Christ's body. Wyclif, on the other hand, maintains that only the predestined can actually possess the right faith. The foreknown, no matter their baptism, bear an indelible sin that marks them as heretics perpetually separated from Christ's body.[114] Again extreme language perhaps, but Wyclif remains much more concerned with matters of present righteousness than eternal status.

It must be remembered that for all his invective Wyclif was not attempting to dismantle the church as it exists in this world; he merely wished to reform it. And in that he was hardly alone. He was cognizant of the fact that the visible church as constituted here on earth comprises both the predestined and the foreknown who have the grace of present righteousness. The wheat and the chaff are allowed to mingle now as they await the final judgment.[115] By no means a Donatist, despite later charges, Wyclif did believe that this mixed church can continue to function no matter the eternal status of its participants. Those among the foreknown may still fulfill their clerical tasks. For Wyclif concedes that by human ordination clerics are constituted in ecclesiastical offices from among both the predestined and the foreknown.[116] He clearly states that a foreknown man can licitly function as a priest and bishop even if he is not a member of Holy Mother Church.[117] Like Judas and his many vicars, God chooses such people and gives them the power to fulfill their office. They can exercise their duties within the church, therefore, even as they are not really of the church.[118] Wyclif is adamant that the foreknown, even in a state of mortal sin, do actually administer sacraments to the faithful.[119] In fact, he will appeal to canon law to confirm that evil priests will not thereby injure the pious faithful. Wyclif no doubt made some provocative comments at times regarding the sacramental ministrations of wicked priests, but he knew very well that Augustine—and all the saints—had condemned the Donatist heresy.[120] Above all else, Wyclif's discussion of an invisible church was a call for reform, not chaos. The notion that there might one day exist only a small remnant church in the midst of general apostasy was accepted by perfectly orthodox sources. As we have seen, Henry of Ghent and Gerard of Bologna both raised the possibility of a church in name only that might deviate from Holy Scripture. It was widely accepted by canonists and theologians alike that the church could even be reduced to a single person as when she existed solely in the Virgin Mary following Christ's Passion.[121]

More practically, however, Wyclif was simply saying that ecclesiastical prelates are not entitled to the blind obedience of their subjects; all directives must be in conformity with divine law. Hence whenever prelates command something that is in conformity with the will of Christ they are to be obeyed insofar as one is chiefly obeying Christ by fulfilling this command. Otherwise, such prelates were to be resisted. Here Wyclif invokes the classic incident when Saint Paul resisted Peter to his face at Antioch (Gal 2:11–14) as an example of what he terms "resistive obedience." Wyclif reads this text in keeping with the greater exegetical tradition, therefore, when he contends that one's obedience to Christ will manifest itself in resistance to the unjust demands of one's earthly superior.[122] So it is that all papal commands must be tested against divine law. If the command is in conformity with divine law, then it ought to be carried out principally out of reverence for Christ. In this sense, therefore, the pope—as one's human superior—is obeyed only indirectly *(non directe)*, inasmuch as one's first allegiance is always to God's law. If, however, the pope were to command something contrary to divine law, then one should obey God by resisting the command, since it is one's duty to resist injustice even unto death. Again this may be called "resistive" or even "indirect obedience," inasmuch as one is obeying God indirectly by resisting what is contrary to divine law. No Christian, therefore, should follow any new tradition that is not founded in scripture, precisely because such newly invented laws violate the freedom that the Christian has been guaranteed in Christ's evangelical law. Hence the faithful must never believe that simply because the pope commands something that it must be done in obedience to God. Wyclif credits Robert Grosseteste with this understanding of obedience, and the aforementioned terminology, although he provides no citation.[123] One recalls that Grosseteste, when bishop of Lincoln in 1253, had refused to obey Pope Innocent IV's command to grant a benefice to his nephew, arguing that obedience to the apostolic see itself prevented his implementation of such a command, inasmuch as "apostolic commands are not, and cannot be, contrary to the teaching of the apostles and their Lord Jesus Christ."[124] Wyclif may well have had this letter of Grosseteste in mind.

Human Laws, Religious Orders, and Doctrinal Development

In the later years of his life Wyclif could be quite critical of the mendicant orders, although he never lost hope in them entirely—at least not the Franciscans. What he had to say about the mendicants was often directly pertinent to his views of scriptural authority and doctrinal development. Some of that material can be found in a tract known as the *De religione*, which comprises what now makes up the first two chapters of *De apostasia* and the first three chapters of *De civili dominio III*. As we shall see, the Franciscan William Woodford responded to the *De religione* with a lengthy refutation in defense of the mendicants.[125] The central question Wyclif addressed was whether the religious orders could find any foundation within Holy Scripture or whether they amount to a superfluous addition to the perfect religion of Christ. Prior to the fallout over transubstantiation Wyclif had enjoyed good relations with some friars (notably the Augustinian Thomas Winterton) and even now appealed to those "I have called beloved sons, those who are not numbered among the apostates, but rather are excellent observers of the good that belongs to the religion of Christ." Indeed, Wyclif claims that the reform he is seeking is for the good of the church and even the friars themselves. As such, he asks the friars to help him in his work.[126] Wyclif regarded the Franciscan rule as an authentic expression of evangelical law.[127] And he commended Saint Bonaventure and William of Ockham for struggling to recover the primitive rule from which their order had fallen away.[128] Yet Wyclif fears that the religious orders now pursue a way of life that is lacking in scriptural foundation and in the process destroying the very religion that Christ had instituted in Holy Scripture.[129] Such anxiety provoked by the mendicant orders—

with their many privileges—was shared across the board by secular theologians throughout the late Middle Ages, from Godfrey of Fontaines in the thirteenth century to Jean Gerson in the fifteenth.

Religious orders are bound by a rule that their members pledge to uphold; that is the most basic fact: *religio-regula*. Wyclif was afraid, however, that such a set of obligations might be seen as supplementing the Christian life as spelled out by Christ in the Gospels as though scripture were somehow deficient. This is the fear that drives the bulk of his criticism. The question is whether it is permissible to go beyond the religion of Christ handed down in Holy Scripture and found some new religion based upon human tradition. Is not the religion that Christ expressly instituted in the Gospels *(in evangelio expresse instituit)* sufficient unto itself apart from the mixture of human ceremonies? If it is, then it would seem that the addition of some new law, some new religion, would not be permissible.[130] This is not to say that Wyclif necessarily wanted to abolish private rites and rules wholesale. For to the extent that they give expression to the evangelical life found in the scriptures they remain acceptable. Wyclif was not wholly opposed to private rites and human laws, therefore, just so long as they did not exceed what is already implicitly grounded in the Gospels *(fundantur implicite in evangelio)*. Thus in a perfectly traditional vein Wyclif contends that every good human law will ultimately be grounded in the Gospels and, conversely, that no human tradition is licit unless it facilitates the observance of Christ's law.[131]

Wyclif had merely required that all orders and expressions of piety must be at least implicitly grounded in Holy Scripture *(implicite fundabilis)*. He clearly does not demand explicit foundation no matter what opponents such as Woodford might charge. In fairness, though, Wyclif admitted that he had not always made himself clear on this point. And that has provided an avenue, he says, for unscrupulous adversaries to attack him.[132] As far as Wyclif is concerned, all genuine human laws are themselves eternal truths that are already implied within Holy Scripture. Human law dictates, for instance, that it is a crime to disturb the peace of the realm, which Wyclif believes is perfectly reasonable. All that Wyclif asks of a human law is that it be justified by eternal principles. His enemies (so he claims) have falsely accused him of saying that all human laws are wicked, or that none of the principles of human laws can be eternal truths, when he has actually maintained the opposite. He insists that all human laws be continually tested against the divine standard, however, for it often happens that human laws can prove to be defective. Actually, Wyclif pursues a very reasonable line of argumentation—basically applying the principle of *epikeia*—when he contends that human laws must not be elevated to universal status, since the law that does no harm today may well lead to injustices tomorrow as new cases arise. The problem is that politicians cannot foresee all the consequences of the laws they pass, which means that we must consistently keep an eye on the divine law, which will always be applicable in every circumstance. Genuine law, therefore, is a truth that directs man as to how he might best serve God. And this is known as divine law *(lex divina)* of which one part is hidden in Holy Scripture where it awaits explication in the form of human law.[133] The whole truth and the law of God have been given in the evangelical writings, even if only implicitly *(implicite)*—again, no demand for explicit formulations. The problem, according to Wyclif, is that the Antichrist and his disciples daily fabricate new rescripts that they place on par with Holy Scripture as if to remedy its supposed insufficiency.[134] Human laws and traditions are not inherently wrong, therefore, but neither must they be exalted at the expense of evangelical law. Wyclif finds that human laws are sometimes necessary in order to manage what is not explicitly laid out in divine law. But when the divine law does suffice, then it would indeed be superfluous to introduce further human laws. The multiplication of rules drawn up by the different religious orders seems to be an example of this very sort of unnecessary excess. Hence Wyclif's call for a pure Christian religion *(religio pura christiana)* in which evangelical counsels and precepts are observed without the addition of later human legislation.[135]

One should not lose sight of the context of Wyclif's remarks on scripture and ecclesiastical traditions when he is disputing with the friars. He is not at leisure to address the greater question of the authority of Holy Scripture relative to doctrinal developments. The question that Wyclif sets himself to answer here is simply whether private religion is more perfect than common Christian religion. By "private," Wyclif tells us that he means an aggregate formed from religious vows and obligations that bind the adherents. By "common," Wyclif refers to the religion clearly described in Holy Scripture *(in scriptura sacra est expressa)*. This is the common religion to which every faithful person must adhere in order to be saved *(de necessitate salutis)*. Wyclif goes on to contend that the Christian religion as conveyed in the Gospels is simpler, more necessary, and more authoritative than any other, and thus more perfect. This Christian religion proves to be the more necessary since it alone, and no other, is required for salvation *(requiritur ad salutem)*. What is more, the fullness of the Christian law is love, which the common Christian religion teaches more fully and concisely, whereas private religion requires papal authorization, which the *lex Christi* obviously does not.[136] This last point is telling for it highlights the intersection between mendicant rights and papal authority inasmuch as the former were secured by the latter. Wyclif is voicing the long-standing secular frustration with the overreach of papal authority so often carried out to the benefit of the mendicant orders. Hence the persistent contrast drawn between the authority of scripture and that of the papacy: the latter must always be subservient to the former.

It is at this point in the discussion that one runs across the sentence that William Woodford would not only single out for particular criticism, but would distort so as to create the caricature of Wyclif as upholding a naive *sola scriptura* policy. Here Wyclif had written, "Now by faith we grasp that every truth is derived from Scripture; and the more necessary some truth is, the more clearly it is described." Were this not the case, it would seem that the Divine Author had not fully provided for the faithful.[137] In the following chapter, I explore what Woodford makes of this, but suffice it to say here that Wyclif was not presenting this as a universal principle designed to cover the whole of Catholic doctrine. He is merely saying that God would not have failed to reveal clearly the perfect way of Christian piety in the Holy Scriptures. If that is the case, then it is fair to ask whether the rules of the mendicant orders can add any level of perfection to what has already been plainly set forth in scripture. This speaks directly to the authority of Holy Scripture, which must contain the fullness of the evangelical life. Any suggestion that it does not—that the mendicant rules may be improving upon it—could only undermine scripture's claim to the unique perfection that forms the basis of its absolute authority. Yet whereas Christ has established the true Catholic order and religion, says Wyclif, the friars seek papal approval for their many novelties.[138] Again, therefore, the papacy is portrayed as a threat to the authority of scripture as it comes to the assistance of the mendicants in the form of legislation that seemingly calls the sufficiency of scripture into question. Indeed, all Wyclif's talk of extraneous and unwarranted additions secured by papal mandates leads one back to thirteenth-century Paris and the battle over the *status ecclesiae* that no pope has the authority to disrupt.

We have seen that Wyclif was no slave to the explicit verbal formulation of the biblical text. Rather, he chose to follow Augustine in the belief that all truth is ultimately found in scripture, "whether explicitly or implicitly," such that scripture remains the final measure of orthodoxy.[139] He was aware, however, that theological speculation unchecked by a sacred and eternal standard could easily lead to heretical conclusions. It is in this vein that he observed how the church fathers had been wary of introducing novel and nonscriptural terminology into theological discourse lest it provide an opening for heretics to corrupt orthodox teaching. When doctrine was sufficiently secure, however, they were willing to allow nonscriptural terms that had since been approved by the church. Such terminology is acceptable precisely because it faithfully expresses scriptural truth. Wyclif only cautioned, therefore, against a recklessness that had scant regard for the parameters set by scripture and the ancient doctors.[140]

Nowhere did Wyclif ever question the legitimacy of the church's great creeds. Never did he call into doubt the propriety of employing nonscriptural terminology such as the *homoousios* of Nicea. In fact, Wyclif's comments on the Western addition of the *filioque* clause to the Nicene Creed offer his most sustained argument regarding the process of doctrinal development relative to scriptural authority. In his *De trinitate* Wyclif readily admits that the Holy Spirit's procession from the Son is not explicitly stated in scripture. What is more, the Council of Constantinople (381) clearly asserts that the Spirit proceeds from the Father.[141] Yet while the Greeks may be upset with the Latins for altering the Creed, one must take into consideration the emergence of heresies that compelled the Western church to act as it did for the preservation of the faith. In 381, says Wyclif, there was no need to add that the Spirit proceeds from the Son because it had not yet been challenged by heretics. The *filioque* clause, therefore, did not amount to an addition of some newly discovered truth but was simply the ancient truth presented in a more explicit form.[142] Actually, says Wyclif, there are many Catholic truths that are taught by the saints and doctors of the church that are not "expressly" posited in scripture. All sorts of things are catholically taught in the church that are not clearly described in the Gospels, such as Christ's descent into hell, matters pertaining to the administration of sacraments, and the publication of creeds. Having said that, Wyclif is hardly deeming scripture an insufficient source of Catholic faith. For the fact remains that every philosophical truth can be found in Holy Scripture, such that the holy doctors, led by reason, will be able to bring to full expression the truth hidden therein. Hence Wyclif will conclude that the Spirit's procession from the Son does indeed "follow from the sense of scripture" if not from the precise words.[143] Wyclif might happily abide the language of the great creeds, therefore, but he regarded the language surrounding the scholastic doctrine of transubstantiation as an extraneous modern addition to the faith, unwarranted by scripture.[144] The problem with transubstantiation was not the word itself but the fact that the word conveyed a concept that was at odds with the greater *sensus scripturae*. It is not a matter of novel words, therefore, but novel concepts that can only be conveyed by these words.

It can be a daunting task to disentangle the many things that Wyclif has said over the years relative to the authority of scripture and ecclesiastical traditions. Yet for all the invective there is a solid and essentially conservative core. Wyclif embraced the calling of the medieval theologian—the Master of the Sacred Page—for whom theology is a science founded upon a divinely authored text. Whether or not his various theological and political conclusions were right or wrong is a separate issue. The point is that his means of arriving at these conclusions, through reliance upon scripture and the fathers, was standard operating procedure for the medieval master. Nor was Wyclif a primitivist clinging to the patristic age to the exclusion of later developments. He not only drew upon the work of fellow theologians such as Aquinas, Lyra, and FitzRalph, but he called upon the glosses of the great canonists to further his arguments based upon church law. With his insistence that all Catholic doctrine be grounded *at least implicitly* in Holy Scripture, Wyclif was not saying anything that contemporary theologians and canonists would not also have embraced. For no matter what later opponents may have charged, Wyclif never demanded *explicit* scriptural warrant for every article of faith. There would have been no reason for him to do so in light of his larger Christological vision of Holy Scripture as the eternal fund of truth by which all other things are themselves true. But then even this expansive conception of Holy Scripture only echoes the sentiments of his predecessors who had come to praise scripture as "the radiance of eternal light, a spotless mirror of the working of God, and an image of his goodness" (Wis 7:26).

Chapter 3

The Ambivalent Friar

William Woodford

Having examined John Wyclif's view on scripture and authority, we can turn now to his critics. This chapter looks at the Franciscan theologian William Woodford and the objections he raised to Wyclif's exegetical program. The principal points of concern are Woodford's views on scriptural authority and exegesis, as well as the authority of extra-scriptural traditions. The question of extra-scriptural truth was of special concern to Woodford as a Franciscan friar. Indeed, Woodford's arguments on authority cannot be fully understood without recognizing that his response to Wyclif forms part of the perennial defense of the mendicant orders against charges of illegitimacy leveled by secular theologians. In fact, it may be fair to say that Woodford's chief concern was the danger that Wyclif's exegetical program posed to the status of mendicant orders.

Woodford earned his doctorate in theology at Oxford in 1373. A few years later, in 1376, he lectured at Oxford against Wyclif's views on clerical dominion. And in 1383, not long after Wyclif had been expelled from the university, he made the case against Wyclif's eucharistic theology. Archbishop Thomas Arundel later asked Woodford to expound on eighteen articles drawn from Wyclif's *Trialogus* that had been condemned in February 1397. He died only a few months after completing that work.[1]

Woodford receives mixed assessments from modern scholars. Anne Hudson finds his work disappointing on the whole, commenting, "Woodford's discussion of Wycliffite positions appears curiously blinkered and beside the point."² Hudson's disappointment is rather mild criticism in comparison to Paul de Vooght's assessment. De Vooght came to the rescue of Wyclif who he believed had been unfairly maligned by Woodford. As far as de Vooght was concerned, although Wyclif was "a fierce defender of Scripture and Tradition, an instinctive enemy of innovation," he was nevertheless a "profoundly Catholic figure" whose image was tarnished by Woodford's baseless accusation that he maintained a *sola scriptura* position and had discarded the tradition.³ According to de Vooght, Woodford never even refutes the real Wyclif since the conception of scripture he attacks does not belong to Wyclif at all. As a refutation, de Vooght reckons it worthless—*égal à zéro*.⁴ Michael Hurley, on the other hand, defended Woodford, noting that he was not even responsible for composing the aforementioned list of eighteen errors; he merely responded to a list that Oxford theologians extracted from the *Trialogus*. What is more, Hurley criticized de Vooght for offering a biased defense of Wyclif that does not examine some of the schoolman's more radical statements.⁵

Eric Doyle later attempted to mediate between the extremes but was clearly far more sympathetic to Woodford. He argued—with good reason—that Woodford's assessment of Wyclif's conception of scripture and ecclesiastical tradition should principally be interpreted as a defense of the religious life in response to the *De religione*. Contrary to de Vooght's thesis, though, Doyle contends that Wyclif was in fact proposing a *sola scriptura* principle, at least in this case. This is not to say that Doyle completely dismisses de Vooght; he just thinks that the issue is more complicated than de Vooght acknowledges. Nevertheless, I cannot agree with Doyle's conclusion that "Wyclif held two principles: *sola scriptura* in a Catholic and traditional sense and *sola scriptura* in a literalist sense." For his own part, Doyle goes so far as to say that there is "nothing new or startling" about Woodford's claim that there are many truths *necessary for salvation* that are not contained in scripture.⁶ Minnis recently revisited this debate and came out squarely in support of Doyle to the point of dismissing de Vooght's reading.⁷ Indeed, the image of the sensible Woodford confronting the radical Wyclif seems to have won the day. In the eyes of Jeremy Catto, Woodford emerges as an eminently confident theologian who "rejected Wyclif's doctrine of *sola scriptura:* many truths were not contained in scripture." For

Woodford, "the tradition of the church was the essential norm for the interpretation of holy writ." Thus Catto believes that Woodford's embrace of a developmental model of ecclesiastical tradition proved to be the best means to refute Wyclif's subjective reading of Holy Scripture.[8] Ghosh echoes these sentiments; he praises Woodford for his "holistic vision of faith and the truths of the faith . . . encompassing scripture, tradition [and] traditional interpretations."[9]

The following discussion should raise some serious doubts as to the validity of the prevailing scholarly assessment. First of all, as the previous chapter should have made clear, Wyclif did not advocate any sort of *sola scriptura* doctrine; this is indeed an invention of Woodford. In fact, Woodford took it upon himself to spin out all sorts of possible scenarios that would result from the adoption of a *sola scriptura* doctrine—a doctrine that he claimed to find in a few decontextualized remarks drawn from Wyclif's criticism of the mendicants. More than that, however, Woodford is hardly a portrait in serenely confident orthodoxy. For when it comes time to make his case Woodford is really not sure where to turn. There is a marked ambiguity in Woodford's conception of scripture, tradition, and authority. In fact, Woodford was ultimately unable to present a consistent response to Wyclif because he himself was torn between alternative modes of authority, none of which could claim his absolute allegiance. Not only does this fact reveal something about Woodford himself—unsure in his footing and lacking a fully coherent vision—but it gives us a glimpse into the larger state of affairs at the end of the fourteenth century.

De causis condempnationis

I begin with Woodford's comprehensive 1397 work, *De causis condempnationis articulorum 18 damnatorum Joannis Wyclif*.[10] Although we cannot look at all eighteen articles in minute detail, we can look at what they reveal about matters of scripture and authority—which is after all the key to the entire debate. Only the last article deals with this topic specifically and thus will be accorded the most thorough analysis. The opening questions concerning the Eucharist set the tone for the entire work, however, as Woodford attempts to paint Wyclif as an enemy of the unbroken Catholic tradition, driven by pride to refute what the saints and doctors have held across the ages. Woodford lists a series of doctors, from Ignatius of Antioch all the way to Giles of Rome, in order to prove that Wyclif—with a temerity that not even Berengar of Tours could match—sets himself against a tradition that has been solidified by both ancient and modern authorities *(antiqui et moderni)*, hence from the time of the apostles until the present. While Berengar and Wyclif may have shared the same distaste for transubstantiation, says Woodford, at least Berengar claimed it was merely erroneous, whereas Wyclif labels the doctrine heretical. Yet it is Wyclif's doctrine of remanence that has been deemed heretical from the apostolic age *(a tempore apostolorum)* down to the present through the succession of fathers and doctors. Woodford might have been content to leave it there, but he says that he feels compelled to refute Wyclif point by point lest the simple be led astray by Wyclif's deceptive efforts to prove his own position true and Catholic.[11] Woodford, like Wyclif's other posthumous opponent Thomas Netter, will insist that beneath every seemingly orthodox statement Wyclif intends only to further his own perverse agenda. This is a vital component of Woodford's strategy: every exegetical move Wyclif makes, no matter how plausible it may seem, must be presented as tainted by his radical disregard for the Catholic tradition.

Having dealt with the Eucharist at length, Woodford examined Wyclif's position—as set forth in the *Trialogus*—regarding the other sacraments. Of principal interest in all this is Woodford's response as it pertains to ecclesiastical tradition. For instance, Wyclif had said that it is presumptuous to define with certainty that children of faithful parents who die without baptism will not be saved (*Trialogus* 4.12). The problem is that no less an authoritative source as Saint Augustine seems to have made it clear that they are damned. Well aware of the saint's view, Wyclif had claimed that Augustine was merely pondering the damnation of unbaptized infants as a possibility, not asserting it as a fact. Yet Woodford sees Wyclif's explanation as a prime example of his willingness to present a new explanation *(nova expositio)* that runs contrary to the saint's intention *(contra mentem Augustini)* and indeed against that of all the ancient doctors. Here Woodford's instinctual response is to appeal, not to present teaching authority, but instead to antiquity. Woodford is certain that "the ancient faith of the church" testifies to the perpetual damnation of all infants who perish without sacramental baptism. "The authority of the gospel" has always been understood this way "from the apostolic tradition and through the succession of fathers coming down to us." Not only does Woodford have the ancient witness of fathers on his side, but also the surest measure of orthodoxy: the testimony of Holy Scripture. Woodford specifically invokes the classic definition of heresy when he accuses Wyclif of interpreting "the Evangelical Scripture in ways other than the Holy Spirit requires and the church understands," thereby marking his exposition as heretical (cf. *Haeresis*, C. 24. q. 3, c. 27).[12]

Later on we will see Woodford invoke the authority of extra-scriptural tradition, but here he charges Wyclif with heresy on terms that Wyclif himself would readily understand, indeed on terms that all medieval theologians understood: what Wyclif was saying ran contrary to the intended sense of Holy Scripture. Woodford is taking his stand here upon scripture and the fathers, and he will do so repeatedly. This bears emphasizing precisely because it is a mode of argumentation that runs along the very same lines as Wyclif. Hence, no matter that he will charge Wyclif with harboring a morbid obsession with Holy Scripture and ancient sources, the fact is that Woodford himself recurs to their authority on a regular basis.

Woodford worked his way through a series of statements that Wyclif made about the sacraments in his *Trialogus* that I will not cover in their entirety. Suffice it to say that he takes Wyclif to task for the various doubts that he raises concerning current ecclesiastical practices. The sacraments of Confirmation and Extreme Unction had often raised concerns for medieval theologians on account of their lack of explicit scriptural warrant. This led Bonaventure to argue (as we have seen) that they had not actually been instituted by Christ. In his *Trialogus* (4.25) Wyclif—who never rejected any of the seven sacraments—had opined that were Extreme Unction a sacrament, then Christ and the apostles would have promulgated it. Evidence for this, however, appears to be lacking. Rather than take the more expansive view of his Franciscan predecessor, however, Woodford makes the case for this sacrament directly on the basis of Holy Scripture. The key verse is James 5:14, which he accuses Wyclif of interpreting in a manner other than the Holy Spirit requires. Again Wyclif's interpretation must for this reason be heretical. Interpreting scripture as he does, Wyclif has set himself apart from the exegetical tradition, according to Woodford, since the doctors from apostolic days to the present have located the sacrament in this verse. Rejecting the correct interpretation of scripture would by itself render Wyclif's remarks heretical. But Woodford also reckons it heretical to claim that nothing is Catholic unless scripture records Christ and the apostles having promulgated it.[13] This last point is crucial to Woodford's argument throughout, since he needs to find a place for religious orders and customs that do not necessarily have a direct apostolic warrant. Yet it also reveals Woodford's own fundamental ambivalence on the whole matter of authority: on the one hand, he wishes to condemn Wyclif for contravening the clear witness of Holy Scripture; on the other, he cannot let the argument rest entirely upon scripture, since that may undercut his larger goal, namely, the defense of the mendicant way of life.

Yet again, though, Woodford will return to clear testimony of Holy Scripture in order to demonstrate Wyclif's heresy. When Wyclif argued that cases for divorce based on consanguinity or affinity are merely human ordinances (*Trialogus* 4.20), Woodford counters that such a position is expressly *(expresse)* contrary to scripture. Willing to wrestle over exegesis with no reference to the larger tradition, Woodford notes that in Genesis the institution of the sacrament of Matrimony prohibits marriage of ascent and descent within the first grade. God, by the institution of marriage, said that a man will leave his father and mother and adhere to his wife. Hence a child marrying his or her parent runs against the divine institution described in scripture. As such, consanguinity within the first grade according to the line of ascent and descent is cause for divorce by divine law. By the time of Leviticus, however, the law extended to the second grade, so that a man cannot marry his sister. Scripture proves that causes for divorce based on consanguinity are divinely introduced and not mere human conventions. Hence Wyclif's article is shown to be "expressly contrary to Holy Scripture and consequently heretical." Again, therefore, scripture is the judge. Woodford will at once affirm the authority of scripture and the church's right to apply biblical injunctions as she sees fit. For, as he continues, he deems it heretical to assert pertinaciously that the church militant has not received from Christ the power to nullify a marriage for sufficient cause *(ex sufficienti causa)*. Woodford is actually defending something very similar to the principle of the canonists, namely, that the pope may dispense against the Gospel for good cause. He notes that one often finds in canon law that the church does, for sufficient reason *(ex sufficiente ratione)*, nullify marriage contracts between people too closely related. Sometimes, therefore, the cause of divorce is indeed based upon divine law *(iure divino)*, while at other times it is based upon human decisions that are nevertheless directed by the Holy Spirit and done for sufficient reason. And yet a further problem with Wyclif's position, according to Woodford, is that it assumes that what was once permitted by God must always stand, such that any alteration is illicit. In other words, Wyclif seems to make no allowance for development. Yet as Woodford charted above, times have changed, so that while it was once permissible for brother and sister to marry that was simply by necessity and was later abolished. As the earth was populated and the Hebrew people set themselves apart from other nations new laws emerged. But these were divinely instituted laws and not mere human inventions. Underlying all this is a common refrain: if Wyclif is right that the practices of the church concerning marriage and divorce are illicit, this would mean that everything the church has deemed just over the years would prove contrary to gospel law and thus be heretical. And that, in turn, would mean that the church that promulgated those laws would also be heretical.[14] This, of course, is regarded as patently impossible inasmuch as the church cannot err. More to the point, however, Woodford the Franciscan friar needs to be especially protective of the legitimacy of alterations to ecclesiastical life. After all, the persistent charge leveled by the secular theologians against the mendicant orders is one of illegitimate innovation.

When Woodford defended the reservation of the sacrament of Confirmation to the bishops he had to contend with the argument that there was no such distinction between bishop and presbyter in the primitive church *(ecclesia primitiva)*. In fact, Saint Jerome had said as much in his commentary on the Epistle to Titus (*PL* 26:596). Here Woodford is willing to admit that at the very beginning of the church *(in principio ecclesiae)*, and in the days following the sending of the Holy Spirit at Pentecost, those who were made priests were called bishops, and bishops were also called presbyters. But, he says, it does not follow from this that there was no difference between the episcopacy and the priesthood with respect to sacramental powers, or that the bishop had no more power to ordain and confirm than a simple priest. What is most interesting here is that Woodford does not turn to a developing tradition to make his case but instead seeks the most primitive witness he can find. For on this matter he chooses to follow Pseudo-Dionysius, who was (supposedly) a contemporary of the apostles and thus knew their intention better than later doctors. Woodford notes that Pseudo-Dionysius distinguishes between three orders, bishop, priest, and deacon, each of which has its own specific operations. As such, there really was a distinction between the episcopacy and priesthood with respect to sacramental power during the time of the apostles.[15] By not appealing to a theory of development here but instead rooting this distinction in the very earliest days of the church, Woodford is attempting to defeat Wyclif on his home court: antiquity. This would appear to be a dangerous move, but it highlights Woodford's conflicted strategy. Wherever possible he should take the fight to Wyclif based upon scripture and ancient sources, but he must also be able to pull back where need be and defend recent developments. Woodford is unable to generate a consistent line of attack precisely because he has failed to work out for himself a coherent basis for orthodoxy as a whole.

As Woodford proceeds to sort out the episode in Acts 9:17 where Ananias laid hands on Paul we find that he will suddenly invoke an extreme version of extra-scriptural truth, although he supports this move with only the vaguest justifications. Here Woodford begins by noting that the mere fact that Ananias was called a disciple does not exclude the possibility that he was a bishop, since the apostles are also called disciples even after the resurrection, at which point they were certainly bishops. Moreover, says Woodford, it is not clear that this imposition of hands was a sacramental confirmation in the first place. For scripture makes it clear that Paul had not yet been baptized at that time, whereas the church maintains that baptism is the gateway to the rest of the sacraments. As Woodford continues, however, he notes that the mere fact that scripture never mentions where Paul was sacramentally confirmed does not mean that he was not confirmed, for neither is there any record in scripture of where Paul and the other apostles were baptized. And it is here that Woodford remarks that "there are an *infinite number* of Catholic truths which cannot be concluded clearly *(evidenter)* by us from what is contained in Holy Scripture, as the last chapter of John makes clear (Jn 21:25)."[16] This is actually an ambiguous remark in light of Woodford's use of the adverb *evidenter,* "clearly/manifestly/plainly." For even if some truth cannot be clearly deduced from scripture that is not to say it therefore lacks all scriptural foundation. At any rate, Woodford never states precisely which unwritten truths are at issue or whether these are truths necessary for salvation. And, of course, if one does not know what these truths are, then there is no way to prove that they have not been written somewhere else in scripture. In fact, Woodford offers no proof of any truths necessary for salvation whose source is outside of scripture.[17] The defense of extra-scriptural truth will play an important role in Woodford's overall argument, but in this instance it seems almost an afterthought that he cannot be bothered to explain. It may be a principle upon which he can rely but not one he always feels comfortable dwelling on.

Woodford's preference for documented ancient sources — as opposed to unverifiable "Catholic truths" — is evident when he answers Wyclif's claim that there had not been any distinction between popes, patriarchs, and bishops in the apostolic era. For here again Woodford has recourse to the most primitive sources, in this case Clement of Rome, a contemporary of the apostles just like Pseudo-Dionysius. Appealing to a canon attributed to Clement (*Audire episcopum*, D. 24, c. 2), Woodford argues that there is a distinction not only between presbyter and deacon but also between presbyter and bishop. Hence priest and deacon were not sufficient at the time of the apostles. Yet Woodford is aware of the fact that many ancient sources mention only the orders of priest and deacon in the primitive church. Perhaps, then, the other orders were instituted later as time progressed. Woodford responds that one must not take all these ancient documents at face value *(verba sonant)*; they are in need of contextualization. He admits that the primitive church did not yet have sacramental rites for all the present orders that the church now recognizes. But that is not to say that the church lacked the orders themselves. To prove this Woodford turns once more to Pseudo-Dionysius whose *De ecclesiastica hierarchia* speaks of psalmists, lectors, and doorkeepers.[18] Hence this primitive apostolic source confirms the antiquity — and thus the inherent legitimacy — of such offices.

This leads to further discussion of development as Woodford notes that there are different ways one can address the apparent absence of these orders in apostolic times. Either one can say that as time progressed *(procedente tempore)*, after the time of the apostles the church established that no one may ascend to superior orders unless he had first received inferior orders. Or one can say — and this is the position Woodford prefers — that although one does not read in scripture that the primitive church had orders other than priest and deacon, the episcopacy was always included in the priesthood. And then, later on, the various inferior and superior orders were propagated. As for pope, patriarch, bishop, and archbishop, the mere fact that these orders are not found in scripture does not mean that they were not part of the church. "For there were many things in the primitive church which are not posited in Holy Scripture." Yet the key factor here is that the move is still to antiquity since Woodford does not regard this as the invention of new orders over time but merely an act of propagation and clarification. The more recent orders are an organic product of scriptural orders, and in that sense already present in scripture even if only inchoately. One might say that the matter was there all along and the form came just a bit later.[19] The point is that Woodford wants to ground all the orders in the primitive church to the maximum extent that he is able. He is unwilling to concede this source of legitimating authority to Wyclif. And yet the irony is that he actually ends up—albeit unwittingly—highlighting his own proximity to Wyclif.

The discussions above also had implications for papal authority. In his 1376 *De dominio civili clericorum* Woodford had made some very strong claims on behalf of the papacy, declaring that the supreme pontiff has by divine law *(ex iure divino)* the plenitude of power, not only in spiritual affairs, but also in the temporal.[20] Here in the *De causis condempnationis* Woodford claims that the papacy was instituted by Christ when he placed Peter not only above the church militant, but above the college of the apostles. And for this Woodford believes that he has explicit scriptural support. In fact, he thinks that papal primacy can be drawn clearly *(clare)* from Holy Scripture. Christ made the apostles into bishops, and then the apostles themselves went on to institute bishops throughout the cities—a fact that Woodford insists is found openly *(palam)* in scripture. The cardinals were instituted by Peter, although not under that name, for in the primitive church those who are now called cardinals were then called presbyters of the Roman Church.[21] Yet again, therefore, we find an appeal to Holy Scripture and antiquity. The first because Woodford believes that papal primacy is clearly *(clare)* derived from scripture; and the second inasmuch as he thinks that the material element of the curia has been in place from the earliest days of the church even as the form underwent alteration. From a purely methodological standpoint, therefore, Woodford has failed to distinguish himself from Wyclif.

As mentioned at the outset, Woodford's principal concern is to secure the legitimacy of the religious orders. Now, as we have seen, Wyclif was not wholly opposed to the religious life. Rather, he voiced many of the common secular arguments against the mendicants. The nuances of Wyclif's position are ultimately beside the point for Woodford, however, inasmuch as he must continue to defend his order against a steady stream of opponents—Wycliffite and otherwise—who challenge its very foundation. In fact, Woodford devoted a fair amount of space to refuting the antimendicant writings of Richard FitzRalph.[22] At all events, Woodford is willing to concede that there is no mention of the canons regular in the apostolic age, for they began under Pope Urban I (d. 230) and were later reformed in the time of Saint Augustine. As for Cluniacs, Carthusians, Cistercians, and Praemonstratensians, they began in what Woodford calls the time of the holy fathers. This epoch also accounts for the Franciscans and Dominicans. The universal church has approved and confirmed them all as holy and especially beloved to God. This is also true, says Woodford, of the Carmelites and Augustinian friars.[23]

That Woodford traces the foundation of the different orders to post-apostolic times, however, does not mean that he thereby cedes the scriptural ground to Wyclif. In fact, Woodford will claim for the orders the unimpeachable authorization of Holy Scripture as he contends that the substantial observances of the religious orders are themselves drawn from the law of scripture. The evangelical counsels of poverty, chastity, and obedience all proceed from the law of the gospel. Having made that case, though, he promptly shifts to a defense of nonscriptural practice. For he then admits that private religion contains certain facets not found in scripture, although pointing out that the common Christian religion also contains diverse traditions that are not contained in scripture. To this end Woodford calls upon Basil of Caesarea's classic list of liturgical and devotional practices (cf. *Ecclesiasticarum*, D. 11, c. 5). He notes that all sorts of holy customs—from genuflexion to the Lenten fast—are not recorded in scripture but have instead been handed down by apostolic tradition.[24] Here he will also appeal to the same text that Henry Totting had made so much of in his defense of extra-scriptural material: Pope Innocent III's 1202 decretal, *Cum Marthae*. And like Totting he thoroughly misunderstands this text when he claims that Innocent had looked outside of scripture for the formula of consecration.[25] Woodford's abrupt change from a scriptural to an extra-scriptural argument for the mendicant orders may not only highlight his own ambivalence with regard to authority. It may also signal his awareness that because arguments from scripture carry the most weight with his fellow theologians he must press that line as often, and as far, as he can. Only then can he appeal to extra-scriptural sources as almost a last resort.

Article 18 brings us most directly to the question of scripture and authority. This condemned article states: "Whatever the pope or his cardinals know how to deduce clearly *(clare)* from Holy Scripture must be believed precisely or must be done according to their admonitions. Yet whatever they might presume to define that goes beyond this must be condemned as heretical."²⁶ Woodford plans to offer a sixfold response to this article. First, he contends that this proposition is contrary to scripture itself and thus must be rejected on that count alone. For there are many things in scripture that are true and must be believed, yet are not contained there literally *(literaliter)*; nor can they be deduced from the literal sense of scripture. Woodford has recourse to the Gospel of John, where the Evangelist notes that Jesus did many more things than could ever be written down (Jn 21:25). Indeed, Christ performed many deeds that are not found in Holy Scripture; consequently there are many truths about Christ that cannot be deduced from scripture. Woodford turns next to the apostle Paul (2 Thes 2:15) who expressly *(expresse)* distinguishes between traditions that are handed down by way of speech *(sermone)* and those handed down in writing *(per scripturam)*, commanding that both be held. Here, then, Holy Scripture itself explains that there are many traditions that must be kept and believed that are handed down by the apostles through oral tradition alone *(solummodo sermone)* and are not contained literally *(ad literam)* in Holy Scripture. Hence Woodford will conclude that many truths are authentic and worthy of belief that the pope and cardinals cannot clearly *(clare)* deduce from scripture.²⁷ Yet Woodford is really confusing the issue. First, Wyclif's view of the literal sense is certainly not confined to "the letter" (*ad literam*) but embraces the full extension of the Divine Author's intended meaning.²⁸ And second, Wyclif does indeed allow for doctrines and laws based upon an implicit—not merely explicit—scriptural foundation. After all, "clear deduction" *(deducere clare)* means to make explicit what as yet remains implicit in the biblical text.²⁹ In fact, as part of what seems to be a deliberate strategy, Woodford never defines precisely what he means here by terms such as "literal" and "clear."

At any rate, Woodford observes that one will also find references to extra-scriptural material as cited within the canonical scriptures themselves. For instance, in Colossians 4:16 the apostle Paul instructs his audience to read the letter written to the Laodiceans. Yet the Epistle to the Laodiceans is not contained in the biblical canon. Woodford lists a series of other examples to the same effect. In 2 Maccabees there is mention of the five books of Jason (2 Mc 2:23), which do not belong to the canon, and offers material on the prophets Jeremiah and Nehemiah, which also lack canonical corroboration (2 Mc 2:1, 2:13). Again, the point of these and other examples is to prove that there are truths worthy of belief that are neither literally contained in scripture nor deduced clearly from scripture. Thus it seems that article 18 actually dogmatizes against scripture itself and must therefore be heretical.[30]

Not only is Wyclif's stance heretical, says Woodford, but it is itself the foundation of many other heresies—notably, Arianism. The Arians had attacked the Catholics for using the word *consubstantial*, which is not expressly stated in scripture. Of course, the Catholic doctors admitted that such words as *homoousios* are not found in scripture but still insisted that this is the faith that has been received from the ancient tradition from the beginning of the church. Article 18 thereby proves to be the foundation of the Arian heresy, precisely because the Arians could not avoid lapsing into heresy when they insisted on this rigid scriptural criterion.[31] Yet, as we have seen, Wyclif specifically allowed for the use of nonscriptural terminology in the creeds.[32] Once again, therefore, Woodford is not doing battle against the real Wyclif but instead the radical *sola scriptura* figure he has invented.

As Woodford continues he finds that Wyclif's article runs contrary to what the holy doctors have to say about ambiguous propositions in scripture. Augustine had responded to the Manichee Faustus, who insisted on reading the words of scripture just as they sound on first hearing *(sicut sonabant prima facie)* and according to the grammatical sense rather than in keeping with the interpretation of apostolic men. Hence the Manichees took literally Christ's command not to swear oaths and thus considered them illicit. Yet Christ himself shows that precepts may be interpreted in many ways and need not be accepted prima facie. Christ excused the disciples for plucking grain on the Sabbath, citing the story of David and the bread of Presence (Lk 6:1–5). Here, then, he did not interpret the divine precept according to its strict grammatical sense.[33] All this is true, of course, but again it amounts to the creation of a straw man since Wyclif never confined the literal sense to the bare grammatical meaning. Indeed, his entire fight with the sophists was over the fact that the *virtus sermonis* transcended the strictures of proper supposition.[34]

Woodford's final point is broken down into a series of smaller arguments all of which are designed to prove the many heresies that follow from article 18. Some of these points had been made at greater length above when tackling the other articles specifically. It is an extensive list that covers everything that Woodford can think of—from central doctrines to mutable laws and liturgical rites. In fact, it is so broad as to be ultimately unhelpful, since Woodford makes no distinction between what is necessary for salvation and what is merely sound custom. At all events, the first point would deny that Peter was bishop of Rome, taught there, and was martyred there since scripture makes no mention of such things. Instead, says Woodford, the church holds them on the strength of the faith of the fathers and apostolic men and through the successors of the fathers down to our own day—not on the basis of the biblical canon. Second, one would have to reject the Apostles' Creed because there is no mention in scripture of the apostles having created it. And yet this doctrine has descended through the succession of the fathers from the time of the apostles themselves. Third, there is nothing in the Gospels of Matthew and John that proves these are in fact their Gospels; we only glean that from the rubrics and prologues that are not actually part of scripture. We do not know these facts from the Evangelists themselves, therefore, but from their successors. Fourth, that God is Three Persons is a doctrine that cannot be deduced clearly *(clare)* from scripture. Woodford turns to Augustine's comment (*De trinitate* 7.4.8) that the term "person" is employed when speaking of the Trinity not because scripture uses it but because scripture does not contradict it. This makes it clear to Woodford that neither Augustine nor the pope could deduce the Three Persons clearly *(clare)* from scripture. Fifth, the Son's divine consubstantiality with the Father cannot be clearly deduced from scripture. Sixth, the apostles were sacramentally baptized, which we ought to believe. Seventh, making the sign of the cross. Eighth, Christ was conceived on 25 March and born on 25 December. Ninth, solemnizing the Lord's Day, since by the grammatical sense of scripture it ought to be Saturday. And so it is with other feast days that come down to us by apostolic tradition and not as scriptural precepts. Tenth, fasting at four times throughout the year. Eleventh, that healthy adult Christians are to abstain from meat during Lent, although Christ did not fast prior to Easter. Twelfth, the form of the consecration of the chalice as found in *Cum Marthae*. Thirteenth, laws regulating marriage under which separation is permitted on the basis of grades of consanguinity and the like. For the various causes for separation cannot be found in scripture or clearly *(clare)* deduced from it. Fourteenth, solemn vows in the reception of holy orders and profession to the religious life. Fifteenth, coronation vows, episcopal vows, and vows upon the reception of university degrees. None of these human laws and customs are contained in scripture; hence they would all be laws of Antichrist. Sixteenth, there should be no archbishops in the church any more than the now-defunct chorebishops. Seventeenth, no Easter, because Christians do not observe the feast of the Pasch at the time prescribed by the Old Testament, nor do they observe it as determined in the New Testament. Indeed, there was great controversy over the observance of Easter until the matter was settled by a miracle. Eighteenth, the church at the time of Gregory was heretical for confirming the veneration of images against Emperor Leo since the images are not in scripture, which even speaks against them. Rather, says Woodford, the church has received this *ex traditione Christi*, when Christ impressed an image of himself in sweat (the legend of Saint Veronica). This comes down to us by a tradition of the primitive church not written in the biblical canon.[35] It must noted here that Woodford has drawn up a list that is purely hypothetical in nature: these are all things that Wyclif would have to reject were he to hold the *sola scriptura* position that he did not in fact maintain.

Woodford's last two points are longer and deserve more attention. In his nineteenth point, he notes that in the time of the first popes—Peter, Linus, and Clement—Christians were not obligated to believe only those things that John the Evangelist had recorded in his gospel. For, according to Jerome and the chronicles, John had written the last of the Four Gospels after completing his Apocalypse, and thus sometime after A.D. 100. In fact, says Woodford, John's Gospel was not placed in the biblical canon during the lifetimes of these popes. Hence what John wrote in his Gospel would not have formed part of Holy Scripture as these men knew it. Following Wyclif's standard, therefore, this would mean that Christians were not bound to believe this material. Woodford anticipates Wyclif's possible response here, namely, that Christians were bound to believe many things not found in scripture at that time simply because the biblical canon was not yet closed. But now that the scriptures are complete there is no obligation to believe what is not contained therein. Woodford is not swayed by this argument, however, for he believes that the principal criterion here is not whether this material ever made its way into the canon but whether it belonged to the apostolic faith. Christians must believe all that the apostles said about Christ, and much of that is still not found in the biblical canon. If evangelical truths existed before such time as they were placed in scripture, then it must be the content, not the form, that determines their value. And if content is the determining factor, then Catholic truths may still exist today even if not located in the biblical canon. For, although all the books of the New Testament might be burned by the enemies of the faith—just as when they burned those of the Old Testament—the faithful would still be obligated to believe them as Catholic truths necessary for salvation *(de necessitate salutis)* that have been evangelized by Christ and his apostles. For these same doctrines have since been dogmatized by the Catholic Church through the succession of the fathers down from the time of the apostles.[36] If Woodford were simply claiming that the full content of the scriptures is also preserved outside of the scriptures and thus will never perish, then he would get no argument from anyone—certainly not Wyclif. Bear in mind that for Wyclif Holy Scripture is the eternal *Liber Vitae,* which transcends its merely material manifestations.[37] Yet Woodford wants to go even further here so as to maintain that are still more Catholic truths—apparently even some that there are necessary for salvation—that are not found in the scriptures. Once again, though, Woodford offers no specific list of extra-scriptural truths that are necessary for salvation. Perhaps this is because he knew there could never be any agreement on such a list even among the few people who might accept the principle.

In his twentieth point, Woodford contends that the church would also lose all the knowledge gleaned from experience regarding the preeminence of the pope and the ordination of the apostles which is not contained in scripture. The Christian laity, therefore, would not be obligated to believe that any given man was truly the pope or genuinely elected since such rules cannot be found in scripture. All authority would collapse if the laity could reject as heretical the notion that Thomas Arundel is archbishop of Canterbury, or Robert Baybroke bishop of London, or Richard II king of England. Indeed, says Woodford, this article would mean the destruction of both spiritual and temporal polity.[38]

Woodford finds that Wyclif's theory actually destroys itself, for it will lead one to conclude that Wyclif's own teachings must not be believed unless they too could be clearly deduced from scripture. The final irony, therefore, is that article 18 cannot itself be deduced from scripture, since it is repugnant to scripture on many counts. Hence the authority of scripture itself proves this article to be heretical on its own merits. Actually, says Woodford, this article is the chief cause of the Lollard heresy; and if the Lollards could be cured of this they would be all the more easily led back into the Catholic truth. It is a marvel that they believe this article, seeing as they themselves teach many things that are neither contained in nor can be deduced from Holy Scripture.[39]

In the conclusion of this treatise Woodford reiterates that we should believe a great many truths received by the universal church whether in written or unwritten form. In fact we ought to believe in truths that follow neither from the contents of Holy Scripture nor even from the apostolic traditions. These would include the fact that the Athanasian and Nicene Creeds are themselves Catholic truth. We should also believe the interpretations given by the approved holy doctors about ambiguous passages of scripture. And we can accept the decisions of general councils that have been legitimately and universally gathered, providing that the church abides by those decisions for a suitably long time. There are also truths demonstrated by the certitude of miracles and those recounted by trustworthy men that are not found in scripture. Although much of this reads like the work of his Franciscan predecessor William of Ockham, what Woodford treats as a generally accepted position Ockham had merely proposed as a possibility.[40]

Woodford actually stands closer to the secular theologian Henry Totting de Oyta who had made of Ockham's hypothesis a fixed system. For the theory that there is some separate deposit of Catholic truth that cannot be found in Holy Scripture remained just that—a theory that no theologian was bound to accept. Most medieval theologians, including Wyclif, would have agreed that some truths that have come down in Holy Scripture have also come down in unwritten forms through the teaching, preaching, and liturgy of the church. Nevertheless, Woodford treated the whole matter of a separate extra-scriptural deposit of Catholic truth as though it were a clearly defined orthodox position held throughout the church, with the result that its rejection amounts to heresy. Yet there was no such agreement on this point; in fact, it is Woodford himself who would be numbered among the minority in this case, not Wyclif.

As Woodford winds up this work, he attacks Wyclif for appealing to Augustine's famous affirmation that all truth is contained in scripture (*De doc. chr.* 2.42.63). Woodford does not believe that Augustine intended this to be taken as a sweeping statement to be applied across the board *(universaliter)*, since the saint would otherwise have contradicted himself on many occasions. Hence Augustine meant that for the most part *(pro maiori parte)* every truth that a Catholic is bound to believe as necessary for salvation is contained in Holy Scripture either explicitly or implicitly. Nevertheless, says Woodford, there are still many truths that must be believed as *necessary for salvation* that cannot be deduced from scripture. And he claims that Augustine himself conceded this point.[41] Actually, it seems to be Woodford who is glossing Augustine in the extreme—and, one might ask, on what authority? For while it is certainly true that Augustine and the rest of the fathers believed that the Creed expresses truths necessary for salvation that are not explicitly stated in scripture, they still maintained that these were ultimately scriptural truths.[42] Certainly, the Augustine transmitted through Gratian's *Decretum* would not support Woodford's reading.[43] The only way that Woodford's argument could work is to so expand the list of truths necessary for salvation—beyond anything the church had actually established to this point—that virtually every aspect of ecclesiastical order and Christian piety becomes a dogma.

Quattuor Determinaciones

Woodford's goal in his *Quattuor Determinaciones*, written in 1389–90, is specifically to defend the legitimacy of the religious orders against Wyclif's attacks in the *De religione*, some of which was examined in the previous chapter.[44] It is the second determination that is of special interest here, for this is where Woodford takes up the question of extra-scriptural tradition. His discussion turns on a single remark made by Wyclif: "Now by faith we grasp that every truth is derived from scripture; and the more necessary some truth is, the more clearly it is described."[45] Woodford considers this sentiment to be at the very root of Wyclif's erroneous program, since it would mean that the faithful need not believe any truth as necessary for salvation unless it were contained in Holy Scripture.[46] At this point Woodford lays down a few ground rules. He supposes that both he and Wyclif are thinking of what is contained in scripture—whether explicitly or implicitly—in the historical, or literal, sense as opposed to the three spiritual senses. This distinction is based on the generally accepted principle that matters of Catholic truth cannot be based upon the spiritual senses but only upon the literal.[47] Woodford will then proceed to offer no less than twenty-eight truths disproving the thesis that the more necessary a truth is to salvation, the more expressly it is posited in Holy Scripture. We need not cover all twenty-eight, a fair number of which appear in Woodford's *De causis condempnationis* treated above.

Wyclif's principle seems to founder at the outset, according to Woodford, for surely the truthful proposition that "God is Three Persons" is more necessary for salvation than the fact that Barabbas was a thief (Jn 18:40) or that Tobias had a dog (Tb 11:9). And yet the triune nature of God is not expressly *(expresse)* stated in scripture, whereas these rather minor facts are therein contained *explicite et expresse*. Needless to say, one can be saved without knowing the minute details of Tobias's life, but one cannot be ignorant of the Trinity.[48] The second truth proceeds along these same lines, namely, that "the Father is consubstantial with the Son." This article of faith is stated explicitly in the Creed but not in scripture. As he did in *De causis condempnationis*, Woodford will note that the Arians had specifically objected to this statement because it was not clearly stated in scripture. The Catholics had conceded that such words as *homoousios* were not to be found in the Holy Scriptures, but they contended that it still belonged to the faith handed down by the ancient tradition from the beginning of the church.[49] Woodford basically has it right, but again it must be remembered that the pro-Nicene party believed that even if the terminology was not precisely scriptural, it certainly conveyed the very same truth that is revealed in Holy Scripture, although more fully manifested (cf. Athanasius, *De decretis* 5.21). Woodford's third truth continues this Trinitarian theme with an appeal to the double procession of the Holy Spirit. Again, this is an article of faith posited in the Creed that it is necessary for every priest to believe in explicitly *(explicite)*, even though it is found only implicitly *(implicite)* in scripture. Indeed, were this truth plainly spelled out in scripture it would not be the source of division with the Greek Christians.[50]

Now, Wyclif dealt specifically with the *filioque* clause as an instance of a doctrine that follows from the implicit meaning of scripture rather than the explicit words.[51] And this single quote that Woodford seizes upon here was concerned solely with the rules of life adopted by mendicant orders. Perhaps Wyclif could have expressed himself more felicitously, but the fact remains that he was merely arguing that God would not have failed to make clearly known to all Christians the ways of holiness needed to attain final salvation. The truths "necessary for salvation" that Wyclif was referring to in this case are concerned solely with the directives of Christian piety: the means to live out the Christian life that are patently and sufficiently expressed in sacred scripture without need of supplementary mendicant rules. Woodford — and the modern scholars who followed him — have decontextualized Wyclif's remarks to the point of distorting them beyond recognition.

At all events, as Woodford continues, he makes the classic point that many heresies arise from an overly literal reading of the scriptures *(sicut sonant prima facie)*. And here Woodford once more seeks counsel from the most ancient sources. One must trust, he says, in the interpretation of apostolic men *(virorum apostolicorum)* who can press through to the orthodox sense of the text.[52] There are also ambiguous propositions in scripture in need of authoritative interpretation. Hence, clearly following his confrère Ockham, he will argue that Christ's words to Peter in Matthew 16:18 were in need of Anacletus's interpretation (recorded in *Sacrosancta*, D. 22, c. 2). Anacletus was himself a disciple of the apostles and therefore would have learned from them the full implications of these words, namely, that Christ bestowed primacy upon the Roman Church. On the other hand, though, having made the case for recourse to the apostolic men, Woodford also holds open the possibility of a new revelation *(nova revelacione)* that will explicate the latent meaning of the biblical text.[53]

In his effort to shore up extra-scriptural authorities Woodford offers an interesting discussion of general councils. Here he establishes the basic criteria by which a general council can be considered authoritative. It must be gathered in the name of Christ; Christ had to have been in its midst; and its decision must proceed from the inspiration of the Holy Spirit. Having said that, however, Woodford does not reckon general councils infallible (as Gerson would later claim). Like Ockham, he admits that a general council can err in its determinations. As a matter of order, though, he cautions that Catholics should not impugn the council's decision if they do not know for a fact that the council has erred and if they have not listened to the opinions of theological experts. He likens the situation to a judge who ought to trust in the testimony of witnesses whom he has no reason to doubt and no means to refute, even though they may in fact be lying. The point is that a general council must be given the benefit of the doubt, although error remains a possibility.[54] This is certainly a reasonable position, and doubtless Wyclif would agree with this in principle. Although Wyclif, as a theological expert himself, would also claim the right to dissent if he located an error—which, after all, Woodford admits is a possibility. When can one trust that the council has spoken the truth? Woodford adopts the traditional answer: it will depend upon its reception. After the council has defined some matter of faith and the definition has been spread abroad by the Church, and after it has been received by the universal church without objection, then it may considered sufficiently authentic *(satis authentica)*, despite the fact—here is

Woodford's larger point—that it does not appear in Holy Scripture. Woodford takes all this to be in line with Christ's promise that the universal church will not err in matters of faith.[55]

Woodford fails to provide an example of a general council defining as a matter of Catholic orthodoxy any doctrine that is not itself found—even if implicitly—in Holy Scripture, although he holds open this possibility. Clearly, though, the council cannot serve as a final authority in itself, since its decisions will attain fully authentic status only after the entire church has received them. Until that happens the possibility of error remains, and who is in a better position to test the validity of its decrees than the *magister sacrae paginae?* Hence if Wyclif rejects the findings of the Blackfriars Synod—which was surely not a general council—he would seem to be exercising his rights during the period of consideration and reception.

If Woodford was not a conciliarist, neither was he a papalist. Hence he seems hard pressed to locate any sort of binding final authority. Following close to Ockham, he makes the point that although the pope along with a general council can make an article of faith *(articulum fidei)* in the strict sense of the term, they cannot make this thing a Catholic truth. Woodford notes that such a truth was Catholic from the beginning of Christ's preaching up until the judgment day. Only Christ can make something a Catholic truth; no mortal pope can do this.[56] What the pope can do, however, is make this an article of faith when he and his council insert this truth under its proper formulation into an authentic creed. Hence a Catholic truth, made so by Christ himself, can then be made an article of faith at some later date by a mortal pope. Again, though, Woodford insists that the term "article of faith" is taken in its strict sense. He does not want to leave the impression that a pope can actually create the truth itself.[57] Woodford's immediate goal here is again to prove that there are Catholic truths formalized in creeds that the faithful are expected to believe even if not found in scripture. But it also reveals more about his basic views of ecclesiastical authority. Not only is there no talk of papal infallibility, but there is the sort of constraint placed upon the papacy relative to the formation of doctrine that one would expect from a theologian responding to the canonists. As the discussion in the previous chapter has shown, his fellow theologian John Wyclif would not have offered a substantially different view of papal authority.

One of Woodford's final arguments turns on the reliability of the biblical text. He makes his point quite plainly: the text of the Bible that we possess suffers from many defects. Hence there are various items contained therein that do not require our firm assent.⁵⁸ This is a curious line of attack, given the fact that Wyclif was no slavish adherent to the biblical codices.⁵⁹ At all events, Woodford runs through a list of textual corruptions and inconsistencies that Jerome has dealt with, as well as the comments of FitzRalph, Lyra, and Peter Brutus, all of whom claim that the Jews tampered with key Christological texts in the Old Testament. Indeed, it was commonly believed that Jews had set about to alter passages that testified to Jesus Christ's messianic status, thereby corrupting the genuine text *(vera littera)*.⁶⁰ For all that, however, Woodford knows that he must meet the objection drawn from Augustine's remarks enshrined in the *Decretum* (*Si ad sacras scripturas*, D. 9, c. 7), that were any lies found in scripture it would lose all its authority. Woodford responds that the saint never meant that the physical codex itself was free from corruptions, since he himself admits such defects (*De doc. chr.* 2.15.22). Rather, Augustine is referring to Holy Scripture in its pristine state when first handed down to its writers under the inspiration of the Holy Spirit. The problems set in with the later texts that suffered the fate of poor translation and willful corruption of the original content.⁶¹

Woodford was quite content to admit the many corruptions that have crept into the biblical codices that the church of his day possessed. That helped make his point that one will have to go outside the text and look to the greater tradition for any reliable communication of the truth. Here Woodford begins with the observation that although the biblical text that we have is corrupted in many ways, Holy Scripture itself remains free from corruption and falsehood in the form that it came down to its first authors. Wyclif would clearly agree with that, as he would with the following statement: "Where the text which we have is generally corrupt and falsified, it is not, as such, part of Holy Scripture."⁶² Wyclif precisely sought to defend the fundamental veracity of scripture—understood as the eternal *Liber Vitae*—from the charges of falsehood stemming from textual corruption. Yet Woodford wants to make an even bolder point. He is not simply saying that any given codex may contain mistakes; he will contend that the whole Bible as we have it is corrupt. Thus he notes that it is easy enough to admit that the humanly constructed book, this tangible volume *(liber artificiatus et codex biblie)*, has suffered corruptions at the hands of false scribes. Yet the truth is, says Woodford, that the biblical text that the universal church possesses is itself defective and corrupt. Here he cites the charge recounted in

Peter Brutus's *De victoria contra Iudaeos* (1.15) that Saint Jerome had translated a corrupted text. And this means, in turn, that the modern scribes following Jerome's version are likewise publishing false texts. Hence it is not simply a matter of the texts deteriorating over time; the very text that the church ought to have received from Jerome is corrupt because Jerome translated a false and corrupt text.[63] Woodford is making the very sort of argument that not only Wyclif but (as we have seen) also Richard FitzRalph and Henry Totting had attempted to defeat. Yet what makes this argument especially curious is that Woodford had himself been compiling a series of arguments against Wyclif that were based on Holy Scripture. Clearly, his own scriptural arguments could only be as reliable as the text they are based upon. Thus in his attempt to undercut the force of Wyclif's appeals to scripture he has undone many of his own refutations. All of which only serves to highlight the ambivalence — if not near-incoherence — of Woodford's entire anti-Wycliffite program.

Woodford is still left to deal with the fact that the saints themselves say that all truths necessary for salvation are contained in Holy Scripture. On this point, he advises reading with discrimination. After all, he says, just as there are universal propositions in scripture to which there must be exceptions, so there are exceptions to be made in the works of the holy doctors. Although the writings of the saints may seem to mean *(videntur sonare)* that all truths useful to salvation are contained in scripture, they are not limiting this to the historical, or literal, sense but may include the mystical senses. And even when they might have the literal sense in mind, they are only referring to the greater part of such truths, since the truths to which Christian wayfarers are bound to assent are for the most part contained explicitly or implicitly in the canon of scripture according to the literal sense.[64]

In fact, Woodford contends that some of these saints are speaking in very broad terms about Holy Scripture, as when they refer to the Book of Life *(Liber Vitae)* rather than the strict confines of the biblical canon. Furthermore, they may be thinking so expansively as to include mystical similitudes that bear some relationship to what is contained in scripture even as the thing itself is not properly found therein.[65] In other words, the saints will employ the term "Holy Scripture" in ways that cover myriad sacred writings as well as those sacred truths only hinted at by the text of the canonical scriptures. In this sense virtually any expression of divine truth might be classified as Holy Scripture. Aware of the fact that he cannot get past the patristic insistence on scriptural authority, Woodford—in what amounts to special pleading—actually winds up bestowing upon scripture the kind of expansive quality found in Wyclif, who had drawn all truth under the auspices of the Eternal Scripture—the *Liber Vitae*.[66]

Woodford concludes the second of his four determinations with a list of things that must be believed beyond what is contained in Holy Scripture. There is nothing speculative about it. Woodford is quite confident in the orthodoxy of what he is proposing, although it must be remembered that this a purely private list that had received no formal approval. At all events, Woodford finds that apart from material immediately furnished by Holy Scripture there are no less than nine other sources of truth. They are as follows:

1. Unwritten traditions of the apostles coming down to us through the succession of the fathers;
2. All things that follow from the contents of Holy Scripture, or from the apostolic traditions, and from those things that consist in well-known fact, or in natural experience;
3. All things miraculously shown to the church, although not found in Holy Scripture;
4. All things determined by a general council (whose assembly meets the aforementioned three criteria);
5. All things that the universal church accepts without any objection;
6. Those things we learn through sense experience;
7. Those we learn through natural reason;
8. Those things we learn through witnesses worthy of trust;
9. Interpretations given by apostolic men regarding ambiguous passages of scripture.

Woodford believes that these nine categories should prove sufficient to eradicate the root of Wyclif's erroneous assertion that it is not necessary to believe anything unless it is contained in Holy Scripture.[67]

Throughout his attempted refutation of Wyclif one finds that Woodford swings between extremes: from scripture and antiquity on some occasions to an expansive extra-scriptural regimen on the other. He certainly adopted a more extensive position on extra-scriptural traditions than previous members of his order such as Saint Bonaventure and William of

Ockham. But there was a lot at stake for him in knocking down, not just Wyclif's basic opposition to the mendicants, but the whole superstructure that supported it. In fact, the very remarks of Wyclif to which Woodford took such offense were specifically directed at religious orders; they were not broad statements of principle intended to cover the whole process of doctrinal formation and development. Yet even as Woodford was invested in promoting the legitimacy of extra-scriptural traditions, his first instincts often took him back to the biblical text when attempting to defend the religious orders. He endeavored to demonstrate that the mendicant orders can ultimately find legitimate foundation in Holy Scripture and the apostolic era. This line of argument seems strange at first insofar as he had attacked Wyclif precisely for overestimating the authority of the primitive church. Yet Woodford was much more deeply invested in antiquity than his own rhetoric allows. What these debates reveal is Woodford's own ambivalence with regard to authoritative sources. Despite the fact that he did not want to get locked into a battle over scripture and antiquity with Wyclif, he ended up making some of his most sustained arguments on that very basis, and often accused Wyclif of heresy precisely for having misread Holy Scripture. The appeal to extra-scriptural tradition, therefore, was always tempered by a recognition of the formidable authority of ancient sources. Woodford may also have realized that some of the more expansive arguments he made for extra-scriptural authority would not necessarily be received by all—or even most—of his fellow theologians.

Chapter 4

Ad Fontes (?)

Thomas Netter

The Carmelite theologian Thomas Netter earned his doctorate at Oxford in 1411 and just a few years later, in 1414, was elected prior provincial of the Carmelites in England. His connection to William Woodford was more tangible than merely a common interest in defeating Wycliffism. Netter had very likely studied with the Franciscan, who resided in London from 1390 to 1396 when the young Netter was living in the Carmelite house. Netter began work on his massive anti-Wycliffite *Doctrinale Antiquitatum Fidei Catholicae Ecclesiae* by 1421 and appears still to have been working on it at the time of his death in 1430.[1] It is by all accounts a very impressive work, notable not merely for its sheer length, but for its combination of formidable erudition and earnest expressions of piety. Anne Hudson regards it as an attempt to "re-establish the orthodox credentials of the English church after the notoriety that an English heretic had gained at the Council of Constance, both in his own right and as the alleged theological begetter of Jan Hus."[2] That is no doubt correct, although at the same time Netter's place within the continuum of medieval Carmelite theology should also be considered when assessing his work. In this vein, Andrew Jotischky writes that "Netter's *Doctrinale* summarises and honours a century of Carmelite historiography in presenting the history of the Church as an unbroken chain whereby the contemporary Church was secured to the firm moorings of the age of the apostles and early councils."³ Thomas Turley has found that Netter, like his fellow Carmelites John Baconthorpe and Guido Terreni, believed in the sufficiency of Holy Scripture. Popes and councils possess authority in their connection to the primitive church and have scripture and the fathers to lead them to the truth. In this vein, though, Turley thinks that Netter, like Terreni, "classicised the primitive church so thoroughly that there was little room for any concept of development."⁴ Ghosh also finds that for Netter the truth of scripture is wholly preserved by the church, which merely proclaims what it has received. The patristic sources form the really authoritative aspect of the interpretive tradition, while the present church simply preserves their explications. Netter is in agreement with Wyclif, therefore, that one can gain access to the true meaning of the biblical text and the most fundamental values of the primitive church.⁵

Within this modern scholarly emphasis on the value of antiquity for Netter, some have offered slightly more nuanced views. Thus Michael Hurley contends—rightly I believe—that Netter did allow for a certain degree of development amid his strict adherence to the immutable ancient faith. Still, Hurley finds that it is the temporal continuity of the church that is of central importance to Netter, as opposed to the merely geographic; the enduring tradition forms Netter's authority rather than the present magisterium.⁶ F. X. Siebel likewise locates the authority of the church for Netter principally in its historic extension, the accordance of testimony from the time of Christ up until the present. Siebel concludes that Netter never fully resolved his position regarding the authority of the present magisterium such that in the end the authority of the church militant rested in its agreement with the apostolic faith.⁷ Most recently, Santiago Madrigal has concluded along similar lines that even as Netter could argue for the authority of ecclesiastical traditions secured by the *ecclesia universalis*, "he is not prepared to grant full powers to a sort of uncontrolled magisterium."⁸

In this chapter we shall see that scripture and antiquity did indeed take center stage for Netter but by no means to the exclusion of development. Netter often manages to weave all three together in a compelling fashion. Yet no matter how impressively researched and documented Netter's many arguments were, closer analysis reveals that even he was ultimately unable to resolve the issue of authority decisively. Netter would appeal to neither papal authority nor to that of a general council when attempting to meet the Wycliffite challenge. Nor, however, was he free to retreat into antiquity alone, since the Wycliffites were able to fight very effectively on that front. And it was for that reason that Netter had to try to muster a coherent doctrine of development in order to counter Wycliffite charges that the present church had forsaken its pristine foundations through the introduction of heretical novelties. The fact is that Netter was fighting a defensive battle against the Wycliffites, who had thrown him back on his heels through their own appeals to the ancient tradition. He knew that he could not afford to get bogged down in disputes over ancient practices; there had to be room for substantial growth. Thus Netter will often invoke the testimony of the universal church, which preserves a line of consistent development. Yet such invocations can seem as vague at times as the Wycliffite Church of the Predestined—a nice idea devoid of any concrete referent. The fact that Thomas Netter—marvelous scholar and debater that he was—could not effectively resolve the matter of authority in the church gives one a sense of the magnitude of the difficulty that everyone faced.

The Apostolic Tradition

In the prologue to book 1 of his *Doctrinale* Netter set the tone for this massive undertaking with his opening words—those of Jesus Christ himself: "My teaching is not my own, but his who sent me" (Jn 7:16). Netter is a man of tradition, passing on what he has himself received. Genuine authority rests in the very roots of faith itself, that which has been believed from the beginning, coming down from Christ and his apostles and then later through the holy fathers and doctors.[9] Netter thereby seeks immediately to differentiate himself from John Wyclif who will only allow "the faith of the scriptures." Clinging to texts alone, Wyclif has pushed aside the faith of the wider church that Jesus Christ and the apostle Paul have handed down in nonwritten form *(non scriptam)*. Yet Netter describes this faith that Wyclif (supposedly) rejects as the very faith that preserves the interpretation of the scriptures from falsehood.[10] As we will see, however, Netter is not going to establish an extra-scriptural tradition that rivals the authority of Holy Scripture. Rather, he will argue for an authoritative interpretive tradition comprising the saints and doctors who can offer inspired guidance through the sacred text. Netter will constantly portray himself as the defender of ancient truth. It is Wyclif who is the innovator. Netter will not construct his edifice of orthodoxy with "newfangled ideas" after the manner of Wyclif but rather upon the "teaching of the church and the most ancient tradition of the holy fathers."[11]

Netter voices his commitment to the authority of scripture in much more explicit terms than Woodford. Indeed, he declares that he will attempt wherever possible to refute Wyclif's heresy from the faith of Holy Scripture. But in order to avoid any distortion of scripture he will turn to the holy fathers and their successors, who from the beginning (a key phrase for Netter—*ab initio*) have provided clear expositions of the text. Moreover, Netter pledges that he will not base his case upon the testimony of a single doctor but rather upon what the greater part has taught from the time of the apostles and has been handed down into the present day. So great is Netter's commitment to the universal church as the bearer of ancient tradition that he states that no one—not even the pope or general council—may turn away from it, since it is itself an article of faith as recorded in the Creed: belief in the Holy, Catholic, and Apostolic Church.[12]

For Netter, Holy Scripture must always be interpreted within the sacred tradition. Wyclif, therefore, will forever be accused of seeking refuge solely in the scriptures, interpreting them in their bare sense *(nude)*, and demanding that this be the test for all matters of doctrine and practice. After all, as Netter points out, Wyclif has often expressed his refusal to accept any papal teaching that cannot be proven from Holy Scripture, which comprises all truth.[13] All this is central to a narrative in which Wyclif takes his place in a long line of heretics, from Marcion to Pelagius, all of whom have attempted to distort scripture with their own mendacious expositions, exchanging its true meaning for their own false sense.[14] Heretics are all of a piece for Netter; they wish first of all to transform Holy Scripture to support their own detestable intentions: "to speak the same words, but to cloak them with an alien sense." Yet heretics will never possess the true words of God, will never grasp their meaning, precisely because they have no access to the secret things of God. "The spirit of the church is the spirit of truth. Every spirit that contradicts the church is the spirit of error."[15] Netter will continually portray Wyclif as the typical heretic—someone who has forsaken the authoritative tradition and thereby rendered himself incapable of grasping the true meaning of the scriptures. And like Woodford before him, Netter warns the unsuspecting reader that even though Wyclif's arguments might appear orthodox enough they are in fact laden with heretical nuances.

Netter will, in other words, construct a consistent narrative in which Wyclif is the consummate outrider. If he is going to be able to separate himself from Wyclif, so as to more effectively attack him, he will have to reinforce this line relentlessly. Hence his readers are informed that Wyclif despises the teachings *(documenta)* of the church, the holy fathers, and the approved councils, whereas Netter consistently returns to the teaching that has come down from the apostles right to our own day—*a tempore apostolorum usque in praesens*. For Netter, the consensus of the fathers is a central point in establishing the authoritative tradition. The church does not accept just any ancient council but only those that have been approved by the holy fathers. This consensus reached by the fathers is then preserved by the church through the line of succession.[16]

Scripture read apart from this great and ancient expository tradition ends up destroying the essential character of Holy Scripture itself. It renders scripture a killing letter because it is divorced from the spirit of Christ (2 Cor 3:6). Holy Scripture must be read in the spirit of the saints, from Paul to Hilary, from Augustine to Isidore; this is where the spirit of the letter is found—within the tradition.[17] Netter readily admits that the most certain way of coming to the truth is through Holy Scripture. Yet if one is to scale the ladder of scripture and reach its peak one will have to rely upon the most faithful expositions of the doctors, since they are worthy of trust in matters of faith. This is especially the case, says Netter, with those who lived closer in time to Christ and the apostles. Greater proximity to the source of divine revelation bolsters one's authority.[18] Primitive sources offer the best testimony to the truth. The rule of the fathers *(regula patrum)* will be the measure by which the Catholic faith and the words of Christ must be interpreted.[19] There can be no doubt that antiquity is for Netter—perhaps in good Carmelite fashion—an indispensable locus of authority. It is such not merely in its ancientness, but because of its inherent sanctity—its proximity to Truth and the Good.

For Netter, antiquity is not simply a reservoir of sayings, therefore, but a spiritual resource that can only be approached in humility; one must exhibit a filial trust in the fathers. And it is just this sort of humility and piety that the prideful Wyclif lacks. It seems that, for Netter, no word so befits Wyclif as pride *(superbia)*.[20] Wyclif's moral failure in this regard is proof that he has no claim to genuine teaching authority, since it has cut him off from the only true source of Catholic faith. Netter the university-trained theologian is no less insistent than Wyclif himself that a genuine calling to the magisterial chair must be answered not only in sheer erudition but also in sanctity. For Netter, a true doctor, or *magister*, is not simply a man with a university degree. Christ does not recognize the title of *magister* among the heretics. Only a faithful schoolman *(scholasticus fidelis)* may rightfully lay claim to the magisterial title. Where the true faith of Christ is lacking there is no magisterium.[21] Here again we see that all sides of the debate acknowledged the inexorable connection between the personal disposition of the exegete and his capacity to arrive at the truth. If it were merely a matter of training and professional skills, Netter would have no grounds upon which to criticize Wyclif, who was by all accounts extremely learned. In fact, Netter himself admits to having been fascinated by Wyclif's metaphysics while a young student at Oxford. No, says Netter, there is more to it all than that. Wyclif's vanity, his pride, has driven him into heresy.

The Nature of the Church

For all of Netter's talk of an ancient tradition preserved across the ages by the universal church, which alone is capable of discerning the meaning of scripture, this concept is not quite so airtight as it might first appear. After all, Wyclif is no less committed in his allegiance to the One, Holy, Catholic, and Apostolic Church confessed in the Creed. The problem rests in determining the precise means by which that church will be able to speak authoritatively. Netter demands obedience to the church, the church that preserves the apostolic tradition against all heretical corruption, but where exactly is that church manifested? In answer to such questions, the first thing Netter rules out is Wyclif's preferred definition of the church as the gathering of all the predestined. Although it should be remembered that Wyclif certainly did allow for a functioning nondonatistic church complete with a law-abiding pope.[22] At any rate, Netter prefers to speak of the church as a mixed body, gathered from both the elect and the reprobate.[23] "The church militant is the congregation of all those who are called and are joined together in Catholic fellowship." The church in this age of darkness will, therefore, contain members of the reprobate so long as they have not been expelled from this society through ecclesiastical censure. On the other hand, the elect may be outside of this community due to heresy or some other grievous crime. The point that Netter wants to make clear is that even the predestined can really, and not just pretendedly *(vere non ficte)*, be ejected from the ecclesiastical community and the body of Christ, even as they do not fall away from the gathering of the elect. The first parents were expelled from paradise by God and yet remained in the Book of Life; they were exiles bereft of blessed fellowship.[24] Catholic fellowship *(societas)* is essential for the church; without it there will be no prayers, no help from the saints, and no assistance from the sacraments. Yet within this community, this fellowship, there currently abide both the good and wicked, the wheat and the chaff.[25]

Fearing that a Wycliffite stress on the invisible hand of predestination will render all earthly authority null and void, Netter emphasizes the visible nature and structure of the church on earth. It is baptismal regeneration, not predestination, that produces the church. The centurion Cornelius (Acts 10) was not a member of the church prior to his baptism even as we assume that he must have been eternally predestined.[26] Hence Netter specifically rejects Wyclif's distinction between those who are *in ecclesia* and those who are *de ecclesia*. The reprobate, says Netter, are indeed "of," and not merely "in," the church.[27] The members are conjoined to Christ through their baptism and reception of the sacraments. They are members of the body of Christ, therefore, not merely because they are counted as such, but because they are such in reality *(non tantum reputatione sed veritate)*. "Baptism creates true members of Christ, not only by reckoning them as regenerated, but because it truly regenerates them."[28] Of course, it is not merely the reception of water that incorporates one into Christ; the three theological virtues of faith, hope, and love serve to join the members to the head.[29] Yet if all people are saved or damned by absolute necessity (which was not Wyclif's position),[30] it would seem pointless to admonish the predestined in the hope that they may remain members of the body of Christ. In point of fact, one may indeed fall away from the final good through sin, just as one may abide by grace. The member is conjoined to Christ through a faith that works through love (Gal 5:6). "Thus everyone who exists in a state of grace according to present righteousness is a true member *(verum membrum)* of the Church of Jesus Christ."[31]

Now, it should be remembered that Wyclif made it clear that no one could judge the eternal status of any prelate; it was one's present moral status that most concerned him. And even here Wyclif contended that corrupt priests continued to function as ministers of Christ's sacraments.³² Nevertheless, it is certainly true that Wyclif believed that personal sanctity—manifested most acutely in adherence to apostolic humility and poverty—was integral to any claim of ecclesiastical authority. Netter, for his part, harbored no illusions as to the sanctity of the church's hierarchy. Indeed, he wants to steer the whole conversation away from personal holiness; he will not fight on Wycliffite ground. Netter insists, therefore, that the successors to the apostles, prophets, and doctors are the leaders of the church by way of their office, not their actions *(identitate non actus sed officii)*. In other words, the successors need not do the very deeds of their predecessors in order to lay just claim to their office.³³ It is in this vein that Netter rejects Wyclif's demand that a true pope follow Peter perfectly in his way of life. In fact, Netter reckons the notion that the greatest power must coincide with the greatest virtue a pagan error. The pope certainly should strive to live a life of great virtue, but it is not necessary. The pope is identical with Peter in terms of his power and his see—*non persona sed officio*. His power is equal to that of Peter even as he might not be his equal in virtue.³⁴ This is the power that Christ personally bestowed upon Peter and his successors as he continues to speak through them.³⁵ These are especially interesting remarks for having been written just one decade after the healing of the papal schism. For (as discussed in a later chapter) the Council of Constance saw fit to depose Pope John XXIII for grave moral failings that had scandalized the church. Of course, this points to one of the larger ironies in the whole battle against the Wycliffites and Hussites: the personal sanctity of ecclesiastical officials did indeed matter to all sides. One need not be a Donatist to expect personal holiness on the part of the man who occupies the see of Saint Peter.

Given Wyclif's attacks on the papacy—nuanced as they may have been but still excoriating at times—Netter feels compelled to defend the papal office itself. To the apostle John, he notes, Christ had commended his beloved Mother (Jn 19:26–27) and to Peter the care of his church (Mt 16:18): to the first the Virgin Mother and to the second the Virgin Bride. In fact, Christ offered his very self to these two disciples when he said to his mother, Mary, "Behold your son," and to Peter, "upon this rock," even as—says Netter—the rock was Christ himself (1 Cor 10:4). Netter was certainly not an ultra-papalist. He relied upon Saint Ambrose's remark that Peter responded on behalf of the rest of the apostles and is for that reason called the foundation. The faith that the Father revealed to Peter is the foundation of the church—not a matter of Peter's flesh but Peter's faith. Thus, according to Netter, it is Peter's faith that will withstand the gates of hell and the onslaught of heretics.[36] Peter does, however, retain some measure of primacy in the church. For immediately after Christ, it is the very person of Peter who functions as the first metaphorical rock upon which the whole church was founded and built.[37] Thus even as Christ is the first rock, Peter remains the rock in a secondary sense inasmuch as he is Christ's vicar.[38] The other apostles may be called the foundation (Eph 2:20), but Peter is still the foundation of the foundations *(Petrus fundamentorum fundamentum)*.[39] Netter offers only the most common and basic line on Petrine supremacy: Peter is the prince of the apostles and the head of the church; first among the apostles by way of authority and prince of the church militant.[40] Hence while it is true that all the apostles were equal in terms of power and honor, Peter the head surpassed the rest in authority of jurisdiction.[41]

Netter will then draw upon the authority of antiquity as he contends that the church fathers long recognized that the pope's guidance and decisions were regarded as indisputable *(pro irrefragibili)*. With the pope lay the mysteries of the faith, and within his breast rests the prophetic insight by which he knows how to choose the good and reject the evil. It is for the pope, therefore, both to determine Catholic truths and destroy heretical wiles.[42] The Roman church is the place whence flows Christian wisdom. "The whole church throughout the world confesses that the Roman see remains hitherto inviolate in the faith, always determines credible truths well-nigh without fault, and mightily vanquishes heretical wickedness." If there really is to be one faith (Eph 4:5), then there surely must be one inspired teacher, a pedagogue for all the faithful. Here Netter turns to Luke 22:32, arguing that Christ's promise has protected the Roman Church from error. This promise made to Peter has ensured that the Roman church would surpass all the other churches in her defense of the faith. "The Roman church remains free from error *(impeccabilem)* in the teaching of Christ."[43] Note that there is no talk here of papal infallibility but only the traditional belief that the church herself will remain steadfast in the faith. Hence Netter does not pursue the infallibilist arguments of his fellow Carmelite Guido Terreni.

Netter has dutifully made his case for the papacy and the church of Rome, perhaps to satisfy Pope Martin V, but it is the universal and apostolic church that stands as the ultimate authority for Netter. This is where he locates the abiding presence of the sacred tradition preserved across the ages. To the universal church belongs the unique prerogative of "infallibly handing down and teaching all the articles of faith, and all else that must be believed as necessary for salvation."[44] Netter turns to the Apostles' Creed as he explores the definition of the church. Here he points out that the very word *catholic* means universal and that this universality can be taken in four ways: extension, instruction, subjection, and care. What Netter wants to make clear, though, is that universality of extension applies not only to place, but more importantly to an extension of time. The church is known to be extended throughout the world as it takes its beginning from Christ's baptism and the inception of his preaching.[45] Locating the inception of the church in Christ's earthly ministry is a key factor in Netter's ecclesiology. Here he is pointedly setting aside the Wycliffite—and ultimately Augustinian—notion of the *ecclesia ab Abel*. In that sense Netter attempts to demystify the church by giving it a datable, and thus genuine historical, point of departure. It is part of his larger effort to maintain the continuity that exists between the primitive community of believers and the present hierarchical church.

Hence certain signs make the Catholic Church recognizable. "It is the whole series of faithful people from the first gathering of Christ on the banks of the river Jordan down to the present day, and thereupon successively descending until the end of the world."[46] And it is essential that one distinguish "the true Church of Christ which possesses the true teaching of the faith" from the heretical sects who likewise claim to be the true church. Indeed, "every heresy wishes to be called the church and go under the name of our Mother." A sure sign will be whether the church in question maintains Catholic unity, which is both temporal and spatial. This is the ancient unity that has been preserved from the time of Christ's baptism—*ecclesia Christi non est nova*. "If some sect arises whose faith is new, and has not been accepted by the ancient fathers, that is not the Church of Christ. If in other parts of the world, where the name of Christ is known, it is unknown, then this not the Church of Christ but a whore and an heretical synagogue."[47]

The Catholic and apostolic nature of the church coincide, precisely because the apostles had established churches in the one faith of Christ throughout the world, teaching in like manner the substance of the faith—*sine dissonantia literae vel syllabae*. Appealing to the legend of the Septuagint translators producing identical volumes from their separate cells, Netter finds it even more miraculous that the apostles, spread abroad as they were, could deliver the faith with its many parts while retaining its integrity and identity of meaning.⁴⁸ It is in this apostolic church that the Holy Spirit is manifested, not only in the scriptures, but also in the living teachings and traditions that the apostles have handed down *(non solis scripturis sed vivis documentis et traditionibus)*.⁴⁹ The *ecclesia Christi* is called apostolic, therefore, because it is founded upon, and instructed by, the apostolic tradition.⁵⁰

To believe in the Catholic Church *(credere ecclesiam catholicam)* is to believe that she has the true faith and sacraments from God. The church is a necessary object of the Christian faith because she renders abundant testimony to Christ. From the time of the apostles into the present age the church consistently bears this true testimony no less now than among the first believers. This testimony is infallible and indestructible. In fact, it predates the scriptures themselves. Prior to the written Gospel narratives there was already that living gospel which Christ and the apostles inscribed within the hearts of men (2 Cor 3:2). This is the very testimony to which the faithful must turn when the heretics attempt to subvert the true meaning of the written text of scripture. Indeed, the *lex Christi* finds its most certain interpretation in the hearts of the faithful, succeeding from generation to generation down from the time of the apostles and continuing forever.⁵¹ Here we see that Netter, in keeping with the greater tradition—including Wyclif—looked beyond the text of scripture itself to content that substantiates and ultimately transcends it: the Gospel of Christ.

Drawing again on Luke 22:32, Netter is concerned this time to affirm the indefectibility of the universal church rather than the Roman church. Peter functions here as a figure for the whole church, says Netter, not merely a particular church, whether in Africa or Rome, but the *ecclesia universalis*. It is noteworthy that Netter specifically distances this indefectibility of the universal church from its gathering in a general council, noting that such meetings are not immune from error. Rather, what Netter has in mind is "the Catholic Church of Christ dispersed throughout the entire world, devolving from the baptism of Christ through the apostles and their successors down to the present day." It is here alone that the faithful testimony is preserved and the truth firmly rooted against all error.⁵² "To believe in the church *(credere ecclesiam)* is to believe that the church bears faithful testimony to Christ and his laws."⁵³ For Netter, the church is always pointing beyond herself to Christ. Netter speaks in stirring tones here to be sure, with an eloquence resonant of deep personal commitment to sacred truth. Yet the universal church that he describes seems to transcend all earthly manifestations. It is rather nebulous inasmuch as it cannot be located specifically in Rome, or in a general council, for it actually owes more to temporal continuity than geographic situation. Who at any given moment can be counted on to speak authoritatively on behalf of this universal church that infallibly hands down the living Gospel? As we shall see, this is a question for which Netter has no final answer.

Church and Scripture

Netter continually attacked Wyclif for spurning the church's authoritative reading of scripture — the very reading that is necessary to defeat the misinterpretations of the heretics. Classic examples are Arius, who used the very words of Christ to deny his divinity ("The Father is greater than me," Jn 14:28); and Sabellius, who rejected the Trinity of persons ("I and the Father are one," Jn 10:30). Netter is well aware that Wyclif has no truck with such heresies, of course, which is why he finds it thoroughly inconsistent of Wyclif to claim the authority of scripture for his own cause even as he rejects the Arians. Perhaps Wyclif will say this is because their readings are distortions of scripture and thus false. But, asks Netter, how will you prove this? And how will you convince the faithful to believe you rather than the heretics? The point is that Wyclif has no foundation upon which he can guarantee the authenticity of his reading of the sacred texts. He feels free to define errors even as he denies that right to the prelates.[54]

The main thrust of Netter's criticism on this front is that Wyclif is a capricious and willful exegete, unattached to an authorized interpretive community. He retreats from human fellowship and the college of ecclesiastical men, says Netter, turning instead to scripture and the private revelation of the Holy Spirit. One will never find the truth in this way. "Written authority does not certify apart from the shared understanding of the church, nor revelation apart from witness. Every other path, other than the one that moves through the apostolic successors by which all believers before us have entered, is sacrilege." It only makes good sense that one would trust in the wisdom of the many rather than one's own. One must always have recourse to the fathers when investigating the scriptures.[55] As Netter sees it, Wyclif has lapsed into the ancient deceit of the heretics, who all claim for themselves the special inspiration of the Holy Spirit. Yet the testimony of the universal church is surely more trustworthy than that of a solitary man—one who has proven himself a liar at that. Wyclif is a radical individualist who imagines that Christ abides with him alone. But true Catholics live in community; the church is a genuine society of believers. Christ said, "I will be with you always"—*vobiscum,* plural, not *tecum,* singular. Christ spoke to the whole Catholic and apostolic church, which cannot be led astray. She will always bear true witness to Christ, for she knows all the mysteries of the bridegroom. The church knows Christ and finds her truth in him. "In a matter of faith I call upon the truth, Christ and the church: Christ speaks and the church attests, for she is a participant in the truth *(participem veritatis).*" One does not turn to men alone but to men as they are inspired by the Holy Spirit, who forever dwells within the church and never leaves her in doubt as to matters of faith.[56] The connection between the bride and bridegroom, the universal church and Christ the Lamb of God, is so intimate that the bride affirms nothing that the bridegroom has not approved. Here, then, we are seeing the Christocentric nature of Netter's ecclesiology come to the fore. He writes, "The bridegroom speaks in the scriptures and the bride testifies that these things are supremely true. Whatever Christ says the church of the holy fathers commends, and then proves by all authority that it is most worthy. In no way does she ever deviate from his words."[57] Netter concedes, therefore, that greater faith should be placed in Christ, but this must never be to the total exclusion of the church, as the Creed itself attests.[58] The schismatic rends the whole church when he divides the body from the head and bride from bridegroom. Wyclif has, according to Netter, driven a wedge between Christ and the apostolic tradition.[59]

Wyclif would not have disagreed with Netter on the vital connection between church and scripture. He is, after all, equally convinced that he is speaking in line with the fathers and the sacred tradition—from Augustine to Lyra. Netter has read Wyclif's works thoroughly, so he cannot have missed the heavy reliance upon canon law and the holy doctors. Rather, he knows that getting locked into a battle with Wyclif over the application of a given chapter from the *Decretum* will go nowhere. That will just bring everything back to a classic magisterial debate between two doctors over the same authoritative sources; and one will still be left to ask where the final answer lies. Yet again, though, Netter cannot really provide any concrete final authority; his point of reference is always this, frankly vague, universal church—of which Wyclif considers himself very much a part. It is true, of course, that Netter appeals to the authority of the church as manifested in the hierarchy, but even hierarchical authority remains nebulous in the end because Netter does not see it issuing infallible judgments either through the papacy (contra Terreni) or through a general council (contra Gerson).

We ought to be clear that the problem for Netter is not that Wyclif extols the authority of Holy Scripture. It is that he (supposedly) clings to scriptural authority to the exclusion of all other forms of authority that can be brought to bear in the interpretation of the Sacred Page. Netter certainly caricatures Wyclif's exegetical methods, claiming that he hastens to the literal sense *(ad literam)* of scripture in the hope that it will protect him. Yet it is the faith of the church that best interprets the senses of scripture and declares the falsity of heretical interpretation. One is not a faithful doctor simply because one produces the faith of scripture. One must follow the faith and authority, not of one particular church, but of the universal church in which the true sense of scripture is correctly maintained. Nor is one reckoned a faithful Catholic for believing in the Trinity according to the articles of the Creed, unless one also believes the Catholic Church, since one must believe whatever she teaches about the Trinity. This is the authority that the Lord himself gave to the church. The church and her faith are inseparable. One cannot honestly confess the whole Creed if one is unwilling to accept the authority of the church, which is itself an article of the Creed.[60]

The dilemma that I have sketched with regard to final concrete authority in the church was not entirely lost on Netter. For while he maintains (as all sides would) that the church is herself perennially indefectible, he also concedes that the clergy and prelates—even when assembled in general council—can err. Where then is the inerrant church? If one says it is the universal church that has endured from the time of Christ's baptism and is diffused throughout the world, Netter admits that one is still left with the problem that such a church cannot possibly be gathered together at one place and time. He advises that we must return once more to the example left to us by the apostles at the Jerusalem council. Peter and James based their decision on the words of the prophets and the ancient histories that will resolve all doubts. In practice this means that one consults the writings of the apostles, their successors, and then the upright men and Catholic doctors even of our own day. Where they speak with one accord, there one will find the truth. There is a natural succession of truth. Just as the apostles drew upon the prophets as fathers of the church, so modern generations turn to the apostles, though not only to them but also to their heirs who have succeeded them down through the ages.[61] This is a very important point, because here we see that Netter, for all the emphasis he places on antiquity, never advises a full retreat into the ancient sources. One can trust the bishops and doctors of one's own day to interpret faithfully the very truth that Christ proclaimed to his apostles. This apostolic truth constitutes an ancient and immutable deposit, but it is not locked away in ancient documents. It continues to live in the authoritative pronouncements of the bishops and doctors in the present day. This unified and consistent testimony is authoritative: this is the voice of the universal and apostolic church. As to where *precisely* this voice can be heard at any particular moment—having just admitted that prelates can err even when gathered in general council— Netter does not say. In all fairness, though, Wyclif could not offer a better answer. Yet one is struck by this very fact: Netter's universal church seems just as elusive as Wyclif's true church. Both Netter and Wyclif accept that there can, in principle, be determinative judgments rendered in this world. But neither one entirely succeeds in locating an actual earthly authority beyond which there can be no appeal in this life.

That the church alone possesses the authoritative apostolic testimony also has clear ramifications for the biblical canon. Only she may definitively determine the books of the Divine Scriptures and certify that their authors are faithful. "Apart from the authority of the church's testimony no book can achieve canonical authority."[62] The question arises, however, as to whether the universal church could now add another book to the canon by way of the subordinate authority of a general council or through the confirmation of the Roman church. It might seem so, since the church possesses no less authority now than she did in antiquity. Wyclif claims this cannot be done. Netter, for his part, also believes that the number of books cannot be increased. Here, though, there is some difference between the two men, although perhaps more of degree than kind. For Wyclif, the New Testament church is uniquely authoritative in the sort of restrictive way that it is not for Netter. Such insistence on the unique status of the primitive church was the stick that Wyclif used to beat the present church into submission. Hence Wyclif did not feel pressed to set forth an elaborate thesis of doctrinal development even as he certainly accepted the principle itself. Yet Netter, for all that he extolled the authority of the ancient church, always found a place for development. Indeed, he had to if he was going to assert the authority of the present church. In this case, therefore, Netter does not find that the church actually lacks the authority to expand the biblical canon but instead argues that the law of Christ has already attained perfection. The church, like a man, has no less power when he reaches full stature than when he was an infant just beginning to grow. During the days of the Old Testament the law of Christ was in its infancy but then reached its fullness at the time of Christ and the apostles. The time for accumulating books, itself part of the growth process, came to a close with the end of the apostolic age. It could no longer grow once it had come to full maturity.[63] Netter is once again in a delicate situation. Wyclif's appeal to the primitive church in these matters will force Netter to articulate a coherent doctrine of development that does not undermine his own stated preference for antiquity.

Having defended the church's inherent rights with respect to the biblical canon, Netter then returns to the familiar ground of apostolic authority. There are, he notes, different grades of authority among the holy writings. Only the *Scriptura Principium*, namely, the scripture of the apostles, has full canonical authority. Books were not received into the canon unless written in apostolic times. The sayings of later saints have their own authority, as do the faithful determinations of the church, but neither of them possesses canonical authority. None of this is to deny the authority of the church with regard to her right to determine the canonical scriptures. It is the church, after all, that renders the Gospels of Thomas and Bartholomew apocryphal. It rested with the fathers who presided over the ancient churches to bring the scriptures into their complete and perfect state. Hence it would be the height of presumption for anyone to reevaluate those books that the fathers had either rejected or received. That hour has passed *(transit ergo hora)* — the canon cannot expand. When a man comes to maturity he puts away childish things (1 Cor 13:11). Netter is adamant about this. Those who believe that the canon can be augmented through the authority of the church are like the Jews still waiting for the Messiah. Thus when it comes to Gregory the Great's famous remark recorded in the *Decretum* (*Sicut sancti*, D. 15, c. 2) that appears to place the four councils on a par with scripture, Netter insists that the saint did not mean they are actually comparable. Rather, they have a certain likeness, as when Christ counseled believers to be perfect like their Father in heaven (Mt 5:48).[64]

Although the early church determined the canon, there is still no sense in which the authority of scripture is derivative. Netter makes it quite clear that the authority of the church is subject to that of scripture. In fact, he specifically rebuked those who misuse Augustine's comment that he would not have believed the gospel unless the authority of the church had moved him. Here we see Netter, the *magister sacrae paginae*, bristling at the arrogance of those who take this remark as an occasion to exalt the authority of the decrees of the fathers over that of the Holy Scriptures. Such efforts are not only inept, says Netter, but downright foolish. After all, Philip was not greater than Christ simply because he led Nathaniel to believe that Jesus of Nazareth was the one predicted in the Law and Prophets (Jn 1:45).[65] Just like Wyclif, therefore, Netter is adamant that ecclesiastical authority must always serve Christ and thus is inferior to Christ's laws and the Holy Scriptures.[66] Indeed, Netter goes so far as to say that the authority of the universal church is subject to the authority of scripture.[67] Yet, as we have seen, none of this may be taken to imply a disjunction between scripture and the church. The Catholic Church is contemporaneous with Holy Scripture, says Netter, stemming as she does from the side of Christ. They are joined as bride to groom, body to head.[68] In fact, the church still plays an indispensable role in promoting and guaranteeing the authority of scripture. Netter contends that it is on account of the church's authoritative witness to Christ that people first come to believe. Having come to belief, however, they will then subordinate the church's authority to that of scripture. It is at that point that authority of the sacred canon takes precedence over the church.[69]

Throughout all of Netter's arguments in support of ecclesiastical authority he never devalues the authority of Holy Scripture. It will always remain the principal source of doctrinal truth. It is especially important, therefore, that in his battle against the Wycliffites Netter defend the scriptural basis of the very ecclesiastical authority that he considers essential for faithful exegesis. Hence he will point out that even as the *auctoritas scripturarum* surpasses that of the church, it is also true that the scriptures in their turn attest to the authority of the Catholic Church. Netter warns, therefore, that elevation of scriptural authority must never become a license to denigrate the authority of the holy doctors. To say that Holy Scripture exceeds the bishops and councils does not mean that the latter are therefore bereft of authority.[70] Having said this, however, we also find that as Netter explores the relationship between scripture and the holy doctors, he insists that the authority of the doctors — real though it is — remains derivative. Although the truth of the scriptures may indeed be found in the books of the saints, such books will never achieve equal authority. The works of the saints serve as witnesses *(testes)* to the truth, whereas scripture offers what is superior: testimony *(testimonium)*. Netter likens the relationship of the church to scripture to that of a herald and his king: what the herald proclaims is the object of belief but only insofar as he expresses the decision of the king.[71]

As just noted above, Netter rejected the notion that the present church could add to the biblical canon. Along similar lines, he will address the question as to whether the church could now create a new article of faith. The case is made that the church could do this on the grounds that the Council of Nicea had added the article on Christ's consubstantiality with God the Father. Here Netter reiterates his position that the church, even while retaining the power she possessed in earlier ages, has nonetheless grown to perfection. Having reached her full stature, she will not grow any more. There can be no new articles of faith, therefore, because with the passage of these fourteen hundred years such an article could not be Catholic, that is, universal. This is linked to Netter's concept of the church's catholicity as being above all something temporal — extending back to the most primitive apostolic beginnings. By that standard, in order for a doctrine to be truly Catholic it would have to have been known by the fathers. But a new article of faith could not have been known, and thus believed, in the patristic era. Thus while such an article could indeed be faithful, says Netter, it could never be Catholic.[72]

When, therefore, the Council of Nicea declared the Son consubstantial with the Father it did not create a new article of faith. It was merely defending the ancient faith against the rise of heresy. This is the very faith that had been received from the apostles and handed down through the succession of fathers.[73] Similarly, at the Council of Ephesus, Saint Cyril invoked the true faith of the apostles against the heresy of Nestorius. The apostles had been ministers of the Word and eyewitnesses to Christ; it was to their faith that Nestorius was being recalled. To paraphrase Netter: *Percepimus fidem antiquam a primis apostolorum temporibus.*[74] Articles of faith have never been added over the history of the church; they have merely been more fully explicated as the times required.

General Councils

While never expressing himself explicitly on the matter of conciliarism, Netter makes it quite clear that general councils are not repositories of infallible teaching. Netter did attend the council of Pisa and actually proved to be a supporter of the *via concilii*, which would have meant deposing the two rival popes and electing one in their place. He was invited to attend Constance, and, though his attendance is not altogether settled, he may have been present as an observer. Kirk Smith, having examined Netter's conciliar theory, concludes that Netter was never really so concerned with the precise parameters of conciliar versus papal power as he was with the council's ability to defeat heresy. He needed to uphold the legitimacy of modern councils in order to secure the legitimacy of their judgments against the Wycliffites and Hussites. In the end, though, Smith finds that Netter's views on conciliar theory were not very consistent. He was never invested in the councils in the same way as many conciliarists; his goal was first and foremost the battle against heresy.[75] Had Netter followed Gerson in asserting the infallibility of a general council as representative of the universal church, he might have found a way through this impasse. As it was, though, Netter proved to be neither a papalist nor a conciliarist. In the end he always fell back on a vaguer notion of the universal church — one that does not possess an infallible voice when gathered in a council.

So it is that even as Netter may have maintained the legitimacy of a given council such as Constance, he distances himself from conciliarism as a principle. For when he treats the matter of councils specifically he will reiterate his belief that the unbroken testimony that comes down from apostolic times renders a more certain judgment in matters of faith than even that of a general synod of bishops. This is based upon the fact that such wisdom cannot be brought together in one place. Netter sees no problem, therefore, in valuing the harmonious possession of the fathers *(concordem possessionem patrum)* over the decree of a general council. In fact, he believes that the great ecumenical councils of the early church always looked beyond themselves to the ancient teachings. They turned to this sacred tradition, as well as to Holy Scripture, when determining matters of faith. It was in this way, says Netter, that the fathers at the first four ecumenical councils were able to defeat the heretics when scripture was set against scripture and reason against reason. They looked to the "ancient faith of the fathers" in order to arrive at the true interpretation of scripture. Hence the council does not determine matters based upon its own authority but rather by the authority of the holy fathers *(auctoritate sanctorum patrum)*.[76]

Netter has consistently stressed the unity of the tradition, the harmonious consent of the fathers passed down through the ages, as the touchstone of orthodoxy. And while he grants that general councils convened together with the papacy do bear a special authority, his qualifications of that authority are often quite debilitating. First of all, these councils are authoritative, says Netter, only to the extent that they are in conformity with the universal church. And Netter is quite clear that the council is not the universal church, nor are its decrees to be equated with the creedal faith. Rather, it is an image of the Catholic Church inasmuch as it comprises participants from all the churches gathered in one place. For Netter, the council functions as sign to truth—*signum* to *res*. In terms of the authority of the council, he concedes that it is similar to the universal church, but it never bears the full weight of the truth itself.[77] The council can achieve the full authority of the sacred tradition only to the extent that it functions as an appointed sign of the truth. With that conception in mind, Netter attacks Wyclif for saying that he would accept no council unless its decisions seem to have received the confirmation of the Holy Spirit. As Netter sees it, Wyclif's stipulation is another example of his "heretical temerity." For Christ had promised to be present among the gathering of believers (Mt 18:20) and to assure them of the assistance of the Holy Spirit in the midst of the sacred council (Jn 15:26). Wyclif has set himself up as the sole arbiter of truth: one man against the whole council, as if he alone possessed the Spirit.[78]

Netter's attack on Wyclif is not very convincing, however, given the fact that he himself has admitted that—despite the assistance of the Holy Spirit—the council can err, and that its decisions are valid only to the extent that they represent the mind of the universal church. Wyclif had made this very point with reference to the classic instances of Rimini (359) and the "Robber Council" of Ephesus (449), which, although convened by emperors, were later repudiated by the wider church. Actually, Netter is aware of the fact that he and Wyclif really are in agreement as to the possibility of conciliar error. Yet if it is always a possibility in principle, how will he contest Wyclif's right to reject the findings of a given council? This is no mere academic question given the Hussite reaction to Constance. The problem with Wyclif's position, according to Netter, is that he impugns the very principle of conciliar authority on the basis of particular failures rather than trust that the assembly should—not must—get it right.[79] Here again Netter will stress the concept of the church as a community. The very fact that councils are large gatherings representing the Catholic multitude imbues them with a genuine—although admittedly not infallible—authority. Against Wyclif's private spirit, therefore, the council is an example of the Holy Spirit active in the community as a whole. The *consensus multorum* brings with it a moral weight that cannot be gainsaid.[80]

Netter places his confidence in the numbers; he is being practical. There is good reason to conclude that a statement is Catholic and orthodox if the unanimous multitude so declares it, even if there are some at the council who are not guided by the Spirit. There may be dissent, but Christ will never desert the whole. Netter drives this point home repeatedly: it is always better to trust in the multitude who are gathered together in Christ's name. Heretics, whether Arius or Wyclif, always stand alone against the assembled faithful, against the whole church.[81] Because Netter will not defend conciliarism as an overarching ecclesiological principle, the best he can do is promote the council as a practical manifestation of the authority possessed by the present church. The authority of the general council is such that all the writings of pontiffs and doctors must yield to it. So great is the authority of the present church, says Netter, that her decisions ought to be obeyed under pain of the charge of obstinacy. Yet when Netter presents the full order of authority he places scripture above all the rest, followed by the authority of the Catholic Church, after which are the definitions of the holy fathers coming down from apostolic times. Netter does not intend by this ranking to sow division between the different levels of authority, since scripture and the church speak with one voice, and the fathers testify to the truth of the gospel writers and apostles.[82]

Although Netter tirelessly insists that the authority of scripture and the Creed surpass a general council, therefore, he does believe that the council is worthy of obedience and reverence as befitting paternal admonition. Indeed, he must say this lest the Wycliffites are permitted to make the whole debate about scripture and the Creed, to the exclusion of later authoritative determinations. The council's teachings should be received with trust, unless—and this is a significant proviso—someone can prove that a superior authority had rightly proscribed what the council now declares. But even so, Netter cautions that a pious son of the church does not insolently revolt against such a decision. He must receive even this teaching with proper modesty and in all deference to its great authority.[83]

Netter does believe that the church has received the assistance of the Holy Spirit whenever she has gathered with full authority in the name of Christ for the purpose of resolving matters of doubt. For, as Ambrose affirmed of the Nicene Council, its definition was no mere human invention but a statement of divine truth *(non humana sententia sed divina)*. The agreement reached by the multitude of the holy fathers at the councils bestowed upon their decisions a fullness of authority.[84] And with respect to the precise relationship of pope and council, Netter contends that papal authority does increase in the context of the council but only in the sense that what he proclaims is accepted by the assembled believers *(in acceptatione credentium auditorum)*. Netter likens the situation to Saint Peter first proclaiming the faith of Christ in Rome and then having his authority increased by Saint Paul's confirmation of that same faith in his Epistle to the Romans. The authority of the pope is enhanced, therefore, when those of lesser authority confirm his teaching.[85]

In very traditional fashion, therefore, Netter makes reception by the church a central principle for evaluating the validity of papal decisions. Needless to say, it is the question of what constitutes true reception that drives the debate. In this instance, though, Netter adopts a commonsensical approach: sheer numbers should be enough to satisfy Wyclif that the truth has been reached. Trusting that in most cases a gathering of bishops will exceed the wisdom of a lone theologian, however, does not make for an ironclad principle of authority. What is more, though, the fact that Netter veers close to full-fledged conciliarism only to pull back at the precipice reveals his underlying ambivalence in questions of authority. He desperately wants to close the door on Wyclif for good but cannot quite bring himself to settle on a single principle that will facilitate this.

Ecclesiastical Offices and Religious Orders

When Netter addressed questions such as the growth of religious orders he needed more than ever to affirm both the legitimacy of development as a concept and the present church's power to authorize the various changes that have occurred during her life. He must do all this, of course, without sacrificing his commitment to antiquity as a standard of orthodoxy. He will offer a sober assessment of development that never, however, goes nearly so far as Woodford on the matter of extra-scriptural traditions. As noted in the preceding chapter, Wyclif had pointed to the fact that in the primitive church there were only two orders: priest and deacon. In response, Netter goes even further than this, arguing that in the very earliest days of the church *(in primaevis ecclesiae)* there were not even deacons. In fact, there was great ambiguity with regard to offices and duties in the primitive church, he says, with no clear distinctions. The priesthood was for a while the only order; deacons were then created to assist the priests. Here we see Netter's frank acknowledgment of development; he is willing to speak of the confused situation that was gradually stabilized. The apostles created the order of deacon to meet the needs of their time. Netter likens the whole situation to God's work in created nature as he reduces the imperfect to final perfection. In this way, then, God is at work in the church adjusting matters to suit different epochs *(secundum aetates diversas)*.[86]

Yet, although Netter allows for some measure of development, it turns out that the different offices have an ancient origin. For Netter contends that even as the titles themselves were not yet in place the basic division was already present. Netter looks back to the priesthood of the Old Law in which there was a distinction between high and inferior priests. Such a distinction was then instituted among Christians in the apostolic age, although the titles were as yet undetermined. The apostles were those who came to be called bishops, while the prophets are now the priests (Eph 4:11).[87] The different orders were soon formally distinguished, however, so as to avoid confusion in the church and establish good governance. Netter calls upon Wyclif to take historical circumstance into consideration, therefore, and recognize that the church had to evolve beyond the most primitive state. "The primeval confusion of priests begat schism, and schism led to blasphemies against Christ. Hence the distinct ordination of priests followed so that schism might be eradicated." Netter is actually exasperated by Wyclif's attachment to the most primitive state: "You speak of the first time of the apostles as though there were no second!" The ancient is certainly good, but there must also be progress. Hence the appeal to Virgil: *Laudamus veteres, sed nostris utimur annis (Eclogue* 3).[88]

Netter knows that he must make the case for progress, lest he get mired with Wyclif in a dispute over which side best represents the most primitive community. Yet Netter can never entirely cede the ancient ground to Wyclif. And this is where his ambivalence reveals itself. The distinction between priest and bishop was established within the age of the apostles. These are not post-apostolic inventions of the later church. The only temporal distinction to be made, therefore, is between the very earliest days of the apostolic age *(in primaevis)* and the later apostolic period. Netter makes it quite clear that already in the apostolic age *(in tempore apostolorum)* the distinction was in place. He also finds a distinction among the bishops themselves in the primitive church *(ecclesia primitiva)*, all of which is borne out by the New Testaments texts. Titus was a bishop but not an *episcopus summus*. For there were already *capitales episcopi* such as the apostle Paul. And Saint Peter was the first among all the apostles, which demonstrates that there was already a distinction in place between pope, patriarch, and bishop.[89]

Apart from the question of the episcopacy, there is the matter of religious orders. Here Netter, the Carmelite friar, draws some careful distinctions when discussing the concept of newness. He notes that scripture itself extols the *via nova* inaugurated by Christ (Heb 10:20) and the New Jerusalem (Rv 3:12). There is no harm, therefore, in a *nova religio*. Indeed, one may rejoice in it. Yet the sort of newness that Netter defends ought not to be equated with something newfangled. In the end the *via nova* and the *nova religio* are really just further extrapolations of ancient truth. Netter looks to the words of William of St. Thierry to make his case: "This novelty is not a novel vanity. Rather, it is the reality of the ancient religion, the perfection of piety founded in Christ, the ancient inheritance of the Church of God that had been shown beforehand from the time of the prophets."[90] In other words, the religious orders are the manifestation in recent days of the ancient truth; they are the explication of the implicit truth that the church has always maintained.

Unwritten Traditions

We have seen that Netter repeatedly emphasizes the authority of the canonical scriptures, even as he maintains that their genuine interpretation will take place in the larger context of the Catholic Church. Does he, then, have any place for unwritten traditions? Netter records that, in London around 1410, some Lollards had denied the perpetual virginity of Mary because this is not clearly described *(expressum)* in Holy Scripture. Many heresies, Netter warns, arise in just this way.[91] Distortion of the scriptures is the chief weapon of heretics across the ages. Thus the apostles themselves not only commanded their flocks to observe the canonical scriptures. They also instructed them to abide by their own living discourse and traditions that were passed down *viva voce* from senior to junior so that the true understanding *(verus intellectus)* of scripture might be preserved.[92] In this case, then, tradition amounts to the authoritative interpretation of Holy Scripture.

In matters of doubt one must move beyond the letter of written law and seek the instruction of the greater authorities. The fathers of the church understand the scriptures through the inspiration of the same Holy Spirit who had been poured into the writers of the scriptures themselves. It is for this reason, says Netter, that the church commends the unwritten discourses *(sermones non scriptos)* and traditions *(traditiones non scriptas)* of the apostles, which, had they been written down, would have been included in the biblical canon. One would not reject the sermons that Paul preached in Athens and in the synagogues simply because they have not been committed to writing. Not having been inscribed on a dead hide *(morticina pellis)* renders these principles no less inspired. Indeed, books are liable to perish, but the word of Christ will never pass away (Mt 24:34). No matter the authority of Holy Scripture, therefore, the Catholic faith must transcend the physical codices. We believe these truths based for most part on the traditions and documents of the fathers that the church has preserved. It must be stressed, however, that Netter is not positing the existence of a separate deposit of Catholic truth that makes up for the deficiency of Holy Scripture. The rites and customs handed down by the fathers, even if not located in the pages of scripture, still express the same gospel found in the written text. It is along these lines that Netter will appeal to Basil of Caesarea's comment that the tradition of the apostles that is not communicated in the scriptures is worthy of equal affection and piety *(Ecclesiasticarum,* D. 11, c. 5).[93] Netter is simply saying, therefore, that the same gospel that comes down to the church fully in Holy Scripture can also be communicated—albeit in different forms— through apostolic sayings and rites. There can be no doubt that on the matter of extra-scriptural tradition Netter proves himself much more sure-footed than Woodford.

As Netter continues he never retreats from his position of affirming the superior authority of Holy Scripture. He admits that scripture does not provide the answer to every question of religious devotion. Nevertheless, the procedure he outlines for ascertaining the truth serves to reinforce biblical authority. Having first begun one's inquiry by searching through the scriptures, one should then see what the church generally thinks about the matter, what is found in the common tradition or in the harmonious institutions of the fathers. One should then accept this as a complete definition as though it were *(tamquam)* found in the scriptures themselves.[94] Holy Scripture, therefore, remains the paradigm. Netter sums up his position: one must first have faith in the canonical scriptures and second in the definitions and customs of the Catholic Church. Turning to the church is perfectly legitimate, for it is in keeping with the very words of the Creed: belief in One, Holy, Catholic, and Apostolic Church. If one is still without an answer from these two main sources, Netter counsels recourse to "studious men and lovers of the truth," although one is not obligated to take this third step.[95]

Netter's discussion of extra-scriptural traditions continues in book 6 of the *Doctrinale*, the whole of which is devoted to a defense of the sacramentals. Here his explicit goal is to demonstrate the value and validity of the church's many rites whether located in scripture or passed down by way of unwritten tradition. Netter took as his text Titus 2:10, "Let them adorn the teaching of God our Savior in all things." Here Netter begins by affirming that the whole substance of what must be believed regarding the Trinity, angels, virtues, sacraments, and laws is all most firmly established in the teaching of Christ *(doctrina Salvatoris)*. Yet the substance of Christ's teaching must then be adorned by the faithful, through their prayers, fasting, hymns, blessings, and so many other acts of devotion that have been passed down across the ages.[96] These are the very things that Netter claims Wyclif has condemned because he could neither prove nor disprove them. Wyclif cannot locate them in Christ's teaching, which is to say, in Holy Scripture.[97] Yet by rejecting these apostolic customs, or garments *(vestes)*, says Netter, Wyclif would thereby leave the *doctrina Salvatoris* bare and unadorned *(nuda)* and so deprive Christ of his due glory.[98] In other words, the church needs her many rites and customs that she acquired over the centuries in order to live out the truths of the faith at a more profound level of devotion. These are not merely incidental accretions that can be scraped off at no cost to the church's spiritual life. They belong to her very lifeblood. Netter once again believes that he has located the source of the problem: it is that Wyclif will accept only those teachings of Christ that can be located expressly *(expresse)* in scripture, which for Wyclif has become synonymous with the *lex Christi*. Not only the Wycliffites, says Netter, but the Taborites of Prague, are now rejecting various ceremonies of the mass, which they dismiss as "human traditions."[99] It need not be repeated that Wyclif had never demanded explicit, or express, biblical testimony for every pious practice in the church. But such a claim was a central component in Netter's efforts to delegitimize Wycliffite biblical exegesis as an irrevocably radical and dangerous methodology.

Because the church's many prayers and ceremonies all serve to magnify faith and worship, then far from diverging from the words of the gospel, or being foreign to the foundation of the apostles, they are indeed quite consonant with them. Wyclif is thus accused of refusing to allow the church to build upon the foundation laid by the apostles (1 Cor 3:10), whereas Netter argues that such a continuation—provided that it is true to the apostolic foundation itself—is perfectly legitimate.[100] The key to all this, for Netter, is continuity. If future practices can be shown to be in accord with the word of Christ and the apostles, then there is really nothing novel about them. Actually, Netter believes that scripture itself testifies to the fact that there is more to be had than what is found exclusively in the biblical canon. He summons the classic texts such as John 21:25, "There are also many other things Jesus did . . . "; and 2 Thessalonians 2:15, "Hold to the traditions which I have handed down to you, whether by word of mouth or by letter." Wyclif cannot hope, therefore, to bind the church to the written word when neither scripture, nor Christ, nor the apostles demand such a thing.[101]

Indeed, it is at this point that Netter attempts to gain some traction and put real distance between himself and his Wycliffite opponents. To that end Netter looks to Christ's words, "go to the sea" (Mt 17:27), as an invitation to discover all those facets of his life that are not clearly described in the scriptures *(scriptis non expressi)*.[102] Here within the tradition of the church are the rites, prayers, and observances coming down from Christ the great high priest and his sons the apostles. They have been maintained among all the churches from antiquity *(ab antiquo)* without variance or contradiction.[103] Taking his cue from Basil of Caesarea once more, Netter notes that if the first fathers of the church kept some of the sacred mysteries secret this was to preserve them from the attacks of heretics and pagans. By limiting access to these mysteries to the congregation of the faithful the fathers were able to preserve their true interpretation free from heretical distortion. The sacramental observances were handed down in creeds by the teachers of the first churches and maintained through long-standing custom by way of the living word—*sine scriptis, vivo sermone*.[104] Netter's consistent affirmation of the authority of Holy Scripture is in no way undermined by anything he has said here in book 6 of the *Doctrinale*. For he confines unwritten tradition to liturgical rites and practices of piety, and simply argues that even as there is not a direct scriptural warrant for all such things, they still remain valid. He has only said what every other medieval theologian would also have affirmed. Netter was certainly not setting up a parallel extra-scriptural source of doctrine that might rival the principal authority of scripture in matters necessary for salvation.

Development of Doctrine

Netter's extensive section on the Eucharist provides much insight into his views on tradition and development of doctrine. Here are some of the central themes that we have already encountered but now employed as part of a direct refutation of Wyclif's objections to the doctrine of transubstantiation. Central to Wyclif's argument was that transubstantiation was a novelty foisted on the church by a handful of scholastics in direct violation of ancient sacred teaching. Wyclif had pointed out that the great creeds of the church (Apostles', Nicene, and Athanasian) never state that the bread and wine cease to exist following the consecration. Hence this teaching must not rise to the level of an article of faith. Netter quickly rebuffs this claim, reckoning it a common tactic of heretics to cloak themselves in the very creeds that convict them. Yet Netter points out that while it is true that someone is reckoned unfaithful for maintaining an error that the words of the Creed specifically address, that does not mean that someone is unfaithful for believing in a Catholic truth that is not openly *(palam)* asserted by the words of the Creed. "After all, the words of the Creed do not expressly *(expresse)* refute every error; nor do they expressly consent to every Catholic truth."[105]

The Wycliffites *(sequaces Wicleffi)* had also pointed to the fact that there is no mention of transubstantiation in Holy Scripture. Yet Netter argues that the church cannot be confined to the precise vocabulary of scripture. Many things are said in the creeds that are not found in scripture, as when we read that Christ is "God from God, light from light." But when the church employs language that is not found in scripture—often in her battle against heresy—the meaning itself is still scriptural *(sensus verbi in scripturis poterit reperiri)*. Hence Netter dismisses the "Lollard" charge that the church is now resorting to newfangled terminology *(nova vocabula)* in matters of faith, for the church is simply following the example of the apostles and fathers. How else will we protect the faith, asks Netter, "unless through the addition of suitable vocabulary?" In fact, he says, one need only peruse the books of Wyclif himself to find all manner of extraneous terminology that has no foundation in scripture or the church's tradition. Netter certainly holds scripture up as the repository of orthodoxy, but he also notes that "we believe many things really happened which scripture does not *expressly* recount."[106] The key word here is "expressly" *(expresse non recolit)*. Again, therefore, Netter is not positing the existence of a separate extra-scriptural deposit of truth; he is simply saying that the church will have to draw out the implicit meaning of the biblical text on occasion. Thus, in answer to Wyclif's charge that his opponents have added to Christ's words when they speak of accidents without subjects, Netter responds that this is perfectly legitimate. "To explain the condition and properties of a thing is not to add to the thing, but rather to express the way in which those [conditions and properties] follow upon the thing in an orderly manner. For, having posited a human being, we do not add anything to him by saying that he is a combination of body and spirit. . . . So it is that [the various aspects of transubstantiation] all follow when one has posited that the body of Christ exists there purely according to its substance."[107] Thus, for Netter, the doctrine of transubstantiation is a perfectly legitimate "unpacking" of the biblical eucharistic texts. One might say that it is the organic unfolding of the dogma embedded in the Sacred Page. Although Wyclif never worked out such a detailed account, he would not have disagreed with the process that Netter has outlined—only the results in this particular instance. Remember that it was not the matter of nonscriptural terminology as such that bothered Wyclif but only the forced imposition of scholastic theories that lack at least implicit scriptural foundation.[108]

The whole process of explication, and thus development, belongs to the long and tested line of patristic biblical exegesis. "This is the *concors testimonium Patrum* which has been handed down from the time of the apostles and preserved through the succession of bishops right up to our own day." Once again, therefore, "this is the Catholic faith even though it may not be expressly *(expresse)* contained in the canonical scripture." The church was not prevented from using the word *consubstantial* against Arius simply because it is not found in scripture. The fathers knew that the reality this word conveyed was indeed contained within scripture. Arius was defeated by the consistent witness of the fathers stretching across the past into the present. In fact, for Netter, to cite one father is in some sense to cite them all. Thus, having quoted Saint Ambrose, Netter will say that "the whole Church is proclaiming her faith with one voice through the instrument of Ambrose."[109]

Wyclif had impugned Duns Scotus for having accepted transubstantiation (understood as substantial conversion) based solely upon the decree of the Fourth Lateran Council.[110] Yet Netter claims that Wyclif has really distorted Scotus's position by making it seem as though he accepted this doctrine only because the church decreed it and not because it is true in itself. In fact, says Netter, Scotus makes it quite clear that it is not in the power of the church to make anything true or false; that power belongs to God. The church merely explicates what has been handed down to her by the Holy Spirit who is the very author of scripture. The faith of scripture does not derive its truth from human explanation, says Netter; rather all human comprehension must be conformed to the inherent truth of the faith and of scripture. Indeed, it is not even by the will of the church fathers that scripture derives its authority but because it is inspired by the Holy Spirit. God, the very author of scripture, reveals its true sense to men and thus compels the church to explicate scripture accordingly. Nor does a papal decretal or conciliar decree derive its meaning purely from human authority as if human beings were free to construct the faith.[111]

There is good reason, moreover, why the church does not adopt the easiest solution to the holy mysteries (e.g., by choosing consubstantiation in the case of the Eucharist). It would have been much easier, for instance, to follow the Arians and conceive of Christ as a creature alone and not also God. But here the easier way was condemned and the more difficult chosen, since the more difficult proved to be the true meaning. And thus the Council of Nicea chose the truth. This understanding of Christ was recognized as true at that time, says Netter, precisely because it had always belonged to the living faith of the church *(animata fides ecclesiae)*. This is the very faith coming down from the time of the apostles through the succession of bishops and the people all the way to the time of the council, even though it had not yet been *expressly* defined as a matter of faith until that point *(non esset expresse definita pro fide)*. Netter notes that when there was some doubt as to a matter of faith at the great councils the fathers would have considered the issue in light of the common faith that has been maintained since apostolic times.[112]

The church must also determine the very means of enunciating the sacred truth if she is to protect it. Netter recalls how John Quidort of Paris had (at least tentatively) espoused the doctrine of impanation, thus presenting another manner of eucharistic presence than the church had decreed. John had said that to adhere to just one way of defending the truth, to the exclusion of all others, was actually injurious to the truth. For Netter, however, the truth itself dictates the way in which it ought to be expressed. The one who believes that the flesh of Christ exists in the sacrament substantially believes the truth, whereas the one who believes in impanation believes the truth in a false way and thus believes nothing *(quia falso modo verum credit, nihil credit)*. "Therefore, the truth must not only be believed, but the truth must be believed in the correct way. . . . If this is the manner and this is the way which the Church holds then it is true and it alone is true; everything else is false." Just as the Law of God posits only one way to righteousness (Ps 118:53) and thereby restricts us lest we go astray and lapse into heretical opinions, so the church proposes only one way to the truth when she defines an article of faith. By her authority she affirms what must be held, and does so precisely because it is the ancient faith.[113]

As for the church's actual method of scriptural exegesis, Netter concedes that she recognizes that diverse meanings can indeed be found within the words of Holy Scripture. But the church chooses one from among them all that is believed to be the most certain so long as it is not at odds with the context of the passage *(circumstancia scripturae)* and does not contradict the true faith. And there is no more certain way of knowing what the true meaning of a given biblical text is than by relying upon what the whole church has unanimously decreed. Thus impanation is an example of a doctrine that clearly contravenes the simple conversion of bread into the body that Christ himself intended and handed down to the church. Indeed, this simple conversion is in accord with both the context of scripture and the true faith that has been held in agreement by the holy fathers. "Rightly, then, is the way [of impanation] repudiated, for it deviates from the truth, and thus from life itself."[114]

We have seen that Netter—like Wyclif—ultimately grounds all doctrine in Holy Scripture, such that the church is never adding anything to the sacred deposit of truth so much as she is clarifying it. It is essential for

Netter that he present a coherent view of doctrinal development if he is going to ward off Wycliffite claims that the ancient truth has been corrupted by the present church. In fact, says Netter, the church has always been driven by the demands of the times to express the ancient faith in new ways. Present exigencies have forced the orthodox to consider these matters in new ways and by that route come to a deeper understanding of the truth. Thus Netter contends that the saints of ages past only turned their attention to clarifying matters of faith when they were under attack. Councils will make new declarations of the faith as the need arises, but they must not be expected to handle every single circumstance of the truth at the same time. Had there been Wycliffites *(Wiclevistae)* in the age of the fathers, he says, the fathers surely would have written against them. In fact, Netter thinks that God did not want to rush matters and reveal everything clearly all at once. God does not personally reveal all things but instead dispenses many things by means of his creatures in due time so that people may grasp the importance of each item. So it was that Christ entrusted many things to be instituted by the apostles and their successors. One might have expected Christ and the apostles to resolve all the questions that would plague later generations, since it is not as if the fathers possessed any greater expertise than they. Yet, as Netter sees it, divine providence is at work as God uses the contingencies of history to work for the greater good. The articles of faith are made clearer as a result of heresy and the attacks upon the Catholic truth. Heretics actually provide the church with an opportunity to declare the faith in a more lucid manner than had once been needed. On this score, Netter appeals to Augustine's comment that the church had not yet offered a complete position on the Trinity until the Arians attacked it. Here, though, Netter sounds a note of caution: the fact that the saints had not yet spoken specifically against Christ's figurative presence in the Eucharist does not mean that any of them ever accepted this. Actually, says Netter, there were many among the people of God who knew the true faith even as they did not take the time to write it down, for there was not yet anyone on the scene to derogate it. Simply because the faith had not yet been perfectly expressed does not mean, therefore, that it was not yet held. The form of the faith's expression might be new, but the content of the faith expressed is still ancient (*Hac ergo forma, non novella fides . . .*).[115]

    The church that Netter is protecting is the church of the apostles, which persists in untrammeled continuity down to his own day. Perhaps it is ironic, therefore, that Wyclif would have agreed with much of what Netter had to say about doctrinal development. Yet unlike Netter, he had no compelling reason to work out theories of development so carefully. Wyclif had the luxury of constantly being on the attack, which relieved him of the burden of generating a full-fledged and sustainable position on development. His remarks on the matter are rare and scattered; they have to be pieced together. Netter, in all his ferocity, was actually put on the defensive by the Wycliffites. He had to make the case that the present church was not a corruption of the ancient ideal but the living manifestation of the very church that the Wycliffites yearned to recover. In the end, though, Netter is left in a precarious position because his final appeal is always made to abstractions: the ancient faith and the universal church. These are indeed infallible loci of truth, but there does not appear to be any infallible conduit on earth through which this truth is channeled. Neither a pope nor a general council can offer the sort of final authoritative ruling that will settle the matter once and for all. For Netter, therefore, while it is true that the universal church is the authoritative interpreter of Holy Scripture, he never settles on a concrete avatar that can decisively manifest the mind of the church at any given moment.

Chapter 5

A Falling Out

Hussites and Their Czech Opponents

There had been a long history of reform in Bohemia that predated John Wyclif and the subsequent dissemination of his works in the region. I cannot delve into the history of Bohemian reform here, but it must be noted at the outset that the Czech reformer Jan Hus (d. 1415) was not a solitary figure; he belonged to a greater native tradition. In fact, two of his later opponents, Stanislav of Znojmo and Stephen Páleč, had been leaders of the Bohemian protest movement. I will have more to say about Stanislav of Znojmo and especially Stephen Páleč, who did not take Hus to task for demanding an end to clerical corruption but rather for his unwillingness to submit to ecclesiastical authority.[1]

Indeed, the matter of ecclesiastical authority proved to be the central issue in the debate between Páleč and Hus. Both in Bohemia and on the Continent as a whole a fierce struggle developed over who would be authorized to define the parameters and methods of reform. The tragic irony is that virtually everyone involved—from Jan Hus to Stephen Páleč and even Jean Gerson—had very similar goals. More than that, however, they shared many of the same exegetical strategies, and ecclesiological assumptions, that would allow them to reach those goals. Yet the Hussites, or Prague Wycliffites as they were often known, were cast as dangerous radicals who had no place in the church that their fellow reformers were constructing.

Reform efforts in Bohemia stretched back to the 1360s and the preaching of Konrad Waldhauser, who railed against clerical abuses such as simony. He was then followed by Jan Milíč, an ascetic who launched relentless attacks on a worldly clergy. It was also Milíč who championed frequent lay communion as a vehicle of spiritual renewal. In his wake came Matěj of Janov, who emphasized the early church as a model for Christian life. He too stressed the importance of lay communion. In his *Regulae Veteris et Novi Testamenti* (1387–93) Matěj contended that it was only through participation in the Eucharist, receiving its sacramental grace, that there could be truly effective moral reform among Christian people. He writes, "There is nothing in the Church of God better, more perfect, more useful and necessary than this daily eating and drinking, which is the common right of all, by everyone who wishes to have this sacrament of the precious Body and Blood, through which, in which, and from which every good is communicated to men from God through Jesus Christ." Merely attending mass is not enough: it is in consuming the consecrated elements that one partakes of the transformative power of the sacrament. And so he chastised those priests who looked upon the Eucharist as a unique clerical privilege that set them apart from the lay rabble.[2] Hus would later compare Konrad Waldhauser, Jan Milíč, and Matěj of Janov to Old Testament prophets and acknowledged his debt to their earlier work.[3]

The drive for reform in the late fourteenth century was not confined to the lower clergy, however. It received support from the higher ranks, beginning with the archbishop of Prague, Arnošt of Pardubice. In 1344 the episcopal see of Prague was raised to metropolitan status and the very able Arnošt duly promoted to archbishop. The statutes issued under Arnošt's authority were wide ranging in their efforts to reform the moral life of the church, both lay and clerical. There were strict sanctions levied against negligent and simoniacal priests. The provincial synod of Prague, held in 1369, offers an extensive list of reforming statutes, some eighty-six in all. Arnošt was succeeded by Jan of Jenštejn, who was not at first receptive to the demands of the reformers but later came around and in 1391 permitted frequent lay communion. Also in 1391 the Bethlehem Chapel was founded, its name—House of Bread—referring to the Word of God. Thus when Hus assumed the chief position there in 1402 he was stepping into a place firmly established within the reform movement. In the same year Zbyněk Zajíc of Házmburk was named archbishop of Prague, and for some years relations between Hus and Zbyněk were good. Yet it was also during this time that tensions between Czech and German masters were mounting and Wycliffism was thrust into the center of the debates. On 28 May 1403 some forty-five Wycliffite articles were condemned at Prague against the wishes of the Czech scholars in the Bohemian nation, among them Stanislav of Znojmo and Stephen Páleč, who argued that these propositions were not heretical. The Pisan papacy would later enlist Archbishop Zbyněk in the anti-Hussite cause, and on 16 July 1410 Zbyněk ordered some two hundred Wyclif volumes consigned to the flames.[4]

Wyclif was clearly at the center of things now. Contemporary sources — both for and against the Hussite movement — attest to this fact. In 1413 Pope John XXIII condemned Wyclif's works, which he claimed were avidly read by the university students and were being taught to the laity in their native tongue.[5] There is no doubt that Wyclif's works were being widely read and copied in Prague.[6] In May 1414 Jean Gerson called upon the archbishop of Prague, Kónrad of Vechta, to rid Bohemia of that heresy born of Wyclif. If disputation did not put the matter to rest, Gerson counseled, then be sure that the heretics go to the stake.[7] Indeed, the sentence issued against Hus at the Council of Constance in 1415 consistently tied him to Wyclif, the *radix virulenta* who had spawned a series of noxious sons. Hus, according to the council, was "a disciple of the heresiarch John Wyclif" and defended him repeatedly in Prague.[8] And some years later Thomas Netter would still be speaking of the Prague Wycliffites *(Wiclevistarum Pragensium)*, laying blame for Bohemian utraquism squarely on the shoulders of "the heresiarch Wyclif."[9]

As Vilém Herold observes, "Wyclif's influence on the Bohemian Reformation is incontestable and one can only debate its relative weight or the extent to which its role was decisive."[10] Following the marriage of Richard II to Queen Anne of Bohemia there was an upsurge in cultural exchange, one example being the creation of Beam Hall at Oxford to accommodate visiting Czech scholars. Hence Wyclif's views were already receiving attention among the Czechs within his own lifetime, for around 1380 his eucharistic theology was criticized in Prague by the Dominican Nicholas Biceps. And it seems that Wyclif's metaphysical works were being read by this time at Charles University. Yet, as František Šmahel observes, it would seem that Wyclif was not really very popular among the Prague scholars in the latter decades of the fourteenth century. Rather, the rise in popularity of his realist metaphysics and works of reform can be dated to the turn of the fifteenth century. Thus we find that Jerome of Prague, who was in Oxford from 1399 to 1401, would return home with copies of Wyclif's *Dialogus* and *Trialogus*, as well as some works on the Eucharist. Wyclif's *De ideis* was especially influential among the Prague masters, a copy of which Hus had made in 1398 and then defended in 1410 amid the burning of Wyclif's works. The younger Stephen Páleč had been a great admirer of Wyclif and composed a commentary on his *De universalibus*. It was only in 1412, when Páleč turned decisively against Hus, that he renounced any attachment to Wyclif. Soon Bohemian proponents of Wyclif's theories were being labeled Wycliffites (*Wyclifitae, Wyclifistae*) by their adversaries. Attacked as the *famosissimus heresiarcha* by his critics, Wyclif was known as the *doctor evangelicus* by his admirers, some going so far as to refer to him as the fifth evangelist. Yet as Šmahel reminds us, one could agree with Wyclif in many areas without accepting all his theories. Without discounting Wyclif's genuine influence on masters such as Jan Hus, Šmahel maintains that there were three versions of Wyclif in Bohemia at the beginning of the fifteenth century: "one authentic, one transformed by his Czech pupils and the third caricatured in the distorting mirror of anti-Hussite propaganda."[11]

Jan Hus and Holy Scripture

Jan Hus was a master of arts by 1396 and then went on to study theology around 1400, receiving three baccalaureates by 1408. Given other pressing concerns, however, he never took his doctorate.[12] Hus did comment on Peter Lombard's *Sentences* from 1407 to 1409, and this work provides some interesting insights into his conception of Holy Scripture. At the outset of his commentary Hus addresses the very nature of scripture, which is called sacred not only because it signifies sacred and holy things but also because it effects sanctity in human beings. The one who makes use of scripture efficiently will be sanctified by it, because scripture teaches people to honor the divine majesty, love the good, hold to charity, and abhor iniquity. Scripture not only sanctifies man, but makes him wise. All the precepts that must be fulfilled, along with the examples of holiness, are found therein. Holy Scripture is, therefore, the most comprehensive of all laws *(lex universalissima)*.[13]

The study of scripture is, for Hus, a matter of affective piety. Live for Christ, Hus counsels, and you will know him well. If you are poor and lacking the first wisdom, rise up from sin and seek after virtue. Indeed, wisdom *(sapientia)* is synonymous with Holy Scripture; to attend to wisdom is to listen to scripture. He who listens closely to scripture will come to understand clearly, and then by understanding to love sweetly, and by loving to fulfill, and finally then to teach those who do not know. All that is necessary for salvation can be found in scripture.[14] Hus then proceeds along traditional lines to praise Lombard's *Sentences* even as — or indeed especially because — Holy Scripture itself is handed down therein. All theology, therefore, ultimately resolves to scripture. An argument *(locus)* based upon the authority of scripture always takes first place. It is the *primus locus* of all arguments, the one to which all others are reduced. Scripture transcends every human authority, since man is not the proper author of scripture but only a fallible disciple of the Divine Author. Hence no man is to be believed unless one first believes in God. We are to seek wisdom from the divine and infallible Author of Truth.[15] And yet Hus never lapses into a naive fideism. For he also commends human reason, noting that it is meritorious to treat with reason *(racione)* the various articles of faith, since no article of the Christian faith can be contrary to reason. If it were so, it would be false, and thus not an article of faith to begin with, since the *Summa Veritas* would never have people believe anything contrary to the truth.[16] The person of Christ is the Truth in whom all truths of scripture are ultimately rooted.

If reason and scripture coincide that is because they both emanate from the same source: the Wisdom, Truth, and Word of God. Scripture is dynamic and alive. Thus in response to Stephen Páleč who had claimed that scripture is an inanimate thing *(res inanimata)*, Hus insisted that it is the very Book of Life. As for Wyclif, so for Hus, scripture has a specifically Christological nature, having been sent into the world by God the Father (Jn 10:36). As an emanation of Christ the Word, Scripture is a living entity, even a person, who speaks the truth. Hus claims that Páleč has made the mistake of equating scripture solely with the inscribed words and characters on the page. He chides Páleč for his attachment to signs and terms that causes him to miss the eternal truths to which they point.[17] Because Hus equates scripture with Christ, he contends that it will judge all men on the Final Day. It is the Truth bestowed upon man by the Holy Spirit who leads him along the path of faith in order that he might determine all things by its eternal standard.[18]

In a tone again quite reminiscent of Wyclif, Hus will state that Holy Scripture is Christ, the Word of God, together with those things that have been revealed through Christ for the sake of man's salvation. Hence every truth that directs man in the service of God is contained in Holy Scripture, although—and this is very important—it may be found therein either explicitly or implicitly *(explicite vel implicite)*.[19] Scripture is a repository of truth, but Hus clearly recognizes that the truth may be very subtly embedded in it. No matter the charges of his adversaries, therefore, he was well aware that the divine truth will not always be presented in explicit formulations. Hus's equation of scripture with Christ the Word also permits him to offer an expansive view of scripture on its lower signifying levels, so that even when functioning as a sign it is not limited to the written codex. Scripture on the level of a sign manifests the Word not only through words and characters but also by way of pictures and sculptures. In fact, Hus finds that images that depict Christ's Passion to the laity may themselves be reckoned as Holy Scripture. No matter the variations here below, however, scripture on its highest level—as Eternal Word—never varies. Hus conceives of scripture as synonymous with Truth itself and thus transcending linguistic and codicological concerns.[20]

Pursuing this line of thought, Hus observes that Holy Scripture is threefold in its construction: the first level is the objective truth *ex parte rei;* the second the truth as it informs the soul; and the third a voice in the air or a word on the page. The first is formally sacred because sanctity inheres within it. It is, in fact, sanctity itself since sanctity formally inheres in Christ the Word. Yet it is also efficiently sacred because it affects sanctity in rational creatures. The second and third levels are not formally sacred, however, but only efficiently such. The third level derives its sanctity from the fact that it signifies the first level of Holy Scripture. And it is because the first level can never be falsified that it will safeguard the true meaning of the Holy Spirit that is conveyed through the characters of the text on the third level. The Spirit's meaning expressed on the page will always be true precisely because it is a manifestation of the highest level of scripture—Christ the Word. Yet it is in the meaning of those words that it is free from all falsehood, no matter that the reader may misconstrue the inscribed words that bear that meaning. The true meaning, says Hus, must not be confined to the external arrangements of words on the page. Here he has recourse to Jerome, Augustine, and Aquinas to the effect that the meaning of scripture cannot be limited to the bare grammatical sense, the mere outward sense; it will be found deep within the marrow. These words correctly understood, metaphors and all, lead the reader up to the highest level such that scripture becomes a mirror *(speculum)* in whose various parts man can see the Trinity. In fact, it then functions as the very path by which the Trinity would lead man into itself. It is in this vein that Hus will defend the veracity of scripture against the charges of the sophists as he chastises anyone who claims that Holy Scripture could be false in its divinely intended literal sense—*de virtute sermonis*. Following along traditional lines—outlined in the introductory chapter—Hus held an expansive view of the literal sense of scripture, which he equated with the intended sense of the Divine Author. Those who say that scripture can be false simply because they can apply some false meaning to its words are admonished to submit themselves to the literal sense *(sensui litterali)*, which the Holy Spirit requires (cf. *Haeresis*, C. 24, q. 3, c. 27).[21] Not only do these remarks bear a striking resemblance to Wyclif, they also (as we shall see) could have been spoken by Jean Gerson himself.

In words reminscent of Nicholas of Lyra, as seen in the introductory chapter, Hus concludes that scripture, which is itself synonymous with theology, is the *profundissima sciencia*. Scripture is the science, the knowledge, by which God is known, by which he is loved, and through which the beloved is attained. Indeed, the Holy Trinity has bestowed scripture upon men that they might be saved. It is the perfect gift descending from the Father of Lights. It has been given to men not according to their own merits but by grace alone. And it is grace that brings us to genuine knowledge of scripture, which should then be read, heard, and preached for the sake of eternal life.[22]

Yet even as Hus extols the authority of Holy Scripture, he never adopts anything like a *sola scriptura* policy—despite the distortions foisted upon him by the likes of Gerson. In point of fact, Hus believed that the *lex Christi* could also be found in canon and civil law, and he had stated plainly that "every true law is the law of God." Righteous human laws may themselves be considered the law of Christ to the extent that they serve God. Following Augustine, therefore, Hus believed that as all truth is found in Scripture, so all just law is an expression of the law of Christ.[23] Nor did Hus ever demand that human law be founded on the explicit words of scripture. In fact, he wrote: "I honor all general and particular councils, decrees and decretals, as well as all laws, canons and constitutions, so long as they are in *explicit or implicit* agreement with the law of God."[24] Along with the whole tradition, therefore, Hus maintained that human statutes must always conform to divine law, which is true in all cases. And, of course, by definition, anything contrary to the truth is illicit. In that sense, then, all human laws should be regulated by divine law.[25] And yet even here Hus recognizes the inherent flexibility of divine law. There are some divine precepts that were not intended to bind men for all time, and they can be changed according to necessity of circumstance or to achieve an equitable goal—thus the principle of *epikeia*. Hus also recognizes the distinction between divine precepts and counsels, the latter of which one is not bound to obey.[26]

Jan Hus and Authority in the Church

As I have shown above, Holy Scripture will form the principal standard of orthodoxy and heresy in the church and thus serve the cause of ecclesiastical reform. In his *Sentences* commentary Hus ran through the standard definitions of heresy given in canon law all to the effect that heresy is the maintaining of a doctrine contrary to Holy Scripture.[27] Later in his 1413 Czech work, *On Simony,* he stuck closely to what he had said about heresy when commenting on the *Sentences,* defining it here as "stubbornly defended erroneous doctrine contrary to the Holy Scriptures." And because heresy is possible only for a rational spirit, it must be a willful opposition to scripture. What is more, however, heresy can be a matter of both word and deed. A person who speaks the truth about a given sin, such as fornication, but then commits it anyway is a heretic in deed, although not in word. Thus one who persists in mortal sin is a heretic inasmuch as he persists in an error contrary to Holy Scripture. Hus recounts three sorts of heresy: apostasy, blasphemy, and simony. This has clear ramifications for church reform, of course, because these grave sins can be brought under the larger umbrella of heresy and judged as such according to the standards set forth in Holy Scripture.[28]

Hus laid out his reform agenda most thoroughly in his *De ecclesia,* which he completed by May 1413 and which was read to an audience of eighty people at the Bethlehem Chapel on 8 June.[29] Hus was certainly influenced by Wyclif's earlier work of the same name, but he did not—despite the claims of some nineteenth-century scholars—merely appropriate this work for himself. The most recent analysis shows that Hus took 23 percent of his text from Wyclif. And while that may still be a fair amount, much of it comprises quotations of scripture and the fathers. Moreover, the way that Hus reworked and applied the material to make his argument demonstrates that *De ecclesia* is very much his own.[30] The bulk of the thirty articles condemned at Constance in 1415 were drawn from *De ecclesia*, along with material from works that deal with similar subject matter. This leads Thomson to conclude that Hus was condemned for his writings about the church.[31] Broadly speaking that is true, of course, but within that larger framework are the specific questions having to do with the authority of scripture, its place in the larger tradition, and the means to judge true and false doctrine.

Hus begins his *De ecclesia* by noting that every Catholic must faithfully believe in the Holy Catholic Church and love her spouse the Lord Jesus Christ. Yet one cannot love one's spiritual mother unless one would know her by faith and so honor her. Hence discerning the true church is the first task. For there is one *ecclesia*, or congregation, that is composed of sheep and another that is composed of goats: one *ecclesia sanctorum* and the other *ecclesia reproborum*. The church of the righteous is Catholic and universal, the gathering of all the predestined past, present, and future. This is the one universal church lasting from the beginning of the world until its end. It is the mystical body of Christ; he is the head and bridegroom who has redeemed the church by his blood so that he might possess her glorious and free from all sin. If much of this sounds quite traditional that is hardly surprising since this first chapter (like the rest of the treatise) is replete with quotations drawn from the church fathers and Gratian's *Decretum*.[32]

Along the lines laid out by Wyclif in his earlier work, Hus finds that many people may appear to be members of the church, but to be *in ecclesia* is not necessarily to be *de ecclesia*. The foreknown are "in" but not "of" the church; they are the tares among the wheat. Conversely, there are some among the predestined who are not in a present state of righteousness and yet still remain "of the church" even as they may not appear to be "in it" for the time being. Hus distinguishes, therefore, between grace according to present righteousness, which even the foreknown may possess; and the grace of predestination that belongs exclusively to those who are truly members of the eternal church. Judas and Paul are prime examples of the former and the latter respectively.[33] In this sense Hus concedes that one can be both just and unjust at the same time *(simul et semel est iustus et iniustus)*, although such a statement needs to be qualified by the fact that he is referring to two different sorts of grace: predestination and present righteousness.[34]

Hus never allowed talk of the elect and damned to lapse into merely speculative doctrine; it has real ramifications for questions of authority in this world. He was driven by an age-old desire for moral reform that for all practical purposes concerns judgment here on earth. A glance at his 1410 *Sermo de ecclesia* is instructive on this front. Here Hus offered a threefold definition of the church. First, if taken in the wider sense *(large)* it comprises all those who profess the true faith, whether they are predestined or foreknown. Second, it is only in the stricter sense *(stricte)* that it includes the predestined alone. And in a third way, the church is made up of the pope and cardinals. Thus when questioned at Constance about the status of the foreknown he said that they were not members of the church in the most proper sense of the word *(catholicae propriissime dictae)*. Yet it is precisely because this strict definition was not exhaustive, as Herold notes, that Hus could indeed affirm the existence of the present institutional church.[35] This must not be forgotten in light of the charges Hus faced at Constance where his subtle views were reduced to a crude Donatism.

In the *De ecclesia* Hus contends that faithful Christians who fulfill the commandments are the greatest in the holy church of God, whereas prelates who break the commandments are the least. The disciples of Antichrist who live in opposition to Christ are marked by pride and avarice rather than by the gospel of Christ. At present all are mixed together, the good and evil, the predestined and foreknown, but they will eventually be separated. Yet even as Hus claims no certainty in determining anyone's eternal status, he is able to draw upon that very uncertainty to attack the authority of the current prelates. Indeed, he says, it would be presumptuous—apart from special revelation—to claim to know whether one is among the predestined and thus a member of the holy church. And as that is the case, then it is certainly wrong for those who live in such opposition to Christ to assert themselves as heads or members of Christ's body. The laity, therefore, are not bound to believe that the prelates belong to the body of Christ unless it is true. For no one is bound to believe something unless God moves him, and God moves no one to believe a falsehood. Here again, though, the speculative quality melts away as Hus contends that the laity have a right to expect good conduct from their pastors as a sign that they are at least members of the church according to present righteousness. Whether the pastor possesses the grace of predestination, however, is a judgment the laity could only render conditionally. Yet if the pastor's crime is manifest, then one should suppose from his works that he is presently unjust and thereby an enemy of Christ. Despite the protests of his opponents, Hus insists that this does not throw the church militant into a state of confusion, precisely because—apart from special revelation—we do not know distinctly who are genuine members of the body of Christ.[36] Thus it must be stressed that Hus is counseling the laity to withdraw their obedience from pastors and prelates who exhibit clear signs of present mortal sin. He is not asking them to come to a conclusion as to their ultimate status, since that is all but impossible to gauge in this present life.

When Hus turns his attention to papal authority he points out that Christ is the sole head of the universal church. Contrary to Boniface VIII's 1302 bull *Unam Sanctam*, therefore, the Roman church must not be identified with the Holy Universal Catholic Church. The pope is the head of the Roman church alone and the cardinals the body—but they are not synonymous with the gathering of all the predestined.[37] The central question of papal authority always comes back to the authority of Holy Scripture, which will remain the principal standard by which all papal claims are judged. Hus argues that the Christian is bound to believe, either explicitly or implicitly, every truth that the Holy Spirit has placed in Scripture. Thus one is not bound to believe the sayings of the saints, or the papal bulls, unless they have spoken from scripture or can at least be grounded *implicitly* in scripture. A man can believe in papal bulls merely by way of opinion, therefore, since the pope and his cardinals remain liable to error. Hence whereas it is unlawful to disbelieve or contradict Holy Scripture, one is free to contradict a papal bull if it commends the unjust, attacks the innocent, or contradicts the commandments of God.[38] Hus was hardly alone when taking issue with some of the more extreme claims of the decretalists, for example, that the pope can do whatever he wishes and no one may question him. Nobody, says Hus, ought to be believed except to the extent that his words are grounded in scripture.[39] Everything that Hus has just said here is so straightforward and conventional as to be completely unremarkable. For it must be noted that Hus neither rejected papal legislation as such nor demanded that it be based on explicit biblical testimony. All he asked is that the pope not act in ways contrary to Holy Scripture—a principle that is clearly spelled out in the *Decretum* (cf. *Sunt quidam dicentes* C. 25, q. 1, c. 6). No one could really argue with that, but one is still left to ask who exactly is in a position to render judgment on the fitness of papal actions. The answer to that question did not come easily to anyone in the early fifteenth century—neither Hus nor his adversaries.

In an extended treatment of Matthew 16:18–19, Hus contends that Christ is the foundation of the whole Church.[40] But that is not to say that there is no place for Peter and successors. There can be genuine popes who are worthy of respect. The true vicar of Peter will conduct himself like the saint, but if his ways are contrary to Peter and Christ, then he will prove to be Antichrist. For no one truly *(vere)* bears the office of Christ and Peter unless he follows their way of life.[41] Writing in the midst of the papal schism—which will itself be settled by papal deposition—Hus's treatise is filled with quotations from canon law to make the case that true vicars of Peter are righteous. The true successor *(verus successor)* of Peter will follow Peter's way of life, while true cardinals only stand in succession of the apostles to the extent that they represent the apostolic life.[42] Actually, as discussed in the next chapter, what Hus has to say about true and false successors is virtually identical to the conciliarist Dietrich of Niem.

Hus insists that he is not attempting to devalue the papacy and cardinals, as his opponent Stephen Páleč claimed; it is simply that any avaricious and illicit commands must be regarded as inherently devoid of authority. As for Stephen Páleč's charge that the Hussites wish to judge all matters by Holy Scripture alone and thus reject the apostles, doctors, and the universal church, Hus responds that this is a lie based upon a distortion of their works; they had merely said that their adversaries would have to offer some scriptural warrant for their claims. After all, says Hus, Páleč himself knows that one should not adhere to any argument unless founded upon scripture or reason. And surely the Hussites do not intend to interpret scripture other than the Spirit requires and as the holy doctors expound—the very ones to whom the Spirit grants understanding. Here Hus has recourse to Nicholas of Lyra, that diligent biblical exegete *(sedulus scripturae expositor)*, who comments that no one should be obeyed who teaches anything contrary to the law of God. Actually, Hus thinks that his fellow master Páleč really does know better and would concede privately what he denies publicly for fear of the pope.[43]

Following the Augustinian principle that all truth is contained in scripture, Hus contends that any deed or precept that proves unhelpful to the church of Christ cannot by definition be contained in scripture either explicitly or implicitly *(explicite vel implicite)*. He concludes, therefore, that a subject would not be obligated to fulfill such a command issued by a prelate, since that would offend against the freedom inherent in the law of Christ. Hus will concede, however, that subjects are bound to carry out the precepts of wicked prelates if these still prove to be the commandments of Christ. In other words—and this is essential—it is the nature of the command itself, not the moral status of the prelate who issues the command, that makes all the difference.[44] Yet if a subject clearly discerns that a command is detrimental to the church and works against the worship of God and the salvation of souls he ought to resist the command of his superior. For such resistance is actually true obedience, not only to God, but also to one's superior, since no superior ought to command anything unless it is good. And, as this is a matter of conscience, the subject is not excused from sin if he obeys his superior in an unjust command.[45] As it was, then, Hus reckoned it blasphemy to say that the pope cannot err and must be obeyed in all things. He therefore attacked one of the more extreme claims of the decretalists: "That the pope is an earthly god who can do on earth as he pleases, ruling over all mankind as he wishes; likewise those who say that he may establish a law contrary to God's law, or that he may rightfully order something against the holy apostles."[46] Hus would hardly have been alone in rejecting such exalted papalism—indeed, his enemies at Constance had likewise discarded the absolutist demands of the monarchical papacy.

Hus Responds to Accusations

As noted at the outset, Jan Hus was seen by opponents to have been fostering the heresy of John Wyclif. Yet no matter the stigma of the "Wycliffite" label, Hus says that he has found Wyclif's writings to be true, not because Wyclif—whom he specifically refers to as a "master of sacred theology"—has said these things, "but because God, Scripture, and infallible reason attest to them." Of course, says Hus, if any error can be found in Wyclif's remarks he would never follow them.[47] He protests, however, that many of Wyclif's books were being burned indiscriminately, even such works as his *De trinitate*, despite the fact that no one had located any heresies within it.[48] Against John Stokes, who claimed that all those who read any of Wyclif's books thereby involved themselves in heresy, Hus points out that people have been reading Wyclif at Oxford for thirty years and at Prague for twenty. Stokes could scarcely find a scholar at these universities who has not read Wyclif and thus (according to Stokes) involved himself in heresy. Furthermore, said Hus, many of Wyclif's books are concerned with neutral subjects such as logic, metaphysics, and the natural sciences rather than the controversial topics of biblical exegesis and ecclesiology.[49] Was Wyclif really a heretic? Hus does not believe so, although he confesses that he can only surmise this, since such things are ultimately hidden from us.[50] The fact is that a good number of Hus's opponents—notably Stephen Páleč—had themselves been enthusiastic readers of Wyclif just a few years earlier. If Wyclif was under a cloud at Prague this was a very recent phenomenon. All of which is to say that the lines separating orthodox and heterodox literature were not only blurred, but, even when firmly determined, were hardly so long-standing as men like Stokes would have people believe.

Hus was his own man and was quite willing to depart from Wyclif on some issues, most notably transubstantiation. Hus's treatment of the Eucharist in his *Sentences* commentary is entirely traditional; there is nothing remotely provocative about it. Here he employed the term "transubstantiation" matter-of-factly, just as he affirmed in another work that the true body and blood are consumed under alien species. Nor did Hus make the case for lay reception of both species, pointing out that the laity do receive both the body and blood under the bread alone in keeping with the doctrine of concomitance. On the question of the evil celebrant—where one might expect something provocative—Hus trots out the standard scholastic authorities to the effect that the presence of Christ's body will not be jeopardized by a wicked priest.[51] At all events, in his response to the list of forty-five Wycliffite errors we see Hus assert his independence. When it comes to the first proposition on the list, the remanence of the eucharistic bread following consecration, Hus answers, "I have never held this, nor do I hold it now, for I follow the meaning of the saints and of the Church." He steers clear of Donatism in article 4, which states that a priest and bishop in mortal sin do not consecrate and baptize. For Hus qualifies this statement, saying that "[the priest] does not do so worthily *(non digne)* . . . yet in some way even the most wicked priest does [consecrate], because God works through him." In other words—and along the most traditional lines—Hus finds that while the priest's moral inadequacy may have negative ramifications for himself, the objective validity of the sacrament is never imperiled. As for the statement that there is no foundation in the gospel for Christ having instituted the mass, Hus admits that there is some truth to this, "for Christ did not clearly describe *(non expressit)* the office of the Mass in the Gospel, although he did grant priests the power to say Mass." And finally, as to whether temporal lords could take away the goods of delinquent clerics, "I will neither assert nor deny it, for perhaps it can have a true sense."[52] We need not trace all forty-five; the above is sufficient to demonstrate that Hus was willing to deal with each proposition on its own merits. But it must also be admitted that divorced from their larger context none of the propositions could be adequately addressed. As we shall see, when a list of errors was put before Hus at the Council of Constance he was never given the time he needed — that anyone would have needed — to address the issues in a proper manner. In fact, the decontextualizing of Hus's work was a principal strategy adopted at Constance and proved to be one of the great injustices of the council.

Opponents of the Wycliffites — whether in England or on the Continent — were consumed with the fear of Donatism, which they regarded as the destabilizing enemy of legitimate reform. And it appears to be part of a deliberate strategy on the part of the anti-Wycliffites to tar Hus with this charge so as to make him appear far more radical than was really the case. Hus was consistently charged with being a Donatist, despite his insistence that the sacraments are not invalidated by evil clerics. For he believed that even when the minister is personally unworthy, and indeed acts unworthily, he still consecrates. When responding to Stephen Páleč, Hus stated that "an evil pope, bishop, prelate, or priest is an unworthy minister of the sacraments, through whom God baptizes, consecrates or otherwise works to the benefit of his church." If God can work through the devil for the good of his saints, then he can certainly operate effectively through some unclean priest. But again, the evil priest does not baptize or consecrate worthily *(digne)* but rather unworthily *(indigne)* and for that reason works to his own damnation.[53] The precision Hus achieves in these formulations is essential to the preservation of his orthodoxy. In fact, the question of correct verbal formulation of theological propositions played a huge role in Hus's eventual condemnation and is considered at greater length in the following chapter.

Anti-Hussite Ecclesiology

Having examined Jan Hus's understanding of the criteria by which authority can be justly exercised in the church, it will be instructive to examine what some of his principal Czech opponents believed about the church and the structures of authority. Turning first to Stanislav of Znojmo and then to Stephen Páleč, one finds that they both had a difficult time offering decisive answers to the questions of ultimate authority in the church. Stanislav of Znojmo promotes a very strong papalist doctrine, but he cannot fully overcome some of the most fundamental problems that papalism faces. He contends that Jesus Christ the Light of the World now shines across the whole earth through a mystical and ecclesiastical composite consisting of the pope as head and the college of cardinals as body; this is called the Roman church. And wherever the pope and cardinals may dwell—not necessarily in Rome itself—there is the Roman church. Possessing the fullness of power, she rules over all other churches and the entirety of Christ's faithful. In the midst of this rather exalted portrait of the papacy and curia, however, Stanislav must still address the possibility of papal defection from the true faith. And it is here that he readily admits that what he calls the "material parts" of the Roman church, namely, the persons of the popes and cardinals, can err gravely in questions of faith and morals. But Stanislav insists that the Roman church in her "formal being" *(esse formale)* will never fall away from the faith, since she always remains the same with respect to her essential form. Thus Stanislav cautions the faithful not to focus their attention on the pope and cardinals in their merely human selves but instead look through them to the formal essence of the Roman church that is at work in them governing the faithful. Simply because the material parts may sin gravely, therefore, does not mean that the Roman church herself has sinned. Stanislav clearly wants to affirm the authority of the institutional church manifested in the hierarchy. Here, then, one is left with an inerrant Roman church that nevertheless remains separable from the very persons who hold its highest offices. The fact that—as Stanislav himself has just admitted—the pope and cardinals can err in matters of faith and morals is precisely what drives Wycliffite and Hussite dissent from what they regard as unjust directives. Nevertheless, Stanislav thinks it is the best of all the ecclesiological options. He certainly objected to limiting the church to a communion of the just and elect, since there is no way—apart from special revelation—to know who is among the elect. Such a system will result in chaos because it would make it impossible to achieve any authoritative judgments in matters of faith. Stanislav also chastised those who claim that the church consists of the whole body of Christians who alone will decide matters of doctrine. There is no way, he notes, that this body could actually be gathered together to render its decision. And, finally, Stanislav takes issue with those who would recur only to scripture. They insist on interpreting it according to their own understanding and cite whatever texts of canon law and the fathers suit their case—all of which results in infinite error and alienation within the church.[54] Stanislav may have accurately depicted the shortcomings in all these approaches, but he still has not solved the problem of ultimate authority.

In a brief tract Stephen Páleč surveyed the various meanings of the word *ecclesia*, contending that ignorance of this subject was leading many into error. There are, he says, a total of six ways in which the word is used. The first simply refers to the material building. In the second sense it is a congregation of the wicked, such as heretics and schismatics. In the third sense it can refer to a general council gathered to define some matter of faith. And here Páleč notes that it is for the councils to enforce ecclesiastical customs and coerce those who thwart those customs and canons (cf. D. 11, c. 7–9). In this vein, Páleč has recourse to Augustine's oft-cited remark that he would not have believed the gospel had the church not moved him. Therefore, says Páleč, it is for councils to determine the contours of the biblical canon. The fourth meaning of *ecclesia* refers to the pope and his cardinals, the patriarch and his primates, the archbishops, and the bishops. In that sense there are many churches, but "the mother of all the churches, the head and mistress, is the Roman Church." And "of this Roman Church the pope is the head, the true and manifest successor of Peter the prince of the apostles, while the college of cardinals is the body." As is so often the case in these debates, there is the appeal to antiquity. Thus we find Páleč turning to the primitive ecclesiastical order in support of his conception of the Roman church. The pope and cardinals, says Páleč, ought to follow the order found in the *ecclesia primitiva*. This means that the pope stands in Peter's place, the cardinals in that of the other apostles, and the priests as the seventy-two disciples. This is the Catholic Church, which, as mother and head of all the rest, possesses the ultimate authority to decide matters of faith and correct all errors. She may judge all and be judged by none. For what she ordains in matters of faith must be obeyed by all. Thus anyone who speaks against the Roman church would thereby be reckoned a heretic. The fifth mode of *ecclesia* refers to the whole congregation of all the predestined or faithful, "who are in the grace of God and are in the spirit of Christ." Yet Páleč is quick to point out that this fifth mode of *ecclesia* possesses no authority to decide ecclesiastical cases, since such a group has never been simultaneously gathered together, nor can it be known precisely who would belong to it. That is why it is necessary for the good governance of the church that all such authority be entrusted to "the true and manifest successors of Peter and the apostles," namely, the pope and his cardinals. Again, it is an appeal to the visible, institutional church hierarchy, for the manifest successors must be regarded as the true successors *(manifestos verosque successores)*. And last, the sixth sort of *ecclesia* refers to the community of all baptized believers who hold to the twelve articles of faith in the Apostles' Creed. This is the church militant comprising the wise and foolish virgins, the wheat and the tares.[55] Páleč, therefore, does affirm a church of the predestined, but it is ultimately of no concern to him, since it does no good here on earth. For now we must think of the church in terms of the church militant, that *corpus mixtum* that will last until the end of the age.

This tract was concise and largely free of polemic, but Páleč also penned a substantial reply to Hus in which he set out to answer his various charges. Páleč must first, in the vein of Woodford and Netter, establish the prevailing narrative. He begins by staking out the high ground, claiming to speak for orthodox Christendom. "The whole community of clergy in Bohemia, together with the community of all the clergy in the world and of all Christianity, consistently hold and believe just as the Roman church and not otherwise, that in every Catholic and ecclesiastical matter one must adhere to the faith, judgment, and determination of the apostolic see and the Roman church."[56] On the offensive, Páleč cries out to Hus, "Look upon your works and be ashamed! You who would rend the rite of ecclesiastical unity, alleging your innocence, but not proving it; would that you might strive to turn your curse into a blessing!" If Hus is so convinced of his own innocence, why does he lurk about in the corners of Prague afraid to make his case before the pope?[57] Let Hus join with all wise Catholics throughout the world and admit that the pope and his cardinals are the true successors of Peter and the apostles. But if Hus and his fellows refuse, how can they dare claim that they desire only to be correctly instructed when they are unwilling to submit to Rome's teaching and discipline?[58]

The opponents of Hus were clearly troubled by the fact that his words were now resounding beyond the privileged walls of the university. When what could have remained a magisterial dispute over scriptural exegesis and the limits of papal authority under canon law turns into a popular cause the situation can—and eventually did—become explosive. For, according to Páleč, Hus's actions are destroying the common peace and discipline of Christ; the whole structure of authority is being brought down. Hus speaks the words of obedience, but his rebellious actions prove him false. His incessant preaching provokes the laity to disobedience toward their prelates and insults the dignity of the priesthood. He hides away in the Bethlehem Chapel, a school of Satan and nest of Wycliffite heretics.[59] Over and against Hus's protests, Páleč says that he calls Hus and his apostles Wycliffites *(Wykleffistas)* precisely because they attempt to excuse the Englishman of heresy even though he was the most dangerous heretic to rise up against the church in all her history.[60]

Intent on portraying Hus as a Donatist, and thus a dangerous radical, Páleč makes the orthodox position clear. Yet, as he does so, Páleč ends up sounding a lot like Hus himself: Hus had clearly stated that an unworthy priest may nevertheless consecrate on account of the divine power at work through him.[61] Here Páleč states that any evil priest or prelate, although unworthy *(indignus)* and ministering unworthily *(indigne)*, is conceded divine cooperating grace such that he truly consecrates, absolves, and ordains. It is the office, not the life, that makes the difference; this man is still a *verus officialis* of Christ. "God is not concerned with the dignity or indignity of the person, but the order, office and power."[62] The question of Donatism goes right to the heart of the ecclesiological debate: the true and false church. Páleč rejects the notion that the church can be limited to the predestined. For Páleč, it is true faith *(vera fides)*, that by which all truths are believed either implicitly or explicitly, which distinguishes faithful Christians from the infidels. "Therefore, all Christians, even the wicked, having a true unformed faith, are faithful and thus true Christians by way of the true faith even if not by way of true life."[63] Thus one need not be in a state of grace—having a faith formed by love—to be counted within the ranks of the church. The dispute here turns more on vocabulary than substance, however, although the implications of the vocabulary are clearly troubling for Páleč. It is the Hussite use of the adjective "true" *(verus)* that bothers Páleč, since it seems to cut right to the heart of legitimate authority. When Hussites distinguish true and false prelates based upon their moral status it appears, at least on the face of it, to deprive the false of any right to carry out their ecclesiastical functions. Now, as we have seen, Hus's position is more subtle than that, inasmuch as he admits that false prelates can administer sacraments and even issue just commands. Nevertheless, Páleč prefers the adjective "unworthy" *(indignus)* because it still maintains the man in the legitimate tenure of his office even as it shows him to be unfit for that office. One could imagine Páleč saying, Yes, I admit that this man is a bad prelate, but he is still a true prelate all the same.

It is in this vein that Páleč accuses Hus of "generally failing to distinguish between truth of office and truth of life." Páleč, for his part, admits that an evil and foreknown pope would amount to a thief, but he would still be a

> true pope by reason of his office and authority, and thus the head of the church. For just as predestination, or grace according to present righteousness, does not make someone pope, so neither does it make one head of the church. Rather, it is the capital and fontal authority of knowing and defining in every Catholic and ecclesiastical matter that makes someone pope and thus head of the church. Such authority, since it is a grace given for the benefit of others *(gratia gratis data)*, can abide along with foreknown status and mortal sin.

The power of the pope is a "spiritual light received from God for the good of others. And so, in the manner of light, it cannot be defiled by what is unclean." Hence there are two things to keep in mind with an evil pope:

> Evil life and sacred office. With regard to his life he is a dead member who does not receive the influx from Christ the head . . . but with regard to his office he is a living member of the church who is capable of conferring the sacraments . . . and directing the church in all matters of faith.

Such a pope can be a member of the holy church because he is a member of the church militant in which the good and the evil are mixed together, the predestined and the foreknown. Hus is not permitted to exclude the foreknown from the church, therefore, precisely because anyone in a present state of grace thereby lives a spiritual life. Such a life is itself supernatural and can only be derived from Christ the head to whom he is united by charity.[64]

For all that, however, Páleč has not really gotten to the heart of the issue. Making Hus out to be a Donatist freed Páleč from having to engage the central point of Hus's position on the papacy. It was not that a foreknown man could not serve as pope, or that he was bereft of power even if in a state of mortal sin. The only question that really mattered with respect to papal authority—that had any concrete ramifications—was whether someone is bound to obey a pope who is commanding an unjust action. And the fact is that nobody would have said that obedience is owed to an unjust command. So we are once again left to ask, who, and under what criteria, can render a determination on the legitimacy of a given papal command—especially in a time of schism? For some two centuries the university masters believed that they had every right, indeed a duty, to offer their considered opinion on such matters. Exercising their magisterial, or teaching, authority in this way might not be finally decisive, but it was clearly part of the larger determinative process.

Páleč was certainly aware of the fundamental rights of the university masters; after all, it was only a few short years earlier that he was defending the condemned theses of John Wyclif. Hence his need now to recast the narrative. Central to Páleč's line of attack, therefore, is that Hus and his Prague supporters have lapsed into a radical subjectivity; they refuse to abide by any of the traditional mechanisms of authority. Hus and his accomplices profess themselves to be "gospel men" *(viri evangelici)*, which stems from the fact (says Páleč) that they reject all canons as mere human traditions and wish to rely solely upon the law of Christ. Of course, this misses the fact that Hus believed that the law of Christ *(lex Christi)* could be located in both canon and civil law.[65] Páleč points out that in matters where scripture is unclear one must abide by the established customs of the church, but Hus surely accepted Páleč's statement that the Christian religion is confirmed "in the truths of the holy doctors, the institutions of the holy fathers, the canons and rules, which one is not permitted to disbelieve." Páleč finds that Hus's apparent resistance to established customs and authorities is itself evidence that he does not truly live by the law of Christ. And where are these authoritative sources manifested? In the decrees of the papacy. No one who is truly faithful to Christ's law, says Páleč, would disobey the Roman church and supreme pontiff. Hus claims not to have sinned against the church, so let him live under her yoke and discipline and submit himself to her determination and definition.[66] Thus when Páleč speaks of the church he means the papacy—here in the midst of a schism and the calling of a general council that will depose the duly elected Pope John XXIII.

This debate, like so many others, will be fought over adherence to sacred tradition. And nothing seems to irk Páleč more than Hus's claim that he is willing to submit his case to the judgments of the apostles and holy doctors. Páleč regards this as specious posturing, as he complains that Hus refuses to recognize the apostolic see, the Roman church, or any other competent judge here on earth. There is no visible authority capable of passing a final ruling whom Hus will recognize. This universal church, which Hus calls the multitude of the predestined, has never been gathered upon the earth. The result, says Páleč, is that Hus will turn to Holy Scripture as his sole judge, having effectively refused any possibility of visible authoritative judgment. And on the subject of Holy Scripture, Páleč refutes the charge that he has reduced scripture to mere letters on the page *(literas exaratas)*. He fires back in tones that Wyclif and Hus would surely approve, contending that he understands Holy Scripture to be "the real Catholic truths contained under those signs. For I know that, although those written signs can be burned and destroyed, the truth of Holy Scripture will never cease, but will abide for eternity." Actually, Páleč claims that it is Hus who plays it false when he cites scripture, the fathers, and the canons. For he does so, not according to the intention of the authors, but only in order to bolster his case based on some superficial reading *(superficiem literae)*.[67] Páleč charges Hus with being tendentious in his use of authoritative sources, therefore, twisting those he introduces to make his case and then deriding as mere human traditions the church's approved canons and decrees used against him. Hus will accept nothing that does not support his errors, while he claims authority for texts that have not been authorized by the church.[68] The battle over authoritative sources will never end unless both sides are willing to recognize some final interpretive judgment issued by some unimpeachable (and thus infallible) authority from whom there is no further appeal.

Páleč presents a solid disquisition on the relationship between scriptural and extra-scriptural authority. He pointedly rejects Hus's position that all judgments of the Roman church must be based solely upon what is contained within scripture. In fact, he says, "there are many judgments handed down to Christ's faithful through the canons, holy councils, and decrees, which are not contained in the texts of the Old and New Testaments." Indeed, the faithful hold many things that are not clearly delineated in scripture but instead come from the institution of the fathers and the customs of the people, which are now accepted as law. It is here that Páleč appeals to a model of development. Expansion and increasing complexity is only natural. Just as the church has grown in the faith successively and by degrees *(gradatim)* from the time of Abraham down to our own day, such that those who came later will have believed in a clearer and more explicit fashion, so too has the church successively increased in her institutions and decrees. "Christ and the Holy Spirit have handed down many judgments successively through the councils and the Roman church that must be held faithfully by Christ's faithful ones, even though these things are not contained in the Bible." The church had to keep growing in order to survive. As heresies arose councils had to respond with new decrees, handing down decisions that are not found in scripture. By rejecting all that is not contained in the Bible, Hus is following the path of the Armenian Christians, says Páleč, who accept only scripture and reject the authority of the saints and holy doctors.[69]

Yet Páleč also makes it clear that the judgments of the Roman church do not contradict scripture. In fact, for Páleč, scripture remains the touchstone—the measure by which to judge extra-scriptural customs. For he says that if any customs are found to be in opposition to scripture they should not be accepted. On the other hand, we should not posit a false antithesis here either, since scripture and the Roman church will always remain in sync with each other. Therefore, says Páleč, one must not doubt that the judgments handed down by the Roman church to Christ's faithful are worthy of belief, since such judgments will always be in keeping with Holy Scripture. For if the church handed down even one judgment that was not consonant with scripture, then the faithful would have no assurance regarding any of her judgments. Yet whatever the Roman church has approved in matters of faith must be accepted by everyone. Indeed, if one questions the authority of the Roman church, then all will be thrown into confusion. It is by the very authority of the church that one receives the Four Gospels; she alone guarantees their authority. It is on her testimony that we ought to believe every single truth contained in these Gospels, since the veracity of the whole rests on the certainty of each part. The church approves the genuine Gospels and rejects those written by heretics. Church and scripture go together, therefore, and it is simply unreasonable to think that the Roman church would hold firmly to something that was not of the faith, or reject something that was. The church is the mystical body of Christ governed and vivified by the Holy Spirit, a body whose spiritual life can never be extinguished by infidelity. Thus to claim that the church could consistently err would be to impugn the Holy Spirit. To Páleč's mind, then, Hus is arrogating to himself supreme authority in the church and thereby establishing himself as one more faithful to the tradition than the whole Christian community. And it is this rupture with the greater community, this prideful individualism, that Páleč returns to again and again. All Hus's talk of being willing to submit himself to the judgment of the church is written off as "a sophistical submission, vocal and not real, humble in word but exceedingly proud in deed." Páleč begs Hus to tell him to whose judgment precisely—outside of his own party—he is actually willing to submit.[70] At the close of this work, though, Páleč implores his former friend to recant and even asks that Hus excuse his rough tone. He has written with great zeal, having sworn an oath to defend the profession of sacred theology and truth. Páleč bids Hus, "Drink sweetly this cup, although bitter, which gushes up from the well of charity." Then might Hus and his fellows come around again to be men of Catholic truth.[71] For all Páleč's frustration with Hus's refusal to submit to authority, it must be admitted that Páleč's own location of legitimate authority seems a bit murky. The "Roman church" that he consistently refers to—here in the midst of a papal schism—looks more like a vague abstraction than a functioning court of appeal.

The Trial of Jan Hus

The record of Hus's trial at Constance makes for disheartening reading.[72] Peter of Mladoňovice, who witnessed the proceedings, recounts that when Hus tried to explain what he had meant by the various propositions extracted from his works (often in distorted fashion) he was repeatedly told to answer simply "yes" or "no" as to whether he accepted them. Hus would then try to explain himself based upon the authority of the holy doctors only to be shouted down. I noted earlier that metaphysical realism had been very important to many of the Bohemian masters—not only Hus but also Stephen Páleč. Yet the Paris master Pierre d'Ailly specifically attacked Hus for his realist metaphysics, asking him whether he believed that universals possess reality apart from particulars. Hus said that he did, and adduced Anselm of Canterbury among others to support his position.

Yet d'Ailly, himself a nominalist, believed that the natural result of Hus's realism would be a denial of transubstantiation. Indeed, Hus was continually linked to Wyclif's theory of remanence, despite his persistent denials. And when faced with the charge that he denied that a priest in mortal sin can administer the sacraments, Hus insisted on qualifying that statement in ways that I have already examined. Here too Hus maintained that the wicked priest really does consecrate but does so unworthily since he is at that moment an unworthy minister of God.[73]

Hus implored the council to let him explain the meaning of the articles brought against him and wished also to defend his reading of the holy doctors. Again and again, Hus said that he would be willing to revoke any article that was proven to him false — if indeed that article was stated as such in his works. What he could not do, however, was abjure an article that he never held, since that would amount to asking that he perjure himself before God and thus face eternal damnation.[74] To the very end Hus claimed that he had never been obstinate but had only desired that the council instruct him from the scriptures. If proven wrong he would recant. Sadly, he never received the fair hearing that was his due. Perhaps there is some consolation in the fact that Hus professed his unwavering commitment to the Catholic tradition up until the very end. Indeed, on his way to the stake he said that he would gladly die safe in the knowledge that he "preached in accordance with the saying and expositions of the holy doctors."[75]

Hus wrote a number of letters while imprisoned at Constance that provide further insight into his thoughts and those of his adversaries. Writing from the Franciscan prison in Constance to Lord John of Chlum, Hus recounted how Páleč had tried to persuade him to recant, arguing that it would be no great shame and would even work to the good. Yet when Hus put the question to Páleč as to what he would do were he sure that the errors ascribed to him were false, Páleč admitted the difficulty of the situation and then began to weep.[76] Along similar lines, Hus recounted to friends in Constance that a certain doctor instructed him that it would be lawful to admit to whatever the council wished even as he knew it to be untrue. To this Hus replied: "Even if the whole world said that to me, I, having reason which I am now using, could not without harm to conscience say that!"[77]

The issue of conscience is crucial to understanding Hus's time at Constance. He was not simply standing on good principle in the way that modern readers might admire; he firmly believed that if he admitted to teachings that he had never held he would be putting his soul at risk. That is what makes the actions of his accusers so contemptible; by refusing to allow extended discussion of the articles, they were forcing him to choose between his earthly life and his eternal soul. And in light of the larger scope of this book we should not lose sight of the fact that conscience is itself an authority of very high order. For although the Catholic is certainly obliged to form his conscience according to the teachings of the church, he still must obey what his own conscience judges to be right. Yet as Hus stood before his accusers at Constance it was not at all clear that he had actually contravened the teachings of the church; that remained to be proved.

At all events, the council was in no mood to accommodate Hus, who recounted how he told Pierre d'Ailly that he merely wished to be instructed as to whether he had done anything wrong. Yet d'Ailly demanded that Hus recant, since he had already received the instruction of fifty Masters of the Sacred Page. Hus wrote to his friends, however, that he had not been defeated from the scriptures or by any other proof. Rather, he says, the council merely issued threats to get him to recant and abjure.[78] Writing to the members of the University of Prague, Hus told them that he had never recanted a word, refusing to do so unless he could be proven wrong by scripture. He told the council that he did indeed detest any false sense that may exist in the condemned articles. Hus asked only that they put aside the errors that they attribute to the articles and retain the truth that he intended by them.[79] As for the fifty doctors, Hus recalls that they rebuked him at the public hearings based upon false abstractions of the articles and were not willing to give him private instruction or even confer with him. They simply told him that he must stand by the council's decision. When Hus attempted to argue based upon scripture and the holy fathers they either mocked him or claimed that he misunderstood the texts.[80]

In his last declaration to the council Hus once more protested that he would not recant false articles that he had never preached, so that he might not lapse into perjury and offend God. And again, if there was a false sense found within those articles that had been properly drawn from his works, he was prepared to repudiate them.[81] Thus to his friends in Constance Hus wrote that he was "not willing to declare that every article drawn from my books is erroneous, lest I condemn the opinions of the holy doctors, particularly of the blessed Augustine. Secondly, concerning the articles ascribed to me by false witnesses, I am not willing to confess that I have asserted, preached, and held them. Thirdly, I am not willing to recant, lest I commit perjury."[82] Hus wanted a chance to explain what he had meant by the words now repeated back to him, but, as we shall see, Jean Gerson made it very clear that the propositions themselves—no matter the author's intention—remained open to condemnation as they stood. The fact that Hus could offer a reasonable explanation of them was irrelevant to the council. It is the most awful irony, then, that Hus was placed in a position by his fellow masters whereby he had either to defend or deny statements based upon the crudest standards of literalism—the very sort of literalism that the medieval theologians themselves deplored.

The trial of Jan Hus at Constance turned more on the question of propositions than ideas; that is to say, it was more about the wording of statements themselves than the legitimacy of the theories that lay behind them. Yet even were one to grant that this was itself a reasonable way to proceed on the grounds that propositions have a life unto themselves—can therefore be dangerous and thus must be accepted or rejected as they stand—there remains the further question as to whether the propositions are an accurate report of the defendant's writings. It must be remembered that the defendant did not choose a set of self-standing propositions that he then submitted to the council for judgment. Instead, his opponents combed through his work and selectively drew phrases out of the text—and out of context—that they deemed heretical, erroneous, ill-sounding, and offensive to pious ears. And even here they could not be counted upon to provide an accurate report of the defendant's statements.

So it was that Páleč had drawn forty-two propositions from Hus's *De ecclesia* that he regarded as "false, full of errors, scandalous, rash, seditious, destructive of the peace of the church, making a wreck of ecclesiastical jurisdiction, foolish, and contrary to scripture, to the universal church and to the tradition of the fathers, and thus heretical." Hus, as one might imagine, claimed that the propositions had been extracted in a false and unfair manner. In this exchange, not only the charges, but even Hus's responses to them, are all over the map. Paul de Vooght records the exchange and offers an evenhanded analysis. Here we find that Hus sometimes offers a fuller explanation that genuinely clarifies his previous statement, sometimes merely quibbles over the precise formulation without offering a substantive correction, and at other times simply rejects a charge because it is an outright lie.[83] For instance, Páleč found fault with the following proposition: "The universal Catholic Church is precisely that of the predestined." Hus responded that he had actually said, "The Holy Catholic Church, that is to say, the universal church, is a gathering of all the predestined. This proposition is found in St Augustine's *De baptismo contra Donatistas*."[84] This does indeed look like a distinction without a difference. Yet when Páleč claims that Hus had said that "the power of a pope who does not imitate Christ should not be feared," Hus does provide a substantial correction. He notes that this proposition cannot be found in his *De ecclesia*. In fact, he points out that he had specifically contended that subordinates are bound to obey their superiors whether they be good or evil. He did say, however, that subordinates should not, out of a servile fear, assist the pope in his abuse of power. Indeed, Hus notes that the cardinals certainly did not fear the power of Pope Gregory XII before they deposed him. Rather, they resisted him precisely because he had abused his power.[85] And finally, when Páleč charged Hus with having written that he had been "received with honor at Constance by the pope and emperor," Hus responds that this is just a lie: "I had been imprisoned before the emperor arrived."[86]

Irony is a word that continuously comes to mind as one considers these episodes. And de Vooght captures the irony of this situation very well, indeed to devastating effect. It is true that Hus defined the church as the gathering of all the predestined; that he did not admit that Christ had instituted a papal primacy consisting of universal and inalienable jurisdiction; and that religious obedience extended only to a just cause. Yet Hus was only offering responses to the very same questions that the conciliarists themselves had been attempting to answer. And their own responses do not look much different from those of Hus. After all, what sort of obedience did the cardinals show to the papacy when they deposed Gregory XII and Benedict XIII and then convoked the Council of Pisa on their own authority? Where was their theory of the universal primacy and jurisdiction of the pope? For in April 1415 they went on to declare the general council superior to the pope.[87] Here again, therefore, we are struck by the deep similarities between the Hussites, or Prague Wycliffites, and their adversaries. And it was the depth of these exegetical and ecclesiological similarities that so unnerved the conciliarists. It was essential that they put some distance between themselves and those they now labeled heretics. So fearful were they that their own reform efforts would be undone by any apparent associations with radicalism, only the most decisive methods of separation could vindicate their own aspirations. De Vooght correctly observes that desperate as the council fathers were to display their rigorous orthodoxy, Hus gave them just such an opportunity. Jan Hus proved to be "the ideal heretic" for them to crush.[88]

The Hussite Utraquists

A central demand within the larger Hussite movement was the restoration of the chalice to the laity so that they too could receive communion under both kinds—hence the term "utraquism." And examination of the debate over the chalice reveals the strange turn that arguments about authority were taking in the fifteenth century. Those who proposed refusing the chalice to the laity were put in the unenviable position of defending a practice that is notably at odds with the established practice of the early church and the explicit testimony of the church fathers. Indeed, defending the refusal of the chalice to the laity is especially dangerous precisely because it implies that the church fathers had been in error and had not fully understood the injunctions of Holy Scripture. But to question the authority of the fathers in matters of biblical exegesis was all but anathema in the Middle Ages—as the English bishop Reginald Pecock would discover a few decades later.

The fathers at Constance were certainly aware that the practice of communion under both kinds had been well established in the early church. Indeed, they recognized that the New Testament itself supports it. Their decision to refuse the chalice to the laity, therefore, constitutes an extreme assertion of the authority of evolutionary custom over the primitive order of the church. The council's official statement concedes that Christ did institute and administer the Eucharist to his disciples under both species of bread and wine. Nevertheless, the custom *(consuetudo)* of communion under one kind was reasonably introduced to avoid danger and scandal. It is freely admitted that in the *ecclesia primitiva* the laity did receive under both kinds, but the custom of single reception serves a good purpose and thus will stand. It must be held as law *(pro lege)* and thus cannot be rejected or changed apart from the authority of the church. To claim that this new practice is illicit must be regarded as erroneous *(erroneum)*, and those who pertinaciously assert the opposite will be confined as heretics *(haeretici)*.[89] Hence custom that evolves under the aegis of reason and is sanctioned by the present ecclesiastical authorities will now take precedence over the practices of the early church—the very church with which the conciliarists claim to be in continuity. Whether withdrawal of the chalice does in fact constitute a legitimate development can be debated, of course, but this reversal of ancient custom also serves to highlight the manner in which "the new orthodoxy" will be enforced. Aware that lay communion cannot rise to the level of heresy, the council has nevertheless closed down all possibility of discussion. For the decree maintains that even if the objection to this statute is not itself heresy, those who do object will nonetheless be treated as heretics *(tamquam haeretici)*.

Jakoubek of Stříbro and Andrew of Brod

Although Hus himself was not an active promoter of utraquism, it was already a widely discussed topic in Prague before he departed for Constance.[90] Like any medieval theological debate, the question of utraquism centered first of all on biblical exegesis. Thus when Andrew of Brod, professor of theology at Prague, wrote against the Hussite Utraquists he attacked their reading of John 6:53–56, where Christ offered his flesh as food and his blood as drink. These words of Christ, said Andrew, cannot be read literally *(ad literam)* but instead must be interpreted in a spiritual manner *(spiritualiter)*. Indeed, says Andrew, there are many words of Christ that should be comprehended in this way: *non ad literam sed spiritualiter*.[91] Disputes over the interpretation of these specific verses aside, Andrew was generally convinced that lay communication under both species is "contrary to the will of Christ, contrary to the understanding of the entirety of Holy Scripture, and runs against the canons of the Holy Mother Roman Church." Everything about the Last Supper indicates that Christ had no intention of offering the chalice to the laity. If he really had willed that lay people receive communion under both kinds he would have invited the Virgin Mary—who is worthier than all the apostles—to the Last Supper. When Christ instructed the disciples, "Drink this all of you" (Mt 26:27) his remarks were directed to those gathered at the table, including Judas, in order to show that he gave himself not only for the good but also for the wicked. Andrew is keen to make this a closed clerical event. Christ was speaking only to the twelve apostles as he consecrated them cardinals and bishops. They, in turn, represented future generations of the priesthood who offer up the sacrifice; they did not represent the laity. If Christ had meant for the laity to have the chalice he would have given the multitudes wine along with the loaves and fishes (Mt 15:32–38).[92]

Andrew admits as he must, however, that the laity did communicate under both kinds in the *ecclesia primitiva*. Yet rather than make the case for legitimate development since those times, he instead finds fault with previous generations. Lay communion was always a mistake in need of correction. Andrew contends that some, such as Saint Cyprian, erringly communicated the laity under both kinds for reasons of simplicity and pious devotion. Only later, when the truth was revealed to the saint through Holy Scripture or a miracle, did he then put an end to this practice.[93] And the fact that lay communion under both kinds is recorded in Holy Scripture itself (1 Cor 11:17–29) is the result of pseudo-prophets having deceived the Corinthian congregation, since there was no directive from Christ that they receive the chalice. Any examples the Utraquists might point to from the primitive church, therefore, are to be dismissed as bad practice soon corrected. The Roman church, says Andrew, considered the many errors that had arisen and came to realize that in the age of the New Law the laity should receive only under the species of the bread. This decision was henceforth sanctioned and confirmed by canons, decrees, decretals, and good custom over many centuries, such that the faithful priest must observe it under pain of anathema. Much of this hinges on the unique status of the Roman church, which Andrew hails as the head of all other ecclesiastical authorities in the world. Inasmuch as she is directed by the Holy Spirit, anyone who opposes her sins against the Holy Spirit. Hence whatever the Roman church observes must be observed by all the faithful, since no member ought to sever itself from the head.[94] Rather than fight the battle over biblical exegesis as such, Andrew believes that he is on firmer ground by appealing to the church's authority, and thus her right, to impose the practices she sees fit at any given time. Yet in placing such emphasis on the present church's authority to impose these laws, Andrew thereby runs the risk of conceding the solid ground of antiquity, which possesses an authoritative status of its own. For Andrew is not simply arguing that the ecclesiastical hierarchy may impose some practice as a legitimate development designed to meet the needs of the present church; he views the withdrawal of the chalice as a corrective measure that sets right errors that had been made in earlier epochs of the church's history.

One of the leading Hussite theologians, Jakoubek of Stříbro, responded at length to Andrew of Brod. As seen above, Andrew had based much of his case on the Roman church's unique authority to establish the customs of the church in keeping with her discernment of the Lord's genuine intention. Jakoubek took issue specifically with Andrew's claim that the present custom *(consuetudo)* of withholding the chalice from the laity is no mere human commandment but rather the usage *(usus)* of the holy church, whose actions—as the Bride of Christ—are always vouchsafed by God. The issue for Jakoubek turns on the proper grounding of custom, which amounts to a solid foundation in the primitive church. "Every custom that runs contrary to the evangelical observance, which has been held since its introduction by the ancient church, is evil." For Jakoubek, withholding the chalice from the laity is just such an evil precisely because it stands opposed to "the ancient evangelical observance of the saints of the church."[95] Thus what Andrew calls *usus* is better termed *abusus,* since it lacks the sanction of the Holy Spirit. For the Spirit would never direct the Bride of Christ to maintain a practice that contradicts the evangelical observance and the institution of Christ. Indeed, this must be a contradiction, since the Holy Spirit is a Spirit of truth and by definition cannot set the church at odds with the Truth, who is none other than Christ himself. The fact is, Jakoubek notes, that Andrew cannot locate any decree of communion under one kind having been issued by the church of the saints gathered together in the name of Christ. And turning to the authoritative sources of canon law, Jakoubek finds nothing in either the *Decretum* or the *Decretales* to support this position. If it is a matter of the authority of the church—something all sides recognize—then the perennial question reappears: *Ubi ecclesia?* Thus when Andrew speaks of the church perhaps he has in mind some sort of fake church *(ecclesia simulata)* that has shut out the sons of God—those who are led by the spirit of Jesus and thus abide by ancient custom. For there is no evidence of the church of the saints *(ecclesia sanctorum)* having consented to the withdrawal of the chalice from the people.[96]

Andrew had appealed to John 16:12 ("I still have many things to say to you, but you cannot bear them now") in order to secure the church's right to institute a policy that does not have direct warrant from Christ. To which Jakoubek—taking his stand on the uniquely authoritative apostolic deposit of faith—responded that it is impossible that Christ would have withheld this wisdom from his immediate disciples only to entrust it to later generations who had never known him in person. In fact, Jakoubek contends that

Andrew does not possess "a scintilla of solid scripture or reason which would contradict the evangelical meaning of the primitive church. Instead, all of his deductions are sophistical and unintelligible."[97] Jakoubek finds that none of Andrew's arguments can hold up under the weight of the *ecclesia primitiva sanctorum*, filled as this church was with the Holy Spirit when she administered the Eucharist under both kinds to the people. By word and deed, says Jakoubek, the primitive church understood that the Gospel texts themselves intended that the people receive the chalice.[98] The primitive church sets the standard, therefore; the present church has no authority to alter ancient practice. This is based not only upon the evangelical foundation of utraquism itself but also on the fact that modern popes, cardinals, and bishops are clearly liable to sin and error—the prevalence of simony being a prime example. Hence the appeal to the *ecclesia primitiva* constitutes a rebuttal of the *ecclesia Romana*, which can err in both word and deed, can both deceive and be deceived.[99] Adopting a rather traditional view, therefore, Jakoubek resolves not only that the primitive church is the best interpreter of scripture, but all legitimate development will have to be apostolic in origin.

The most effective card the Utraquists have to play is that of continuity. They believe that the true church must be in perfect continuity with the apostolic church and that such continuity is best exemplified in eucharistic practice. On the other hand, of course, it can be objected that genuine continuity is manifested in apostolic succession, which thereby secures the authority of the bishops to establish doctrine and discipline. Andrew of Brod will argue for the latter as he charges that the Utraquists stand guilty under the words of the fathers, as recorded in the *Decretum*, which affirm that those who act against established custom must be coerced. As one might expect, Jakoubek rejects such an invocation of custom precisely because it is the Utraquists who are "observing the law of Christ and thereby following the example of the primitive Church."[100] Far from acting against the established custom of the church, therefore, the Utraquists are upholding it against those who would contradict both the gospel and the apostolic tradition.[101] It is the withdrawal of the chalice that constitutes a tradition harmful to faith, charity, devotion, and salvation, since it is clearly beneficial for the laity to receive it.[102] Here, then, one comes back to the centuries-old principle that development is legitimate only if it does not disrupt the fundamental *status ecclesiae*.

Along with the practice of the primitive church, Jakoubek places a great deal of emphasis on the precise words of Christ at the Last Supper— the words that the primitive church honored and the present church is forsaking. He notes that when Christ offered the bread to his disciples he specifically told them to eat, just as the chalice was offered for the purpose of drinking. Christ in his infinite wisdom instituted this spiritual and sacramental way of drinking his blood under the species of the wine for the great benefit of souls. And it is because Christ instituted the sacrament in just this way that those who receive the bread alone do not drink Christ's blood in a sacramental manner. Jakoubek certainly realizes that Christ is never without his own blood. Yet he insists that this does not mean the reception of the bread is thereby tantamount to reception of the blood as spiritual drink. Christ promised his body as food only to those who came to the species of the bread, and his blood as drink to those who received the cup. Simply because the whole living Christ is present in the species of the bread does not mean that his blood is also there in a sacramental manner. Hence the body is only received spiritually and sacramentally in the species of the bread, and the blood spiritually and sacramentally in the chalice. In fact, were this not the case, Christ's dual form of institution would seem superfluous.[103] Any appeal to scholastic theories of concomitance to bolster the notion that the laity receive the blood under the species of the bread is brushed aside as irrelevant to the main issue at hand. This is itself a lesson in the weighing of authoritative sources. Modern theologians may indeed command respect, but they really offer no more than opinions that one is under no obligation to follow. In this instance, therefore, Jakoubek—adopting the conventional understanding of relative authority—contends that one is perfectly free to reject the opinions of the *moderni scholastici* such as Aquinas, Bonaventure, and Lyra if they have contradicted the Law of God. Better in such instances to adhere to the saints of the *ecclesia primitiva* who possessed the spiritual gifts in greater abundance.[104]

Jakoubek looked back even beyond the primitive church to the words of Christ himself. It is Jesus Christ who had personally instituted this practice *(per se ipsum personaliter)* and then through his own primitive church had commanded what was to be done then and in future generations. Communion under both kinds is not merely one more custom of the primitive church that the later church might feel free to change. It is a direct precept of Christ for every Christian. This is made clear in the Gospels, the

Epistles, and throughout the whole ancient church *(ex evangelio, et epistola, et per totam antiquam ecclesiam)*.¹⁰⁵ Christ willed communion under both kinds for every Christian precisely because this is the best way for the people to be united sweetly and intimately to their Lord. It is by eating and drinking that they abide in Christ and he in them (Jn 6:56).¹⁰⁶ As far as Jakoubek is concerned, therefore, this is a matter of salvation that is grounded upon the sure foundation of the Lord's promise rather than shaky human opinions about sacramental concomitance. Better to build upon the divine covenant, therefore, and receive body under bread and blood under wine as Christ offered them.¹⁰⁷

This direct appeal to the unique and surpassing personal authority of Christ and his promise is echoed by Nicholas of Dresden, who argued that one may never enact a custom that runs contrary to the Truth—Christ himself. Christ is the *Veritas* and he has instituted communion under both kinds: the Truth is immutable. The Truth cannot be dismissed in favor of contrary custom. A legion of doctors, Nicholas insists, cannot undo Christ the Truth, since in all matters his word is infallible.¹⁰⁸ Quite simply put: *Quod enim Dominus jubet, servus bonus non mutat.*¹⁰⁹ This means, in turn, that any of the so-called reasonable customs that Constance claims the right to institute will have to prove themselves consonant with Holy Scripture, which is itself the repository of Christ's own words.¹¹⁰ And similar to Jakoubek, Nicholas also refused to concede that the bread is transubstantiated into the blood of Christ. Rather, bread is transubstantiated into body alone and wine into blood alone.¹¹¹

Anti-Hussite Reflections on Development

Some opponents of the Utraquists were willing to disparage the practices of the primitive church in order to establish the obligatory nature of current laws. The author of an anonymous anti-Hussite work came to the defense of the modern church and the legitimacy of its current practices along similar lines. He had no desire to romanticize the primitive church. In fact, he would have to strip the *ecclesia primitiva* of her veneer of perfection in order to undercut the surpassing authority accorded her by the Utraquists. His point is unequivocal: things are a lot better now than they used to be! First of all, the author defines the *ecclesia primitiva* as pertaining to the rites and customs observed by the community of the faithful from the time of the apostles until the papacy of Sylvester (hence until the Donation of Constantine). The *ecclesia moderna*, on the other hand, refers to the rites and customs of the church from Sylvester's time into the present day. Now the fact is, says this author, that things were done in a much simpler and cruder way in the primitive church than in the modern. That Saint Paul's First Epistle to the Corinthians records the primitive church communicating under both kinds has no hold over modern practice. The modern church improves things as she goes—streamlining some things and completing others. "In the modern church all things are reduced to a better form *(ad meliorem formam)*, to one species," this author writes. "There are many things that the apostles and their followers omitted which the modern church has since fulfilled."[112]

The author then addresses Jakoubek's specific claim that the *ecclesia moderna* must follow the customs of the *ecclesia primitiva* on the grounds that the primitive church was in a better moral state than the modern one. The primitive period, the Hussites insist, was a superior time given its holiness of life, miracles, and saints. His response to this generally held principle was, however, quite blunt: no greater good should be reduced to the lesser. And the modern church is the greater good in matters of governance and ecclesiastical dispensation regarding matters of faith. Indeed, the *ecclesia moderna* does all things in a more dignified and laudable manner than the *ecclesia primitiva* had done. What is more, it would not only be unjust to reduce the modern to the primitive; it would also be impossible. Antiquity must not be the sole criterion; the church preserves many things that have not been handed down from the apostles even as they are approved by long-held custom; communion under one kind is a prime example. The fact that miracles were more frequent in the primitive church does not prove that her ways were superior. As it happens, people in the modern church are more firmly rooted in the faith and thus are no longer in need of convincing miracles. As for the presence of simony and avarice, they do not prove the inferiority of the modern church as such, since these remain the crimes of individual men and cannot be imputed to the church as a whole.[113] This author makes no apologies for setting aside ancient ways. The church was within her rights to change this practice when she saw that it was not so beneficial for the laity; it was the reasonable thing to do. Yet having made this argument for legitimate alteration of earlier practices, the author returns to the most primitive source of all: the Last Supper. The change, he insists, was not contrary to the constitution of Christ. Like Andrew of Brod, he asserts that Christ had instituted communion under both kinds solely for the priest to offer at the altar for the sins of the world. He then left lay communication to be arranged by the church as ecclesiastics saw fit. Hence it is ultimately the authority of Christ himself that supports the church's current practice.[114] Here, then, the matter comes around again to biblical exegesis and the need to discern the intended sense of the Divine Author who in this case speaks directly to the church as represented by the apostles. Yet it would appear that the early church had misunderstood what Christ had intended if indeed the chalice was never meant for the laity.

Also writing against Jakoubek, Maurice of Prague employed a standard argument against opponents of a given church practice: if you are right, then the church has been wrong for all these years, and many are thereby damned. If Jakoubek is correct and communion under both kinds was commanded by Christ, then the laity themselves stand condemned for neglecting this command. If the command really is stated explicitly in scripture as the Utraquists claim *(explicite sit in sacra scriptura positum)*, then there is no excuse for not communicating in this way. If it is a precept of Christ, and thus *lex divina*, the laity are not excused. Nor are they excused even if their prelates taught them to receive under only one kind. Maurice notes as an example that if a prelate teaches people that Christ is not divine, and they believe this, they would actually be guilty of a grave sin, since ignorance of divine law is no excuse. Of course, all the priests would also stand condemned since they failed in their care of souls. Hence the entire lay and clerical population would be damned. Defining heresy in classic fashion as an assertion contrary to some truth that is asserted in Holy Scripture, Maurice finds that all the adult clergy and laity for the longest time would have erred in the faith and have maintained heresy. For they have apparently held and believed an assertion contrary to the divine law and the precept of Christ. And yet this would run contrary to the Creed, since the church could not be "one" if not united in a common faith. And she could not be "holy" if all the adults were tainted by heresy. Such a heresy, Maurice concludes, could never have been introduced into the universal church, since it would then have been believed by all. Maurice will take his stand on the classic theory that the whole church cannot lapse into apostasy at any given time. There will always be some people, he says, who oppose heresy. By this reasoning, then, communion under one kind cannot be an error since it has been believed by all people for such a long time. With recourse to Christ's promise that the gates of hell would not prevail against the church (Mt 16:19), Maurice is sure that the Lord would never have allowed his entire church to lapse into heresy for so many centuries.[115]

Finally, in an ironic twist, Maurice accuses the Hussites of creating an article of faith where none exists. In fact, he bases his argument on the sufficiency of scripture for the determination of salvific truth. The Hussites, says Maurice, have made communion under both kinds a matter of divine law—a precept of Christ and a truth of scripture. By treating this as a Catholic truth necessary for salvation, however, they are guilty of adding material to Holy Scripture (Rv 22:18).[116] In other words, it is the Hussites who are expanding the scope of heresy and orthodoxy by insisting on doctrines that are not grounded in scripture. They seem to be doing the very thing that they abhor the most! The result of all this is that the Hussites are leading the people astray by teaching them to transgress a laudable and approved custom of the universal church. They condemn Holy Mother Church as she is represented by the general council, choosing their own will and attempting to alter sacred custom.[117] This is a very clever line of attack. Maurice attempts to bring the Utraquists to heel precisely by lessening the importance of the chalice itself and thereby making this a debate over ecclesiastical discipline rather than theological dogma. Recall that the council did not raise this to a matter of dogmatic status; that is why rejection of the decree could not actually be considered a heresy. The error rested in the refusal to recognize the church's right to determine good practice. According to Maurice, therefore, all the trouble can be traced to the Utraquist insistence on generating what amounts to a false theological debate.

The debate over the chalice points to one of the greater ironies in the larger discussion of authority. For in this instance opponents of the chalice were placed in the position of having to defend a practice that they themselves admitted had only the most tenuous grounding in the ancient tradition. Indeed, the fathers at Constance acknowledged that the laity had received the chalice for centuries. Hence the anti-Utraquists are forced, not merely to wrangle over biblical passages with little patristic support, but even to denigrate the practice of previous generations. This is the most interesting turn of events, for it had always been "the orthodox" who called out "the heretics" for having forsaken the path trod since apostolic times.

Now it seems that the heretics are more traditional than the orthodox. At any rate, this remains a battle over correct exegesis: what did Christ intend by his words, and are they subject to reinterpretation? The Hussites contend that Christ's intention is both clear and fixed; he had one meaning all along that is not subject to revision. Anti-Utraquists are likewise seeking the intended sense of Christ's words but find in them a certain degree of flexibility—a flexibility that Christ himself would have foreseen and thus approved. Where, then, will one locate the final authoritative determination on Jesus Christ's intended meaning? For conciliarists such as Jean Gerson, the general council will, under the guidance of the Holy Spirit, render this infallible determination. It is to Gerson and the conciliarists, therefore, that we turn in the next chapter.

Chapter 6

Approaching Final Authority

Gerson and the Conciliarists

As noted in the previous chapter, an ardent desire for the reform of the church in head and members was not confined to Hussites and Wycliffites. Indeed, leaders of the conciliarist movement, such as Pierre d'Ailly and Jean Gerson, sought to enact sweeping changes within the late medieval church. Of special concern here, then, is how those who were simultaneously reformers and anti-Wycliffites envisioned the role of Holy Scripture in the determination of authority. What should become clear throughout is that Jan Hus was consigned to the flames at Constance despite the fact that he held views regarding scripture, ecclesiastical tradition, and the papacy that ran very close to conciliarists themselves. One finds that some modern scholars, who certainly understand the thought of d'Ailly and Gerson very well, do not seem to recognize the proximity of the conciliarists and their opponents. For example, Louis Pascoe concludes that for Gerson the primitive church proved to be the most authoritative exegetical standard.[1] And Mark Burrows contends that, at Constance, Gerson increasingly relied upon the tradition of the early church. Biblical texts must be read in the context of the tradition, thus preserving the "traditioned sense," as Burrows calls it.[2] This is all true, but these scholars fail to mention that the Wycliffites and Hussites were doing the very same thing. Thus even as it was convenient for Gerson to portray his enemies as proponents of a radical *sola scriptura* policy it was a massive distortion—one that we should not permit to cloud our own assessment of the issues. These were magisterial disputes in which all sides appealed not only to Holy Scripture but also to patristic testimony and canon law in order to make their case for universally sought-after reform of the church. Again, therefore, it must be stressed that it was precisely because these masters had so much in common by virtue of their extensive training that the disputes were so fractious—especially fractious because seemingly irresolvable (unless by brute force).

To get an immediate sense of some similarities with regard to the crucial matter of papal authority, let us look briefly at a few statements issued by the council and other orthodox proponents of ecclesiastical reform. The decree *Haec sancta*, issued at the Council of Constance in 1415, declared that a general council, gathered in the Holy Spirit, receives its authority directly from Christ. All people of any rank, indeed even the papacy itself, are bound to obey it in matters of faith.[3] The council also decreed that a newly elected pope must make a public confession "to maintain the Catholic faith according to traditions of the apostles *(traditiones apostolorum)*, of the general councils, and of the other holy fathers, chiefly those of the eight universal councils. . . . And [that he] will preserve the faith unchanged *(immutilatam)* to the last dot, and will confirm, defend and preach it to the point of death."[4] Not only was the pope bound under the authority of tradition in matters of doctrine, but he was obligated to lead a morally upright life befitting the successor of the chief apostle. Hence the council had seen fit to depose Pope John XXIII not only for the crime of simony but also because "he has notoriously scandalized God's church and the Christian people by his detestable and dishonest life and morals."[5] Thus Jean Gerson—in keeping with his belief in the infallible judgment of the council—had stated quite plainly that a general council can depose a sitting pope for any notorious crime that brings scandal upon the church.[6] Such emphasis placed by the conciliarists on the moral conduct of the pope—even to the point of being grounds for deposition—must be borne in mind when assessing their criticism of the Wycliffite agenda. The call for papal sanctity could not in itself be a sign of dangerous radicalism given what Gerson and the council had formally decreed.

The determinations at Constance were positively mild in comparison to the work of the conciliarist Dietrich of Niem. His orthodoxy never in question, Dietrich espoused views regarding the papacy and its authority within the church that are basically identical to those of Hus and Wyclif. A brief examination of one of his central works should demonstrate the fundamental agreement on matters of ecclesiastical authority that continued to exist between the so-called heretical and orthodox camps. Dietrich contended that the true church, which knows one origin and watches over the sanctity of her dwelling place, is the one that—in imitation of Christ—despises temporal things and preserves the original faith of the primitive church.[7] Here again we find the perennial appeal to the normative influence of the *ecclesia primitiva,* which proved every bit as dear to the Wycliffites and Hussites. This is the *ecclesia Christi,* says Dietrich, the congregation of spiritual people.[8]

Dietrich then goes on to draw a distinction between the universal Catholic Church and the apostolic church. The former gathers her members from all quarters: from Greeks and Latins, men and women, noble and peasant, rich and poor, all of whom are believers in Christ. For Christ is the sole head of this body that is the universal church. And that means that the pope cannot be head of this church but only the vicar of Christ here on earth—and then only on the condition that he does not err in his use of the keys. In fact, the pope appears to be a dispensable figure, since it is in the universal church that man will find salvation even were there no pope to be found in the world, precisely because this church is founded solely upon the faith of Christ. As for the apostolic church, it is just one particular church included within the universal Catholic Church. This means, in turn, that the pope is merely the head of the Roman church, which can indeed fall into heresy and schism. No doubt, then, the Roman church is ultimately inferior to the universal church. Dietrich's claims regarding papal authority relative to the church bear a striking resemblance to Wyclif's limitation of the papacy to headship of the Roman church.[9]

Dietrich does allow for the papacy as an institution, but he holds popes to a very strict standard of moral and spiritual conduct. He sounds a lot like Wyclif and Hus who had contended that the pope must govern the church according to the law of Christ if he is to be considered Christ's vicar on earth. For Dietrich will insist that Christ did not bestow such exalted power upon the papacy irrespective of the man who holds the office. Christ conceded no such dignity eternally but rather only to those who love him with a whole heart. Even Saint Peter—to whom the papacy was principally given—would not have received the commission to feed the sheep had he not repented of his mortal sin in denying Christ. The fact is, says Dietrich, that the pope is just a man, dust from dust, a sinner who is still capable of sin. If he does sin he must show true contrition and confess. The pope is no angel, Dietrich reminds us, nor is he is a saint. Nor does Dietrich acknowledge the distinction whereby the pope could err as a man but not as pope. Even the pope as pope is still a man, Dietrich insists, and thus can sin precisely because he is a man. The authority of his office does not preserve him from sin, since authority is conveyed to the good and evil alike. When he ascends to his office the pope receives a dignity, but dignity does not bring with it the sanctifying effects of the Holy Spirit. Only the grace and love of God can induce that, not mere authority. The papal see does not make a man holy, therefore, since the place does not sanctify the man but rather the man the place. All of this, then, is virtually identical to Wyclif's earlier refusal to equate the papacy with the Holy Catholic Church when he insisted that only the latter is immune from error even as the pope remains a fallible human being.[10]

Speaking in ways that any Wycliffite might approve, Dietrich reckons it nothing short of ridiculous to say that one mortal man, if he be a fornicator, a simoniac, or a liar, could claim for himself the power to bind and loose sins on earth and in heaven. Nor can human judgment presume that such a man is holy when his evil works testify to the contrary. Genuine ecclesiastical authority remains integrally connected to sound morals. This means that even a man who has been canonically elected must not be tolerated if he scandalizes the church with his wicked deeds. Instead, he should be treated as a putrid member infecting the whole body and thus cast down from his high post.[11] Along these lines, Dietrich contends that the pope can be deposed for an evil way of life, public scandal, heresy, and any mortal sin whatsoever by which he scandalizes the universal church, such as public fornication and simony.[12]

Dietrich pins the bulk of his argument on the aforementioned distinction between the universal and the apostolic church. In the case of two or three men contending for the papacy (as was the case) Dietrich contends that it is not a mark of the universal church, or an article of faith, to believe that any given man is the pope. In point of fact, the Apostles' Creed does even not stipulate belief in the papacy. The faith of the universal church centers on Christ. It is not located in the pope who, as any other man, can fall away from the faith. Belief in the church, for Dietrich, means belief in the universal church—the church of Christ, not the pope. There are evil men within the apostolic church, he warns, who are not members of the universal Catholic Church, which is itself the communion of saints *(communio sanctorum)*. Actually, Dietrich is quite certain that someone existing in a state of mortal sin is neither in nor of the universal Catholic Church, which is founded upon charity.[13]

In light of all this, Dietrich not surprisingly claims that the general council is superior to the pope in authority, dignity, and office. The council can limit the power of the pope since it represents the universal church; it is the council that has been granted the keys of binding and loosing. The council can abolish papal rights, and from this council there can be no appeal. The council can elect the pope and depose him. It can establish new laws and nullify old ones. Its constitutions and statutes are immutable and indispensable for anyone inferior to it. And this means that the pope cannot dispense against the council, or change, or otherwise interpret the council's decisions. These decisions must be treated as the very gospel of Christ over which the pope has no jurisdiction.[14] It is the general council, therefore, that will form the locus of final authority in the church.

Calls for the reform of the papacy were not confined to the Continent, as we see in the words of the English theologian Richard Ullerston. It should also be noted that Ullerston had, in 1401, publicly defended the idea of translating the Bible into the vernacular. A few years later, in 1408, he drew up the *Petitiones* for the English delegation at the Council of Pisa, a document that sought to curtail papal power and attack abuses of papal prerogatives.[15] His statements give us a glimpse into what a solidly orthodox English theologian had to say about the papacy at the opening of the fifteenth century. Article 3 of the *Petitiones* states that the pope must promote the law of Christ *(lex Christi)* above every other law. Indeed, failure to do so would prove that he is not the true Vicar of Christ *(verus Christi vicarius)*. For Christ did not raise Peter to this position of authority in the church so that he might then institute some other law above the gospel. Nothing, Richard insists, may diminish the honor and authority of the Gospels. In fact, it is precisely because the law of Christ surpasses all others that the Vicar of Christ should be chiefly expert in it. Richard can only lament that in these days human laws have now overtaken the Gospels, which carry no more weight than the verses of Cato and the proverbs of Seneca. The only exception apparently are Christ's words to Peter and his successors—"Whatever you bind and loose . . . " (Mt 16:19)—which are now cited at the expense of the law of Christ.[16] If one did not know otherwise, there would be every reason to believe that these words had been written by another English theologian, John Wyclif, who also had lamented the forsaking of Christ's law amid of a sea of papal rescripts.

Pierre d'Ailly: The Role of the Theologian

Pierre d'Ailly (d. 1420) had been the chancellor of the University of Paris in 1389 and served as a mentor for his younger contemporary Jean Gerson. With regard to his larger theological vision, Louis Pascoe places d'Ailly within the tradition of Robert Grosseteste and Saint Bonaventure in equating theology with Christ as he is revealed in Holy Scripture. Theology does not proceed from human reason, according to d'Ailly, but from the truths that are divinely revealed in scripture. As the theologian has no evident knowledge of these truths, however, he must receive them on faith. It is along these lines, therefore, that d'Ailly rejected the Thomist attempt to establish theology as a subaltern science.[17] If the masters at Oxford and Prague saw themselves as members of a long and distinguished line of theological experts whose duty it was to test the orthodoxy of ecclesiastical legislation, so did their adversaries in Paris. To advise, and even to correct, their superiors was a sacred task that all these masters championed. For his part, Pierre d'Ailly certainly had a very high view of the university theologian. This was especially pertinent in a time of crisis such as the papal schism. D'Ailly emphasized the role of theologians in the general council: the *sacrae theologiae doctores* who have the authority to preach and teach throughout the whole earth—*autoritas praedicandi aut docendi ubique terrarum*. They surely have more authority, d'Ailly believed, than some ignorant bishop or abbot. The right to represent the church, therefore, falls chiefly to those who have the requisite wisdom.[18] In other words, genuine authority could not be exercised apart from deep knowledge of scripture and the tradition of the church. D'Ailly did retain respect for the institution of the papacy and recognized that the pope has supreme jurisdiction in matters of faith. Yet he still maintained that theologians were entitled by their office to examine questions pertaining to the faith even as their authority is ultimately subject to the papacy. It cannot be for the pope alone to decide such matters, however; canon law provides for an appeal from the pope to a council.[19]

In fact, d'Ailly had argued that the teaching office of the theologian amounted to something akin to an ordination, which entitled the university theologian to take his place in the ecclesiastical hierarchy. In terms reminiscent of Ockham, he argued that because the theologian's office was concerned with Holy Scripture—which is itself synonymous with theology—it was for the theologian to judge matters of heresy and orthodoxy. This is because the assertion of Catholic truth based upon scripture implies the condemnation of its opposite. And, in keeping with Ephesians 4:11, "some apostles... some teachers," d'Ailly located a teaching office even within the apostolic church: not only bishops, but theologians too, were successors of the apostles. In this vein d'Ailly argued that no judicial decision is authentic unless preceded by a scholastic definition rendered by theologians. The license to teach *(licentia docendi)* gave the theologian the right and duty to render determinations of orthodoxy and heresy, even as d'Ailly acknowledged that only the bishop has the judicial power to enforce the judgment.[20]

With a high view of theologians, whose entire discipline revolved around Holy Scripture, d'Ailly naturally could be quite critical of the canon lawyers. He did find some good in them, however. He believed that some were honorable practitioners of their discipline—those who sought justice for the poor and defended the church against her enemies. But others he found to be self-serving and divisive. In fact, he felt that they were largely to blame for the ongoing papal schism because they rejected the solutions put forward by the theologians on the grounds that they could not be squared with canonical legislation.[21] In a sermon delivered at the Council of Constance, d'Ailly warned against extolling human laws over the divine law in matters of faith. In words echoing Wyclif some forty years earlier, d'Ailly argued that human laws should always be subject to the divine in such cases. Human traditions, therefore, must never be preferred to divine commandments. Each science has its own style *(stilus)*, its own procedural method *(modus procendi)* suitable to its endeavor. Thus the *stilus theologicus* ought to be employed in cases of faith, rather than the *stilus juridicus*. And, because the science of canon law is a subaltern science that must be subjected to the science of theology, so too must the *stilus juridicus* be subordinated to the *stilus theologicus* in matters of faith. D'Ailly believed this to be in keeping with the great general councils in which the fathers proceeded theologically, not legalistically, when defining matters of faith. At Constance, therefore, the statements of the theologians should be allowed to shine forth as the light of faith upon the lamp stand and not be hidden under a bushel (see Mt 5:15).[22]

D'Ailly again extolled the theologians in a work that addressed the question as to whether someone could rule justly even if not learned in divine law. Some say that erudition in human law is enough, evinced by the fact that the papacy promotes more lawyers than theologians to high ecclesiastical office.[23] D'Ailly responds to this assertion by quoting Christ's words, "Every scribe who has been trained for the kingdom of heaven [i.e., the church militant] is like the master of a household who brings out of his treasure what is new and what is old" (Mt 13:52). This, says d'Ailly, refers to the treasure of wisdom that is nothing other than the documents of the Old and New Testaments. Hence the one who rules in the kingdom of the church should be well schooled in both testaments, which means that he will rule justly only by way of divine law.[24] For d'Ailly, the authority of the theologian is directly tied to the authority of scripture. Divine law and Holy Scripture are for all intents and purposes synonymous. The prelate who is ignorant of scripture, and thus divine law, will thereby sin in his governance. All of which is to say that the prelate ought to know Holy Scripture since his principal duty is to teach and preach this sacred text.[25]

D'Ailly laments, however, that many in his own day believe that training in civil and canon law is more useful to the prelate than instruction in Holy Scripture. In defense of this position they cite the famous remarks of Hostiensis who had hailed canon law as the *scientia scientiarum* designed for the governance of both the temporal and spiritual spheres. They note too his contention that the composite science is worthier than the simple, thereby exalting canon law over theology.[26] Prelates, they say, should employ the more useful science.[27] And, according to the canonist Guido de Baysio, the science of law is older and thus worthier. For law has been imposed from the inception of the human race, beginning with Adam and Eve and continuing with Moses.[28]

In response to these arguments d'Ailly notes, first of all, that "theology is the most perfect and stable wisdom, whereas human law is imperfect, fluid and unstable. Hence a prelate who neglects the wisdom of theology ought not adhere to human law."[29] Indeed, theology is the truest and most concordant science to which nothing may be added or subtracted, whereas the science of law is forever in flux.[30] Here d'Ailly is appealing to the principle of authoritative texts: theologians read scripture, which is perfect, whereas canonist read the law books, which are constantly being revised. It comes as no surprise, therefore, that d'Ailly is incensed by Hostiensis's statement about law being the "science of sciences" and reckons it not only false, but even heretical, to place canon law ahead of theology. For although human constitutions are useful in many respects, the fact is that prior to the existence of human law God had already bestowed divine laws. In tones reminiscent of Wyclif who had anchored all law in the Person of Christ as revealed in Scripture, d'Ailly notes here that prior to the creation of the decretals there already existed the most complete laws of justice. The laws of Moses and Christ found within the Old and New Testaments constitute the wisdom and infinite justice of Almighty God, established for the perfect governance of the universe. Indeed, Christ himself is the consummation of the law (Rom 10:4).[31] Of course, all of this is biblical and thus the province of the theologian rather than the lawyer.

Addressing the related question as to whether the church of Peter ought to be governed by law, d'Ailly immediately focuses on Christ. The law of Christ *(lex Christi)* is the entire gospel teaching. By the term "gospel," d'Ailly tells us, he is including not only the teaching of the Four Gospels but the New Testament generally, that is, the gospel proclamation as Saint Paul understands it (2 Tm 1:11). This law of Christ—which d'Ailly believes to be synonymous with the gospel—can actually be understood in many ways. In fact, as d'Ailly describes this law, it bears some resemblance to Wyclif's multilayered scripture. For d'Ailly contends that in one sense this law pertains to the truth of the teaching whether in the mind, writing, or voice. Or it can refer to the truth as an object of intellectual cognition. Hence the very knowledge of what one must do or refrain from doing is no less properly called law or precept or prohibition, since the truth itself enunciates what is to be done or not done. Finally, the law of Christ may be called infused faith, or the act by which a rational creature firmly assents to the truths of the Christian faith.[32] Actually, the law need not even take exterior form. The virtue of justice subsists in the mind—not in writing or voice—but it is still the law, or rule, of a just life. For even when no written or vocal version of the law exists there is still law itself.[33] The audible voice and the legible document are really only law in an equivocal sense. They are referred to as law by way of a figure of speech, or a trope, by which the truth of the thing itself is imposed upon the image. Thus when the jurists define law, says d'Ailly, they do so according to its less proper meaning, namely, as a written document.[34]

In his *Recommendatio Sacrae Scripturae*, d'Ailly examined the relationship between scripture and the church. He chose as his theme Matthew 16:18 and immediately appeals to Augustine's *De civitate Dei*, where, says d'Ailly, the two cities signify the two churches: that of God and the devil — the former comprising the good and the latter the evil. The first is founded upon the rock for all eternity, whereas the latter is founded upon sand. D'Ailly contends that the rock in Matthew 16:18 is none other than Christ himself, such that his church rests upon the firmest possible foundation. Indeed, it was upon the rock of Christ that Peter himself was then solidly grounded. This, says d'Ailly, is the literal sense of the text *(secundum literalem sensum)*. Yet according to the spiritual meaning *(spiritualem intellectum)*, the rock is the Divine Scripture and the sacred teaching of Christ, itself so solid as to merit Christ founding his church upon it. Nothing could be so firm as the sacred sayings, the divine testimonies. However many sayings of Christ there are, however many testimonies of Christian teaching, there are that many foundations of the Christian church. Sacred Scripture, therefore, is founded eternally upon the testimonies of Christ and in that way comes to serve as the rock upon which the church is built. Wisdom builds a house for herself (Prv 9:1), which is none other than the Catholic Church built upon the truths of Holy Scripture. If scripture is the foundation, then the windows are the speculative men: the preachers and doctors through whom the sun's rays of truth spread light and dispel blind ignorance. The columns are the active men: the pastors and leaders through whom the edifice of Christ is sustained. Nevertheless, as it was for Wyclif and Hus, so also for d'Ailly, scripture itself still forms the entire foundation upon which the house is built. All throughout history as heresies, torments, and temptations have besieged the church the Catholic doctors have always fought victoriously by relying upon the faith of Holy Scripture. Even in the darkest days, therefore, the church will never ultimately capitulate to heresy and schism, secure in the promise of Matthew 16:18 that the gates of hell will not prevail. Indeed, there have been times when the church may have existed only in Abel, Enoch, or Abraham, but the city of God will always be defended by the words of divine eloquence. For d'Ailly, Holy Scripture is the inexorable bond that holds together Christ and his church, exemplified most patently by his determination that the rock *(petra)* is at once Christ and scripture.[35]

As d'Ailly continues his analysis of the church, he argues that the church militant can be understood in two ways. On the one hand, there is the universal church, which is unique, and outside of which there is no salvation: Christ is the head of this church which is his body (Col 1:18). On the other hand, one can think of the particular church of which there are many, as in Paul's words, "all the churches greet you" (Rom 16:16). As for the universal church, this is sometimes taken for all the faithful who are currently alive. In its broadest sense, however, the church can refer to all the faithful from the beginning of the world until the end of the age. Speaking of the church in broad terms, d'Ailly echoes Wyclif rather than Netter when he says that she comprises not only the church of Christ but also the synagogue of Moses and those who lived in the time of natural law. This is the classic Augustinian *ecclesia ab Abel*. In a more specific sense, though, the church is the congregation of all the faithful from the time of Christ and the apostles until the present day, thereby distinguishing her from the synagogue. Likely under the influence of Ockham, d'Ailly claims that this is what Augustine had in mind when he said that he would not have believed the Gospel unless the authority of the church had moved him. Taken in this way, the church is of greater authority than the Gospel, inasmuch as the Gospel writers existed as parts within the whole church.[36] D'Ailly insists, however, that Augustine was not speaking of the Roman church here but the universal church. Indeed, it would be absurd to say that the authority of any particular church ought to be believed more than the Gospel. Rather, Augustine was thinking of the church that succeeded from the time of Peter to his own day, thereby comprising all the apostles, Gospel writers, and saints through whom the Gospel is received into the church and the teaching of Christ proclaimed.[37] Nor does scripture ever speak of the church as simply comprising the congregation of clerics, even as the clergy misappropriate the name church *(ecclesia)* when calling themselves ecclesiastics.[38]

Wyclif would surely have endorsed much of what d'Ailly had to say about Holy Scripture, the role of the theologian, and the universal church. But Wyclif's emphasis on the church of the predestined did not figure into d'Ailly's reform program. D'Ailly writes that the church militant can properly be taken as the universal church described thus: "The Church is every faithful man, or all faithful men, naturally living in mortal body."

The faithful are those who, by act or habit, believe either implicitly or explicitly, or know enigmatically, all Catholic truths. And, again like Ockham, d'Ailly contends that the church could abide in just one person alone, as when the church was in Abel, or at the time of the Passion when the whole church, and the whole faith of the church, remained solely in the Virgin Mary.[39] Thus one can be confident that the universal church—even if not every single part of it—is never deformed by error but instead is always conformed to the law of Christ through a living faith that has been formed by hope and charity.[40] The similarities between d'Ailly and Wyclif (as well as Hus) are striking: asserting the principal authority of theology over canon law, demanding that human laws and traditions be grounded in divine law, and privileging the universal church over the Roman. Such proximity between conciliarist and heretic is perhaps even more evident as we turn to Gerson.

Jean Gerson: Theologians, Canonists, and Biblical Exegesis

Jean Gerson no less than his teacher Pierre d'Ailly believed that the theologian occupied a special place of authority in the church, one that surpassed that of the canon lawyer. He too adopted the position that it was for theologians to decide what constitutes Catholic truth and heresy, while jurists merely decide what penalty applies in each case.[41] Gerson rehearsed arguments that point out the uselessness of canon law. It creates all manner of trouble and disrupts the peace of the church. Canon law is really superfluous anyway since care for one's neighbor and the worship of God are dealt with sufficiently in other faculties. Indeed, the principle of justice is expressed in human laws that are grounded in moral philosophy and known to natural reason. Thus between evangelical law and civil law it would seem that everything has been covered. Having said that, however, Gerson does find a place for canon law within the life of the church. For he believed that when correctly implemented it could be an expression of the divine will. Nonetheless, canon law will always remain subervient to theology by the very nature of things.[42]

Canon law does serve a purpose in a fallen world. For although it is true that there would have been no canon law in the state of unfallen nature—since the law would have been sufficiently inscribed on the human heart—

the canons were later multiplied to keep up with human transgressions. Lawyers are now needed, therefore, in order to institute penalties against the incorrigible. It is in this way that they help to shoulder the burden of governing the church since the theologians cannot do it all: they are busy explaining and defending divine, or evangelical, law. In this vein, Gerson notes that there are four sorts of things that pertain to divine (evangelical) law. First, there are those things that are expressly *(expresse)* contained in the text of the canonical scripture, such as the fact that God created the heavens and earth. The second category comprises those things that clearly *(clare)* follow by way of a necessary and evident conclusion for all who use reason to examine the contents of scripture. The third pertains to the things that, although they do not follow by way of an evident consequence apparent to human reason, are nonetheless judged the best consequence by those who are well trained in the sacred scriptures. Fourth, there are matters that are certain by way of a revelation made to the church. Such things might be made known expressly through prophets or miraculous attestations. They may also be revealed implicitly through the common attestation of the whole church or a general council, as well as through some legitimate succession. Gerson gives no example of this sort of truth, however, and we see that it is principally scriptural truth that concerns him.[43] Beyond these four sorts of truth there are many matters in need of further explication that cannot be expressly deduced from scripture. Such matters are not necessary for salvation, but they are still needed for the proper governance of the church; this is where the lawyers come in. Sacramental confession serves as a good example. The sacrament was established by divine law, to be sure, but questions of time and circumstance belong to the sphere of positive law since these things do not follow clearly from evangelical law.[44]

Canon law may be useful, therefore, but it will always remain inferior to both divine and natural law, since it depends upon human tradition more than pure revelation or natural evidence.[45] Gerson actually remained quite close to Wyclif and Hus who had insisted that all human laws were ultimately subject to the standards of divine law. Indeed, Gerson believed that divine law as it is revealed in Holy Scripture will serve as the basis for church reform.[46] Thus he could contend that if some human law, be it canon or civil, could not be concluded from divine law, then its transgression would not be a matter of mortal sin. And if some prelate were to claim that such a statute had the strength of divine law, then it would be right for the theologian to resist him to his face and tell him that he is not walking according to the truth of the gospel (see Gal 2:11–14). This again rests on the theologian's expertise, since he is conversant in the divine law, which has been sufficiently explicated in scripture. Hence if a person does sin mortally for having transgressed some ecclesiastical precept, his fault does not lie in breaching the church's precept as such but rather because the church's precept has given expression to the divine law.[47] In that sense, ecclesiastical law, itself the province of the canonist, is again shown to be derivative of the higher divine law revealed in scripture that is the domain of the theologian.

Christ willed that within his mystical body, the church, there would be doctors assigned to a variety of teachings and laws. Yet Gerson makes it clear that the canonists practice the inferior science; the science of human positive laws cannot match that of the evangelical. If one wonders who could more easily do the job of the other—the theologian or the canonist—it is the former. The theologian is better equipped for the study of the canonical science than vice versa precisely because theology is the higher science and canon law the subaltern. It is easier, says Gerson, to deduce conclusions from principles than to gain knowledge of the principles from conclusions. Canon law derives its principles from the higher science of theology. Gerson is clearly irked, therefore, by those lawyers who imagine that positive laws may assume the level of immutable and indispensable obligation as though on par with evangelical law. Some canonists, he laments, cling to these human traditions as if they were the gospel itself.[48]

In ways reminiscent of Wyclif and Hus, therefore, one finds Gerson complaining that the virtue of divine law is often forgotten these days as mere human traditions render God's commandments invalid. The light yoke of Christ and the law of liberty are thrown aside to make room for the burdensome collections of human laws and institutions that only weigh down the Christian. The list is long: papal canons, provincial and diocesan constitutions, rules of the religious orders, university statutes, and imperial edicts. If, asks Gerson, Adam could not keep one simple precept, what chance do we have of keeping all these? Indeed, we can scarcely fulfill the divine laws that God in his mercy kept to a small number. Here Gerson looks to Peter's speech in Acts 15 where he sought to relieve the early Christian community of burdens of the Jewish law.[49] It is in this vein that Gerson calls upon Christians to imitate Christ's kindness, remembering that he condescended to human weakness by giving us a law that we could bear.[50] Gerson is also quite close to Ockham when lamenting that the canon lawyers and popes have placed excessive burdens on the faithful, thereby infringing upon their evangelical freedom.[51] This is a consistent refrain among all the medieval theologians, namely, that the perfect law of the gospel that they have been entrusted to explicate has been overwhelmed by a steady torrent of humanly devised rules and obligations.

Posthumus Meyjes recalls that Gerson criticized the canonists for their "positivism," that is, their obsession with legal sanction for every aspect of conduct. It is true that canonists are needed to regulate the church's power and wealth, but in Gerson's view these things are nonessential to a church that was created as a pure spiritual entity. Aware that such talk sounded dangerously close to Marsilius of Padua and John Wyclif, however, Gerson steered away from the precipice, noting that just because the church could have done without power and wealth is not to say that these things are inherently illegitimate. They belong to a natural historical development, therefore, but recognition of this fact did not stop Gerson from criticizing the hierarchy if it became consumed with temporal power and privilege. He reminded them that the church was healthiest when poor and simple.[52] Thus we find Gerson chastising ecclesiastical judges for handing out stiffer penalties than their secular counterparts. Excommunication should be a purely spiritual rod that is wielded only against contumacious offenders of the faith, such as heretics and schismatics. But now it is being used for the protection of temporal holdings. In these instances the ecclesiastical judge binds the soul with the most grave bonds of excommunication, while the secular judge merely detains the body.[53] This sounds remarkably like Wyclif's admonition that excommunication was not invented for the sake of exacting money for the clergy but to frighten the delinquent that they might be saved and to thrust poisonous sinners out of the church. But what should be employed in love has been turned into nothing more than a way to exact temporal goods.[54]

For all his criticisms, however, Gerson regarded the science of canon law as a legitimate component of the church's gradual process of development. Evangelical and canon law once spoke with one voice, according to Gerson, before there came to be two distinct faculties of theology and decretists. In the *ecclesia primitiva* evangelical and canon law were joined together, even though the first pertained more to God and the second to neighbor. In later years, however, as the church spread abroad, it was only fitting that there would be an increase in decrees and decretals for the sake of the church's governance and the regulation of her temporal goods. The primitive church was not as yet occupied with such temporal concerns, but times change and traditions must change to meet them—*pro varietate temporum et locorum traditiones istas variare necesse est*. As new situations arose there was need for new solutions offered by canonical legislation, although it is still true that evangelical law is sufficient for the perfection of one's soul. Gerson patently rejects the argument that because prelates in the primitive church did not employ decretals to bring men to God such things are therefore unfitting in modern times *(moderno tempore)*. Coming to the defense of canon law, therefore, Gerson contends that the *vox Christi* can be heard in both theology and canon law. Yet he is careful to point out that the *lex evangelica* rings through theology immediately while resonating through canon law only in a mediated fashion.[55]

Gerson did find a place for canon law, therefore, but it does not possess an absolute authority; it must be qualified depending upon the situation. When dealing with human positive law within the decrees and decretals one must adhere to the Aristotelian principle of equity *(epikeia)*, and thus adapt to different times, places, and persons. The truth exists immutably in divine and natural law but not so human law. In fact, one must beware that the divine commandment of charity is not rendered void for the sake of merely human traditions. Here Gerson affirms the basic rule that "legislation should not follow from the bare text of the law, but must represent the intention of the lawgiver." This is why it is so important when looking at the decrees and decretals to distinguish between what is purely divine law, what is purely natural, and what is human or positive law. Confusion here will inevitably lead to error as one fails to separate the precious from the common, the necessary from the unnecessary, the incommutable from the commutable, the law that obligates and the one that does not. In hard cases, where human traditions prove insufficient, recourse must be had to divine law, which is itself the origin, rule, and exemplar of all other laws.[56] So much of what Gerson has to say about law in its various dimensions runs very close to Wyclif and Hus. In fact, Gerson seems to be aware of this at times as he rallies to defend canon law's place in the life of the church. Yet this is indicative of the inherent tension that all the anti-Wycliffite writers must contend with as they seek to separate themselves from their opponents.

The Theologian and Holy Scripture

That theologians are the authentic examiners of doctrine is formally grounded, for Gerson, in the reception of their doctorate. He appeals to the precise words spoken by the university chancellor to the recipient: "I, by apostolic authority, grant you the license of reading, reigning, disputing, and teaching in the Sacred Theology faculty here and in every land in the name of the Father, the Son, and the Holy Spirit."[57] When it comes to the reform of the church the theologian will take the lead. And this is directly tied to the preeminence of Holy Scripture, since it is scripture that contains divine law and the theologian—*magister sacrae paginae*—is principally a biblical exegete. Gerson, moreover, looked specifically to the university theologians, as opposed to the otherwise corrupted theologians within the papal curia, to render judgment on matters affecting Christian society.[58] This may even bring the theologian into opposition with papal authority. The theologian has an apostolic role to fulfill; he follows in succession from the apostle Paul and thus has the right to correct the successors of Peter (Gal 2:11–14).[59] As Brian McGuire has noted, Gerson was convinced that the Paris theological faculty "remained at the core of the Church's *magisterium* or teaching authority" and thus had every right to weigh in on the validity of papal decretals.[60] This sense of authority is in keeping with Gerson's understanding of himself as a "public intellectual," as Daniel Hobbins phrases it; the theologian, unlike the canon lawyer, is uniquely suited to address contemporary issues in all their complexity.[61]

There is much more to being a theologian than merely receiving a license that formally recognizes one's professional skills. Gerson, no less than John Wyclif, believed that biblical exegesis is a spiritual discipline. As we have seen, Wyclif—like Augustine and Bonaventure—laid great emphasis on the exegete's conformity to Christ. For Gerson, no less, exegetes must not only be intellectually gifted but also humble in their judgments and immune from vice. They must be erudite not only by way of human reason and effort but also by divine revelation and the inspiration of the Holy Spirit.[62] Gerson warns fellow theologians not to stray from scripture lest they are led into error like the pagan philosophers. Theology is a deeply spiritual calling that requires repentance and prayer so that one may penetrate the mysteries of scripture. For Gerson, the theologian occupied a place of honor and sanctity comparable to that of virgins, widows, and the religious. In fact, the theologian's prayer is more effectual than the layman's owing to his clearer view of divine truth and deeper spirituality.[63]

It is precisely because Gerson took so seriously the calling of theologian that he worked to reform the theological curriculum at the University of Paris. He lamented that where there should be just one faith and one law—a common truth coming down from the Holy Spirit—there is instead endless contention among the different orders, each one following its own doctors. Christendom is being torn asunder in these fruitless and vainglorious quests for intellectual superiority.[64] Actually, his complaints run very close to Wyclif's lament that charity had been forsaken in the universities, which are now consumed with envious disputes. Whereas the universities ought to have been defending orthodoxy they have become hotbeds of heresy.[65]

Gerson was not alone in his call for reform. Nicholas Clamanges also railed against the vain disputes of the schoolmen who should instead be preparing pastors for the care of souls. Clamanges believed that the student would need to be trained in the ways of piety, the devout *affectus*. This would achieve the sort of personal reform *(reformatio personalis)* that would lead to better pastoral care *(cura animarum)*. The theologian, for Clamanges, should be a teacher above all else, communicating the faith to people in ways they can comprehend. Under the inspiration of the Holy Spirit the theologian will adopt a specifically theological rhetoric *(theologica rhetorica)* that combines the best of classical rhetoric with theological insight. All the while *scientia* would be combined with *caritas*.[66]

Gerson certainly had a place for the intellective powers, but shorn of the affective they resulted in empty and vain curiosity. The virtues of love and faith were essential for attaining true knowledge of God. *Devotio* and *scientia* could never be divorced from one another in Gerson's quest for a true mystical theology.[67] In a letter to Pierre d'Ailly, Gerson declared that the time had come for the *reformatio* of the theology faculty. The theologians were now wasting their time with useless teachings *(doctrinae inutiles)* to the neglect of materials necessary for salvation. They show contempt for the Bible and the holy doctors. And all the while they are derided by other faculties who are convinced that the theologians are lost in their own fantasies and know nothing of solid moral and biblical truth. In fact, the other masters cannot even fathom what they are saying and do not even care to know any more of their absurdities. As a result of all this, many are being scandalized, and the faith of the church is not edified. Reform would put an end to the sophismata; it would also entail the reading of all four books of Lombard's *Sentences* rather than (as was the norm in this period) remaining fixed on only the first book. And, of course, there would be greater emphasis placed on the study of scripture.[68] Gerson chastised the prelates and religious orders who had set aside "the sacred writings of our law" for the sake of human traditions.[69] Appealing to Pseudo-Dionysius, he spoke of the limits set down by Holy Scripture, which has been revealed to us— boundaries beyond which no one should dare to teach.[70] Because Holy Scripture is at the center of his craft the theologian must know it inside and out. He will be expected to hold with a certain and explicit faith many things that a simple illiterate man could rationally—though not pertinaciously— doubt: facts such as whether Tobias had a dog or Aaron a beard.[71] The theologian should not be a detached expert, however, but should serve as a guide for his fellow Catholics. Gerson realized that not all people had the means to interpret scripture with full precision, and thus he envisioned a Dionysian hierarchy whereby revelation descended as the erudite taught the less learned.[72]

Given the fact that Holy Scripture is the highest authority in the church, Gerson was also willing to admit that if a person lacking authoritative status *(simplex non auctoritatus)* were sufficiently skilled in the Sacred Scriptures, such that he is worthy of greater trust in a matter of doctrine than a papal declaration, one would have to follow his interpretation of the biblical text. After all, the Gospel commands greater confidence than the pope. Hence if this otherwise "nonauthorized" man were to teach some truth contained in the Gospels that the pope did not know, or had erred in discerning, then this man's judgment should be preferred. So too would one have to trust this man if, in the midst of a general council, he opposed a conciliar ruling, having realized that the greater part was in opposition to the Gospel. In short, Holy Scripture always take precedence over present ecclesiastical authorities. Gerson admits that in the earliest days of the church militant—the age of the apostles and their immediate successors—there were many unwritten traditions received from Christ that would have had greater authority at that time than a written Gospel. Yet following the authorization of the Four Gospels, one must place more trust in them than any human authority.[73] Gerson, therefore, actually runs much closer to Wyclif on this point than to William Woodford.

Throughout all the tumult caused by the schism, and certainly in his battle against the Hussites, Gerson never relinquished his fundamental belief in ecclesiastical hierarchy itself even when individual members of that hierarchy may have proven to be errant and corrupt. In fact, it remained central to Gerson's whole conception of determinative exegetical authority. Ecclesiastical power, he argued, is by necessity founded upon a supernatural gift; like the baptismal character, this gift renders one worthy and capable of exercising power. While sanctifying grace is surely fitting for those who have received this power, it can subsist without it. The denial of this basic principle, he says, was the error of the Waldensians that is now renewed by Wyclif and his followers. Their position was justly condemned, he maintained, lest the hierarchical order of ecclesiastical authority were to remain unstable and uncertain, since no one would know whether their prelates are deserving of love or hatred. Even less necessary is the grace of predestination, says Gerson, which these heretics claim is essential for the title and right of power.[74] Having said all that, it must be remembered that Gerson and the council deposed Pope John XXIII on account of the scandal that his immoral life caused the Catholic faithful.

In the face of Wycliffite criticism of the prelacy, therefore, Gerson sought ecclesiastical stability specifically in the church's hierarchy. Certain that Christ will always remain with his church, Gerson saw him at work through the various members of the hierarchical structure. Appealing to 1 Corinthians 12:4–11, he notes that there are different grades and spheres of operation, such that God might work all things in all as each person manifests a different gift of the Spirit. The complex structure that the church now manifests is itself a natural growth from her primitive foundations. All these various offices and functions were planted in the church by Christ as though in a nursery; over time they sprout and come to fruition.[75] Legitimate developments were present incohatively in the primitive church and matured over time, but none must be allowed to compromise the hierarchical structure that Christ had instituted.[76] Gerson believed that by his ordained power *(de potentia Dei ordinata)* God has bound himself to the church hierarchy. Hence reform will take place within that structure, from the papacy and episcopacy right down to the parochial clergy.[77] It is along these lines, then, that Gerson rejected the notion that the church might survive only among a few faithful laymen or even just one woman; there would always remain some orthodox priests and bishops.[78]

If Gerson was bent on protecting the authority of the ecclesiastical hierarchy from Wycliffite and Hussite criticism, he was likewise keen to safeguard the rights of the secular clergy against the infringements of the friars. For Gerson, it was all of a piece: he needed to protect the divinely established order of the church. In 1409 Pope Alexander V (himself a Franciscan) issued the bull *Regnans in excelsis* in which he condemned a series of arguments leveled against the friars by the secular theologians. In the following year, however, the Paris theological faculty pronounced the bull intolerable on the grounds that it would disrupt the state of the church. Once again, the old charges, dating back to the mid-thirteenth century, emerged: the friars were overturning the primitive order of prelates and curates. Gerson, in keeping with his Dionysian principle of illumination through hierarchy, claimed that the pope could not—by issuing blanket privileges to the friars—alter the structure that Christ had established. As it turned out, the seculars got their wish when John XXIII rescinded the bull that very year.[79] Thus, whereas Gerson might defend legitimate development that allowed the church to move beyond the strict confines of pre-Donation ecclesiology, the *status ecclesiae* remained essentially unalterable. In this sense Gerson aligned himself with secular theologians spanning two centuries, from Godfrey of Fontaines all the way to John Wyclif, who had resisted papal intervention on behalf of the friars. In fact, there seems to be precious little difference between Gerson's opposition to the papacy in this instance and Wyclif's complaint that the novelties of the friars are forced on the church by unwarranted papal interference.[80]

The Determination of the Literal Sense

A central feature of the debates with the Wycliffites turned on the literal sense of scripture—how it was defined and how located. Indeed, given the equation of the literal sense and the divinely intended sense adopted by the medieval theologians, it stands to reason that virtually all disputes over orthodox doctrine would turn on Holy Scripture's literal sense. So it was that Gerson complained that the truth is under attack, not only in Britain, Prague, and Germany, but even in his home country, France. He reports that the heretics are claiming that their statements are founded upon the literal sense of Holy Scripture. This, he tells us, is the only authority they are willing to accept, thereby rejecting the decrees and decretals that they have labeled apocryphal and contrary to Christ. So it is, then, that Gerson feels compelled to examine what constitutes the literal sense of scripture and how it may be investigated.[81] Gerson actually had a great deal of confidence in one's ability to discern the literal sense of scripture. He believed in the clarity of scripture and blamed the heretics for muddying the waters. Gerson specifically attacked Wyclif and Hus for "taking refuge in glosses" when they are pressed to make their case. It is a tactic of evasion, says Gerson, a deliberate effort to distort the literal sense of the text.[82] Gerson thereby casts himself as the defender of scriptural clarity against heretics who will mire the whole discussion in a glut of provisos and extraneous explanations. As it stands, though, Gerson holds out little hope of converting his opponents, offering the standard description of heretics: They are depraved in their intellect through error, and in their affections through incorrigibility and pertinacity. True to form they prefer their own sense to the judgment of wiser and more prudent men.[83]

Gerson presented a detailed account of his exegetical methodology in a rejoinder to the Parisian master Jean Petit, who had defended the murder of the duke of Orleans at the order of the duke of Burgundy in 1407. Petit had argued that this was a case of legitimate tyrannicide, which meant that the commandment "Thou shalt not kill" could not be strictly applied in this instance. Instead, he claimed, it had to be read through the Aristotelian principle of equity *(epikeia)*, which allowed for the spirit of the law to be fulfilled rather than slavishly adhering to the letter. Basing his argument on 2 Corinthians 3:6, "The letter kills, but the spirit bring life," Petit concluded, "*c'est-à-dire que tenir le sens litéral en la Sainte Ecriture est occîre son âme.*" This matter was brought for examination to the Council of Constance, with seventy-five masters rendering opinions on Petit's exegesis. Much of the support for his exegesis rested on the fathers, especially Gregory the Great's remark that not all passages of scripture ought to be read literally *(iuxta litteram)*, since a mere surface reading might lead to error rather than edification (*Moralia* 1.3). Petit equated the literal sense of scripture with the bare grammatical meaning, which he then felt free to dismiss. Yet Gerson argued that this means of bypassing the so-called literal sense—on the grounds that it is absurd—could quickly become a license to make a text say whatever the reader likes. When the words of the biblical text are no longer trusted to reveal the true meaning there will be no end to capricious interpretations. Indeed, if the literal sense was no longer considered reliable, then the very authority of scripture would be at stake.[84]

For Gerson, as for most late medieval exegetes, the literal sense of the text is identical to the intention of the author. He writes: "The literal sense of any discourse is the sense which the speaker himself principally and directly intends. Hence it is the same thing to say that one should not hold to the literal sense as to say that one should not grasp the intention of the speaker. Yet since the Holy Spirit is the one who speaks in Holy Scripture, it is erroneous to say that the literal sense is not true sometimes and thus should not always be held."[85] Gerson insists, therefore, that scripture be shown proper reverence, which means affirming that its literal sense—its intended sense—is never false.[86] The key here, for Gerson, is that the letter *(littera)* and the literal sense *(sensus litteralis)* are not always the same, since one thing is signified through the terms of the letter *(per terminos litterae)* and another through the things signified *(res significatas)*. And because the Holy Spirit speaks in the latter way at times, it is simply false to equate the grammatical sense of the text with the literal sense, since the sacred letter expresses the intention of the speaker by way of things, not terms.[87]

It should be noted that Gerson does allow for a *duplex sensus litteralis*. The histories of David and Solomon not only symbolize Christ, therefore, but also offer moral instruction when read as simple narrations. Yet there are also instances when a text might reduce from a double literal to a single literal sense over time. This is the case with Genesis 17:14, where the uncircumcised boy will be removed from the people of God. At one time it both taught the intellect insofar as it was figurative and induced right action insofar as it was preceptive. Considered from the perspective of the New Law, however, this verse has only one literal sense: the figurative. For with the advent of Baptism, the Holy Spirit does not intend for Christians to practice circumcision. Hence a proposition that once had a double literal sense now has only one sense here in the age of grace.[88]

This emphasis on context in determining the literal sense—the sense of the text as it is meant to be understood—is central to Gerson's exegetical program. Christ revealed the true literal sense of the Old Testament, but the Jews refused to accept it. Thus when Paul said that the letter kills (2 Cor 3:6) he was referring to what the Jews considered to be the letter or literal sense.[89] The Jews and the sophists are making the same mistake, for they are both locked into a strictly grammatical reading of the letter.

Modern sophists—members of the arts faculty—follow the logic of the speculative sciences, but scripture has its own logic and grammar.[90] One must be attuned to the subtleties of scriptural discourse if one hopes to see its inherent logic. Here, then, Gerson praised Henry Totting de Oyta's prescription that in order to attain the literal sense one must consider the context; the modes of speaking—be they figures and tropes; and finally the various customs of discourse *(usus loquendi)* employed by the holy doctors and the expositors of scripture.[91] Thus Gerson can remark that "Holy Scripture explains its own rule through itself in accordance with different passages of scripture and in keeping with the holy doctors."[92]

Perhaps it is ironic, therefore, that in his struggle against Wycliffites and Hussites, Gerson stressed the authority of Holy Scripture in ways that would have made Wyclif proud. Everything revealed by God is true, says Gerson, and Holy Scripture has been divinely revealed by God, whose Word is found in every part of scripture.[93] Holy Scripture is the rule of faith, and, provided that scripture is rightly understood, there is no authority that can be admitted against it.[94] In the examination of doctrines, says Gerson, we attend principally to whether the doctrine is in conformity with Holy Scripture. For scripture was handed down to us as a sufficient and infallible rule for the governance of the whole ecclesiastical body until the end of time. It is such a perfect rule, or exemplar, that any doctrine that does not conform to it must be rejected as heretical or suspect.[95] The canon of Holy Scripture, and each of the things that are literally asserted in it, form the first standard of Catholic truth. Hence one may not dissent from the contents of scripture as they are understood by the Holy Spirit, since it is the Holy Spirit's intention that constitutes the true literal sense.[96] Wyclif could not have said it better! For indeed, Wyclif extolled scripture as the one Word of God, the eternal mirror of divine majesty that forms the foundation for all Catholic doctrine.[97]

And much like Wyclif some four decades earlier, Gerson was clearly irked by the logicians who claimed to have located errors in the narratives of the biblical authors. In fact, Wyclif had devoted a good bit of his own *De veritate sacrae scripturae* to combatting the sophists of the arts faculty and thus defending the veracity of scripture's literal sense.[98] Now Gerson would respond to those sophists who had rebuked Mark the Evangelist for having said that "people from the *whole region* of Judea and *all the people* of Jerusalem were going out to [John the Baptist]" (Mk 1:5–6). Apparently the *tractatores logicae* were scandalized by this statement and found fault in such a form of speech. For by the "force of logic and the propriety of speech" this appears to be false inasmuch as Mark chose to employ "universal discourse" in this instance.[99] It is here that Gerson contends that one must distinguish between two sorts of logic: that which is employed by the natural and speculative sciences, which may simply be called logic; and another logic that Gerson calls rhetoric. Both sorts have their own rules of discourse. The first demands proper speech *(sermonis proprietatem)* and thus rejects the use of metaphor and figurative language in its attempt to be as precise as possible. Yet the other form of logic, which is called rhetoric, fittingly employs figures and tropes, which is helpful to the moral sciences. There is no need, therefore, for prophetic texts, historical narratives, and moral discourse to abide by "the strict rules of the first logic; it is enough that one follows the common manner of speaking *(modus loquendi communis)*."[100] Gerson insisted that theological texts would not be bound to the rules of the first sort of logic. Theology has its own manner of speaking and thus could never be false *de virtute sermonis*. Indeed, to claim otherwise would rightly be rejected as blasphemous by faithful Catholics.[101]

It is in this vein that Gerson attacks those who import the rules of the first logic into the discussion of morals, speaking in ways that are clearly scandalous and false according to the common manner of speaking and the principles of rhetoric even if true by the rules of the first logic. Hence where logicians might employ indefinite propositions, which may be true in the realm of the first logic, they are regarded as universal in moral and political discourse and thus prove false. It is precisely for this reason that propositions can be condemned as erroneous even as they may be true *de vi vocis* and according to the first logic. The reason for such severe sanction is Gerson's concern that people who are not used to hearing such discourse might be scandalized.[102]

For Gerson, therefore, it is nothing less than blasphemy and heresy to assert that the literal sense of scripture might ever be false. As noted above, this turns on Gerson's distinction between the letter *(littera)* and the literal sense *(sensus litteralis)*. Echoing Wyclif almost verbatim, Gerson contends that the literal sense is what the Holy Spirit principally intended, and it can be elicited from the context of the letter of scripture.[103] That is why Gerson insists that the literal sense of scripture must not be taken according to the force of logic or dialectic but more fittingly according to common usage of speech found in rhetoric that allows for tropes and figures of speech. Scripture has its own form of logic.[104] And it is because scripture has its own logic that schoolmen must submit their reasoning to what Gerson will term scripture's "literal theological sense." Masters of the Sacred Page have an obligation first and foremost to scripture itself. The university masters must act responsibly and conduct themselves with the decorum befitting their exalted status. Reverence for scripture's manner of speaking precludes statements that, while not false, are nonetheless scandalous, offensive to pious ears, or bad-sounding. Indeed, the scholar would have to revoke such an assertion.[105] Gerson cautions, therefore, against theologizing with extraneous terms, or novel and foreign meanings; stick to the terms generally employed by the doctors.[106] The schoolmen certainly have an important role to play in determining the correct sense of scripture, but they must not abuse their freedom. They will need to follow the lines of acceptable discourse.[107] Such admonitions were never more important to Gerson than in his struggles against the Wycliffites and Hussites whom he portrayed as irresponsible masters untethered to any sense of controlling authority outside of their own personal whims. The previous chapters should have demonstrated that this was a false portrayal. Yet as Gerson narrowed the range of acceptable theological discourse — by actually rejecting appeals to the broader doctrinal context in order to explain complex theories — he hoped to reduce his opponents to silence.

Echoing the words of his mentor Pierre d'Ailly, Gerson argued in his own *Eight Rules on Theological Style* that when it comes to the condemnation of errors precedence must be given to divine laws *(iura divina)* over the human; the commandments of God must not be rendered void for the sake of human traditions. Human laws and tradition always remain subject to the divine. In fact, says Gerson, all laws — even civil — must ultimately conform to the divine.[108] He would get no argument from Wyclif and Hus there, of course, but Gerson is setting out these parameters precisely in order to condemn these men and their disciples. Every science has its own style, its unique *modus procendi*, which is proper to it. The Council of Constance, therefore, in condemning the errors of Wyclif and Hus will follow the theological style, just as the fathers had done in previous councils when addressing matters of faith.[109]

Constance condemned sets of specific propositions attributed to Wyclif and Hus. When it came to the condemnation of errors, Gerson believed that more attention should be given to the extirpation of the actual errors than the correction of those who err, since it is correction of the former that is of greatest benefit to the faith itself and the public good. Thus, even as the two condemnations occur simultaneously, the condemnation of error is naturally prior to the correction of the errant, since no one can be corrected unless the error itself is first known. Gerson maintains, moreover, that errors can be condemned without the people who asserted the errors being present for the proceedings. The condemnation should proceed from the common deliberation of the theologians in which there is an open inquiry into that which not only attends to the statements themselves, but also the rationale behind such statements. Yet—and this is a major factor in Gerson's consideration of theological error—condemnation does not ultimately depend on whether the proposition itself can be proven to be theologically sound. Gerson is very attentive to the way simple Christians will hear such statements and thus be scandalized—hence his refusal to permit Hus the right to defend decontextualized statements.[110] It is in this vein, therefore, that Gerson insists that the council must chiefly consider the meaning of a statement taken according to the common understanding—*communem intelligendi modum*. As such, Gerson states: "If an assertion possesses an erroneous or scandalous sense, or one that is offensive to pious ears, it can reasonably be condemned notwithstanding the fact it may possess some true sense according to the strict rules of grammar and logic." Indeed, says Gerson, this only stands to reason since an entire book can be condemned on account of some errors despite the fact that it contains many truths.[111] Hence the authorial intention standing behind a given statement is not finally of any importance.

In his sermon *Prosperum Iter* Gerson states that the general council should diligently examine, reprove, and condemn heretical and erroneous assertions that create public scandal in matters of faith and morals, including, therefore, lay communion under both kinds.[112] Here he also states that the council can condemn many propositions along with their authors despite the fact that the propositions may possess a logical meaning or could be otherwise explained. In fact, he says, this is just the problem that the council faces with many articles of Wyclif and Hus some of which can be defended in their logical or grammatical sense.[113] D'Ailly too maintained that even as a doctrine may in fact be true when taken as it was intended, nevertheless it should not be simply asserted *(simpliciter asserenda)* if it appears false apart from the further exposition needed to expose its true meaning.[114] All the trouble, as far as Gerson is concerned, stems from the failure to recognize that theology has its own logic and literal sense that differs from the speculative sciences. It is precisely by observing this rule, he says, that the University of Paris has been preserved from so many of the errors infecting other universities; its schoolmen are compelled to conform their speech to the rule of faith.[115]

In principle, Gerson believed that Wycliffite and Hussite propositions will have to be judged against the greater backdrop of the whole tradition. The fact that such propositions might find scriptural support is in itself not sufficient. "The general council can and should condemn many propositions and assertions of this sort even though they cannot be clearly reproved from the bare expressed text of Holy Scripture alone apart from the expositions of the doctors or the well-known custom of the church."[116] Yet in fact Gerson ruled out Hus's appeal to the tradition in order to justify statements that, in any event, had been extracted from works that often supported his claims with copious citations of patristic sources and canon law. The notion that the Wycliffites and Hussites were shackled to the "bare expressed text of Holy Scripture" is a concoction of Gerson's own making. It is a rhetorical device designed to put maximum distance between himself and adversaries who were, in truth, advocating positions virtually identical to his own.

At any rate, it was precisely Jerome of Prague's failure to distinguish clearly between logic and rhetoric that was condemned at Constance. In the sermon preached prior to Jerome's execution in 1416, the bishop of Lodi chastised Jerome for not recognizing that "the genus of demonstration is one thing in logic, another in rhetoric. For logic demonstrates by immediate propositions and expository syllogisms. Rhetoric, for its part, 'remonstrates' by praise and reprimand." It was along these lines, therefore, that Gerson was troubled by Jerome's failure to keep the arts and theology separate—a master of arts meddling in another discipline.[117] Hence, as Kaluza points out, Hus and Jerome ran into such trouble at Constance because their undefined propositions, while true perhaps for logicians and grammarians, were indefensible in the realm of theology, where they were taken as universal propositions.[118] And because the matter at hand was the propositions as they stood, as opposed to how they might be explained in an orthodox manner, Hus's plea that he be allowed to qualify his remarks fell on deaf ears. All the contextualization that Gerson otherwise insisted upon to make sense of biblical and patristic texts was denied to Jan Hus at this most crucial point in his life.

The Battle over the Tradition

When arguing against the Wycliffites and Hussites Gerson was quite clear that Holy Scripture is the rule of faith, and, provided that it is rightly understood *(bene intellectam)*, there is no authority that can be admitted against it: no human reason or custom. In fact, Gerson readily conceded that this principle is admitted both by the orthodox and the heretics. Everything will have to turn, therefore, not on the authority of scripture as such, but on authoritative hermeneutics. And a central component of hermeneutics, for Gerson, is contextualization. Yet in light of the discussion above, the irony is transparent as Gerson informs the reader that only when scripture is treated in its entirety, rather than artificially isolating particular parts, will its inherent truth emerge. Since the Author of scripture is none other than the Holy Spirit he would never assert a false proposition. Appealing to Augustine (*De doc. chr.* 1.37.41), Gerson notes that were any falsehood found therein, the entirety authority of Holy Scripture would waver.[119] The fact that each proposition must be compared with other parts of scripture in an effort to locate their agreement has direct application to his battle against heresy. Gerson charges the Hussites with a tendentiously selective reading of the biblical text, as they pick and choose the passages that make their case for communion under both kinds. If, for instance, some will latch on to Christ's words, "Whoever believes and is baptized will be saved" (Mk 16:16) they might think that faith alone, apart from the other virtues, is sufficient for salvation. But by that same token Gerson could cite the words, "If anyone eats of this bread he will live forever" (Jn 6:58), thereby upholding the sufficiency of bread apart from wine in the Eucharist. The point is that the literal sense of scripture manifests itself contextually, balancing the meaning of different passages.[120] Thus, says Gerson, Holy Scripture ought to receive reverent and humble exposition in each of its parts and partial assertions, reading one passage in light of another. The intended meaning of scripture is often discovered by examining other passages, allowing the intention of the speaker to emerge and thereby circumvent apparent lies and contradictions.[121] This method is hardly unique to Gerson. It is a basic exegetical principle that his opponents also readily accepted,[122] and thus moves one no closer to resolving the greater problem.

Even if Gerson might sometimes accuse his adversaries of basing their case solely upon explicit biblical testimony he knew that was not really true. In fact, Gerson's greatest dilemma in his fight against heresy is not that his opponents reject the sacred exegetical tradition. It is that they actually *do* accept this tradition. He laments that the Hussite Utraquists are haphazardly citing so many doctors in order to bolster their argument. For his part, Gerson demands that authorities be critically evaluated, since not all sources carry the same weight. It is not simply a matter of lining up authorities; for some are more authoritative than others.[123] Even glosses chosen from among the greatest of the church fathers are not inherently decisive; they still must be contextualized. Holy Scripture, says Gerson, needs to be interpreted not only in its original words, but even in its expositions. The Utraquists can find a gloss in which Augustine seems to claim that reception of the chalice is necessary for salvation, but one can just as easily find a passage in which he appears to say the opposite. Taking isolated texts at first sight *(prima facie)* proves nothing. One must examine the competing texts in the context of other writings in order to resolve the contradictions.[124]

Yet we are still left to ask, where may one turn in what looks like an exegetical stalemate if each side can call upon yet one more saint, one more decretal? For Gerson, Holy Scripture, in its reception and authentic exposition, finally resolves into the authority, reception, and approbation of the universal church. Even here, though, Gerson by no means abandons the principal authority of the ancient sources. In fact, he believes that one must look especially to the primitive church, which received scripture and its understanding immediately from Christ, by the revelation of the Holy Spirit at Pentecost, and on many other occasions.[125]

If the literal sense of text is equated with the author's intended sense, and thereby forms the orthodox sense for both Gerson and his opponents, where does one turn to get a handle on it? Gerson argues that the literal sense of scripture will ultimately have to be judged by the church, which is herself inspired and governed by the Holy Spirit. The individual Christian, says Gerson, is not free to follow just any interpretation he might choose.[126] In fact, Gerson contends that if the literal sense has been openly determined and received by the church one is not obliged to engage in arcane arguments with the heretics but may have immediate recourse to the judicial statutes of punishment.[127] The literal sense of scripture is inseparable from the greater tradition. It was first revealed through Christ and the apostles and was elucidated by miracles; thereafter confirmed through the blood of the martyrs; and later made clearer by the arguments of the holy doctors against the heretics. Then came the determination of the holy councils, such that what had been discussed by the doctors might be officially defined by the church.[128]

While Gerson certainly privileges the ancient church, he has confidence in the present church to uncover the meaning of scripture. In fact, he believes that the literal sense of scripture can be defined within the decrees and decretals as well as the records of the councils. And if so defined it must be judged to pertain to theology and Holy Scripture no less than the Apostles' Creed. For Gerson, therefore, if the literal sense of scripture is the divinely intended meaning, then there is no reason why that sense will not be more fully revealed by later documents produced by the tradition. This does not amount to a separate extra-scriptural source of Catholic truth but simply a further explication of scripture itself, which is the ongoing work of the church. The literal sense so defined must not be spurned as though it were founded on a merely human or positive constitution. It is on this very point that the heretics err, says Gerson, for they think that statements of the doctors, councils, and popes are apocryphal or false unless located expressly in Holy Scripture.[129] As Christoph Burger points out, Gerson always remains true to his conservative principles of reform. Abuses in the church may never be allowed to threaten the basic hierarchical structure. The right of the hierarchy to interpret the literal sense, with the advice of the theologians, must remain unchallenged despite the presence of wicked prelates.[130]

Throughout it all Gerson never loses sight of the unique authority of scripture. He makes it clear that the literal sense is "sufficiently expressed in the books of Holy Scripture." It is true that it can also be found within the works of the doctors but then only insofar as they are drawing conclusions that clearly follow from scripture. In this vein Gerson can point to the Creeds, which of themselves add nothing to Scripture but merely express its literal sense — namely, the divinely intended sense — in a compendious form.[131] Hence one cannot accept the conclusion of Posthumus Meyjes that Gerson saw the church as a "second source of revelation," if that implies that this second source must supply doctrine that is otherwise lacking in Holy Scripture.[132] Rather, for Gerson, the church at any given time in her history is capable of faithfully revealing the literal sense of scripture in the course of inspired reflection and commentary. It is not a matter of addition, but disclosure.

It is true that Gerson recognized the unique authority of the primitive church, given her proximity to Christ. But he was not going to allow the debate with the Wycliffites and Hussites to turn into a battle over antiquity. That was a battle he could not win. This is why he insisted that the church is governed even now by the infallible rule of the Holy Spirit. When it comes to the exposition of scripture, therefore, the custom of the universal church—guided as she is by the Spirit—is owed greater reverence than the authority of any single doctor or saint.[133] Gerson clearly saw the futility of battling the heretics over glosses; each side will marshal a plethora of unimpeachable sources and the debate will never end. Recourse must be had to a living authority, namely, the voice of the Holy Spirit speaking through the universal church. Ultimately, Gerson put his trust in a general council. The council—under the guidance of the Holy Spirit—is the authentic examiner and final judge of doctrines touching the faith. For any one person in the church of whatever dignity, even papal, is subject to infirmity and thus can both deceive and be deceived.[134] The general council would be the authoritative entity that could finally silence the Wycliffites and Hussites.

So it was, then, that Gerson had found the ultimate locus of authority in the church. He regarded the general council as a perfect representation of the church hierarchy, which was itself instituted by God, thereby rendering the council infallible.[135] In keeping with medieval corporation theory, Gerson believed, as Oakley points out, that "final authority in the church . . . inheres in the whole body of its corporate membership." As such, the *plenitudo potestatis* will not be limited to the pope but will always abide in the universal church as a whole and thus in the general council that represents the church.[136] Yet one should not lose sight of the fact that the sort of conciliarism sketched by Gerson, and proclaimed at Constance in the *Haec Sancta* decree, was itself quite controversial and ultimately short-lived. The very concept of conciliarism was portrayed by its fifteenth-century opponents, such as Juan de Torquemada, as belonging to the radical school of Marsilius of Padua.[137] Actually, Torquemada set forth what became a very influential argument, namely, that *Haec Sancta*—asserting as it did conciliar supremacy over the papacy—was invalid since it was enacted prior to the assembly of all three papal obediences.[138] The fortunes of conciliarism waned in the aftermath of the council of Basel, culminating in the 1460 bull *Exsecrabilis* in which Pope Pius II condemned the notion that one might be able to appeal from the Roman pontiff—the very vicar of Jesus Christ—to a future general council.[139]

Gerson did not place the blame for all the church's strife solely on the shoulders of the heretics. There was plenty of blame to go around, but much of that blame would be directed at an entire academic culture that Gerson believed had lost all sense of proportion in assessing the relative authority of its sources. There seems to be a dangerous fascination with the written word. One can only marvel, says Gerson, at the authority accorded a single published gloss of some dead doctor. His writings are cited as authoritative in the schools and the courts, despite the fact that this same man would have no such prestige were he alive. All the while, though, the determination of an entire university on some passage of scripture or law will scarcely be received. It is as if a dead document now has greater authority than the living witness. Nor is Gerson moved by the romanticization of some previous generation's piety, as if that epoch were free from all the corrupt affections that plague current masters. For there is no reason why such passions could not have distorted the judgment of the dead in their own day.[140]

Gerson has seen that his own world—the world of academia—created this heretical monster. The Prague masters were fully convinced of their own authority. Indeed, from Godfrey of Fontaines to John Wyclif, the theologians, by virtue of their universally recognized license, believed that they had every right—indeed a sacred duty—to defend the truth no matter the opposition. Gerson, d'Ailly, and Netter, all eminent theologians devoted to Holy Scripture and the sacred tradition, had met their match. Their Wycliffite and Hussite opponents know the fathers and the decrees backward and forward. When these "heretics" cite text after text they are doing what every university master has been trained to do. When they reject some recent ruling as nonbinding, because insufficiently authoritative, they are not retreating into the subjectivity of personal inspiration. Instead, they are following the most traditional course of all: entrenching themselves *in auctoritatibus sacris*.

Chapter 7

The Enduring Dilemma

We have observed a protracted debate among medieval university masters that seems at times almost impossible to resolve. Perhaps Jean Gerson's confidence in the infallibility of a general council could offer the ultimate measure of authority that would put an end to these persistent debates about the intended meaning of scripture and the testimony of the fathers. But, as I noted, the triumphs of conciliar theory were short-lived. The notion that ultimate authority rested in a general council was no longer viable by the time of the Council of Florence (1439) and was then decisively rejected two decades later by Pope Pius II (1460).[1] At this point, by way of a coda, the whole situation might be further illuminated by a small "case study" drawn from the English heresy debates as they continued into the middle of fifteenth century. This brief examination confirms not only the seemingly intractable nature of the problems that the late medieval church still faced but also the lingering—even unavoidable—irony that surfaces in orthodox responses to perceived heresy.

When the English theologian and bishop Reginald Pecock arrived on the scene to do battle with the Wycliffites the prospect for resolving these controversies looked no closer than it had been generations earlier. Aware that the debates seemed fruitless at times, Pecock proposed some innovative solutions, one of which was to address his Lollard opponents in the vernacular, thereby eschewing the recognized authority of scholastic Latin discourse. More than that, however, Pecock set out to ground orthodoxy on a new foundation—namely, the judgment of reason. He did this because he believed that the constant back-and-forth over scripture and the fathers was a dead end. Yet it was precisely his attempt to find some way through the impasse that led to his own heresy conviction in 1457.[2] What Pecock proposed is certainly of interest, and it has received due scrutiny by modern scholars. Of greater import, however, is the response Pecock's program elicited, especially from the Augustinian friar John Bury. Thus, after a concise look at what Pecock had to say, I turn to Bury, whose full-throated attack on this hapless bishop provides us with a fascinating glimpse into the orthodox conception of scriptural authority deep into the fifteenth century.

Reginald Pecock

All sides of the debates that I have tracked throughout this book believed that their own reading of scripture was consonant with the ways of the apostolic church and the teachings of the fathers. Thus in his appeal to natural reason over antiquity, Pecock was swimming against the tide; in fact, veneration for the fathers was only increasing among Pecock's English colleagues. As R. M. Ball has noted, Pecock's disparagement of the fathers was extremely offensive to his younger opponents. Not only were their preaching and theology heavily indebted to patristic sources, but they also had a deep affection for mystical writers such as Pseudo-Dionysius, Richard Rolle, Walter Hilton, and Bridget of Sweden that made them uneasy with his rationalism as well. Thomas Gascoigne, for one, had been influenced by Thomas Netter and shared his interest in the church fathers.[3] As we will see, such heavy reliance upon antiquity and divine illumination was clearly not Pecock's way to truth. The previous debates examined, whether involving Wyclif and Netter or Hus and Páleč, were conducted according to certain assumptions that all these university masters shared: the unique and perfect truth of the scriptures, the special illumination of the fathers, and the necessity of divine guidance in the ways of biblical interpretation. Pecock would end up discarding some of the most basic features that marked the medieval *magister sacrae paginae*.

In his *Reule of Chrysten Religioun* Pecock found that in those sections of Holy Scripture that recount things already apparent to natural reason we need only believe what is written to the extent that it accords with natural reason.[4] In fact, he would go on to contend that it is only to the extent that the famous doctors follow reason that their explanations are to be accepted. Indeed, one must not follow the doctors any further, since reason always takes precedence. This principle also bears upon Pecock's belief in doctrinal development—one that provides little if any room for the guidance of the Holy Spirit across the ages. No, for Pecock, the question of development pertains to what reason has shown to these doctors. Thus what reason demonstrates may still increase over time and new findings hitherto unknown will later emerge. The problem today, Pecock laments, is that matters are simply left to scripture and the doctors without resolving them on the ground of reason. Such a simplistic reliance upon antiquity has taken over the schools, says Pecock, as scholars trust in these sources without going all the way to the foundation upon which these authorities have, or should have, been basing their arguments.[5] Such sentiments were bound to antagonize Pecock's more traditionally minded opponents, such as Gascoigne and Bury, with their innate respect for biblical eloquence and patristic authority.

In his *Repressor of Over Much Blaming of the Clergy* Pecock did affirm that the truth that human reason cannot attain apart from divine revelation is grounded upon Holy Scripture.[6] Moral laws, on the other hand, such as love of God and neighbor, can be known by the judgment of human reason just as sufficiently as they are taught by scripture. After all, the pagan philosophers discovered these things by their own natural intelligence. Yet Pecock goes even further when he contends that scripture often provides insufficient teaching in some matters, such as marriage and usury, telling us very little about the precise nature of what it enjoins and prohibits. Scripture forbids usury so that we can see that it is unlawful, but it tells us little or nothing about what exactly constitutes usury. While scripture may command us to be just to our neighbor, it is reason that teaches the nature of justice. In fact, were scripture destroyed—as may have happened once before during the Babylonian Captivity—natural reason could still know the moral truths.[7] These are the sorts of remarks that would later be attacked by John Bury, inasmuch as Pecock seems dismissive of the uniquely sacred way in which scripture imparts all truth. Although most would have accepted the confluence of natural reason and divine revelation in the basic statutes of the moral law, none would have followed Pecock in deeming scripture insufficient in these matters. This is what so infuriated men such as Bury.

As Pecock traced the outlines of history, he noted that before God gave any positive law to the Jews they were living by moral truths known by natural reason. And these are the same moral truths to which Christians were bound in the time of the New Testament. Even after the Jews received the ceremonial law, this did not signal the abrogation of the moral law. Nor did Christ revoke the moral law; only the positive law changed with respect to the sacraments in the time of the New Testament. The sacraments were the only law that Christ added, therefore, while he kept the law of nature and reason intact. The point of all this, for Pecock, is that the moral law is not grounded in scripture but instead in the law of nature that is written in the human soul.[8] So it is that whenever Christ and the apostles speak of moral truths they are presupposing these same truths when calling upon people to return to them. And if they are presupposed, then clearly such truths cannot be not grounded in the sayings of scripture, Christ, or the apostles.[9] Here again, Pecock seems to be driving an artificial wedge between scripture and reason, thereby creating a chasm that renders scripture all but unnecessary in matters of moral theology.

There was a long-standing medieval tradition that emphasized personal sanctity as a prerequisite for attaining genuine knowledge of spiritual truths. The piety and affections of the exegete were as important for Wyclif as they were for Gerson. For Pecock, however, genuine scholarship need not be a moral enterprise. Thus in the face of such traditional claims put forward by the Wycliffites, Pecock argued that experience has proven that even a vicious man is capable of attaining a genuine understanding of scripture. To find the true meaning of scripture is a labor of intellect rather than morals. The brighter vicious man might indeed grasp the meaning before the slower-witted virtuous man. For no truth can be known without argument, whether it be a matter of the law of nature or law of faith. Nor does God necessarily withhold his grace from the wicked. In fact, God bestows his gift of understanding Holy Scripture upon the good and the bad alike— sometimes even more upon the worse man.[10]

Yet Pecock is ultimately not interested in quibbling over biblical exegesis at all. For he will go so far as to contend that the positive law of faith—which scripture does ground and teach—is not so worthy in itself, or even necessary to serve God and merit eternal reward, as the judgment of reason, which is itself the moral law of nature. Pecock makes it quite clear that Holy Scripture, with respect to the positive laws of faith, is not so inherently valuable as the law of nature. For there is no law of faith except the positive law of faith, and this law pertains only to the new sacraments. On the other hand, the judgment of reason—understood as the process of the making of syllogisms—is the cause of all human understanding in matters of faith or otherwise. This means that scripture amounts only to the knowledge caused by the judgment of reason, and thus is not so worthy as the judgment of reason itself.[11] Such remarks have led modern scholars such as Everett Emerson to conclude that even as Pecock recognized that it was the function of scripture to ground matters of faith that are not to be based on reason, he still regarded moral philosophy as even more important than scripture in attaining salvation.[12] Along these lines, Ghosh notes that Pecock has set aside both personal sanctity and sacred tradition as a means to doctrinal clarity in favor of a rational analysis of morality conducted by a cadre of erudite clerics.[13]

It was in this vein that Pecock seemed to conflate faith and reason rather than simply recognize their mutual complementarity. He insisted that understanding one's faith is itself meritorious; the amassing of evidence is good in God's sight. Basing belief on sufficient evidence is a reasonable act and thus virtuous.[14] As Vivian Green writes, "Pecock does not at any time deny the necessity of faith but he beats the bounds with certain qualifications which challenge its importance and even reduce its significance."[15] And along these lines E. F. Jacobs concluded that for Pecock "faith then is a kind of knowing (kunning), and involves the use of the reason; and just as it is the function of scripture to teach and reveal the truths of the faith, so conversely it is to be inferred that the scriptures must be reasonable if they are to be believed."[16]

Such an exaltation of reason to the detriment of both faith and scripture was simply intolerable to Pecock's contemporaries, who were outraged by his deprecation of the sacred interpretive tradition. When Pecock eventually faced trial Archbishop Bourgchier declared that he had "manifestly presumed to contravene the sayings of the more authentic doctors." Pecock was also convicted of heresy based upon the most fundamental principle of all: he had interpreted scripture in a manner other than the Holy Spirit requires (cf. *Haeresis,* C. 24. q. 3, c. 27). In short, Pecock had set himself apart from the church and her holy doctors. When Pecock finally abjured his positions and consigned his books to the fire, he was forced to agree that his crimes resulted from "presuming of mine own natural wit, and preferring the judgement of natural reason before the Old and New Testaments, and the authority and determination of our mother, Holy Church."[17]

As noted above, Pecock's preference for the capacities of reason over the testimony of the saints was especially odious to his fellow theologians. Thomas Gascoigne took issue with Pecock for claiming that the sayings of the doctors are not to be believed unless they can be proven by natural reason; and that the sense of Holy Scripture is confined to that which the author of the text first intended, which itself must be judged by human reason.[18] He also noted that Pecock had preached in London that the sayings of saints, such as Jerome and Augustine, are worthy of no greater belief than those of any other wayfarer. Gascoigne, for his part, took a traditional stance when he contended that the saints spoke and wrote under the inspiration of the Holy Spirit; that they possessed more grace and knowledge than other wayfarers; and that their sayings were recognized among the ancient fathers as "authentic, which is to say, worthy of belief"—*autentica, i.e., credulitate digna.*[19] Here again is another fundamental axiom that all sides of the Wycliffite debates over the years had accepted: the special inspiration, and hence the unique authority, of the fathers. To claim otherwise would have been unthinkable. Present arguments found their authority precisely when they were grounded in the testimony of the fathers.

The Response of John Bury

Now we can turn to the Augustinian friar and theologian John Bury who composed his *Gladius Salamonis* in 1458–59 as a direct refutation of Pecock's views on natural reason expressed in the *Repressor of Over Much Blaming of the Clergy.*[20] Here we see that it was not simply Pecock's appeal to reason as such that so incensed Bury but the exaltation of reason at the expense of Holy Scripture. Bury's tract is a sustained argument for the absolute sufficiency and superiority of scripture in ways that may even outdo

Wyclif himself. Here in the *Gladius Salamonis* Bury contends at the outset that God has instituted Holy Scripture as the foundation of all divine laws and truths that may otherwise be discovered by natural reason. Holy Scripture, which is itself synonymous with theology, according to Bury, is sufficient to lead man to God. Thus no matter what natural reason may be capable of, it is the unique task of scripture to achieve this end. In fact, Bury makes this case first from scripture itself, turning to Ecclesiastes, "The sayings of the wise are like goads, and like nails firmly fixed are the collected sayings that are given by one shepherd. Anything beyond these my child, you do not need" (12:11–12). And from Hebrews, "Long ago God spoke to our ancestors in many and various ways by the prophets, but in these last days he has spoken to us by a Son" (1:1–2). This, according to Bury, makes it quite clear that nothing more than Holy Scripture is required. Now, he does not go so far as to argue that scripture offers a precise directive on every single matter. Rather, he notes that it is sufficient for a science—in this case theology, which is equated with scripture—to manifest general principles through which the specific conclusions contained therein can be deduced, even if the science does not itself hand down every single conclusion as such. It is in this sense that Bury contends that the principles of all actions that lead man to God are either the natural virtues that perfect men in a human way or the supernatural virtues that are infused into men so as to perfect them in a divine way. Yet both sorts are sufficiently handed down in the Old and New Testaments, notably in Deuteronomy, the Books of Solomon, the Gospels, and the Canonical Epistles. Here, then, in Holy Scripture, one will find the sufficient foundation for all actions that lead man to God.[21]

Bury clearly rejects Pecock's claim, therefore, that there are moral principles that do not derive from scripture and thus are even presupposed by it. For Bury contends that all human morals are either infused or acquired, and yet both types of morals are most perfectly handed down in Holy Scripture. Scripture is never redundant, as Pecock implies, since it most perfectly demonstrates even those acquired virtues that might otherwise be known by the light of natural reason. This is because scripture presents them under the light of revelation *(in lumine revelationis)*, thereby excluding the darkness of ignorance so that they might be known perfectly.[22] And along these lines, Bury insists that Holy Scripture actually forms the basis for all law: that of nature, the synagogue, and the church. The law of nature is found in Genesis and into Exodus; that of the synagogue from Exodus up to the Gospels; and the law of Christ's church contains the teachings of the apostles.[23]

It is evident as Bury speaks of scripture that he is not confining himself to written texts. Instead, he has in mind the whole positive disclosure of the divine will to mankind across the ages. Hence, in contrast to Pecock's claim that scripture did not exist prior to Abraham, and thus could not have provided the foundation of the moral life that preceded it, Bury argues that Holy Scripture originated where the first positive law was given to man by God. Scripture began, therefore, with Adam. The upshot of this is that from the very first believer to the last there will always be one law—Holy Scripture. Thus scripture began with the inception of natural law. For Bury contends that, although the law of nature was prior to the written version of the Old Testament, it did not actually precede the Old Testament itself. Rather, the essence of the Old Testament was already in place much as the rules of grammar exist before anyone puts them into writing. Hence Bury can claim with confidence that Holy Scripture existed prior to the hands and pens of the scribes who wrote it down.[24] For Bury (as also for Wyclif), Holy Scripture can be described in the traditional terms of the eternal *Liber Vitae*, which precedes and transcends any physical manifestation of its contents.

Bury is clear that no part of divine law given to man can be lacking a foundation in scripture, for however much of the law of nature has been inscribed on the heart of man it is that much more firmly and certainly set down in scripture. In fact, every law given to man can be reduced to evangelical, Mosaic, and natural law—any one of which is founded in scripture. We find also in Bury, therefore, an unwillingness to separate fully the natural and the divine law. In a sense all true law is divine law, and no part of divine law given to man can lack foundation in scripture. For Bury will argue that the law of natural justice through which we universally discern good from evil is nothing other than the impression of divine light. All law is ultimately derivative of divine law *(lex divina)*, and divine law is perfectly revealed in Holy Scripture. Only the divine law so revealed possesses the full sufficiency and certitude to lead man to perfection.[25] Thus Bury considers moral philosophy to be a subclass of theology, which means that what is founded in this derivative philosophy is thus more perfectly revealed in the general theology of Holy Scripture. And this, in turn, means that it is reasonable to look for moral teachings within scripture itself, since whatever relates to partial perfection subsists more perfectly in the whole than in the part.[26]

Bury is not content merely to ground all law in Holy Scripture. For not only is scripture the source of all truth, but that truth can be accessed by the simple and pure of heart apart from any university education. Contrary to Pecock who had rejected the Wycliffite appeal to special illumination, therefore, Bury will make the case precisely for the light of divine grace as a means to true knowledge. He contends that although the natural law founded in the judgment of reason is indeed very useful for those Catholics who are not immediately illuminated by divine revelation, it is not universally necessary for all people. Appealing to Augustine, he points to the apostles as a prime example. Indeed, Bury goes so far as to say that revelation alone *(per solam revelationem)* will suffice for some people apart from moral philosophy founded upon the judgment of human reason.[27] Illiterate and uneducated men *(illiterati viri et simplices)* have reason to praise God for having learned the most certain rules of life, not by way of natural philosophies and human teachings, but from the holy fathers, prophets, and apostles. This fact, says Bury, is evident throughout the Old and New Testaments. Deeply distrustful of human reason operating apart from the guidance of divine inspiration, Bury finds that every teaching of our own invention, and all human philosophy, is prone to error and certainly bears the suspicion of such. Hence God in his mercy leads the faithful, not by way of the rational investigations, but through the holy fathers and the Sacred Scriptures.[28] Everything that Pecock had tried so hard to undo in Wycliffite argumentation—the whole notion of pious illiterate men filled with divine grace in no need of a university degree—is now being dismantled by John Bury the Oxford-trained theologian.

It is Pecock who is the enemy now. His error bears a fraudulent sweetness meant to seduce simple unlearned souls. For nothing could be sweeter in the ears of men than the (false) exaltation of their own natural reason. Pecock's entire program is designed to appeal to human vanity, telling the people that their reason need not be led by the Spirit or informed by the scriptures, such that they could serve God perfectly by their own industry. According to Bury, Pecock proves himself worse than Sabellius, Arius, and even Wyclif, for none among them would oppose the very Spirit of Truth with such fury. Other heretics may have corrupted the church's great doctrines, but only Pecock has struck at the very root of the Catholic faith itself; for he alone has questioned the most certain and constant witness of Holy Scripture. Take away the most steadfast testimony of the scriptures, asks Bury, and what do you have of Christ? What do you know of the Trinity; of the remedy of the sacraments; and the power of redemption? Pecock has turned away from the apostles and apostolic men. He refuses to accept the sense of the patriarchs and prophets, choosing instead his own moral philosophy and the judgment of his own reason.²⁹ It seems fair to say that when Bury looked at Wyclif he at least recognized the image of a medieval theologian, however distorted by heresy this image might be. Pecock does not even register on the spectrum.

For all his invective, however, one is still left to ask how Bury has furthered the cause of anti-Wycliffism. It seems that in his zeal to attack Pecock he may have lost sight of the larger battle. Mishtooni Bose captures the situation perfectly: "In characterizing Pecock as the enemy of scripture and responding to him on precisely those terms, he himself runs the risk of appearing to be an advocate of the supreme authority of scripture over ancillary traditions in a manner recalling Wyclif, at least as the latter's hostile opponents—such as Pecock himself—had been content to characterize Wycliffite thought." Moreover, as Bose points out, in focusing so intently on Holy Scripture, Bury may be "painting himself into a corner" as he narrows the field of legitimate discourse and thus renders the debate that much more intractable.³⁰

Pecock met the usual end for the medieval heretic who is forced to abjure his previous statements and suffer the time-tested accusation of having preferred his own opinion to that of scripture and the church. Except in Pecock's case it was not so much a question of having followed some novel reading of the biblical texts so as to ignore the received, and thus authoritative, interpretation. Rather, it was that he challenged the very means of authority by which the truth of the text was revealed. The typical medieval master charged with error or heresy believes that he has correctly understood the biblical text as the holy doctors would have it; he is the one in accord with the tradition while his accusers have gone astray. Hence it will come down to a battle over the authoritative sources: scripture, patristic writings, and canon law. Pecock, however, was not the typical medieval master. His approach to the task of theology was actually an attempt to bring "medieval theology" itself to a close. For here was someone who did not—much to Gascoigne's vexation—see the inherent value attached to a tradition that is embodied in the fathers and holy doctors. Those whose writings Wyclif and Hus armored themselves with against all comers are the very ones that Pecock is content to discard if they do not meet the test of sound reason. Perhaps this is the final irony, then, for it may prove that Wycliffite doctrines of authority were really much closer to the "orthodox" position after all. The battle over heresy and orthodoxy would continue to be fought over scripture and the fathers.

Crisis at the Heart of the Medieval Church

How could these debates ever be brought to a decisive conclusion? It is clear that what so frustrated Woodford, Netter, Páleč, and Gerson was the express claim on the part of the Wycliffites and Hussites that they would submit to the authority of the church only to refuse to obey the judgments of this prelate or that synod. Such an attitude seemed to render all talk of authority farcical inasmuch as authority itself will be at once everywhere and nowhere. If everyone is free to choose his own judge nothing can be resolved. When everyone believes in the One, Holy, Catholic, and Apostolic Church, the battles will never end until some entity can speak authoritatively for that church and do so here and now.

Both Woodford and Netter believed that popes and councils could err, and thus in principle are subject to correction. Nevertheless, they counseled that in practice one ought to accept the judgments presently handed down by lawfully constituted synods and duly appointed prelates. This seems to be a matter of common sense if one hopes to avoid utter chaos. And yet these men also recognized that the reception of such judgments played an important role in securing their legitimacy. There is a time for scrutiny—and this is where the trouble begins. The authority of councils and prelates is real, but so is that of the university masters. It is a different sort of authority in that the master cannot authorize an article of faith or enact a canonical statute, but he does have the right, indeed the duty, to weigh in on the decision-making process. Such assertions of magisterial authority did not begin with Wyclif and Hus, of course; this line was actively pursued by the theologians at Paris a century earlier. Indeed, challenging the legitimacy of a papal bull was hardly some novel practice invented by a rogue theologian in late medieval Oxford.

Guido Terreni concluded—in the midst of his battles against heresy—that the church could locate the final and authoritative reading of scripture in the infallible judgment of the pope. Under the inspiration of the Holy Spirit the pope could be counted upon to declare the truth. Without much support in its own day, this theory was clearly not going to prevail in the midst of the papal schism. Yet the principle that some kind of infallible judgment could be attained, that there was some entity capable of rendering such a judgment, did prevail in the form of conciliarism. Hence the fundamental belief that the faith of the church could not fail (Lk 22:32) would be manifested not in the papacy, as Terreni might have it, but in the general council representing the universal church. No matter which solution one may prefer, here then are two serious attempts to solve the central problem of final authority in the medieval church. As it turned out, however, conciliarism began to unravel with the disintegration of the Council of Basel. As for papal infallibility, it would have to wait until 1870 to achieve full dogmatic status,[31] and even now there is much discussion as to its precise application.

Having said that, though, the Council of Constance seemed to have brought a protracted crisis to a close, asserting its own authority not only to end the schism, but to condemn the Wycliffites and Hussites once and for all. That such crises existed, however, can be traced to the greater ambiguities that were almost built in to the late medieval church as a whole. Brian Tierney has demonstrated how such uncertainty manifested itself among the fourteenth-century canonists. On the one hand, they were intent on affirming the pope as the source of all authority; Joannes Andreae went so far as to refer to the pope as "the lord of the world." And yet, as Tierney concludes, the canonists ultimately failed "to integrate those claims into a coherent theory of ecclesiastical authority that could be applied consistently in all actual and foreseeable circumstances."[32] They found it very difficult to reconcile their concept of the church as the *collectio fidelium*—a corporation bearing its own inherent authority—with the sort of papal absolutism they sought to promote. The result, then, was "a real uncertainty in the face of the fundamental problems concerning the juristic structure of the Church and the interrelation of its various forms of government."[33] This constitutional dilemma is paralleled by the problems facing the medieval theologians—problems that the Wycliffites and Hussites by no means created even as they rendered them more acute.

One of the most essential and persistent elements of the Wycliffite and Hussite reform programs was the claim that papal power—in the form of jurisdictional prerogatives, dispensations, and penalties—now far exceeded the rightful mandate granted to the Petrine office as conceived by biblical and patristic sources. Neither Wyclif nor Hus sought to abolish the papacy, nor did they even demand explicit scriptural warrant for every ecclesiastical law enacted by the pope. Yet in asking for at least some implicit biblical foundation as Wyclif and Hus did, they were hardly alone. Nor were they alone in lamenting the expanding power of the canonists in the service of the papacy.

These were the perennial concerns of the medieval theologians—concerns that were vociferously echoed by the likes of Pierre d'Ailly and Jean Gerson. These Parisian masters were no less committed to the principal authority of Holy Scripture and the rights of the theologians than their Oxford and Prague counterparts. And it might also be added that these Parisian secular masters could be quite protective of their own rights over against mendicant claims backed by the papacy: witness the hostile reaction to the papal bull *Regnans in excelsis*. Yet despite the striking if not overwhelming similarities between the different camps, the Wycliffites and Hussites were branded as ideological extremists who exalted their own simplistic biblical literalism over the received traditions of the church.

One is still left to ask how it came to this; why was Jan Hus dispatched to the stake by his fellow university masters? No doubt this is a grievous example of the *odium theologicum;* finally there was an opportunity to silence a fractious colleague, indeed obliterate him. Yet this ultimate act of injustice was decades in the making. Perhaps it was the culmination of so much growing frustration with the inability to resolve the church's problems—problems that had reached crisis proportion with the outbreak of the papal schism. If sensible reform were going to proceed, then the more intemperate voices would have to be quashed. Nothing was going to be accomplished so long as a few privileged masters could pen inflammatory tracts from their comfortable college lodgings. In the eyes of Woodford and Netter—master and student it seems—irresponsible theologians like Wyclif were, if not the sole threat to the church, nevertheless significant contributors to the disarray. Whether their perception is accurate or not, they concluded that the time had passed for merely requesting more temperate rhetoric on the part of their fellow masters. Opponents of the Wycliffites and Hussites realized that if they hoped to gain some traction against their colleagues they would have to discredit them entirely. Some only came late to that conclusion— a good example being Stephen Páleč, who had once protested the condemnation of Wycliffite theses at Prague.

Everyone wanted to see the implementation of genuine reform, but someone would have to assert control over the reform process itself. Central to achieving reform, therefore, entailed gaining a decisive victory over these otherwise uncooperative colleagues. Thus one would have to generate an alternative narrative wherein Wyclif and Hus become dangerous radicals who have forsaken the Catholic tradition, who have excluded themselves from the patrimony of the saints, and thus have forfeited their right to be heard. And one can add to this another element—the discussion of which must be saved for another day—namely, the fear of popular heresy and political insurrection. Once Wycliffite ideas spill out of the university into the town, and are no longer couched in proper and authoritative Latin but instead in the vulgar tongue, there is no way to predict where it will all end. One recalls, for instance, Páleč's charge that Hus's preaching was fostering rebelliousness and anticlericalism among the laity. And, of course, it is true that the Hussites did emerge as a formidable force in the decades following Jan Hus's death, even winning the right to the chalice in Bohemia.

In the end, though, we are brought back to the central fact that the theological and ecclesiological controversies that began in the fourteenth century, and then reached their logical conclusion perhaps in the sixteenth century with the (regrettable) fracturing of the Western church, were largely the result of doctrinal and institutional uncertainty. This allowed for a measure of freedom and flexibility that was surely beneficial to Christendom; the glories of the whole scholastic enterprise depended upon such elasticity. Nonetheless, the acceptance of this indeterminacy meant that when conflicts erupted, as they inevitably must, there were precious few fixed means to solve them, few in the way of absolute standards by which cases could be resolved. One would have to wait until the crisis of authority had rent the fabric of the church beyond repair before such measures could be put into place. The Council of Constance (1414–18) belonged to a very different world than the Council of Trent (1545–63), which issued formal definitions on everything from the biblical canon to the process of justification and the nature of the sacraments. Hence, so long as the church offered few in the way of final determinations, it may be difficult to speak even of dissent, let alone heresy, in the case of the late medieval university masters.

Notes

Chapter 1. Facets of Authority in the Late Medieval Church

1. C. 24, q. 3, c. 27; in *Corpus iuris canonici*, 2 vols., ed. E. Friedberg (Leipzig, 1879; reprint, Graz, 1960), 1:997–98: "Heresis grece ab electione dicitur, quod scilicet eam sibi unusquisque eligat disciplinam, quam putat esse meliorem. Quicumque igitur aliter scripturam intelligit, quam sensus Spiritus sancti flagitat, a quo scripta est, licet ab ecclesia non recesserit, tamen hereticus appellari potest." Cf. Jerome, *Comm. in Epist. ad Galatas*, *PL* 26:417a.

2. *Summa de haeresibus et earum confutationibus*, ed. Iodocus Badius Ascensius (Paris, 1528), *De haeresibus generatim*, ch. 4, f. 4v: "Opinio etenim illa haeretica quae expresse et euidenter scripturae sacrae aduersatur, sic quod est contra expressum textum novi vel veteris testamenti. Haec enim est scriptura canonica et catholica eminentissimae auctoritatis. . . . Vnde scriptura canonica nil continet nisi verum." For more on Terreni's understanding of scriptural authority, see Ian Christopher Levy, "Guido Terreni: Reading Holy Scripture within the Sacred Tradition," *Carmelus* 56 (2009): 73–106.

3. *Contra Faustum* 11.5, *CSEL* 25/1:320.

4. *Epistola* 82.1, *PL* 33:277.

5. *Lectura Ordinaria super sacram scripturam*, ed. R. Macken (Leiden, 1980), 5.

6. *Lectura Ordinaria*, 6.

7. *Lectura Ordinaria*, 6–8.

8. *Summa quaestionum ordinarium* (Paris, 1520; reprint, St. Bonaventure, NY, 1953), a. 9, q. 2, f. 71v.

9. *Summa quaestionum ordinarium*, a. 9, q. 3, f. 72v: "Ideo absolute dicendum quod huic scientiae principaliter credendum est propter dei auctoritatem, et nulli alii nisi in quantum ex virtute dei refulgente circa ipsum constet eum mediatorem dei in hoc fuisse."

10. *Summa quaestionum ordinarium*, a. 10, q. 1, f. 73r–73v: "Aut enim intelligitur comparatio scripturae ad ecclesiam quae vere est ecclesia et merito et reputatione. Aut reputatione tantum. Primo modo omnino credendum est aequaliter scripturae et ecclesiae, quia in nullo discrepare possunt. Secundo autem modo dicendum, quod simpliciter et absolute magis credendum est sacrae scripturae quam ecclesiae, quia veritas ipsa in scriptura immobiliter et impermutabiliter semper custoditur."

11. *Summa quaestionum ordinarium*, a. 10, q. 1, f. 73v.

12. *Summa quaestionum ordinarium*, a. 10, q. 1, f. 74r: "Sic certe fidelis sacra scriptura cognita et in ipsa Christo invento plus verbis Christi in ea credit quam cuicumque praedicatori, quam etiam ecclesiae testificanti, quid propter illam iam credit ecclesiae, et si ipsa quaedam contraria scripturae diceret, ipsi non crederet, et ideo talis robur fidei in auctoritate huius scientiae perfectissime consistit."

13. B. M. Xiberta, *De scriptoribus scholasticis saeculi XIV ex ordine Carmelitarum* (Louvain, 1931), 75–76. See also Beryl Smalley, "Gerard of Bologna and Henry of Ghent," *Recherches de Théologie Ancienne et Médiévale* 22 (1955): 125–29.

14. Twelve questions from the *Summa Magistri Gerardi Bononiensis* have been edited by Paul de Vooght in his *Les sources de la doctrine chrétienne* (Bruges, 1954), 269–483.

15. *Summa*, q. 5, a. 1, p. 356.

16. *Summa*, q. 5, a. 1, pp. 356–57.

17. *Summa*, q. 5, a. 1, p. 357.

18. *Summa*, q. 5, a. 1, pp. 357–58: "Sed iste modus dicendi non uidetur bene racionabilis. Primo quidem quia, credens recte, non credit ecclesie nec scripture, nisi propter auctoritatem dei. Vnde utrobique credit ipsi deo et auctoritati eius est unica est. Propter quod, inconuenienter distinguitur de auctoritate ecclesie et scripture in hic casu, quia una est non diuersa. . . . ita quod in hoc inspeccio scripture comparatur auditui uiue uocis, non auctoritas ecclesie auctoritati scripture, quia ex hoc dari patet quod ecclesia non predicat nisi sacram scripturam."

19. *Summa*, q. 5, a. 1, p. 359.

20. *Contra epistolam Manichaei quam vocant Fundamenti* 5, *PL* 42:176–77.

21. *Summa*, q. 5, a. 1, pp. 359–60.

22. See Jean Leclercq, "L'Idéal du théologien au Moyen Age," *Revue des Sciences Religieuses* 21 (1947): 121–48.

23. *De doctrina christiana* 2.42.63, *CCSL* 32:76–77.

24. *De magistro* 11.38, *CCSL* 29:196.

25. *De doctrina christiana* 1.40.44, *CCSL* 32:31–32.

26. *De perfectione evangelica*, Q. 2, a. 1, in *Opera Omnia*, 10 vols. (Quaracchi, 1882–1902), 5:125–26.

27. *Collationes in Hexaëmeron* 3.4–3.9, in *Opera Omnia*, 5:343–45. See also Jacques Guy Bougerol, "Une theologie biblique de la Revelation," *Antonianum* 48 (1973): 95–104; Henry Donneaud, "Le sens du mot *theologia* chez Bonaventure,"

Revue Thomiste 102 (2002): 271–95; and Zachary Hayes, *The Hidden Center: Spirituality and Speculative Christology in St. Bonaventure* (New York, 1981), 192–93.

28. *Breviloquium, prologus*, in *Opera Omnia*, 5:207.

29. *Breviloquium, prologus*, pp. 201–2.

30. *Principium quinque in sacram scripturam* 2.6–2.13, in *Peter of John Olivi on the Bible*, ed. David Flood and Gedeon Gál (St. Bonaventure, NY, 1997), 44–47.

31. *Principium* 4.3, p. 180.

32. *Principium* 3.7–3.8, p. 80.

33. *Compendium sensus litteralis totius divinae scripturae, prologus*, ed. Philbert Seeboeck (Quaracchi, 1896), 1–7.

34. *PL* 113:25c–26d.

35. *PL* 113:26d–27a.

36. *PL* 113:27b.

37. *PL* 113:27d.

38. *PL* 113:28a. Cf. Grosseteste, Dictum 3, MS. Bodley 798 (SC 2656), fol. 4va. See also Gianmaria Zamagni, "Ermeneutica e metafisica: I due Prologhi della Postilla litteralis di Nicola di Lyra O. F. M.," *Dianoia* 12 (2007): 57–85.

39. *Biblia Sacra iuxta Vulgatum Versionem*, ed. Robert Weber (Stuttgart, 1969), 364–66. See also E. F. Sutcliffe, "Jerome," in *The Cambridge History of the Bible*, 3 vols., ed. G. W. H. Lampe (Cambridge, 1969), 2:83–93.

40. *PL* 19:787–93.

41. *PL* 59:157–64. See D. J. Chapman, "On the Decretum Gelasianum: De Libris Recipiendis et non Recipiendis," *Revue Benedictine* 30 (1913): 187–207, 315–33; and Gilbert Dahan, *L'Exégèse chrétienne de le Bible en Occident médiéval XII–XIV siècle* (Paris, 1999), 57–61.

42. *Summa Theologiae* 1, q. 89, a. 8. See P. Synave, "Le canon scripturaire de Saint Thomas d'Aquin," *Revue Biblique* 33 (1924): 522–33; and Ceslaus Spicq, "Le canon des livres saints au XIII siècle," *Revue des Sciences Philosophiques et Théologiques* 30 (1942): 424–31.

43. *Didascalicon* 4.2, ed. C. H. Buttimer (Washington, DC, 1939), 71–72; *De sacramentis christianae fidei*, prologue 7; *PL* 176:186c–d; *De scripturis et scriptoribus sacris* 6; *PL* 175:16a.

44. *Opus Minus*, in *Rogeri Bacon Opera quaedem hactenus inedita*, ed. J. S. Brewer, Rolls Series 15 (London, 1859), 330.

45. Dahan, *L'Exégèse chrétienne de le Bible*, 223–38.

46. *Opus Tertium*, in *Rogeri Bacon Opera*, ed. Brewer, p. 94: "Septima causa quare oportet nos scire rationes linguarum est pro sensu literali sciendo, et spirituali eliciendo veraciter ex literali. . . . Nam si litera est falsa, sensus literalis et spiritualis sunt falsi."

47. See Alastair Minnis and A. B. Scott, *Medieval Literary Theory and Criticism, c. 1100–1375* (Oxford, 1988); and Alastair Minnis, *Medieval Theory of Author-*

ship (London, 1984). See also Ian Christopher Levy, "The Literal Sense of Scripture and the Search for Truth in the Late Middle Ages," *Revue d'Histoire Ecclésiastique* 104 (2009): 783–827.

48. *Summa Theologiae* 1, q. 1, a. 10.

49. *Summa Theologiae* 1, q. 1, a. 10. Cf. Augustine, *Confessiones* 12.42, *CCSL* 27:240–41.

50. *De potentia* 4.1, in *Opera Omnia*, 34 vols. (Paris, 1871–80), 13:119.

51. For a history of the controversy, see Henri de Lubac, *Exégèse médiévale: Les quatre sens de l'Écriture*, 2 vols. (Paris, 1959–64), 2/2:277–85.

52. Mark F. Johnson, "Another Look at the Plurality of the Literal Sense," *Medieval Philosophy and Theology* 2 (1992): 117–41. See also Thomas Prügl, "Thomas Aquinas as Interpreter of Scripture," in *The Theology of Thomas Aquinas*, ed. Rik Van Nieuwenhove and Joseph Wawrykow (Notre Dame, IN, 2005), 386–415.

53. *PL* 113:28c–29a.

54. *PL* 113:33d–34c.

55. *PL* 113:34d.

56. *PL* 113:31d–32a.

57. See Katherine Walsh, "Richard FitzRalph," in *Dictionary of National Biography*, 60 vols., ed. H. C. G. Matthew and Brian Harrison (Oxford, 2004), 19:917–22; Walsh, *A Fourteenth-Century Scholar and Primate: Richard FitzRalph in Oxford, Avignon, and Armagh* (Oxford, 1981), 133–72; Walsh, "Preaching, Pastoral Care, and Sola Scriptura in Later Medieval Ireland: Richard FitzRalph and the Use of the Bible," in *The Bible in the Medieval World: Essays in Honour of Beryl Smalley*, ed. Katherine Walsh and Diana Wood (London, 1985), 251–68.

58. *Summa Domini Armacani in questionibus Armenorum* 1.1, ed. Johannis Sudoris (Paris, 1511), f. 2r.

59. *Summa* 1.2, f. 2r. For a fuller discussion, see Minnis, *Medieval Theory of Authorship*, 100–102; and Alastair Minnis, "'Authorial Intention' and the 'Literal Sense' in the Exegetical Theories of Richard FitzRalph and John Wyclif," *Proceedings of the Irish Academy* 75 (1975): 1–31.

60. *Summa* 6.11, f. 43r–43v.

61. *Summa* 6.6, f. 41r.

62. *Summa* 6.12, f. 43v–44r.

63. *Summa* 7.3–7.4, f. 45v–46r.

64. *Summa* 1.13, f. 5v.

65. *Summa* 1.14, f. 6r.

66. *Summa* 19.21, f. 157v.

67. *Summa* 19.19, f. 156v–157r. Cf. Augustine, *Contra Faustum* 11.5, *CSEL* 25/1:320; and *De doctrina christiana* 2.9–15, *CCSL* 32:40–48.

68. *Summa* 19.20, f. 157r.

69. Albert Lang, *Heinrich Totting von Oyta* (Münster, 1937), 6–43. See also Frank Rosenthal, "Heinrich von Oyta and Biblical Criticism in the Fourteenth Century," *Speculum* 25 (1950): 178–83.

70. *Henrici Totting de Oyta Quaestio de Sacra Scriptura et de Veritatibus Catholicis*, ed. Albert Lang (Münster, 1953), 10.

71. *Quaestio de Sacra Scriptura*, 10–11.

72. *Quaestio de Sacra Scriptura*, 11–12. Cf. Jerome's preface to the Pentateuch in *Biblia Sacra iuxta Vulgatum Versionem*, 3–4; and Augustine, *De civitate Dei* 18:53, *CCSL* 48:652–53.

73. *Quaestio de Sacra Scriptura*, 17–18.

74. *Quaestio de Sacra Scriptura*, 18–19.

75. *Quaestio de Sacra Scriptura*, 22–23.

76. *Quaestio de Sacra Scriptura*, 59–61.

77. *Quaestio de Sacra Scriptura*, 43–46.

78. *Quaestio de Sacra Scriptura*, 52–54.

79. *Quaestio de Sacra Scriptura*, 55–56.

80. See Nicholas of Lyra, *Postilla super Totam Bibliam*, 4 vols. (Strassburg, 1492; reprint, Frankfurt am Main, 1971).

81. *PL* 113:38c.

82. *PL* 113:39d–40a.

83. *PL* 113:40b.

84. *PL* 113:52d–54d.

85. *PL* 113:55a–d.

86. *Chartularium Universitatis Parisiensis*, 4 vols., ed. Henry Denifle (Paris, 1889–97), 2/1:506: "Et quia sermo non habet virtutem, nisi ex impositione et usu communi actorum vel aliorum, ideo talis est virtus sermonis . . . "

87. Zénon Kaluza, "Les sciences et leurs langages," in *Filosofia e teologia nel Trecento: Studi in ricordo Eugenio Randi*, ed. Bianchi Luca (Louvain-la-Neuve, 1994), 197–258. For further discussion of this statute and its ramifications, see William J. Courtenay, "Force of Words and Figures of Speech: The Crisis over *Virtus Sermonis* in the Fourteenth Century," *Franciscan Studies* 44 (1984): 107–28; J. M. M. H. Thijssen, "Once Again the Ockhamist Statutes of 1339 and 1340: Some New Perspectives," *Vivarium* 28 (1990): 136–67; and Maarten Hoenen, "Virtus Sermonis and the Trinity: Marsilius of Inghen and the Semantics of Late-Fourteenth-Century Theology," *Medieval Philosophy and Theology* 10 (2001): 157–71.

88. M.-D. Chenu, *Introduction a l'étude de Saint Thomas d'Aquin* (Paris, 1950), 109–25; and Chenu, "'Authentica' et 'Magistralia': Deux lieux théologiques aux XII–XIII siècles," *Divus Thomas* 28 (1925): 257–85. See Bacon, *Opus Minus*, in *Rogeri Bacon Opera*, 327–28.

89. J. de Ghellinck, "Pour L'Histoire du Mot 'Revelare,'" *Recherches Sciences Religeuses* 6 (1916): 149–57.

90. Dahan, *L'Exégèse chrétienne de le Bible*, 67–68.

91. John Van Engen, "Studying Scripture in the Early University," in *Neue Richtungen in der hoch- und spätmittelalterlichen Bibelexegese*, ed. Robert Lerner and E. Müller-Luckner (Munich, 1996), 17–38.

92. Karlfried Froehlich, "Christian Interpretation of the Old Testament in the High Middle Ages," in *Hebrew Bible/Old Testament: The History of its Interpretation*, vol. 1, pt. 2, ed. Magne Saebø (Göttingen, 2000), 496–558.

93. *Collationes in Hexaëmeron* 19.10–19.14, pp. 421–22.

94. *Principium* 1.28, p. 27.

95. *Principium* 5.15, p. 148.

96. *Summa Theologiae* 1.1, q. 1, a. 8. See Augustine, *Epist.* 82.1, *PL* 33:277.

97. *Summa Theologiae* 2.2, q. 1, a. 8.

98. *Ad Romanos* c. 8, l. 5. See also Nicholas Halligan, "The Teaching of St. Thomas Aquinas in regard to the Apostles," *American Ecclesiastical Review* 145 (1961): 32–47.

99. *Summa de haeresibus (De haeresibus generatim)*, ch. 7, f. 7v: "Quamuis autem sanctorum doctorum scripta extra canonem Bibliae sint tractanda, et legenda, et cum debita reuerentia suscipienda, non tamen sunt sicut summae auctoritatis et inuioabilitatis, quin liceat eis contradicere, et circa ea dubitare: vbi per scripturam sanctam euidenter et expresse non probantur, nec firmantur, nec per ecclesiam auctorizantur, ac determinantur: firmam veritatem et indubiam continere: vnde per dicta sanctorum extra canonem Bibliae praecise non conuinceretur opinio haeretica. Nam vbi non est infallibilis veritas, ibi non est fides certa et indubia, cum certa fides veritati infallibili innitatur, immo circa talia non est assensus infallibilis, nec indubius, nec adhaesio firma. Ex quo enim non est certa et infallibilis veritas, ibi non est fides certa et indubia, et semper assentitur cum dubio et cum formidine falsi."

100. *De Spiritu Sancto* 27.66, ed. Benoît Pruche, *Sources chrétiennes* (Paris, 1968), 478–86; *PG* 32:187–90. See Heiko Oberman, *The Harvest of Medieval Theology* (Durham, NC, 1983), 369–71.

101. George Florovsky, "The Function of Tradition in the Early Church," in *Eastern Orthodox Theology*, 2nd ed., ed. Daniel B. Clandenin (Grand Rapids, MI, 2003), 97–114. Quote at p. 111.

102. *Summa Theologiae* 2.2, q. 1, a. 9.

103. *Summa Theologiae* 2.2, q. 1, a. 10.

104. *Collationes in Hexaëmeron* 16.2, p. 403.

105. *Collationes in Hexaëmeron* 13.2, p. 388.

106. *De perfectione evangelica* q. 2, a. 2, pp. 145–47.

107. *Sent.* 4.23.2, in *Opera Omnia*, 15 vols. (Paris, 1864–71), 6:137: " . . . ideo haec duo sacramenta a Christo fuerunt insinuata, sed post a Spiritu sancto fuerunt instituta."

108. *Sent.* 4.23.2, p. 137.

109. Leo Rosato, "Ioannis Duns Scoti doctrina de scriptura et traditione," in *De Scriptura et Traditione*, ed. P. C. Balić (Rome, 1963), 233–52; Eligius Buytaert, "Circa Doctrinam Duns Scoti de Traditione et de Scriptura Sufficientia Adnnotationes," *Antonianum* 40 (1965): 346–62; Gerardo Cardaropoli, "La Sacra Scrittura nel Pensiero di G. Duns Scoto," *Antonianum* 48 (1973): 123–44.

110. *Ordinatio, Prologus*, in *Opera Omnia*, ed. P. C. Balić (Vatican City, 1950–), 1:59–61.

111. *Ordinatio, Prologus*, in *Opera Omnia*, ed. Balić, 1:61–62.

112. *Ordinatio, Prologus*, in *Opera Omnia*, ed. Balić, 1:62.

113. *Ordinatio, Prologus*, in *Opera Omnia*, ed. Balić, 1:65–66.

114. *Ordinatio, Prologus*, in *Opera Omnia*, ed. Balić, 1:68–69.

115. *Ordinatio, Prologus*, in *Opera Omnia*, ed. Balić, 1:87: "Unde multae veritates necessariae non exprimuntur in sacra Scriptura, etsi ibi virtualiter contineantur, sicut conclusiones in principiis; circa quarum investigationem utilis fuit labor doctorum et expositorum." See Origen, *In Genesim Homilia* 2, *PG* 12:163–64.

116. See above, *Ordinatio*, in *Opera Omnia*, ed. Balić, 1:87.

117. *Ordinatio* 1, d. 11, q. 1, in *Opera Omnia*, ed. Balić, 5:7: "Ad rationem illam de Evangelio dico quod 'Christum descendisse ad inferna' non docetur in Evangelio, et tamen tenendum est sicut articulus fidei, quia ponitur in *Symbolo apostolorum*. Ita multa alia de sacramentis ecclesiae non sunt expressa in Evangelio et tamen ecclesia tenet illa tradita certitudinaliter ab apostolis, et periculosum esset errare circa illa quae non tantum ab apostolis descenderunt per scripta sed etiam quae per consuetudinem universalis Ecclesiae tenenda sunt."

118. *Ordinatio* 1, d. 11, q. 1, in *Opera Omnia*, ed. Balić, 5:8: "Nec Christus in Evangelio docuit omnia pertinentia ad dispensationem sacramentorum; dixit enim discipulis suis (in Ioan.): *Adhuc habeo multa vobis dicere, sed vos non potestis portare modo; cum autem venerit ille Spiritus veritatis, docebit vos omnem veritatem.* Multa ergo docuit eos Spiritus Sanctus, quae non sunt scripta in Evangelio: et illa multa, quaedam per scripturam, quaedam per consuetudinem Ecclesiae, tradiderunt."

119. *Sent.* 4, d. 11, q. 3, in *Opera Omnia*, 26 vols. (Paris, 1891–95), 17:375–76: "Ad argumenta pro prima opinione et secunda. Ad primum, concedo quod etiam in creditis non sunt plura ponenda sine necessitate, nec plura miracula quam oportet. Sed cum dicitur in minori, veritas Eucharistiae posset salvari manente pane vel sine transubtantatione, dico quod bene fuisset Deo possibile instituisse, quod corpus Christi vere esset praesens, substantia panis manente, vel cum accidentibus, pane annihilato, et tunc fuisset ibi veritas Eucharistiae, quia et signum verum signatum verum; . . . Ad secundum, dico quod non est aliquis articulus arctandus ad intellectum difficilem, nisi ille intellectus sit verus; sed si verus est et probatur evidenter esse verum oportet secundum illum intellectum tenere articulum. . . . Et tunc ad tertium, ubi stat vis, dicendum quod Ecclesia declaravit istum intellectum esse de veri-

tate fidei in illo Symbolo edito Innocentio III in Concilio Lateranensi, *Firmiter credimus*, etc. sicut allegatum est superius, ubi explicite ponitur veritas aliquorum credendorum, magis explicite quam habebatur in Symbolo Apostolorum, vel Athanasii, vel Niceni. Et breviter, quidquid ibi dicitur esse credendum, tenendum est esse de substantia fidei, et hoc post istam declarationem solemnem factam ab Ecclesia." With regard to Scotus's navigation of the orthodox readings of transubstantiation see David Burr, "Scotus on Transubstantiation," *Mediaeval Studies* 24 (1972): 336–60.

120. *Sent.* 4, d. 11, q. 3; in *Opera Omnia* (Paris, 1891–95), 17:376: "Et si queras quare voluit ecclesia eligere istum intellectum ita difficilem hujus articuli, cum verba Scripturae possent salvari seccundum intellectum facilem, et veriorem secundum apparentiam de hoc articulo; dico, quod eo Spiritu expositae sunt Scripturae quo conditae. Et ita supponendum est, quod Ecclesia Catholica eo Spiritu exposuit, quo tradita est nobis fides. Spiritu scilicet veritatis edocta, et ideo hunc intellectum eligit, qui verus est. Non enim in potestate Ecclesiae fuit facere istud verum vel non verum, sed Dei instituentis, sed intellectum a Deo traditum Ecclesia explicavit directa in hoc, ut creditur, Spiritu veritatis."

121. *Rep. Par.*, 4, d. 11, q. 3, n. 13, in *Opera Omnia* (Paris, 1891–95), 24:120: "Teneo igitur istam opinionem ibi positam ab Innocentio, quod substantia panis non maneat, sed quod transubstantiatur in corpus Christi, non propter rationes praedictas, quia non cogunt. . . . Et hoc principaliter teneo propter auctoritatem Ecclesiae, quae non errat in his, quae sunt fidei et morum, cujus Vicario primo dixit Christus: *Ego rogavi pro te . . .* "

122. *Dialogus* 1.2.1, in *Monarchia S. Romani Imperii*, 3 vols., ed. M. Goldast (1614; reprint, Graz, 1960), 2:410–11. See *Ego solis*, D. 9, c. 5; Friedberg 1:17; and *Noli frater*, D. 9, c. 9; Friedberg 1:18. Ockham would most likely have been reading the glossed *Decretum*. See, therefore, *Decretum Gratiani Emendatum et Annotationibus Illustratum vna cum Glossis* (Paris, 1601), cols. 33–36. For instance, the gloss on *Ego solis*, D. 9, c. 5, notes that other writers must not be believed, no matter how holy they may be, unless what they have written is supported by the canonical texts: "Aliis autem scriptoribus non est credendum, etsi sancti sint: nisi quod scripserint probauerint per canonicas auctoritates." And it would be impious *(nefas)* to say that scripture could deceive; thus we ought to defend its contents with our very life, thereby quoting from the canon *Sunt quidam dicentes* (C. 25, c. 6, q. 1): "Nefas dicere quod scriptura mentiatur . . . immo quod in eis dicitur, defendere debemus vsque ad sanguinis effusionem, vt 25.q.1.sunt quidam." And the gloss on *Noli frater*, D. 9, c. 9, distinguishes the authority of the canonical scripturas from that of the bishops who are subject to correction: " . . . quia ab auctoritate canonum distinguuntur, vnde reprehendi possunt, si contra veritatem scripta sunt."

123. *Dialogus* 1.2.2; Goldast 2:411–12.

124. *Dialogus* 1.2.3; Goldast 2:412–14. See *Palam est*, D. 11, c. 9; Friedberg 1:25.

125. *Dialogus* 1.2.5; Goldast 2:415–16.

126. *Quaestio de Sacra Scriptura*, 12–13. See also Paul de Vooght, "La décrétale cum Marthae et son interprétation par les théologiens du XIV siècle," *Recherches de Science Religieuse* 42 (1954): 540–48.

127. *Decr. Greg. IX*, L. 3, t. 41, c. 6; Friedberg 2:637.

128. *Quaestio de Sacra Scriptura*, 61–62.

129. *Quaestio de Sacra Scriptura*, 62–63. Cf. Augustine, *Contra epistolam Manichaei quam vocant Fundamenti* 5, *PL* 42:176–77.

130. *Quaestio de Sacra Scriptura*, 66.

131. *Quaestio de Sacra Scriptura*, 68.

132. *Quaestio de Sacra Scriptura*, 69: "Licet omnes veritates catholice fundate sint in canone biblie, non tamen omnes tales explicite continentur in biblia nec ex solis contentis in ea formaliter inferri potest."

133. *Quaestio de Sacra Scriptura*, 70: "Consequencia patet per hoc: quia tam veritates in biblia expresse quam formaliter ex eis inferibiles sufficienter fundate sunt. Similiter et auctoritas ecclesie sufficienter fundata est in ipsa. Hoc patet ex dictis in questione prima; igitur veritates, que tenentur ex auctoritate ecclesie sufficienter in ipsa sunt fundate et sic patet consequencia."

134. *Quaestio de Sacra Scriptura*, 74: " . . . quod nichil addendum est scripturis divinis, quod aliquomodo sit eis dissonum vel quod non sit consonum alicui vero sensui scripture . . ."

135. For detailed discussions, see Manuel Santos Noya, "Schrift, Tradition, und Theologie bei Marsilius von Inghen," in *Marsilius von Inghen: Werk und Wirkung*, ed. Stanisław Wielgus (Lublin, 1993), 73–91; Philipp W. Rosemann, *The Story of a Great Book: Peter Lombard's Sentences* (Peterborough, ON, 2007), 127–36; Paul de Vooght, *Les sources de la doctrine chrétienne*, 210–12.

136. Marsilius von Inghen, *Quaestiones super Quattuor Libros Sententiarum*, 2 vols., ed. Manuel Santos Noya (Leiden, 2000), 1:71–72: " . . . quia scientia iuris canonici habet pro subiecto hominem catholicum dirigibilem ad vitam aeternam per ecclesiae statua et est de veritatibus expressis in libris iuris canonci et extravagantibus eorum. Sed sacra theologia habet Deum pro subiecto prout est finis vitae viatoris fide formata attingibilis . . . et traditur in libris Bibliae vel in se vel in suis principiis . . ."

137. *Quaestiones super Quattuor Libros Sententiarum*, 75–76.

138. Rosemann, *The Story of a Great Book: Peter Lombard's Sentences*, 130–31.

139. Astrik Gabriel, "The Ideal Master of the Mediaeval University," *Catholic Historical Review* 60 (1974): 1–40; Gabriel le Bras, "Velut splendor firmamenti: Le docteur dans le droit de L'Église médiévale," in *Melanges offerts à Etienne Gilson*

(Toronto, 1959), 372–88; Jacques Verger, "Teachers," in *A History of the University in Europe*, 4 vols., ed. Hilde de Ridder-Symoens (Cambridge, 1992–2011), 1:144–68.

140. G. H. M. Posthumus Meyjes, "Quasi Stellae Fulgebunt: On the Position and Function of the Doctor of Divinity in Mediaeval Church and Society," in *In Divers Manners: A St. Mary's Miscellany to commemorate the 450th anniversary of the founding of St. Mary's College, 7th March 1539*, ed. D.W. D. Shaw (St. Andrews, 1990), 11–28.

141. Roger Gryson, "The Authority of the Teacher in the Ancient and Medieval Church," *Journal of Ecumenical Studies* 19 (1982): 176–87.

142. Guy Fitch Lytle, "Universities as Religious Authorities in the Later Middle Ages and Reformation," in *Reform and Authority in the Medieval and Reformation Church*, ed. Guy Fitch Lytle (Washington, DC, 1981), 69–97.

143. *Tractatus brevis de periculis novissimorum temporum* 2, in *Bettelorden und Weltgeistlichkeit an der Universität Paris*, ed. Max Bierbaum (Münster, 1920), 9–13.

144. *De perfectione evangelica* Q. 2, a. 2, pp. 153–55.

145. *Exceptiones contra librum qui incipit Manus que contra Omnipotentem tenditur* 17, ed. Bierbaum, 200–203.

146. See the classic article by Yves Congar, "Aspects ecclésiologiques de la querrele entre mendicants et séculars," *Archives d'Histoire doctrinale et littérature du Moyen Age* 28 (1961): 35–151.

147. M. S. Kempshall, *The Common Good in Late Medieval Political Thought* (Oxford, 1999), 258–60.

148. Quodlibet 3, q. 10, in *Les philosophes belges*, vol. 2, ed. M. de Wulf and A. Pelzer (Louvain, 1904), 218.

149. Quodlibet 12, q. 6, in *Les philosophes belges*, vol. 5, ed. J. Hoffmans (Louvain, 1932), 105.

150. Ian P. Wei, "The Self-Image of the Masters of Theology at the University of Paris in the Late Thirteenth and Early Fourteenth Centuries," *Journal of Ecclesiastical History* 46 (1995): 398–441. See also Alan Bernstein, "Magisterium and License: Corporate Autonomy against Papal Authority in the Medieval University of Paris," *Viator* 9 (1978): 291–307; Mary Martin McLaughlin, *Intellectual Freedom and Its Limitations in the University of Paris in the Thirteenth and Fourteenth Centuries* (New York, 1977), 238–45.

151. Henry Denifle, "Quel livre servait de base a l'Enseignement des Maitres en Théologie dans l'Université de Paris," *Revue Thomiste* 2 (1894): 149–61.

152. Thomas Prügl, "Medieval Biblical *Principia* as Reflections on the Nature of Theology," in *What Is "Theology" in the Middle Ages?*, ed. Mikołaj Olszewski (Münster, 2007), 253–75; quote at p. 270.

153. *Peter Aureoli Scriptum super Primum Sententiarum, Prooemium* 3–4, ed. Eligius Buytaert (St. Bonaventure, NY, 1952), 135–37. See p. 136: "Quod sit tantum scientia eorum, quae in Biblia scribuntur. Ulterius videtur quod sit talis habitus, quo

sciatur tantummodo quid est scriptum in Biblia, et quid intellexerunt Prophetae et Apostoli, et alii compositores divinorum librorum. . . . ergo scire quid scriptum est in divinis libris, et quid intellexerunt scribentes, erit actus verae scientiae dictae theologia."

154. R. James Long, "'Utrum iurista vel theologus plus proficiat ad regimen ecclesiae': A *Quaestio disputata* of Francis Caraccioli. Edition and Study," *Mediaeval Studies* 30 (1968): 134–62. See the transcribed text on pp. 155–56: "Hoc autem potest maxime theologus melius quam iurista. Cum enim theologia vel sit idem quod fides vel de fide, ad eam spectat maxime docere quid credendum. . . . Informacio eciam morum maxime ad ipsam spectat, quia ipsa tradit principaliter Christi vitam, que disciplina morum fuit . . . "

155. *Dialogus* 1.1.2; Goldast 2:400–401. See p. 400/60–64: "Ad tractatores illius scientiae, cuius auctor immediatus Deus est, a quo est tota fides nostra, principaliter pertinet distinctio ante dicta. Talis autem theologia: quia scriptores scripturae diuinae nihil penitus conscripserunt ex humano ingenio sed solum ex diuina inspiratione . . . "

156. D. 9, c. 3–10; Friedberg 1:17–18.

157. Gabriel Le Bras, "Les Ecritures dans le Décret de Gratien," in *Zeitschrift der Savigny-Stiftung für Rechtsgeschichte: Kanonistiche Abteilung* 27 (1938): 47–80. See *Dictum post* D. 36, c. 2; Friedberg 1:134: "Ecce, quod sacrarum litterarum oportet episcopum habere peritiam"; and the rubric for D. 37. c. 2; Friedberg 1:135: "Reprehenduntur sacerdotes, qui omissis euangeliis legunt comedias."

158. D. 15, c. 3; Friedberg 1:36–41.

159. Brian Tierney, "'Only the Truth Has Authority': The Problem of 'Reception' in the Decretists and in Johannes de Turrecremata," in *Law, Church, and Society: Essays in Honor of Stephen Kuttner*, ed. Robert Somerville and Kenneth Pennington (Philadelphia, 1977), 69–96.

160. D. 19, c. 1; Friedberg 1:58–60.

161. *Dictum post* D. 19, c. 7; Friedberg 1:62: "Hoc autem intelligendum est de illis sanctionibus uel decretalibus epistolis in quibus nec precedentium Patrum decretis, nec euangelicis preceptis aliquid contrarium inuenitur."

162. Huguccio Pisanus, *Summa Decretorum: Distinctiones I–XX*, ed. Oldřich Přerovský (Vatican City, 2006), 317–18: "Nam etiam statuta potest reuocare inspecta causa, dummodo non tangat precepta ueteris uel noui testamenti uel articulos uel ea que sunt necessaria ad salutem uel que pertinent ad generalem statum ecclesie."

163. Rufinus, *Summa Decretorum*, ed. Heinrich Singer (Paderborn, 1963), 42.

164. C. 25, q. 1, c. 6; Friedberg 1:1008: "Sunt quidam dicentes, Romano Pontifici semper licuisse nouas condere leges. Quod et nos non solum non negamus, sed etiam ualde affirmamus. Sciendam uero summopere est, quia inde nouas leges condere potest, unde Euangelistae aliquid nequaquam dixerunt. Ubi uero aperte Dominus, uel eius Apostoli, et eos sequentes sancti Patres sententialiter aliquid diffinierunt,

ibi non nouam legem Romanus Pontifex dare, sed pocius quod predicatum est usque ad animam et sanguinem confirmare debet. Si enim quod docuerunt Apostoli et Prophetae destruere (quod absit) niteretur, non sentenciam dare, sed magis errare conuinceretur."

165. Rufinus, *Summa Decretorum*, 13–14.

166. *Decretum Gratiani . . . cum Glossis* (Paris, 1601), 1781: "Nam si [Romanus Pontifex] vellet aliquid statuere contra Euangelium, vel contra Apostolos, vel prophetas: haereticus esse conuinceretur."

167. *Summa Parisiensis*, ed. Terence McLaughlin (Toronto, 1952), 230.

168. Gabriel Le Bras, *Histoire du droit et des institutions de l'Eglise en occident: L'Age classique, 1140–1378* (Paris, 1965), 514–16.

169. Walter Ullmann, *Medieval Papalism: The Political Theories of the Medieval Canonists* (London, 1949), 50–55.

170. John Hackett, "The State of the Church: A Concept of the Medieval Canonists," *Jurist* 23 (1963): 259–90.

171. J. A. Watt, "The Use of the Term 'Plenitudo Potestatis' by Hostiensis," in *Proceedings of the Second International Congress of Medieval Canon Law*, ed. S. Kuttner and J. Ryan (Vatican City, 1965), 161–87.

172. Kenneth Pennington, *Popes and Bishops: The Papal Monarchy in the Twelfth and Thirteenth Centuries* (Philadelphia, 1984), 65–70.

173. Thomas Izbicki, "La Bible et les canonists," in *Le Moyen Age et la Bible*, ed. Pierre Riché and Guy Lobrichon (Paris, 1984), 371–84.

174. Hermann Schuessler, "Sacred Doctrine and the Authority of Scripture," in Lytle, ed., *Reform and Authority in the Medieval and Reformation Church*, 55–68.

175. Rufinus, *Summa Decretorum*, 93.

176. Brian Tierney, *Foundations of the Conciliar Theory: The Contribution of the Medieval Canonists from Gratian to the Great Schism*, enl. new ed. (Leiden, 1988), 184–98.

177. D. 40, c. 6; Friedberg 1:146: "Si papa suae et fraternae salutis negligens reprehenditur inutilis et remissus in operibus suis . . . quia cunctos ipse iudicaturus a nemine est iudicandus nisi deprehendatur a fide deuius . . . " My emphasis.

178. Brian Tierney, "A Scriptural Text in the Decretales and in St. Thomas: Canonistic Exegesis of Luke 22:32," *Studia Gratiana* 20 (1976): 363–76.

179. C. 24, q. 1, c. 9. *Decretum Gratiani . . . cum glossis*, 1721–22: "Sed certum est, quod papa errare potest. 19 dist. Anastasius. 40 dist. Si papa . . . "

180. Brian Tierney, *Ockham, Conciliar Theory, and the Canonists* (Philadelphia, 1971), 14. See the quote from Pembroke MS. 72, f. 147va: "Ego autem credo quod idem sit de quolibet crimine notorio quod papa possit accusari et condemnari si admonitus non vult cessare. Quod enim ecce, publice furatur, publice fornicatur, publice committit simoniam . . . nunquid sic scandalizare ecclesiam non est quasi heresim committere."

181. Tierney, *Ockham, Conciliar Theory, and the Canonists*, 14–24.

182. D. 40, c. 6. *Decretum Gratiani . . . cum glossis*, col. 242: "Certe credo quod si notorium est crimen eius, quandocumque, et inde scandalizatur ecclesia, et incorrigibilis sit: quod inde possit accusari. . . . Hic tamen specialiter fit mentio de haeresis, ideo quia et si occulta esset haeresis, de illa posset accusari: sed de alio occulto crimine non posset. Item numquid papa posset statuere, quod non posset accusari de haeresi? Respondeo, quod non, quia ex hoc periclitaretur tota ecclesia: quod non licet."

183. *Expositio ad Galatas*, *CSEL* 84:15. Cf. Cyprian, *Epist.* 71, *PL* 4:410b–c. For Jerome, see *PL* 26:340c–341c.

184. *Biblia latina cum glossa ordinaria*, 4 vols., ed. Karlfried Froehlich and Margaret Gibson (Strassburg, 1480; reprint, Turnhout, 1992), 4:357.

185. See Karlfried Froehlich, "Fallibility instead of Infallibility? A Brief History of the Interpretation of Galatians 2:11–14," in *Teaching Authority and Infallibility in the Church: Lutherans and Catholics in Dialogue VI*, ed. Paul C. Empie, T. Austin Murphy, and Joseph A. Burgess (Minneapolis, 1980), 259–69, 351–57. See also Thomas M. Izbicki, "The Authority of Peter and Paul: The Use of Biblical Authority during the Great Schism," in *The Companion to the Great Western Schism (1378–1417)*, ed. Joëlle Rollo-Koster and Thomas M. Izbicki (Leiden, 2009), 376–93.

186. The classic study is Brian Tierney's *Origins of Papal Infallibility: 1150–1350* (Leiden, 1972).

187. *Quaestio de infallibilitate Romani pontificis*, ed. Michele Maccarrone, in "Una questione inedita dell'Olivi sull' infallibilità del papa," *Rivista di Storia della Chiesa in Italia* 3 (1949): 309–43, esp. pp. 338–40. See also Tierney, *Origins of Papal Infallibility*, 93–130.

188. *Quaestio de infallibilitate Romani pontificis*, 342–43.

189. *Guidonis Terreni Quaestio de magisterio infallibili Romani pontificis*, ed. B. M. Xiberta (Münster, 1926), 13. See also Tierney, *Origins of Papal Infallibility*, 238–72; Thomas Turley, "*Ab Apostolorum Temporibus*: The Primitive Church in the Ecclesiology of Three Medieval Carmelites," in *Studia in Honorem Alphonsi M. Stickler*, ed. Rosalio Castillo Lara (Rome, 1992), 559–89; and Takashi Shogimen, "William of Ockham and Guido Terreni," *History of Political Thought* 19 (1998): 517–30.

190. *Quaestio de magisterio infallibili Romani pontificis*, 13.

191. *Quaestio de magisterio infallibili Romani pontificis*, 13–14.

192. *Quaestio de magisterio infallibili Romani pontificis*, 15–16.

193. *Quaestio de magisterio infallibili Romani pontificis*, 26: "Ergo multo forcius, si esset papa hereticus, propter immutabilem veritatem Dei et fidei datam a Deo benediccionem toti ecclesie et populo christiano non permitteret Deus enim eum determinare heresim aut aliquid contra fidem."

194. *Quaestio de magisterio infallibili Romani pontificis*, 28–29.

Chapter 2. The Indignant Master: John Wyclif

1. For a succinct biography and an overview of his thought, see Anne Hudson and Anthony Kenny, "John Wyclif," in *Dictionary of National Biography* 60:616–29. See also Andrew Larsen, "John Wyclif, c. 1331–1384," in *A Companion to John Wyclif: Late Medieval Theologian*, ed. Ian Christopher Levy (Leiden, 2006), 1–65.

2. Kantik Ghosh, *The Wycliffite Heresy* (Cambridge, 2002); Alastair Minnis, *Translations of Authority in Medieval English Literature* (Cambridge, 2009), 107–8; and Alastair Minnis, "'Authorial Intention' and the 'Literal Sense' in the Exegetical Theories of Richard FitzRalph and John Wyclif," *Proceedings of the Irish Academy* 75 (1975): 1–31.

3. Beryl Smalley, "The Bible and Eternity: John Wyclif's Dilemma," *Journal of Warburg and Courtauld Institutes* 27 (1964): 73–89; Michael Hurley, "'Scriptura sola': Wyclif and His Critics," *Traditio* 16 (1960): 275–352.

4. Paul de Vooght, *Les sources de la doctrine chrétienne* (Bruges, 1954), 168–200. But see also Mary Dove, "Wyclif and the English Bible," in Levy, ed., *A Companion to John Wyclif*, 365–406; and Ian Christopher Levy, *John Wyclif: Scriptural Logic, Real Presence, and the Parameters of Orthodoxy* (Milwaukee, 2003), 81–122.

5. The fullest study is Gustav Benrath, *Wyclifs Bibelkommentar* (Berlin, 1966). See also Beryl Smalley, "Wyclif's *Postilla* on the Old Testament and His *Principium*," in *Oxford Studies Presented to Daniel Callus* (Oxford, 1964), 253–96; Beryl Smalley, "John Wyclif's *Postilla super Totam Bibliam*," *Bodleian Library Record* 5 (1953): 186–205. Recently Pamela Gradon has surmised that similarities found in the comments in Wyclif's *Postilla* and those in his sermons may be traced to Wyclif's private notes written in his own Bible. See her "Wyclif's *Postilla* and His Sermons," in *Text and Controversy From Wyclif to Bale: Essays in Honour of Anne Hudson*, ed. Helen Barr and Ann M. Hutchison (Turnhout, 2005), 67–77.

6. Benrath, 101 n. 44: "Nam scriptura canonica incipit a principio incorruptibili cum dictitur *In principio creavit deus celum et terram* et cet. Ideo consonum fuit, ut virgo incorrupta scriberet ultimum librum scripture canonice."

7. Benrath, 112 n. 91: "Eiusdem auctoritatis, utilitatis, et reverencie est lex vetus cum nova, quia iste due sunt una, quia unius ecclesie."

8. Benrath, 113 n. 97: "Sed formam diligendi habemus, cum Christus dilexit nos, ut instar sue dileccionis invicem diligamus, gratuite namque efficaciter et recte dilexit nos."

9. Benrath, 99 n. 30: "Est ergo lex evangelica infallibilis, quid a deo immediate tradita, utilis, quid ad vitam ducit eternam, compendiosa, quia in duobus mandatis includitur, et bona ac honorabilis, quia finis omnium alarium."

10. Benrath, 262 n. 670.

11. *De veritate sacrae scripturae* 11, 3 vols., ed. Rudolf Buddensieg (London, 1905–7), 1:232.

12. *De veritate sacrae scripturae* 11, 1:233: "Quantum ad codices oportet capere eos ut correctos ex sensu et autoritate ecclesie; quantum ad sentenciam oportet capere ipsam a capite; et illa est fides ac sacra scriptura."

13. *De veritate sacrae scripturae* 11, 1:233–34.

14. *De veritate sacrae scripturae* 11, 1:234.

15. *De veritate sacrae scripturae* 11, 1:235: " . . . cum codices non sunt nisi supposicione pro tempore necesarii, semper autem sensus requiritur, et sic necesse est in tota matre ecclesia esse fidem catholicam, cum Christus, qui non potuit frustrari a sua peticione, rogavit, ut non deficiat fides Petri."

16. *De veritate sacrae scripturae* 11, 1:238.

17. *De veritate sacrae scripturae* 9, 1:189: "Illa enim mentalis intelleccio est verius scriptura quam lineacio membrane, que non est scriptura sacra, nisi per habitudinem ad illam, nec scriptura mentis est sacra, nisi per scripturam obiectivam, quam concipit. illa enim est primo sacra, in qua omnes catholici comunicant, cum sit una comunis fides toti ecclesie."

18. Jeremy Catto, "Wyclif and Wycliffism at Oxford: 1356–1430," in *History of the University of Oxford*, vol. 2, ed. J. I. Catto and Ralph Evans (Oxford, 1992), 175–261; quote at p. 209.

19. Minnis, *Translations of Authority*, 107.

20. Ghosh, *Wycliffite Heresy*, 55–59.

21. Dove, *Wyclif and the English Bible*, 374–76.

22. *De veritate sacrae scripturae* 11, 1:244: " . . . sed codices quoscunque non plus oportet in particulari credere, quam oportet credere bestias vel alia sensibilia quecunque. Illis autem codicibus correctis credimus tamquam signis scripture autentice."

23. *De veritate sacrae scripturae* 11, 1:236–37. See 1:237: "Item multi preter quatuor ewangelistas scripserunt ewangelia, ut patet de Nichodemo, cuius autoritas videtur racionabiliter debere capi, et quia fuit fidelis et sanctus et quia interfuit." On the status of Enoch, see Augustine, *De civitate Dei* 18.38, *CCSL* 48:633–34.

24. *De veritate sacrae scripturae* 11, 1:238: " . . . quod non obest, sed consonat, veritates fidei asseri per poetas, et per omnia genera hominum eciam Sarracenos . . . nec sunt veritates tales ideo fides, quia ab eis dicte, sed quia a deo dicte."

25. *De veritate sacrae scripturae* 11, 1:241.

26. *De veritate sacrae scripturae* 11, 1:241: "Autores tamen veteris testamenti credimus ex inspiracione interna locutos fuisse ex ore domini . . . quod efficax eorum scriptura sonat ex integro caritatem et in nullo ambicionem temporalium, sed ex integro desiderium celestium conformiter racioni."

27. *De veritate sacrae scripturae* 11, 1:242: "Ex quo patet esse probabile, quod multi libri apocrifi, sum sint libro vite inscripti, sunt scriptura sacra tantum a nobis

credenda explicite vel implicite, sicut nostra scriptura canonica; patet ex hoc, quod probabile est, multos tales libros esse sacras veritates libro vite inscriptas." For instance, the Gospel of Nicodemus can be found in the early fifteenth-century Latin Bible: British Library Royal I. E. IX.

28. *De veritate sacrae scripturae* 11, 1:243: "Unde si codices alii continent veritatem, credamas illam, quia est in nostris codicibus."

29. *Trialogus* 3.31, ed. Gotthard Lechler (Oxford, 1869), 239: "Unde isti particulares codices cum sua sacra sententia sunt implcite fides scripturae.... Et est istis patet quod scriptura sacra sit verissima secundum quamlibet ejus partem, quia si sit scriptura sacra, tunc habet pro sensu sententiam Jesu Christi, et ille non potest esse falsus nec aliquem in sensu decipere."

30. *Trialogus* 3.31, p. 240.

31. *Trialogus* 3.31, pp. 241–43. See *Haeresis*, C. 24, q. 3, c. 27; Friedberg 1:997–98.

32. *De veritate sacrae scripturae* 8, 1:168.

33. *De logica* 1.5, ed. Michael Henry Dziewicki (London, 1893), 14: "Proposicio large loquendo est ens complexe significans; et sic, quia omne quod est significat complexe se esse, omne quod est satis bene potest dici proposicio."

34. See Laurent Cesalli, "Le 'pan propositionnalisme' de Jean Wyclif," *Vivarium* 43 (2005): 124–55; Alessandro D. Conti, "Wyclif's Logic and Metaphysics," in Levy, ed., *A Companion to John Wyclif*, 67–125, esp. 78–86; and Stephen E. Lahey, *John Wyclif* (Oxford, 2009), 79–82.

35. *De veritate sacrae scripturae* 6, 1:108–9.

36. *Trialogus* 3.31, pp. 238–39: "Sed ut loquar strictius, notanda est tibi aequivocatio de *scriptura*. *Primo* enim scriptura sacra signat Jesum Christum librum vitae, in quo omnis veritas est inscripta, juxta illud Johannis x: 'non potest solvi scriptura, quem Pater sanctificavit et misit in mundum.' *Secundo modo* signat veritates in ipso libro vitae inscriptas, sive sint rationes exemplares aeternae sive veritates aliae temporales. Et *tertio modo* famosius quo ad vulgus signat aggregatum ex codicibus legis Dei et ex veritate quam Deus ipsis imponit; sed hoc nudum scriptum materiale non didici vocare scripturam sacram, quia illi codices non sunt sacri, nisi illis assit sententia sacra."

37. *Trialogus* 3.25, pp. 215–16.

38. *Trialogus* 3.30, p. 235.

39. *De veritate sacrae scripturae* 6, 1:109–10: "Ymmo tota trinitas et per consequens ipsummet verbum divinitus misit se ipsum, humanitus est homo nobilis, quo abiit in regionem longinquam accipere sibi regnum et reverti. iste liber non potest solvi ... ordinavit spiritus sanctus in correctis codicibus hoc relativum 'quem' et non 'quam' ... deus ergo fecit dictam scripturam sanctam quoad humanitatem, et genuit vel causavit sanctam quoad divinitatem. et patet ex fide scripture, quod oportet esse scripturam summe autenticam preter signa sensibilia."

40. *De veritate sacrae scripturae* 6, 1:111: "... ymmo a cane solubilis et corrigibilis a scurra sicut maculabilis, et omnis scriptura foret a quotlibet hominibus hereticabilis."

41. See Ian Christopher Levy, "John Wyclif's Neoplatonic View of Scripture in Its Christological Context," *Medieval Philosophy and Theology* 11 (2003): 227–40. Minnis (*Translations of Authority,* 212) is not convinced by this analysis and sees instead "an impulse towards Monophysitism in some of Wyclif's statements."

42. Minnis, "'Authorial Intention,'" 13–14.

43. *De veritate sacrae scripturae* 6, 1:119–20: "Quamvis autem quilibet sensus, quem habet litera, possit de virtute sermonis dici congrue literalis, doctores tamen communiter vocant sensum literalem scripture sensum, quem spiritus sanctus primo indidit, ut animus fidelis ascendat in deum."

44. Ghosh, *Wycliffite Heresy,* 36.

45. *De veritate sacrae scripturae* 6, 1:121–23.

46. *De veritate sacrae scripturae* 6, 123–24.

47. *De veritate sacrae scripturae* 6, 1:124: "Quandoque autem contendebam distingwendo hos quatuor sensus ex opposite per rangas inutiles, vocando sensum non solum veritatem, quam autor asserit de scriptura, sed aggregatum ex illo et modo intelligendi nostro, post vero visum est michi modum loquendi esse infundabilem et superflue onerosum."

48. Benrath, 76 n. 176: "Nec obest scripturam habere multos sensus litterales, quorum unum sit principalis et alius principalior, ut patet per Apsotolum Hebr 1 allegante textum Parali. 22 dictum de Salomone ad litteram de Christo."

49. Benrath, 371. Cf. Lyra, *PL* 113:31d–32a.

50. Benrath, 371–72: "Quando autem apostolus et alius autor exprimit quemcumque sensum scripture alterius, tam autencticus est ille sensus sicut est aliquis sensus litteralis, cum non sunt gradus autorisacionis sensuum scripture. Apostolus igitur sciens plenum sensum antiqui testamenti tam autentice sicut Moyses, Salomon vel alius autor citra deum, dat tantum fidem quecumque sensum pretenderit, sicut aliqua alia autoritas quacunque littera intellecta."

51. Benrath, 362: "Quidam autem nituntur tales proposiciones scripture esse falsas de virtute sermonis cuius sunt quotlibet proposiciones figurative. . . . Unde supposito pro principio, quod non sit aliquid accidens diccioni positum ab auctore scripturae sine notando misterio, devenerunt sancti ad veritates secretissimas absconditas in scriptura, et sic per illud Johannis 7 et 14 notatur, quod Christus est duplicis nature secundum quarum unam fecit reverenciam patri dicendo, quod doctrina vel sermo non fuit suus, significat illam originaliter vel auctoritative, sed patris mittentis."

52. *De benedicta incarnacione* 7, ed. Edward Harris (London, 1886), 115: "... nec debent tales predicaciones abici de virtute sermonis quod sunt figurative, quia per idem negaretur hoc—Ego et Pater unum sumus—Pater et Filius et Spritus

Sanctus sunt unus Deus, etc.—cum in prima sit equivocacio, et in secunda concepcio personarum."

53. *De veritate sacrae scripturae* 4, 1:82: "Istis premissis dico, signa recitata sunt vera, si sunt partes scripture sacre, quia sunt signa imposita ab autore huius scripture ad signandum veritatem adequatam suo integro; ideo non licet lacerare scripturam sacram, sed allegere eam in sua integritate ad sensum autoris."

54. *De veritate sacrae scripturae* 4, 1:80: "Quantum ad tales instancias oportet capere scripturam in sua integritate pertinenter ad sensum autoris, et tunc invenitur undique, quod sit vera." *De veritate sacrae scripturae* 19, 2:112: "Quantum ad secundum obiectum sepe dictum est, quod tota scriptura sacra est unum dei verbum, et quelibet pars eius debet ingrossari usque ad illud verbum integrum, quod beati in patria vident multiudinem veritatum a deo dictarum."

55. *De veritate sacrae scripturae* 5, 1:103: "Ideo soleo dicere, quod quelibet pars scripture sacre est vera de virtute sermonis divini. Que quidem virtus est verbum ac eius virtus et sapiencia incarnata." *De veritate sacrae scripturae* 31, 3:242: "Ideo oportet, primo capere ewangelium Cristi et apostolorum ac ad eius regulam scripturas alias concodare. Conclusio autem finalis tocius scripture et cuiuslibet partis sue est, quod Cristus, deus et homo, est humani generis secundum modum congruentissimum redemptor, tocius salutis autor et ultimus premiator."

56. *Fasciculi Zizaniorum Magistri Johannis Wyclif cum Tritico*, ed. W.W. Shirley, Rolls Series 5 (London, 1858), 7. For more on this debate, see Ian Christopher Levy, "Defining the Responsibilities of the Late Medieval Theologian: The Debate between John Kynyngham and John Wyclif," *Carmelus* 49 (2002): 5–29.

57. *Fasciculi Zizaniorum*, 26: " . . . quia multae sunt propositiones Scripturae, quas volo negare de vi vocis, sed concedere sensum quem auctores Scripturae principaliter intendunt." P. 42: " . . . et ita de multis aliis quarum [sensus] ad intentionem Scripturae satis planus est, sed tamen significatio sermonum quam praetendunt est erronea."

58. *Fasciculi Zizaniorum*, 31.

59. *Fasciculi Zizaniorum*, 41–42.

60. *Fasciculi Zizaniorum*, 195: "Sed, ut reportatum est de isto doctore, ipse omnem modum loquendi sacrae Scripturae vocat proprium, et verum, ad sensum exteriorem vel grammaticalem sonum. . . . Et si secundum verum esset, periret multorum distinctio de sensu propositionum sacrae Scripturae, in quo fiunt, et ad quem fiunt, scilicet de sensu ad quem positae ab auctore fuerunt, et sensu in quo fiunt; scilicet quo sonant secundum grammaticam, vel ad idioma quo proferuntur. Sed quod periret talis distinctio, modica forte cura videretur doctori recitato. Ideo clare ostendetur de multis, quod in sono exteriori et grammaticali quem prima facie exprimunt cuicunque audienti, vel natae sunt exprimere quantum est ex ipsis terminis praecise, quod non sunt verae."

61. *Fasciculi Zizaniorum*, 196: "Quare videtur quod non semper sensus literalis Scripturae sacrae est significatio grammaticalis, vel sonus exterioris literae. Alia exempla multa possent adduci de moralibus et figurativis dictis sacrae Scripturae; in quibus sensus moralis vel allegoricus est sensus literalis, et non sensus quem exprimit sonus grammaticalis."

62. Cf. Wyclif, *De veritate sacrae scripturae* 6, 1:121–24.

63. *De veritate sacrae scripturae* 6, 1:111–12: "Veritas enim est ibi permanencior, quia eterna et indelebilis, liber est serenior, quia candor lucis eterne et speculum sine macula, Sap. Septimo." *De veritate sacrae scripturae* 1, 1:1–2: "... tum quia [scriptura] est fundamentum cuicunque opinioni catholice, sed et exemplar est speculum ad examinandum et extigwendum quemcunque errorem sive hereticam pravitatem."

64. *De civili dominio* 1.44, ed. Reginald Lane Poole and Johann Loserth (London, 1885/1900–1904), 437: "Non enim licet hereticare aliquid nisi docendo quod sit Scripture sacre contrarium. . . . Ex quibus patet quod solus theologus debet hereticare dampnabile; solum enim iste scit quid est hereticum, qui scit esse Scripture sacre contrarium. Et per idem cum nove constituciones, que non fundantur in Scriptura sacra, sunt superflue et inique."

65. *De veritate sacrae scripturae* 27, 3:63.

66. *De veritate sacrae scripturae* 20, 2:146–47.

67. *Sermones* 28, 4 vols., ed. Johann Loserth (London, 1887–90), 1:257: "... et videtur Hostiensi et multis decretis quod sic, in tantum quod universali ecclesia expurgata de heresi canonista et non theologus debet eligi in prelatum. Sed tenendum est ex fide, cum nemo peccat nisi ex defectu fidei, theologorum autem est auditui populi fidem detegere, quod nullus foret prelatus ecclesie vel custos anime nisi theologus."

68. *De veritate sacrae scripturae* 24, 2:268.

69. *De veritate sacrae scripturae* 20, 2:129.

70. *De veritate sacrae scripturae* 20, 2:131.

71. *De veritate sacrae scripturae* 24, 2:235.

72. *De veritate sacrae scripturae* 20, 2:134–35.

73. *De veritate sacrae scripturae* 15, 1:403: "Non negatur tamen, sed conceditur, quod licet episcopis, Petri vicariis, condere statuta ad edificacionem ecclesie, qualia debent supponi esse, quecunque statuerint, nisi statuorum et scripture sacre contrarietas clamet oppositum; sed quod statuta huiusmodi, in quantum a papa edita, sint paris autoritatis cum ewangelio, videtur michi sapere expressam blasfemium."

74. *De veritate sacrae scripturae* 15, 1:395: "Quelibet pars scripture sacre est infinitum maioris autoritatis quam aliqua epistola decretalis, patet sic: quelibet epistola decretalis est condita per aliquem papam, Cristi vicarium cum suis subditis; quelibet pars scripture sacre immediate et proxime autorizatur per deum, igitur conclusio."

75. *De civili dominio* 3.17, p. 331: "Licet enim dominus papa potest interpretari scripturam sacram ad sensum quem Sanctus Spiritus intenderat et sancti doctores

exposuerant, non tamen quomodocunque voluerit. . . . Sicut ergo dominus papa non habet ius condendi scripturam sacram plus quam scriptor, sic non habet potestatem papa interpretandi, quomodocunque voluerit, sed si in hoc erravit, peccat turpiter."

76. *De veritate sacrae scripturae* 24, 2:268: "Nam verum est, quod sacri canones scripture sacre sunt maxime necessari et primo omnium adiscendi, cum omnes alie regule sunt deo et ecclesie suc odibiles, nisi quanto fundantur in scriptura sacra."

77. *De veritate sacrae scripturae* 21, 2:176. See *Sunt quidam dicentes,* C. 25, q. 1, c. 6; Friedberg 1:1008. For more on Wyclif's views of the papacy, see Ian Christopher Levy, "John Wyclif on Papal Election, Correction, and Deposition," *Mediaeval Studies* 69 (2007): 141–85; and Levy, "John Wyclif and the Primitive Papacy," *Viator* 38 (2007): 159–89.

78. *De veritate sacrae scripturae* 11, 1:262–64. See 1:262: "Si enim licet tractare de potestate dei sacratissima et infinitissima, multo magis de potestate Cristi vicarii." See also 1:263: " . . . sicut scriptura sacra est ex integro vera, sic est ex integro tractabilis a doctore catholico."

79. *De ecclesia* 2, ed. Johann Loserth (London, 1886), 32: "Item, in maiori libertate est christianitas posita tempore legis gracie . . . ergo multo magis extenso merito Christi Jesu secundum legem perfecte libertatis."

80. *De veritate sacrae scripturae* 27, 3:71.

81. *De civili dominio* 1.43, pp. 370–73.

82. *Sermones* 45, 3:392–93: "Non enim accipi debet vel credi consilium apostolorum nisi de quanto creditur quod Spiritus Sanctus confirmavit eorum sentenciam. Sed cum multi concurrentes ad modernum concilium sunt (ut plurimum) apostate stolidi et ignari, blasphema foret lex et regula que dictaret quod generaliter standum est et credendum iudicio pluris partis . . . cum maior pars apostatarum talium de facili heresi et destruccioni ecclesie consentiret . . . ideo blasphema est regula quod si maior pars talium sentencie cuicunque consenserit, tum est vera, laudabilis aut tenenda; quod si glossetur, semper credendum est maiori parti collegii habenti maioritatem racionis . . . multi namque corrupti communiter sese inficiunt ex consensu. Nec est plus articulus fidei quod non errent in concilio quam in vita."

83. *Fasciculi Ziȝaniorum,* 58–59.

84. *De veritate sacrae scripturae* 2, 1:20–22.

85. *Fasciculi Ziȝaniorum,* 110–14.

86. Consider, for instance, Wyclif's appeal to Johannes Teutonicus's *Glossa ordinaria* on the *Decretum* in his *De civili dominio* 2.11, pp. 121–22. Cf. *Glossa ordinaria* (Paris, 1601), cols. 1768–69.

87. Ghosh, *Wycliffite Heresy,* 7.

88. *De veritate sacrae scripturae* 15, 1:386–87. Wyclif is referring specifically to the bull of Pope Nicholas III, *Exiit qui seminat* in *Sexti Decretal,* L. 5, t. 12, c. 3; Friedberg 2:1120–21.

89. *Fasciculi Ziζaniorum*, 462–63.

90. *De veritate sacrae scripturae* 12, 1:275: "Unde doctor de Lyra, licet novellus, tamen copiosus et ingeniosus postillator scripture." *De veritate sacrae scripturae* 4, 1:73: "Unde sanctus Thomas parte prima Summe . . . ecce, quante sancti doctores laborarunt ad excusandum scripturam sacram a falsitate."

91. *De apostasia* 3, ed. Michael Henry Dziewicki (London, 1889), 49: "Item, si sine auctoritate scripture licet variare vocando sacramentum, quod ipsa vocat panem, non panem sed quantitatem vel aliam vanitatem (et non est finis potencie sic glosantis), videtur quod totam scripturam sacram pari auctoritate poterit sic glosare et sic totam fidem scripture antiquam pervertere et novam inducere, ut totam historiam gestorum Christi negare ad literam et glosare ad suum oppositum; et sic de aliis que in biblia inseruntur."

92. *Fasciculi Ziζaniorum*, 119: "Intelligo autem dicta mea in ista materia secundum logicam Scripturae, nec non secundum logicam sanctorum doctorum et decreti Romani ecclesiae, quos suppono prudenter fuisse locutos. Non enim valet scandalizare totam Romanam ecclesiam . . . et non obstante errore glossantium, ista fides mansit continue in ecclesia, etiam apud laicos." *Fasciculi Ziζaniorum*, 128–29: "Ista autem septem testimonia sic inficiunt glossatores, quod dicunt tacite omnia talia dicta sanctorum debere intelligi per suum contrarium, et sic negari finaliter cum Scriptura."

93. *De veritate sacrae scripturae* 14, 1:356.

94. *De veritate sacrae scripturae* 13, 1:316: "Prima: longe plura mala orta sunt per tacenciam veritatis, quam per eius promulgacionem . . . cum igitur omnis omissio culpabilis in obligato dicere verbo et opere, veritatem sic tacencia . . . diccio autem veritatis numquam est culpabilis, licet forte quandoque per accidens ipsam concomitetur indiscrecio et sequatur illacio mali pene." *De veritate sacrae scripturae* 13, 1:318: "Tercio videtur, quod veritatis tacencia principaliter propter periculum subtraccionis comodi temporalis vel perturbacionis auditorii ex veritatis displicencia gravati testatur timorem servilem."

95. See Hurley, "'Scriptura sola': Wyclif and His Critics," 350; Minnis, "'Authorial Intention,'" 25; Ghosh, *Wycliffite Heresy*, 60.

96. *De veritate sacrae scripturae* 9, 1:198: "Unde solebam dicere, quod virtuosa disposicio discipuli scripture specialiter stat in tribus, scilicet in autoritatis scripture humili acceptacione, in sui et racionis conformacione et sanctorum doctorum testificacione."

97. *De veritate sacrae scripturae* 9, 1:201.

98. *De veritate sacrae scripturae* 16, 2:20: "Et patet, quomodo ex conformitate sensus cristiani ad sensum Cristi oportet intelligere scripturam . . . sic necesse est, cristianum conformare logicam logice Cristi."

99. *De veritate sacrae scripturae* 22, 2:184: "Oportet enim, cristianum esse per assimilacionem quodammodo ipsum Cristum."

100. *De veritate sacrae scripturae* 20, 2:143–44.

101. *Sermones* 59, 1:386: "Et tercia conclusio patet eo quod oportet quemlibet salvandum fructuose facere sentenciam verbi Christi . . . sed tercium connectit perfeccionem ultimam, cum faciens sic sermones Christi deificatur."

102. *De ecclesia* 1, ed. Johann Loserth (London, 1886), 2: "Quamvis autem ecclesia dicatur multipliciter in scriptura, suppono quod sumatur ad propositum pro famosiori, scilicet congregacione omnium predestinatorum." For a more detailed study of Wyclif's doctrine of predestination and his soteriology generally, see Ian Christopher Levy, "Grace and Freedom in the Soteriology of John Wyclif," *Traditio* 60 (2005): 279–337.

103. *De ecclesia* 1, pp. 3–4. Cf. Augustine, *De doctrina christiana* 3.32.45, *CCSL* 32:104–5.

104. *De ecclesia* 1, p. 5: "Prima, quod nullus vicarius Christi debet presumere asserere se esse caput ecclesie sancte catholice, ymmo nisi habuerit specialem revelacionem, non assereret se esse aliquod membrum eius."

105. *De ecclesia* 1, p. 7.

106. *De ecclesia* 1, pp. 7–8.

107. *De ecclesia* 1, pp. 17–18.

108. *De ecclesia* 1, p. 19: "Ex istis septimo sequitur quod dominus papa, si predestinatus est et exercet pastorale officium, est caput tante militantis ecclesie quantum regit. . . . Hoc autem debet supponi in domino Romano pontifice, nisi factum doceat evidenter oppositum."

109. *De ecclesia* 2, p. 43.

110. *De ecclesia* 3, p. 49.

111. *De ecclesia* 3, p. 62.

112. *De ecclesia* 4, p. 72.

113. *De ecclesia* 6, pp. 139–40.

114. *De ecclesia* 18, pp. 415–16.

115. *De ecclesia* 17, p. 409: "Secundo modo sumitur ecclesia mixtim pro predestinatis et prescitis dum sunt in gracia secundum presentem iusticiam . . . Et ista ecclesia vocatur mixtim granum et palea."

116. *De ecclesia* 4, p. 72: "Conceditur tamen quod ordinacione humana clerici constituuntur in officiis ecclesiasticis tam predestinati quam presciti."

117. *De ecclesia* 6, p. 140: "Et patet quod homo potest esse episcopus, dominus et minister ecclesie, eciam prescitus, existens in gracia secundum presentem iusticiam, sed homo non est cum hoc membrum sancte matris ecclesie."

118. *De ecclesia* 19, pp. 442–43.

119. *De ecclesia* 19, pp. 448–49. See p. 448: "Videtur autem mihi quod prescitus eciam in mortali peccato actuali ministrat fidelibus, licet sibi dampnabiliter, tamen subiectis utiliter sacramenta." See, for instance, *Si fuerit*, C. 1, q. 1, c. 30; Friedberg 1:371.

120. *Sermones* 4, 1:25: "Sed difficultes si infideles vel heretici possunt baptizare fideles (ut Augustinus discuit de Donatistis). . . . Deus non obstante indignitate persone quod suum est perficit, quia aliter in confeccione eucaristie et ministracione cuiuscunque sacramenti aliterius foret ecclesia perplexa." See Ian Christopher Levy, "Was John Wyclif's Theology of the Eucharist Donatistic?" *Scottish Journal of Theology* 53 (2000): 137–53.

121. *De potestate papae* 3, ed. Johann Loserth (London, 1907), 45. See Brian Tierney, "A Scriptural Text in the Decretales and in St. Thomas: Canonistic Exegesis of Luke 22:32," *Studia Gratiana* 20 (1976): 363–76.

122. *Sermones* 2.43, p. 311: "Sic enim dicit Apostolus ad Gal. II, 12 tradens nobis formam obediencie, quod *in facie resistit Petro, quia reprehensibilis erat*. Quanto magis resisteretur prelato hodierno plus patule oberranti? Ideo sepe vocavi illam resistenciam obedienciam, et illam necesse est quemcunque fidelem addiscere."

123. *De ordine christiano* 5, in *Opera Minora*, ed. Johann Loserth (London, 1910), 138: "Si autem prelatus precepiat quod lex Domini non precepit, que precipit quidlibet faciendum, obediendum est, mandatis illius prepositi resistendo, cum usque ad mortem fidelis debet mandatis illis resistere. Et illam obedienciam vocat Lincoloniensis obedienciam resistivam vel obedienciam indirectam, quia, ut ipse declarat, quelibet creatura dicit usque ad mortem generaliter Dei voluntatem, et ut sic obediendum est illi creature sed principaliter Domino suo." A search on the Electronic Grosseteste Database did not result in any plausible matches for *obediencia resistiva* or *obediencia indirecta*.

124. Letter 128 in *Roberti Grosseteste Episcopi Quondam Lincolniensis Epistolae*, ed. H. R. Luard (London, 1861), 432–37 at 433: "Apostolica enim mandata non sunt nec possunt esse alia quam Apostolorum doctrinae et Ipsius Domini Jesu Christi." See also Brian Tierney's discussion of this letter in "Grosseteste and the Theory of Papal Sovereignty," *Journal of Ecclesiastical History* 6 (1955): 1–17.

125. See Eric Doyle, "William Woodford on Scripture and Tradition," in *Studia historico-ecclesiastica: Festgabe für Luchesius G. Spätling, O.F.M.*, ed. Isaac Vazquez (Rome, 1977), 481–502.

126. *De apostasia* 1, pp. 42–45. See p. 44: " . . . vocavi filios karissimos, non sunt de dictis apostaticis; sed excellenter observantes illud bonum religionis Christi."

127. *De civili dominio* 3.9, pp. 125–26.

128. *De ordinacione fratrum* 2, in *Polemical Works in Latin*, 2 vols., ed. Rudolf Buddensieg (London, 1883), 1:92–94. See also Ian Christopher Levy, "Texts for a Poor Church: John Wyclif and the Decretals," *Essays in Medieval Studies* 20 (2003): 94–107.

129. *De apostasia* 1, p. 2: "Isti autem vocantur sic famose religiosi, licet in scriptura infundabiliter; quod nomen tocius religionis quam Christus in fide scripture instituit, est extinctum."

130. *De civili dominio* 3.2, p. 13.

131. *De civili dominio* 3.2, pp. 18–20.

132. *Sermones* 32, 3:262–63: "In ista materia alibi dixi diffusius quomodo nulla circumstancia que non est implicite fundabilis in scriptura constituit aliquam religionem vel ordinem laude dignum. Sed catuli ceci nolunt videre distincciones atque sentenciam per quas sue argucie deliterent et fortisan in penam peccati mei hoc evenit."

133. *Sermones* 32, 3:263–64: "Dixi enem sepe quod universalia legum hominum, immo ipse leges hominum, sunt veritates eterne in scriptura planius implicate. . . . Et sic de multis aliis principiis legum civilium, que leges non possunt iustificari nisi ab eternis principiis . . . et sic dixi quod lex in sua generalitate est veritas directiva hominis ut debite serviat Deo suo, et hoc genus legis est generaliter lex divina cuius una pars in scriptura sacra absconditur. Et applicant explicite, ut debite serviant Deo suo."

134. *Sermones* 32, 3:266: "Credimus autem ex fide quod licet tota veritas et lex Dei sit in prioribus scriptis evangelice implicite, Deus tamen eternaliter ordinavit quod sint secundum illam mensuram adeo implicite. . . . Antichristus cum suis discipulis fabricat cotidie novas scripturas quas dicit equivalere scripture sacre vel ipsam superaddere, ac si vellet constitutere novum mundum."

135. *De civili dominio* 3.2, pp. 30–32.

136. *De apostasia* 1, pp. 9–10.

137. *De apostasia* 1, p. 10: "Nam ex fide capimus quod omnis veritas est ex scriptura, et ut necessarior est expressior; aliter enim autor religionis summe potens, sciens atque benivolus foret inprovidus, nisi religionem cariorem magis exprimeret."

138. *Trialogus* 4.33, pp. 361–64.

139. *Trialogus* 3.31, p. 240: 'Et cum secundum Augustinum omnis veritas sit in scriptura sacra vel explicite vel implicite, patet quod nulla alia scriptura capit auctoritatem vel valorem, nisi de quanto sua sentencia a scriptura sacra sit derivata." See Augustine, *De doctrina christiana* 2.42.63, *CCSL* 32:76–77.

140. *De veritate sacrae scripturae* 13, 1:309: ". . . quod sancti doctores in primitiva ecclesia racionabiliter formidabant in materia fidei introducere novellos terminos preter scripturam propter veneni formidinem, quod abscondi posset ab hereticis. Verumptamen detecto sensu et limitata significacione terminorum ab ecclesia, satis secure potest catholicus uti terminis, licet non fuerint in textu scripture exemplati . . . vel si exceditur, caveamus de terminis concernentibus materiam fidei, et sequamur antiquos doctores et sanctos magis probabiles, sed pre omnibus scripturam sacram."

141. *De trinitate* 17, ed. Allen DuPont Breck (Boulder, CO, 1962), 173–74.

142. *De trinitate* 17, p. 178: "Pro isto notandum quod secundum diversitatem temporum et pululaciones heresum erant diversa concilia diversas hereses dampnancia."

260 Notes to Pages 91–93

143. *De trinitate* 17, p. 179: "Secundo dico quod multa catholica sunt docta per sanctos et doctores ecclesie qui non sunt expresse posita verbaliter in scriptura. . . . Patet enim quotlibet esse docta catholice in ecclesia quae non sunt expressa in evangelio, ut patet de descensu Christi ad inferos, de quotlibet condicionibus sacramentorum, et edicionibus symbolorum et conciliis diversis. Sed quia in scriptura sacra est omnis veritas philosophica et in sanctis doctoribus racione duce veritas philosophica occulta est sepius manifesta, ideo dico tercio quod eque expresse sequitur ex sensu scripture quod spiritus sanctus procedit ex filio sicut et procedit ex patre."

144. *Sermones* 48, 3:507: ". . . quanto magis moderna ecclesia fugeret a seductivo satrapa capere tam terminos extra fidem scripture quam eciam sentenciam a scripture extraneam. Nam isti termini *accidens* et *subiectum* ad sensum loquencium in ista materia sunt satis extranea."

Chapter 3. The Ambivalent Friar: William Woodford

1. See Jeremy Catto, "William Woodford," *Dictionary of National Biography*, 60:179–80.
2. Anne Hudson, *The Premature Reformation: Wycliffite Texts and Lollard History* (Oxford, 1988), 46–49, quote at 48.
3. Paul de Vooght, *Les sources de la doctrine chrétienne* (Bruges, 1954), 254–64.
4. De Vooght, *Les sources de la doctrine chrétienne*, 203–9.
5. Michael Hurley, "Wyclif or Woodford?" *Carmelus* 49 (2002): 31–46. This is a review article of Paul de Vooght's *Les sources de la doctrine chrétienne* unpublished until this late date.
6. Eric Doyle, "William Woodford on Scripture and Tradition," in *Studia historico-ecclesiastica: Festgabe für Luchesius G. Spätling, O.F.M.*, ed. Isaac Vazquez (Rome, 1977), 481–502. Doyle (p. 491) cites Congar (*Tradition and Traditions* [London, 1966], 87–88) to support this claim about extra-scriptural truths necessary for salvation. In point of fact, though, Congar specifically limits purely extra-scriptural material among the medieval theologians to liturgical rites and customs. If oral tradition were invoked in support of Catholic doctrine it was shown that this same doctrine could nonetheless be located in scripture under another form.
7. Alastair Minnis, "Tobit's Dog and the Dangers of Literalism: William Woodford O. F. M. as Critic of Wycliffite Exegesis," in *Defenders and Critics of Franciscan Life: Essays in Honor of John V. Flemming*, ed. Michael F. Cusato and G. Geltner (Leiden, 2009), 41–52, esp. pp. 46–50.

8. Jeremy Catto, "Wyclif and Wycliffism at Oxford: 1356–1430," in *History of the University of Oxford*, 2:175–261; quotes at p. 197. See also pp. 205–6.

9. Kantik Ghosh, *The Wycliffite Heresy* (Cambridge, 2002), 78.

10. *De causis condempnationis articulorum 18 damnatorum Joannis Wyclif*, in *Fasciculus rerum expetendarum et fugiendarum prout Orthuino Gratio . . . editus est Coloniae*, A.D. MDXXXV, ed. Edward Brown (London, 1690), 190–265.

11. *De causis condempnationis*, 191–94.

12. *De causis condempnationis*, 204–5. See Wyclif, *Trialogus* 4.12, pp. 285–87. On the fate of unbaptized infants, see *Firmissime, De Cons.*, D. 4, c. 3; Friedberg 1:1362. For the definition of heresy, see *Haeresis*, C. 24, q. 3, c. 27; Friedberg 1:997–98.

13. *De causis condempnationis*, 231. See Wyclif, *Trialogus* 4.25, pp. 333–35.

14. *De causis condempnationis*, 212–14. See Wyclif, *Trialogus* 4.20, pp. 315–18.

15. *De causis condempnationis*, 206–7. Psuedo-Dionysius, *De ecclesiastica hierarchia* 5, *PG* 3:499–530.

16. *De causis condempnationis*, 207: "Infinita enim sunt vera catholica, quae non poterant nobis concludi evidenter ex contentis in sacra scriptura, ut patet Johannis ultimo." Emphasis mine.

17. See de Vooght's criticisms in *Les sources de la doctrine chrétienne*, 203–5.

18. *De causis condempnationis*, 209–10. See Pseudo-Dionysius, *De ecclesiastica hierarchia* 3, *PG* 3:423–46; and *Audire episcopum*, D. 24, c. 2; Friedberg 1:92.

19. *De causis condempnationis*, 209–10. See p. 210: " . . . quia multa fuerunt in ecclesia primitiva, quae non sunt posita in sacra scriptura."

20. The edited text is printed in Eric Doyle, "William Woodford's 'De dominio civili clericorum' against John Wyclif," *Archivum Franciscanum historicum* 66 (1973): 49–109; see p. 87.

21. *De causis condempnationis*, 216.

22. *De causis condempnationis*, 237–50.

23. *De causis condempnationis*, 216.

24. *De causis condempnationis*, 216–17. See *Ecclesiasticarum*, D. 11, c. 5; Friedberg 1:24–25.

25. *De causis condempnationis*, 258–59. See p. 259: " . . . Cum Marthae: de forma qua utitur ecclesia Romana in consecratione sanguinis: quia illa (ut ibi patet) non habetur in sacra scriptura . . . quod nullibi in scriptura habetur completa forma . . . et quod hoc credi debet." For *Cum Marthae*, see *Decr. Greg. IX*, L. 3, t. 41, c. 6; Friedberg 2:637.

26. *De causis condempnationis*, 257: "Quod quicquid Papa vel Cardinales sui sciunt ex sacra scriptura deducere clare, illud duntaxat est credendum, vel ad sua monita faciendum. Et quicquid ultra praesumpserint, sit tanquam haereticum contemnendum."

27. *De causis condempnationis*, 257–58.

28. See Wyclif, *De veritate sacrae scripturae* 6, 1:121–23.
29. See Wyclif, *Trialogus* 3.31, p. 240; *De civili dominio* 3.2, pp. 18–20; *Sermones* 32, 3:262–63.
30. *De causis condempnationis*, 258.
31. *De causis condempnationis*, 259.
32. See Wyclif, *De trinitate* 17, p. 179; *De veritate sacrae scripturae* 13, 1:309.
33. *De causis condempnationis*, 260.
34. See Wyclif, *De benedicta incarnacione* 7, p. 115; and texts in Benrath, *Wyclifs Bibelkommentar*, 362.
35. *De causis condempnationis*, 261–63. See p. 263: "Sed hoc habetur ex traditione Christi, non scripta in sacra scriptura . . . et ex traditione ecclesiae primitivae, non scripta in Canone Bibliae."
36. *De causis condempnationis*, 263–64. See p. 264: "Unde et veritates evangelicae erant veritates evangelicae duiu antequam positae erant in sacra scriptura."
37. See Wyclif, *De veritate sacrae scripturae* 11, 1:242–43.
38. *De causis condempnationis*, 264.
39. *De causis condempnationis*, 264–65. See p. 264: "Et nihilominus iste articulus destruit seipsum. . . . Sed istum articulum non deducit ex sacra scriptura nec deducere potest, cum multipliciter repugnet scripture et multipliciter veritati. . . . Et aestimo, quod istius articuli credulitas est magna causa, et maxima doctrinarum Lollardorum. Et aestimo, si essent curati de ista mala credulitate, quod faciliter reducerentur in omnibus ad Catholicam veritatem."
40. *De causis condempnationis*, 265: "Debemus etiam credere multis veritatibus ab universali ecclesia receptis, sive scribantur, sive non. Debemus etiam credere multis veritatibus, quae ex contentis in sacra scriptura non sequuntur, nec ex tradicionibus apostolicis." Cf. Ockham, *Dialogus* 1.2.5, Goldast 2:415–16.
41. *De causis condempnationis*, 265: "Multae tamen sunt veritates credendae de necessitate salutis, quae ex sacris scripturis deduci non possunt, ut ipsemet [Augustinus] concedit, et ut ecclesia concedit." Emphasis mine.
42. See the discussion of the role of scripture among the church fathers in J. N. D. Kelly, *Early Christian Doctrines*, 5th ed. (London, 1977), 36–48.
43. Cf. D. 9, c. 3–10; Friedberg 1:17–18.
44. *Quattuor Determinaciones Fratris Willelmi Woodford de Ordine Fratrum Minorum contra Wyclyff in Materia de Religione*, ed. M. D. Dobson (unpublished Oxford B. Litt. thesis, 1932).
45. See Wyclif, *De apostasia* 1, p. 10.
46. *Quattuor Determinaciones*, 42: "Proxima destruenda radix est quod omnis veritas est contenta in scriptura sacra et [eo] expressius quo necessarior est ad salutem . . . sic quod non oportet fidelem credere aliquam veritatem tamquam necessariam ad salutem nisi ipsa sit contenta in scriptura sacra."

47. *Quattuor Determinaciones,* 42: "Suppono eciam hic in principio quod Magister Iohannes loquitur hoc in hac materia sicut ego loquor cum eo, de contineri in sacra scriptura explicite vel implicite, in sensu suo historico vel litterali."

48. *Quattuor Determinaciones,* 45–46.

49. *Quattuor Determinaciones,* 46–47.

50. *Quattuor Determinaciones,* 48.

51. See Wyclif, *De trinitate* 17, p. 179.

52. *Quattuor Determinaciones,* 65–66.

53. *Quattuor Determinaciones,* 70. Cf. Ockham, *Dialogus* 3.1.4.15, Goldast 2:859–60.

54. *Quattuor Determinaciones,* 89–90. Cf. Ockham, *Dialogus* 3.1.3.8, Goldast 2:824–25.

55. *Quattuor Determinaciones,* 91.

56. *Quattuor Determinaciones,* 91: "Patet hec, nam veritas que fuit catholica a principio predicacionis Christi et semper erit vsque ad iudicium, et quam Christusmet fecit esse catholicam, non potest papa mortalis facere esse catholicam veritatem, vt constat." Cf. Ockham, *Dialogus* 1.2.11, Goldast 2:418–19.

57. *Quattuor Determinaciones,* 92: "Ergo verum antiquitus catholicum quod Christus fecit esse verum catholicum, potest papa mortalis nouiter facere esse fidei articulum, proprie loquendo de fidei articulo, quod fuit probandum."

58. *Quattuor Determinaciones,* 93: "Ille biblie textus quem nos communiter habemus, multos et diuersos patitur defectus, et diuersa sunt in illa contenta quibus non oportet fidem indubiam adhibere."

59. See Wyclif, *De veritate sacrae scripturae* 11, 1:235–38.

60. *Quattuor Determinaciones,* 93–96.

61. *Quattuor Determinaciones,* 97–98.

62. *Quattuor Determinaciones,* 174: "Vnde vbi textus quem nos communiter habemus est corruptus et falsatus, ille non est, vt talis, pars sacre scripture."

63. *Quattuor Determinaciones,* 175: "Et ideo dico, quod non solum omnino textus quem omnino consimilem habet communitas ecclesie, est corruptus, sed eciam textus quem habet et habere deberet ex translacione Ieronomi, est corruptus et falsus, quia textum corruptum et falsum Ieronimus transtulit."

64. *Quattuor Determinaciones,* 176: " . . . ideo consequenter dico quod auctoritates sanctorum [que] videntur sonare quod omnes veritates sunt contente in sacra scriptura que sunt utiles ad salutem, non sunt intelligende auctoritates ille de sensu historico vel litterali precise, sed secundum illum vel alios sensus scripture, vel si intelliguntur pro maiori parte talium veritatum, quia veritates quibus Christiani viatores tenentur fidem adhibere pro maiori parte, explicite vel implicite continentur secundum sensum litteralem in canone scripture."

65. *Quattuor Determinaciones,* 176–77.

66. See Wyclif, *De veritate sacrae scripturae* 11, 1:242–43.
67. *Quattuor Determinaciones*, 100–101.

Chapter 4. Ad Fontes *(?)*: Thomas Netter

1. For a detailed account of Netter's life, see Richard Copsey, "Thomas Netter of Walden: A Biography," in *Thomas Netter of Walden: Carmelite, Diplomat, and Theologian (c. 1372–1430)*, ed. Johan Bergström-Allen and Richard Copsey (Faversham, Kent, and Rome, 2009), 23–111. Kevin Alban has recently published *The Teaching and Impact of the "Doctrinale" of Thomas Netter of Walden (c. 1374–1430)* (Turnhout, 2010), which emphasizes the central place of traditional Carmelite spirituality in Netter's thought. This is a fine study that appeared too late for me to incorporate its findings in my own work.

2. Anne Hudson, "Thomas Netter," in *Oxford Dictionary of National Biography*, 40:444–47.

3. Andrew Jotischky, *The Carmelites and Antiquity: Mendicants and Their Pasts in the Middle Ages* (Oxford, 2002), 189.

4. Thomas Turley, "*Ab apostolorum temporibus*: The Primitive Church in the Ecclesiology of Three Medieval Carmelites," in *Studia in honorem Alphonsi M. Stickler*, ed. Rosalio Castillo Lara (Rome, 1992), 559–80.

5. Kantik Ghosh, *The Wycliffite Heresy* (Cambridge, 2002), 182–89.

6. Michael Hurley, "A Pre-Tridentine Theology of Tradition, Thomas Netter of Walden," *Heythrop Journal* 4 (1963): 348–66.

7. F. X. Siebel, "Die Kirche als Lehrautorität nach dem 'Doctrinale Antiquitatum Fidei Catholicae Ecclesiae' des Thomas Waldensis (um 1372–1431)," *Carmelus* 16 (1969): 3–70.

8. Santiago Madrigal, "The Place of the *Doctrinale* of Thomas Netter of Walden in the History of Ecclesiology," in Bergström-Allen and Copsey, eds., *Thomas Netter of Walden*, 201–30; quote at 224.

9. *Doctrinale Antiquitatum Fidei Catholicae Ecclesiae* I, *Prologus*, ed. B. Blanciotti, 3 vols. (Venice, 1757–59; reprint, Farnborough, 1967), 1:5b–c.

10. *Doctrinale* I, *Prologus*, 1:5c–d.

11. *Doctrinale* I, *Prologus*, 1:6c: "Non erigam aedificium novellorum conceptuum cum Wicleffo; sed documentum Ecclesiae, et Sanctorum Patrum traditionis antiquissimae. Mea vero doctrina non erit mea, sed ejus qui misit."

12. *Doctrinale* I, *Prologus*, 1:6a: " . . . Quod major pars Patrum a tempore Apostolorum successive usque ad nos sensit et tradidit: a qua professione nullus sub poena perfidiae potest declinare fidelis: etiam nec Papa, nec Generale Concilium."

13. *Doctrinale* I, *Admonitio*, 1:11b.

14. *Doctrinale* I, *Admonitio,* 1:12a–13a.

15. *Doctrinale* I, *Admonitio,* 2:7a: "Prima ergo doctrina omnium haereticorum est transformare Scripturas sacras ad detestabiles sensus suos: eadem verba dicere, sed alieno sensu vestire." 2:7e: "In hoc cognoscimus spiritum veritatis, et spiritum erroris. Spiritus Ecclesiae, est spiritus veritatis. Spiritus omnis, qui contradicit Ecclesiae, est spiritus erroris."

16. *Doctrinale* I, *Admonitio,* 1:13d–14b.

17. *Doctrinale* I, *Admonitio,* 1:15a.

18. *Doctrinale* II, 2.22, 1:356b–357a. See 1:357a: " . . . et inter eos illi sunt aptiores in materia fidei qui Christi et Apostolorum temporibus viciniores erant."

19. *Doctrinale* II, 2.22, 1:359d.

20. *Doctrinale* II, 2.24, 1:368a.

21. *Doctrinale* II, 3.68, 1:610e: "Ecce apud infidelem et haereticum Christus non recognoscit nomen Magistri. . . . Non enim potest ibi fidelis vendicare magisterium, ubi non contingit cum vera fide probare discipulum."

22. See Wyclif, *De ecclesia* 19, pp. 442–49.

23. *Doctrinale* II, 2.8, 1:275b.

24. *Doctrinale* II, 2.9, 1:279e–280e.

25. *Doctrinale* II, 2.9, 1:280e–281a.

26. *Doctrinale* II, 2.9, 1:282e.

27. *Doctrinale* II, 2.12, 1:300b.

28. *Doctrinale* II, 3.28, 1:389c–390a.

29. *Doctrinale* II, 3.28, 1:390e.

30. See Wyclif's *De universalibus* 14, ed. Ivan Mueller (Oxford, 1984), 346–49. Here he patently rejects the notion of absolute necessity since it would render God the author of sin and make a mockery of moral virtue, which depends upon human freedom.

31. *Doctrinale* II, 3.28, 1:392c–e.

32. See Wyclif, *De ecclesia* 1, p. 19; *De ecclesia* 2, p. 43; *De ecclesia* 19, pp. 442–49.

33. *Doctrinale* II, 2.12, 1:295d.

34. *Doctrinale* II, 3.35, 1:427d.

35. *Doctrinale* II, 3.35, 1:429c–d.

36. *Doctrinale* II, Prologus, 1:241a–242a. See Ambrose, *De incarnatione dominicae sacramento* 4–5, *PL* 16:827a–b.

37. *Doctrinale* II, 1.6, 1:267a.

38. *Doctrinale* II, 1.6, 1:268b.

39. *Doctrinale* II, 1.6, 1:269d.

40. *Doctrinale* II, 1.1, 1:243–46.

41. *Doctrinale* II, 1.2, 1:249d.

42. *Doctrinale* II, 3.47, 1:488a–d.

43. *Doctrinale* II, 3.48, 1:493c–494e.
44. *Doctrinale* II, 2.25, 1:370a.
45. *Doctrinale* II, 2.17, 1:327b: Adhuc autem de prima universalitate Ecclesiae notari oportet, non eam tantum esse extensionem loci, sed et temporis . . . et a baptismo Christi, initio praedicationis ejus, durasse, et duraturam esse usque ad finem mundi."
46. *Doctrinale* II, 2.17, 1:327e.
47. *Doctrinale* II, 2.17, 1:328a–329a.
48. *Doctrinale* II, 2.18, 1:329c–e.
49. *Doctrinale* II, 2.18, 1:330a.
50. *Doctrinale* II, 2.18, 1:330d.
51. *Doctrinale* II, 2.18, 1:332a–333b. See 333b: " . . . lex Christi habebit certissimum interpretamentum suum in cordibus fidelium, succedentium sibi ipsis ab initio nascentis Ecclesiae, et temporibus Apostolorum, usque sempiternum."
52. *Doctrinale* II, 2.19, 1:334b–c.
53. *Doctrinale* II, 2.20, 1:345b: " . . . eo quod credere Ecclesiam, est tantum credere Ecclesiam habere testimonium fidele de Christo et legibus ejus."
54. *Doctrinale* II, 2.19, 1:335b–336b.
55. *Doctrinale* II, 2.19, 1:339d: "Dum tamen scripta authoritas non certificat sine concordi intellectu Ecclesiae; nec revelatio sine teste. Omnis alia via quam per successores Apostolicos, qua omnes ante nos credentes intrabant, est sacrilega."
56. *Doctrinale* II, 2.19, 1:336c–337d.
57. *Doctrinale* II, 2.25, 1:371b–c.
58. *Doctrinale* II, 2.25, 1:373c.
59. *Doctrinale* II, 2.25, 1:370d–e.
60. *Doctrinale* II, 2.22, 1:360c–d: "Non ergo inde est fidelis Doctor, quia fidem Scripturae producit, nisi etiam fidem et authoritatem sequatur, non unius particularis, sed universalis Ecclesiae, in qua sola sensus Scripturarum verus habetur."
61. *Doctrinale* II, 2.19, 1:338a–d.
62. *Doctrinale* II, 2.20, 1:345b–346a.
63. *Doctrinale* II, 2.20, 1:346a–d. See 1:346c–d: "Non posse jam augeri librorum numerum, quia lex Christi jam attigit ad perfectum. . . . Elapso autem Apostolico tempore, non potuit crescere amplius, nisi quis dicat eam hactenus imperfectum."
64. *Doctrinale* II, 2.20, 1:347c–348c. For Gregory, see *Ep.* 1.9.25, *PL* 77:478a.
65. *Doctrinale* II, 2.21, 1:349a–b: "Nec tamen hic laudo supercilium, quod quidem attollunt, volentes occasione hujus dicti, decretum Patrum in Ecclesia majoris esse authoritatis, culminis, et ponderis, quam sit authoritas Scripturarum. Quod quidem non tam videtur ineptum, quam fatuum; nisi talis quis dicat Philippum fuisse majorem Christo." Cf. Augustine, *Contra epistolam Manichaei quam vocant Fundamenti* 5, *PL* 42:176.

66. *Doctrinale* II, 2.21, 1:349c: "Omnis ergo Ecclesiastica authoritas cum sit ad testificandum de Christo et legibus ejus, vilior est Christi legibus, et Scripturis Sanctis necessario postponenda."

67. *Doctrinale* II, 2.21, 1:348c: "Quod authoritas universalis Ecclesiae subdita est authoritati Scripturarum tam novi quam veteris testamenti."

68. *Doctrinale* II, 2.21, 1:351a: " . . . tum quia universalis Ecclesia Catholica non est Scriptura sacra posterior, sed coaeva ipsi, et ejus latori Christo, sicut sponsa sponso, corpus capiti."

69. *Doctrinale* II, 2.21, 1:349e.

70. *Doctrinale* II, 2.21, 1:350d–e.

71. *Doctrinale* II, 2.21, 1:351b–d. See 1:351c: "Libri ergo quod sunt ex authoritatibus suis habent ut testes sint, quamvis testimonium, quod inducunt, authoritatem habeat Scripturarum, vel inferioris cujusquam. Fides autem ut est Ecclesiae Catholicae, in hoc accedit fidei Scripturarum, quod non licet de ipsa dubitare."

72. *Doctrinale* II, 2.22, 1:353a–e. See 1:353e: "Talis ergo articulus etsi posset esse fidelis, non tamen esset Catholicus."

73. *Doctrinale* II, 2.22, 1:353e–354a.

74. *Doctrinale* II, 2.22, 1:354c–d.

75. Kirk Stevan Smith, "An English Conciliarist? Thomas Netter of Walden," in *Popes, Teachers, and Canon Law in the Middle Ages*, ed. J. R. Sweeney and Stanley Chodorow (Ithaca, 1989), 290–99. On Netter's role at Pisa and at Constance, see also Copsey, "Thomas Netter of Walden," 35–37, 56–58.

76. *Doctrinale* II, 2.19, 1:342b–343c.

77. *Doctrinale* II, 2.26, 1:376a–b: " . . . non tamen est universalis Ecclesia; nec ejus decretum, ut sit fides Symbolica; sed Ecclesiae Catholicae imago propinquior . . . ideo est universalis Ecclesiae in authoritate multum consimilis, quamvis secundum rei veritatem disparis ponderis."

78. *Doctrinale* II, 2.26, 1:376c–377a.

79. *Doctrinale* II, 2.26, 1:377c–378c.

80. *Doctrinale* II, 2.26, 1:379e–380a.

81. *Doctrinale* II, 2.27, 1:386c–e.

82. *Doctrinale* II, 2.27, 1:385a–b.

83. *Doctrinale* II, 2.27, 1:384b–c.

84. *Doctrinale* II, 2.27, 1:381d–82d. See Ambrose, *De fide* 1.8, *PL* 16:541.

85. *Doctrinale* II, 2.26, 1:378e–379a.

86. *Doctrinale, De sacramento ordinis,* 116, 2:681a–682a.

87. *Doctrinale, De sacramento ordinis,* 116, 2:686a–d.

88. *Doctrinale, De sacramento ordinis,* 117, 2:690a–b.

89. *Doctrinale, De sacramento ordinis,* 118, 2:694d–695e.

90. *Doctrinale, De sacramentalibus*, 89, 3:574a–e. See William of St. Thierry, *Epistola ad Fratres de Monte Dei* 1.1, *PL* 184:310: "Sed haec novitas non est novella vanitas. Res enim est antiquae religionis, perfectae fundatae, in Christo pietatis, antiqua haereditas Ecclesia Dei, a tempore a Prophetarum praemonstrata."

91. *Doctrinale* II, 2.23, 1:362d.

92. *Doctrinale* II, 2.23, 1:363c: "Idcirco, cum mandarent fidelibus observare Scripturas Canonicas, mandabant eis cum iis observare sermones suos vivos et traditiones, quas scribere non vacabat: sed viva voce alter alteri, et senior traderet juniori: qui semper ad verum intellectum ducerent Scripturas, nulla exa parte patientes eas perverti."

93. *Doctrinale* II, 2.23, 1:363e–364e.

94. *Doctrinale* II, 2.23, 1:365a.

95. *Doctrinale* II, 2.23, 1:365b–c.

96. *Doctrinale, De sacramentalibus, Prologus*, 3:3b–c.

97. *Doctrinale, De sacramentalibus, Prologus*, 3:4a.

98. *Doctrinale, De sacramentalibus, Prologus*, 3:5c.

99. *Doctrinale, De sacramentalibus, Admonitio*, 3:7a–b.

100. *Doctrinale, De sacramentalibus, Admonitio*, 3:10a–11a. See 3:11a: "Dicerem tamen verba superaedificata praecum solemnium, non a verbis Evangelii esse diversa, nec a fundamento Apostolorum esse aliena, sed consona."

101. *Doctrinale, De sacramentalibus, Admonitio*, 3:28c.

102. *Doctrinale, De sacramentalibus, Admonitio*, 3:301e.

103. *Doctrinale, De sacramentalibus*, 45, 3:303c.

104. *Doctrinale, De sacramentalibus*, 45, 3:304a–d.

105. *Doctrinale, De sacramento eucharistiae*, 2:234d–235b. See 2:235b: "Nec ergo omni errore verba symboli expresse repugnant, nec omni veritati catholicae expresse consentiunt." See Wyclif, *De eucharistia tractus maior* 5, ed. Johann Loserth (London, 1892), 140. For more on Netter's eucharistic theology, see Ian Christopher Levy, "Thomas Netter on the Eucharist," in Bergström-Allen and Copsey, eds., *Thomas Netter of Walden*, 273–314.

106. *Doctrinale, De sacramento eucharistiae*, 2:451b–452e.

107. *Doctrinale, De sacramento eucharistiae*, 2:397a–d.

108. See Wyclif, *De veritate sacrae scripturae* 13, 1:309.

109. *Doctrinale, De sacramento eucharistiae*, 2:405e–406e. See 2:405e: "Et hoc dixit esse fidem catholicam, etsi non ipsum expresse Scriptura Canonica contineret."

110. See Wyclif, *De eucharistia tractus maior* 9, p. 274.

111. *Doctrinale, De sacramento eucharistiae*, 2:390a–391e. See Duns Scotus, *Sent.* 4. d. 11, q. 3.

112. *Doctrinale, De sacramento eucharistiae*, 2:392b–d. See Augustine, *De baptismo contra Donatistas* 4.6, *PL* 43:159.

113. *Doctrinale, De sacramento eucharistiae*, 2:393a–d. See 2:393b: "... quia falso modo verum credit, nihil credit.... Idcirco enim non solum verum credendum, sed vere credendum est verum." For John of Paris, see John Hilary Martin, "The Eucharistic Treatise of John Quidort of Paris," *Viator* 6 (1975): 195–240. For Wyclif on John of Paris, see *De eucharistia* 7, p. 222.

114. *Doctrinale, De sacramento eucharistiae*, 2:394b–e.

115. *Doctrinale, De sacramento eucharistiae*, 2:453e–456c. Compare Netter's words to those of Vincent of Lérins, *Commonitorium* 22.7, *CSEL* 64:177: "... ut cum dicas noue, non dicas noua." See also Augustine, *Enarratio in Psalmum* 54, *PL* 36:643.

Chapter 5. A Falling Out: Hussites and Their Czech Opponents

1. Howard Kaminsky, *The History of the Hussite Revolution* (Berkeley, 1967), 37–39; Matthew Spinka, *John Hus' Concept of the Church* (Princeton, 1966), 172–75.

2. R. R. Betts, "The *Regulae Veteris et Novi Testamenti* of Matěj Z Janova," *Journal of Theological Studies* 32 (1931): 344–51.

3. Vilém Herold, "How Wycliffite was the Bohemian Reformation?" trans. Zdeněk V. David, *Bohemian Reformation and Religious Practice* 2 (1998): 25–37. Herold has carefully documented, for instance, the points of agreement between Hus and Milíč.

4. Thomas A. Fudge, *The Magnificent Ride: The First Reformation in Hussite Bohemia* (Aldershot, 1998), 46–73; Zdeněk V. David, *Finding the Middle Way: The Utraquists' Liberal Challenge to Rome and Luther* (Washington, DC, 2003), 18–23; Vilém Herold, "Wyclif's Ecclesiology and Its Prague Context," trans. Zdeněk V. David, *Bohemian Reformation and Religious Practice* 4 (2002): 15–30. For an edition and analysis of the reform measures enacted under Pardubice, see Rostislav Zeleny, "Councils and Synods of Prague and their Statutes," *Apollinaris* 45 (1972): 471–532, 698–740.

5. Katherine Walsh, "Wyclif's Legacy in Central Europe in the Late Fourteenth and Early Fifteenth Centuries," in *From Ockham to Wyclif*, ed. Anne Hudson and Michael Wilks (Oxford, 1987), 397–417.

6. See Anne Hudson, "Wyclif's Works and Their Dissemination," in *Studies in the Transmission of Wyclif's Writings* (Aldershot, 2008), 1–16; and "From Oxford to Prague: The Writings of John Wyclif and his English Followers in Bohemia," *Slavonic and East European Review* 75 (1997): 642–57, reprinted in *Studies in the Transmission of Wyclif's Writings*.

7. Vilém Herold, "Jan Hus: A Heretic, a Saint, or a Reformer?" *Communio Viatorum* 45 (2003): 5–23. See also Walter Brandmüller, "Hus vor dem Konzil," in

Jan Hus zwischen Zeiten, Völkern, Konfessionem, ed. Ferdinand Seibt (Munich, 1997), 235–42.

8. *Decrees of the Ecumenical Councils*, 2 vols., ed. Norman Tanner (London, 1990), 1:426–27.

9. *Doctrinale Antiquitatum Fidei Catholicae Ecclesiae, De sacramento eucharistiae*, 2:518c–519a.

10. Herold, "How Wycliffite was the Bohemian Reformation?," 25.

11. František Šmahel, "'*Doctor evangelicus super omnes evangelistas*': Wyclif's Fortune in Hussite Bohemia," *Bulletin of the Institute of Historical Research* 43 (1970): 11–34; quote at 29. On the matter of metaphsical realism at Prague, see Vilém Herold, "Platonic Ideas and 'Hussite Philosophy,'" trans. Zdeněk V. David, *Bohemian Reformation and Religious Practice* 1 (1996): 13–17; and "Štěpán of Páleč and the Archetypal World of Ideas," trans. Zdeněk V. David, *Bohemian Reformation and Religious Practice* 5.1 (2004): 77–87.

12. Howard Kaminsky, "John (Jan) Hus," in *Dictionary of the Middle Ages*, 13 vols., ed. Joseph Strayer (New York, 1982–89), 6:364–69.

13. *Magister Johannis Hus Super IV. Sententiarum, Incepcio* 1.5–6, in *Opera Omnia*, 3 vols., ed. W. Flašhans and M. Komínková (Osnabrück, 1966), 2:5–6.

14. *Super Sent., Incepcio* 1.7–8, pp. 2:6–7: "... postulet sapienciam (i. sacram scripturam), que omnibus satisfacit, quia quidquid queritur ad salutem, totum iam adinpletum est in scripturis."

15. *Super Sent., Incepcio* 1.11, pp. 2:9–10. See p. 2:10: "Homo enim, non-deus, non est proprie auctor, sed discipulus fallibilis ipsius auctoris (sc. Dei). . . . 'Si quis vestrum indiget sapiencia postulet a Deo' sc. tamquam a primo auctore veritatis infallibiliter informante." It was a traditional practice to extol Lombard's *Sentences* as a work that explicated the truths found already in Holy Scripture. See Philipp W. Rosemann, *The Story of a Great Book: Peter Lombard's Sentences* (Peterborough, ON, 2007), 65–66.

16. *Super Sent., Incepcio* 1.12, p. 2:11: "Non enim est aliquis articulus Cristiane fidei contrarius, sed consonus racioni; quia si foret racioni contrarius, foret falsus et sic non articulus fidei Cristiane: cum summa Veritas non necessitat ad credendum falsum contrarium veritati."

17. *Contra Stephanum Palecz*, in *Opera Omnia Magistri Iohannis Hus (Polemica)*, vol. 22, ed. Jaroslav Eršil (Prague, 1966), 259: "Nescis, bone fictor, quia Scriptura sacra est liber vite per se iudicans? Quid ergo ad verbum, bone fictor, si verba vocalia vel scripte litere sive exarrati caracteres, quos vocas Scripturam sacram, sunt res inanimata? Iam rebus dimissis conversus es ad signa vel terminos, retrocedens sicut cancer." We will look at Páleč's own work later and thus return to this issue below.

18. *Contra Stephanum Palecz*, 260: "Ecce, ista Scriptura cum Christo, qui est sacratissima Scriptura, iudicabit et me et fictorem in die iudicii. . . . Et estimo, quod

non negabit fictor, quin Scriptura sacra, que est Veritas a Spiritu sancto homini indita, principalius dirigere debet humanum iudicium."

19. *Super Sent., Incepcio* 2.3, p. 2:14: "Et sic scriptura sacra est verbum Dei Christus . . . Ex quo sequitur, quod omnis veritas directiva hominis, ut debite serviat Deo suo, est scriptura sacra vel explicite vel implicite credenda ab hominibus teneantur firmiter et credantur."

20. *Super Sent., Incepcio* 2.3, p. 2:15: "Ex quo patet quod ymagines Christi passionem eius notificantes sunt scriptura sacra tam laycis intelligentibus quam eciam literatis; 2 patet, quod omnia ydiomata, quibus passio Christi vel alia Christi veritas designatur, similiter scripture talium ydiomatum sunt sacra scriptura."

21. *Super Sent., Incepcio* 2.3, pp. 2:16: "Et patet, quam stulti sunt, qui dicunt, quod scriptura sacra de virtute sermonis foret falsa. . . . Ergo desistant a tali sensu temerario et subiciant intellectum suum sensui litterali quem Spiritus sanctus flagitat."

22. *Super Sent., Incepcio* 2.4–7, pp. 2:17–20. Cf. Lyra, *PL* 113:25c–27d.

23. Paul de Vooght, *Les sources de la doctrine chrétienne* (Bruges, 1954), 218–30. *Replica Magistri Joannis Hus contra anglicum Joannem Stokes*, in *Les sources*, 228 n. 7: " . . . jura humana justa sunt inclusive in jure divino, immo sint lex Christi de quanto sunt utilia deservientia legi Dei."

24. Thomas Fudge, "The 'Law of God': Reform and Religious Practice in Late Medieval Bohemia," *Bohemian Reformation and Religious Practice* 1 (1996): 49–72; emphasis mine. See Hus quote at pp. 55–56: "Veneror etiam omnia concilia generalia et specialia, decreta et decretales, et omnes leges, canones et constitiutiones, de quanto consonant explicite vel implicite legi dei."

25. *Magistri Iohannis Hus Questiones*, ed. Jiří Kejř, *CCCM* 205 (Turnhout, 2004), 21: "Quidquid lege humana statuitur, si non est legi Dei conforme, est illicitum. Patet, cum lex divina sit vera et omne, quod dissonat a vero, non est verum et per consequens illicitum, igitur conclusio vera." See also p. 22: "Omnes leges humane debent regulari lege divina."

26. *Magistri Iohannis Hus Questiones*, 20–21. See p. 21: "Aliquid lege divina preceptum potest mutari secundum necessitatem temporis aut locum aut epykeiam."

27. *Super Sent.* 4.13, pp. 586–88.

28. *On Simony*, translated from the Czech by Matthew Spinka, in *Advocates of Reform: From Wyclif to Erasmus*, ed. Matthew Spinka (Philadelphia, 1953), 196–99.

29. Matthew Spinka, *John Hus' Concept of the Church* (Princeton, 1966), 252.

30. *Tractatus de ecclesia*, ed. S. Harrison Thomson (Boulder, CO, 1956), xxxiii. See also Herold, "Jan Hus: A Heretic, a Saint, or a Reformer?," 13.

31. *Tractatus de ecclesia*, xx. For the articles, see *Enchiridion Symbolorum*, 36th ed., ed. Henry Denzinger and Adolf Schönmetzer (Rome, 1976), 1201–30.

32. *Tractatus de ecclesia* 1, pp. 1–7.

33. *Tractatus de ecclesia* 3, pp. 15–17.

34. *Tractatus de ecclesia* 4, p. 27. This conception of *simul et semel est iustus et iniustus* has nothing whatsoever to do with the Lutheran doctrine of *simul ius et peccator*, which is grounded in the principle of justification by faith alone.

35. Herold, "Wyclif's Ecclesiology and Its Prague Context," 26–27.

36. *Tractatus de ecclesia* 5, pp. 33–38.

37. *Tractatus de ecclesia* 7, pp. 43–44. For *Unam Sanctam*, see Denzinger, 870–74; and *Etravag. Commun.* L. 1, t. 8, c. 1; Friedberg 2:1245–46.

38. *Tractatus de ecclesia* 8, p. 56: "Et isto modo tenetur quilibet christianus credere explicite vel implicite omnem veritatem, quam sanctus spiritus posuit in scriptura. Et ideo modo non tenetur homo dictis sanctorum preter nec bullis papalibus credere, nisi quid dixerint ex scriptura vel quod fundaretur implicite in scriptura."

39. *Tractatus de ecclesia* 15, p. 125.

40. *Tractatus de ecclesia* 9, pp. 60–61.

41. *Tractatus de ecclesia* 9, p. 70.

42. *Tractatus de ecclesia* 14, pp. 112–15.

43. *Tractatus de ecclesia* 16, pp. 132–35. See pp. 132–33: "Postea contra partem nostram accumulat plura mendacia ille doctor: primum mendacium quod *solam scripturam sanctam in talibus materiis pro iudice habere volumus*. . . . Hoc tamen debet scire doctor, quod nec sibi nec omnibus sibi adherentibus volumus in fidei consentire materia, nisi de quanto se fundaverunt in scriptura vel racione."

44. *Tractatus de ecclesia* 19, p. 177.

45. *Tractatus de ecclesia* 19, p. 179.

46. *On Simony*, 199.

47. *Contra Stephanum Palecz*, 267: "Ego enim fateor, quod sentencias veras, quas magister Iohannes Wicleff, sacre theologie professor, posuit, teneo, non quia ipse dicit, sed quia Deus, Scriptura vel racio infallibilis dicit."

48. *Defensio libri de trinintate*, in *Opera Omnia (Polemica)* 22:54.

49. *Contra Iohannem Stokes*, in *Opera Omnia (Polemica)* 22:60, 66–67. See p. 66: "Tota universitas Oxoniensis ab annis trigenta legit, tenuit et studuit libros ipsius magistri Iohannis Wigleff."

50. *Contra Iohannem Stokes*, 22:62: "Ego autem non credo nec concedo, quod magister Iohannes Wigleff sit hereticus, sed nec nego, sed spero, quod non est hereticus, cum in occultis de proximo debeo meliorem partem eligere."

51. *Super Sent.* 4.8–13, pp. 553–88. See also *De corpore Christi*, in *Opera Omnia*, 1:23–27.

52. *Responsiones Magistri Johannis Hus ad articulos Johannis Wiclif*, in *Mistr Jan Hus*, ed. Jan Sedlák (Prague, 1915), 305–7.

53. *Contra Stephanum Palecz*, 238: "Concedimus enim, quod malus papa, episcopus, prelatus, vel sacerdos est indignus minister sacramentorum, per quem Deus baptizat, consecrat vel aliter ad profectum sue ecclesie operatur."

54. *Magistri Stanislai de Znoyma Tractatus de romana ecclesia,* in *Miscellanea Hustica,* ed. Jan Sedlák (Prague, 1996), 312–17.

55. *Magistri Stephani de Palec De aequivicatione nominis ecclesia,* in *Miscellanea Hustica,* pp. 356–63.

56. *Magistri Stephani de Páleč Antihus* 1, in *Miscellanea Hustica,* p. 369.

57. *Magistri Stephani de Páleč Antihus* 1, p. 376.

58. *Magistri Stephani de Páleč Antihus* 5, p. 425.

59. *Magistri Stephani de Páleč Antihus* 10, pp. 482–83.

60. *Magistri Stephani de Páleč Antihus* 11, p. 492.

61. *Responsiones Magistri Johannis Hus ad articulos Johannis Wiclif,* 305–7.

62. *Magistri Stephani de Páleč Antihus* 2, p. 381: " Ecce quam clara testimonia, quod quidquid sacredos malus vel prelatus cum fide pro officio suo, licet indignus sit indigne ministret, tamen divina gracia cooperante ratum esse conceditur, et per consequens quilibet talis vere conficit, vere consecrat, vere absolvit, vere ordinat . . . cum in talibus deus non sequitur dignitatem persone vel indignitatem, sed ordinem, officium et potestatem."

63. *Magistri Stephani de Páleč Antihus* 2, p. 385: "Ergo omnes christiani eciam mali, veram fidem habentes informem, sunt fideles et per consequens veri christiani illa scilicet veritate fidei, licet non veritate vitae."

64. *Magistri Stephani de Páleč Antihus* 4, pp. 411–14.

65. See *Replica Magistri Joannis Hus contra anglicum Joannem Stokes,* in Paul de Vooght, *Les sources de la doctrine chrétienne,* 228 n. 7.

66. *Magistri Stephani de Páleč Antihus* 6, pp. 438–40.

67. *Magistri Stephani de Páleč Antihus* 8, pp. 457–60. See p. 460: "Si enim dicta doctorum et scripturarum et canones allegas non ad intencionem illorum auctorum, sed ad confirmandos tuos errores secundum superficiem litere, nonne false allegas, non intencione docendi sed subvertendi?"

68. *Magistri Stephani de Páleč Antihus* 11, p. 493: "Consimiliter vos habetis in scripturis, quod scripta vel dicta, que sunt pro vobis, etsi non sunt atentica . . . decreta et instituta, dicta sanctorum, que ecclesia approbavit, et dicta catholicorum glosatorum et tractatorum sacre scripture cum ignominia repellitis, tradiciones humanas appellantes . . . probis reputis et scripturas autenticatis, que tamen sunt fabulose vel ab ecclesia non auctorizate."

69. *Magistri Stephani de Páleč Antihus* 8, pp. 461–62: "Ex quibus patet, quod non omnes sentencie a fidelibus tente in sacra scriptura veteris et novi testamenti exprimuntur, sed alique ex institucione patrum et alique ex consuetudine populi pro lege venerunt que nullatenus sunt contempnende. . . . Ideo multe sunt cause fidei et beneficiales, quarum decisio non continetur in scriptura novi et veteris testamenti. . . . nichil volentes pro fide tenere, nisi quod in biblia continetur, in hoc induentes habitum Armenorum, qui solis auctoritatibus biblie et non aliis auctoritatibus ecclesie sanctorum vel doctorum approbatorum stare volunt."

70. *Magistri Stephani de Páleč Antihus* 8, pp. 462–66. See pp. 462–63: "Alius sensus de conformitate est talis, quod sentencie romane ecclesie sint non contrarie, sed in veritate vel rectitudine consone scripture sacre, ipsi scripture non repugnantes. . . . Non est autem in dubium, quin quamcunque sentenciam romana ecclesia tradidit christifidelibus ad credendum vel tenendum, illa non est contraria, quin ymmo in veritate et rectitudine sit consona sacre scripture veteris et novi testamenti."

71. *Magistri Stephani de Páleč Antihus* 13, p. 507.

72. Peter of Mladoňovice, *John Hus at the Council of Constance*, trans. Matthew Spinka (New York, 1965).

73. Peter of Mladoňovice, *John Hus at the Council of Constance*, 166–72.

74. Peter of Mladoňovice, *John Hus at the Council of Constance*, 213–21.

75. Peter of Mladoňovice, *John Hus at the Council of Constance*, 228–33.

76. *The Letters of Jan Hus*, trans. Matthew Spinka (Manchester, 1972), Letter 86, p. 185.

77. *The Letters of Jan Hus*, Letter 89, pp. 193–94.

78. *The Letters of Jan Hus*, Letter 91, pp. 196–97.

79. *The Letters of Jan Hus*, Letter 93, pp. 198–99.

80. *The Letters of Jan Hus*, Letter 101, pp. 209–210.

81. *The Letters of Jan Hus*, Letter 98, p. 206.

82. *The Letters of Jan Hus*, Letter 99, p. 207.

83. Paul de Vooght, *L'Hérésie de Jean Huss* (Louvain, 1960), 359–60.

84. De Vooght, *L'Hérésie de Jean Huss*, 337. See Augustine, *De baptismo contra Donatistas*, *PL* 43:123.

85. De Vooght, *L'Hérésie de Jean Huss*, 344. Cf. Hus, *Tractatus de ecclesia* 19, p. 177.

86. De Vooght, *L'Hérésie de Jean Huss*, 358.

87. De Vooght, *L'Hérésie de Jean Huss*, 361–62.

88. De Vooght, *L'Hérésie de Jean Huss*, 370.

89. *Decrees of the Ecumenical Councils*, ed. Tanner, 1:419; and also Denzinger, 1198–1200.

90. Helen Krmíčková, "Utraquism in 1414," trans. Zdeněk V. David, *Bohemian Reformation and Religious Practice* 4 (2002): 99–105; quote at p. 105.

91. Andrew of Brod, *Contra communicationem plebis sub utraque specie* 1, in *Rerum concilii oecumenici constantiensis*, 6 vols., ed. Hermann von der Hardt (Frankfurt and Leipzig, 1697–1700), 3:392–94.

92. *Contra communicationem* 2, Hardt 3:394–97.

93. *Contra communicationem* 6, Hardt 3:404–5.

94. *Contra communicationem* 13, Hardt 3:412–13.

95. *Jacobellus contra Brodam De communione sub utraque specie* 1.47, Hardt 3:522–23: "Quia omnis consuetudo, contra observantiam evangelicam ab antiqua ecclesia tentam introducta, est mala."

96. *Jacobellus contra Brodam* 1.47, Hardt 3:524–25.
97. *Jacobellus contra Brodam* 1.50, Hardt 3:528–29.
98. *Jacobellus contra Brodam* 2.27, Hardt 3:578–79.
99. *Jacobellus contra Brodam* 1.29, Hardt 3:490–91.
100. *Jacobellus contra Brodam* 2.25, Hardt 3:574: "... quod ministrantes et suscipientes sanguinem Christi sub specie vini, in hic observando legem Christi instar primitivae ecclesiae." See *In his rebus*, D. 11, c. 7; Friedberg 1:25.
101. *Jacobellus contra Brodam* 2.25, Hardt 3:575.
102. *Jacobellus contra Brodam* 2.25, Hardt 3:577. Here cited is D. 12, c. 4; Friedberg 1:28: "Consuetudines, que fidei non offitiunt, ut a maioribus traditae sunt, observentur."
103. *Jacobellus contra Brodam* 1.11, Hardt 3:456–57.
104. *Jacobellus contra Brodam* 2.26, Hardt 3:577–79.
105. *Jacobellus contra Brodam* 2.28, Hardt 3:578–79.
106. *Jacobellus contra Brodam* 2.28, Hardt 3:580.
107. *Jacobellus contra Brodam* 2.28, Hardt 3:580–81.
108. Nicholas of Dresden, *Apologia pro communione plebis sub utraque specie* 4, Hardt 3:608–9.
109. *Apologia* 2, Hardt 3:596.
110. *Apologia* 4, Hardt 3:611.
111. *Apologia* 3, Hardt 3:602.
112. *Tractatus Specialis* 1.2, Hardt 3:693–94.
113. *Tractatus Specialis* 1.15, Hardt 3:713–16.
114. *Tractatus Specialis* 1.16, Hardt 3:717–18.
115. *Responsio ad illam demonstrationem Jacobi de Misa, De communione laicali sub una specie* 2.6, Hardt 3:876–79.
116. *Responsio* 2.6, Hardt 3:880.
117. *Responsio* 2.6, Hardt 3:880.

Chapter 6. Approaching Final Authority: Gerson and the Conciliarists

1. Louis Pascoe, "Jean Gerson: The 'Ecclesia Primitiva' and Reform," *Traditio* 30 (1974): 379–409.
2. Mark Burrows, "Jean Gerson on the 'Traditioned Sense' of Scripture as an Argument for an Ecclesial Hermeneutic," in *Biblical Hermeneutics in Historical Perspective: Studies in Honor of Karlfried Froehlich for His Sixtieth Birthday*, ed. Mark Burrows and Paul Rorem (Grand Rapids, MI, 1991), 152–72.
3. *Decrees of the Ecumenical Councils*, 2 vols., ed. Norman Tanner (London, 1990), 1:409.
4. *Decrees of the Ecumenical Councils*, ed. Tanner, 1:442.

5. *Decrees of the Ecumenical Councils,* ed. Tanner, 1:417.

6. *Prosperum Iter,* in *Oeuvres Complètes de Jean Gerson,* 10 vols., ed. P. Glorieux (Paris, 1960–73), 5:477: "Concilium generale ... papam potest deponere pro quocumque crimine de quo notorie et incorrigibiliter scandalizat Ecclesiam."

7. Dietrich von Niem, *Dialog über Union und Reform der Kirche 1410 (De modis uniendi et reformandi ecclesiam in concilio universali),* ed. Hermann Heimpel (Leipzig and Berlin, 1933), 5: " . . . que temporalia ad instar Christi despicit, que originem fidei et fundamenta primitive ecclesie custodit." See also Paul de Vooght, "L'Ecclésiologie des adversaires de Huss au Concile de Constance," *Ephemerides Theologicae Lovaniensis* 35 (1959): 5–24.

8. *De modis uniendi et reformandi,* 6.

9. *De modis uniendi et reformandi,* 7–8. See p. 8: "Et solet dici ecclesia Romana. . . . Et hec errare potest et potuit, falli et fallere, scisma et heresim habere, eciam potest deficere; et lec longe minoris auctoritatis videtur esse universali ecclesia, ut dicetur inferius." Cf. Wyclif, *De ecclesia* 1, pp. 7–8.

10. *De modis uniendi et reformandi,* 20–21: "Ecce ponatur papa. Est homo de humo, limus de limo, peccator et peccabilis, filius ante duos dies pauperis rustici. Erigitur in papam. Numquid iste absque aliqua penitencia peccatorum, absque confessione, absque cordis contricione fit angelus impeccabilis, fit sanctus? Quis eum sanctum fecit? Non spiritus sanctus, quia dignitas non solet trahere spiritum sanctum, sed solum Dei gracia et caritas, non auctoritas, que communicatur bonis et malis. Quia ergo angelus papa esse non potest, ergo papa ut papa est homo, et ut homo sic est papa, et ut papa potest peccare, et ut homo potest errare." Cf. Wyclif, *De ecclesia* 1, p. 19; *De civili dominio* 1.43, pp. 370–73; and Hus, *Tractatus de ecclesia* 9, p. 70, and 14, pp. 112–15.

11. *De modis uniendi et reformandi,* 22–26. See p. 25: "Ridiculum enim est dicere, quod unus homo mortalis dicat se potestatem habere in celo et in terra ligandi et solvendi a peccatis, et quod ipse sit filius perdicionis, simoniacus, avarus, mendax, exactor, fornicator, superbus, pomposus, et peior quam diabolus."

12. *De modis uniendi et reformandi,* 42–43. See p. 42: "Et ideo dixi, quod papa est deponendus propter malum vivere, propter publicum scandulum, propter heresim, propter quodcumque mortale peccatum, quo scandalizatur universalis ecclesia, sicut est fornicacio publica, sicut est simonia."

13. *De modis uniendi et reformandi,* 35–36. See p. 35: "Et ideo apostoli symbolum componentes non dixerunt: Credo sanctum papam vel Christi vicarium, quia fides universalis Christi non est in papa ... quod mali quantumcunque eciam sunt in ecclesia apostolica, non tamen sunt in ecclesia catholica, que est sanctorum communio, quia certum est, quod existens in mortali peccato nec est in ecclesia nec de ecclesia catholica, que fundata est in caritate."

14. *De modis uniendi et reformandi,* 39–40.

15. See Margaret Harvey, "Richard Ullerston," in *Dictionary of National Biography* 55:867–68. See also Anne Hudson, "The Debate on Bible Translation, Oxford 1401," *English Historical Review* 90 (1975): 1–18.

16. *Petitiones quoad reformationem ecclesiae militantis* in *Rerum Concilii Constantiensis*, ed. Hermann von der Hardt, 1:1138–41.

17. Louis Pascoe, *Church and Reform: Bishops, Theologians, and Canon Lawyers in the Thought of Pierre d'Ailly: 1351–1420* (Leiden, 2005), 208–25. Cf. Aquinas, *Summa Theologiae* 1, q. 1, a. 2.

18. Francis Oakley, *The Political Thought of Pierre d'Ailly: The Voluntarist Tradition* (New Haven, 1964), 154.

19. Francis Oakley, "Pierre d'Ailly and Papal Infallibility," *Mediaeval Studies* 26 (1964): 353–58.

20. Douglass Taber, "Pierre d'Ailly and the Teaching Authority of the Theologian," *Church History* 59 (1990): 163–74.

21. Pascoe, *Church and Reform*, 237–41.

22. *Sermo factus Constantie in concillio generali, dominica in medio quadragesime*, in *Tractatus et Sermones* (Strassburg, 1490; reprint, Frankfurt, 1971), cols. 8–9. Cf. Wyclif on "human laws" in *De civili dominio* 3.2, pp. 18–20; and "human traditions" in *De veritate sacrae scripturae* 20, 2:129–31.

23. *Utrum indoctus in Jure Divino possit juste praesse*, in *Johannes Gerson Opera Omnia*, 5 vols., ed. Louis Ellies Du Pin (Antwerp, 1706; reprint, Zurich, 1987), 1:646d.

24. *Utrum indoctus*, 1:647a.

25. *Utrum indoctus*, 1:653d–654a. Cf. 1:649b.

26. *Utrum indoctus*, 1:654b–c. Cf. Hostiensis, *Summa Aurea, proemium* (Venice, 1581; reprint, Turin, 1963), 6–8.

27. *Utrum indoctus*, 1:654c.

28. *Utrum indoctus*, 1:655a.

29. *Utrum indoctus*, 1:655a–b: "Quia theologia est sapientia perfectissima ac stabilissima: Jus autem humanum imperfectum est, fluidum et instabile. Igitur Praelatus, negelecta Theologiae sapientia, non debet Juri humano adhaerere."

30. *Utrum indoctus*, 1:655c.

31. *Utrum indoctus*, 1:656a.

32. *Utrum Petri Ecclesia Lege reguletur*, in *Johannes Gerson Opera Omnia* 1:664a–b: "Unde Lex Christi seu regula dicitur tota doctrina Evangelica."

33. *Utrum Petri Ecclesia Lege reguletur*, 1:664d. Cf. Wycif, *De veritate sacrae scripturae* 6, 1:108–9; and *Trialogus* 3.31, pp. 238–39.

34. *Utrum Petri Ecclesia Lege reguletur*, 1:664d–665a: "Patet: quia vox, vel scriptura, Lex non dicitur, aut regula; nisi ea figura, vel tropo qua nomen est et veritas imagini imponitur, vel signo, sicut imago Regis, Rex dicitur."

35. *Recommendatio Sacre Scripture*, in *Quaestiones magistri Petri de Ailliaco cardinalis cameracensis super libros Sententiarum* (Strassburg, 1490; reprint, Frankfurt, 1968), unpaginated.

36. *Utrum Petri Ecclesia Lege reguletur*, 1:665d–666b. Cf. Ockham, *Dialogus* 1.1.4; Goldast 2:402–3.

37. *(De resumpta) Utrum Petri Ecclesia Rege gubernetur. Lege reguletur. Fide confirmetur. Jure dominetur,* in Johannes Gerson, *Opera Omnia*, 1:692b.

38. *Utrum Petri Ecclesia Lege reguletur*, 1:666b.

39. *Utrum Petri Ecclesia Lege reguletur*, 1:666c: " . . . sed in uno solo potest, vel potuit stare Ecclesia. Nam, ut dicit Augustinus super Psal. cxxviii. *Aliquando in solo Abel Ecclesia erat*. Et ut quidem aliquando, scilicet tempore Passionis Christi, tota Ecclesia, et tota Fides Ecclesiae Christianae, in Maria Matre Christi remanserat." See Augustine, *Enarr. In Ps.* 128.2; *CCSL* 40:1882.

40. *Utrum Petri Ecclesia Lege reguletur*, 1:671c: " . . . hoc est, quod universalis Ecclesia nunquam per erorem Legi difformatur; sed semper Legis Christi regulae confirmatur, non solum per Fidem mortuam, sed etiam per Fidem, Spe et Charitate formatam."

41. *De examinatione doctrinarum*, in *Johannes Gerson Opera Omnia*, 1:18b: "Theologo de veritate Catholica, aut opposita haeresi; Juristae de poenis et modo judicii confert partes suas." See also Glorieux 9:472.

42. *Pro licentiandis in decretis (Dominus his opus)*, ed. Glorieux, 5:219–20.

43. *Pro licentiandis in decretis (Dominus his opus)*, ed. Glorieux, 5:224.

44. *Pro licentiandis in decretis (Dominus his opus)*, ed. Glorieux, 5:224–25.

45. *De potestate ecclesiastica*, in *Opera Omnia*, 2:252a. See also Glorieux 6:244.

46. See David Zachariah Flanagin, "God's Divine Law: The Scriptural Founts of Conciliar Theory in Jean Gerson," in *The Church, the Councils, and Reform: The Legacy of the Fifteenth Century*, ed. Gerald Christianson, Thomas M. Izbicki, and Christopher M. Bellitto (Washington, DC, 2008), 101–21.

47. *De vita spirituali animae*, ed. Glorieux, 3:162. Cf. Wyclif, *Sermones* 32, 3:263–64; and Hus, *Magistri Iohannis Hus Questiones*, 20–21.

48. *Pro licentiandis in decretis (Dominus his opus)*, ed. Glorieux, 5:226–28.

49. *De vita spirituali animae*, ed. Glorieux, 3:129.

50. *De vita spirituali animae*, ed. Glorieux, 3:167.

51. John Morrall, *Gerson and the Great Schism* (Manchester, 1960), 46–47.

52. G. H. M. Posthumus Meyjes, *Jean Gerson: Apostle of Unity* (Leiden, 1999), 220–27.

53. *De vita spirituali animae*, ed. Glorieux, 3:177–78.

54. Cf. Wyclif, *De veritate sacrae scripturae* 36; 3:39–40.

55. *Pro licentiandis in decretis (conversi estis)*, ed. Glorieux, 5:172–73.

56. *Pro licentiandis in decretis (conversi estis)*, ed. Glorieux, 5:177–78.

57. *De examinatione doctrinarum*, in *Opera Omnia* 1:10b. See also Glorieux, 9:462.

58. Louis Pascoe, *Jean Gerson: Principles of Church Reform* (Leiden, 1973), 89–92. *Dominus his opus habet* quoted in Pascoe, 92 n. 30: " . . . theologi proprio nomine dicuntur hi qui notitiam profitentur et habent eorum quae proprie dicuntur esse ad theologia hoc est de jure divino, seu evangelico quod idem est, et qui illud sciunt elucidare, defendere, roborare."

59. *An licet in causis fidei a papa apellare* quoted in Pascoe, *Jean Gerson*, 91 n. 27: "Ex quibus palam elicitur quod Summus Pontifex qui succedit Petro in apostolatu reprehendi potest publice per doctorem theologum qui in officio praedicationis succedit Paulo." *De vita spirituali*, in Pascoe, *Jean Gerson*, 91 n. 28: "Quod si quis praelatorum vellet hujusmodi legem aut diceret habere robus legis divinae, sibi fas esset per theologos aut alios hoc cognoscentes resistere in facie et dicere quod non recte ambulat ad veritatem Evangelii." See also Meyjes, *Jean Gerson: Apostle of Unity*, 334–35.

60. Brian Patrick McGuire, *Jean Gerson and the Last Medieval Reformation* (University Park, PA, 2005), 213.

61. Daniel Hobbins, "The Schoolman as Public Intellectual: Jean Gerson and the Late Medieval Tract," *American Historical Review* 108 (2003): 1308–37.

62. *De necessaria communione laicorum sub utraque specie*, in *Opera Omnia* 1:458b: "Scriptura Sacra in expositione partium suarum requisivit et requirit homines primo praeditos ingenio; secundo exercitatos studio; tertio humiles in judicio; quarto immunes ab affectato vitio." See also Glorieux, 10:56. Cf. Wyclif, *De veritate sacrae scripturae* 9, 1:201; *De veritate* 16, 2:20; *De veritate* 22, 2:184.

63. Pascoe, *Jean Gerson*, 107–9.

64. *Contra curiositatem studentium*, ed. Glorieux, 3:239.

65. Cf. Wyclif, *Dialogus sive speculum ecclesie militantis* 26, ed. A.W. Pollard (London, 1886), 54.

66. Christopher Bellitto, *Nicolas de Clamanges: Spirituality, Personal Reform, and Pastoral Renewal on the Eve of the Reformations* (Washington, DC, 2001), 111–26.

67. Steven E. Ozment, *Homo Spiritualis: A Comparative Study of the Anthroplogy of Johannes Tauler, Jean Gerson and Martin Luther (1509–16) in the Context of Their Theological Thought* (Leiden, 1969), 51–53. See Gerson's *De mystica theologia speculativa*, quoted in Ozment, 51 n. 3: "Contemplatio namque, si nude consideretur sine dilectione vel affectu subsequente, iam arida est, inquieta est, curiosa est, ingrata est, inflata est."

68. *Gerson a Pierre d'Ailly* (Bruges, 1 April 1400), ed. Glorieux, 2:26–28. See also Monika Asztalos, "The Faculty of Theology," in *A History of the University in*

Europe, 4 vols., ed. Hilde de Ridder-Symoens (Cambridge, 1992–2011), 1:409–41, esp. 436–38.

69. *Contra curiositatem studentium*, ed. Glorieux, 3:230.

70. *Contra curiositatem studentium*, ed. Glorieux, 3:233. Cf. Pseudo-Dionysius, *De divinis nominibus* 1; *PL* 122:1113.

71. *Quae veritates sint de necessitate salutis credendae*, in *Opera Omnia* 1:25d–26a. See also Glorieux, 6:187.

72. Mark Burrows, *Jean Gerson and De Consolatione Theologiae* (Tübingen, 1991), 88–124.

73. *De examinatione doctrinarum*, in *Opera Omnia* 1:11b–c. See also Glorieux, 9:463.

74. *De potestate ecclesiastica et de origine juris et legum*, in *Opera Omnia* 2:227c–d.

75. *De Auferibilitate Sponsi*, ed. Glorieux, 3:296–97. See 3:297: "Fuerunt enim primitus velut in quodam seminario vivifico positi in Ecclesia per Christum et postdum, crescente Ecclesia, discretio talium magis innotuit velut si botrus vinae se in folia et flores et ramos explicuerit."

76. Louis Pascoe, "Jean Gerson: The 'Ecclesia Primitiva' and Reform," *Traditio* 30 (1974): 379–409.

77. Francis Oakley, "Gerson as Concilarist," in *A Companion to Jean Gerson*, ed. Brian Patrick McGuire (Leiden, 2006), 179–204, esp. 190–92.

78. Morrall, *Gerson and the Great Schism*, 80.

79. Robert Swanson, "The 'Mendicant Problem' in the Later Middle Ages," in *The Medieval Church: Universities, Heresy, and Religious Life: Essays in Honour of Gordon Leff*, ed. Peter Biller and Barrie Dobson (Woodbridge, Suffolk, 1999), 217–38, esp. 229–34. See also Nancy McLoughlin, "Gerson as a Preacher in the Conflict between the Mendicants and Secular Priests," in McGuire, ed., *A Companion to Jean Gerson*, 249–92.

80. Cf. Wyclif, *De apostasia* 1, pp. 9–10; and *Trialogus* 4.33, pp. 361–64.

81. *Propositiones de sensu litterali sacrae scripturae*, in *Opera Omnia*, 1:2a–b. See also Glorieux, 3:334.

82. *Circa damnationem propositionum Joannis Parvi*, in *Opera Omina* 5:930c: ". . . quia sic se fundabant Haeretici, prout vidimus in Wiclef, et Huss, qui dum urgebantur, confugiebant ad glosas."

83. *Propositiones de sensu litterali sacrae scripturae*, in *Opera Omnia* 1:4c: "Ratio est, primo, quia praeferunt sensum suum judicio prudentiorum et sapientiorum." See also Glorieux, 3:337.

84. See the excellent analysis by Karlfried Froehlich, "'Always to Keep to the Literal Sense in Holy Scripture Means to Kill One's Soul': The State of Biblical Hermeneutics at the Beginning of the Fifteenth Century," in *Literary Uses of*

Typology from the Late Middle Ages to the Present, ed. Earl Miner (Princeton, 1977), 20–48.

85. *Circa damnationem*, 5:926c: "... quod sensus litteralis cujuscumque locutionis, est ille sensus quem principaliter et de directo intendit ipse loquens. Unde idem est dicere: Non est tenendus sensus litteralis; et dicere: Non est capienda intentio loquentis. Cum igitur Spiritus sanctus sit ille qui in sacra Scriptura loquitur; erroneum est dicere, quod sensus litteralis non sit verus aliquando, et non semper tenendus."

86. *Circa damnationem*, 5:930d: "Secundo, quia sacrae Scripturae debetur talis reverentia, quod non licet eam credere esse falsam in aliquo sensus literali."

87. *Circa damnationem*, 5:927a–b: "... fallax ergo est hoc Argumentum: Iste est sensus grammaticalis litterae; igitur sensus litteralis: quia littera illa sacra reprimit intentionem loquentis, non per terminos, sed per res significatas."

88. *Circa damnationem*, 5:927c: "Nec habeatur pro inconvenienti, quod aliqua Propositio olim habebat duplicem sensus litteralem; nunc vero, tempore gratiae, unicum."

89. *Circa damnationem*, 5:928b.

90. *Circa damnationem*, 5:928b.

91. *Circa damnationem*, 5:928a. Cf. Totting, *Quaestio de Sacra Scriptura*, 55–56.

92. *Circa damnationem*, 5:930c: "Primo, quia Scriptura sacra exponit suam regulam per semetipsam, secundum diversos passus Scripturae, et juxta sacros Doctores."

93. *Quae veritates sint de necessitate salutis credendae*, in *Opera Omnia* 1:22b: "Omne revelatum a Deo est verum; et quod Scriptura Sacra divinitus est a Deo revelata sic quod in omni sua parte est verbum Dei quod transire non potest." See also Glorieux, 6:182.

94. *De necessaria communione laicorum sub utraque specie*, in *Opera Omnia* 1:457b: "Scriptura Sacra est fidei regula, contra quam bene intellectam non est admittenda auctoritas vel ratio hominis cujuscumque; nec aliqua consuetudo, nec constitutio, nec observatio valet si contra Sacram Scripturam militare convincatur." See also Glorieux, 10:55.

95. *De examinatione doctrinarum*, in *Opera Omnia* 1:12d–13a: "Attendendum in examinatione doctrinarum primo et principaliter, si doctrina sit conformis Sacrae Scripturae, tam in se, quam in modi traditione ... quoniam Scriptura nobis tradita est tanquam regula sufficiens et infallibilis, pro regimine totius ecclesiastici corporis et membrorum, usque in finem saeculi. Est igitur talis ars, talis regula, vel exemplar, cui se non conformans alia doctrina vel abjicienda est ut haeretica, vel de haeresi suspecta, aut sicut impertinens ad religionem prorsus habenda." See also Glorieux, 9:465.

96. *Quae veritates*, 1:22a–b. See also Glorieux, 6:181–82.

97. Cf. Wyclif, *De veritate sacrae scripturae* 1, 1:1–2; *De veritate sacrae scripturae* 6, 1:111–12; *De veritate sacrae scripturae* 19, 2:112.

98. Cf. Wyclif, *De veritate sacrae scripturae* 1, 1:1–19; and *Fasciculi Zizaniorum*, 462–63.

99. *De duplici logica*, ed. Glorieux, 3:58: "Igitur logicae virtus et sermonis proprietas videntur falsitatis arguere evangelistam Marcum qui hoc universali sermone usus est."

100. *De duplici logica*, ed. Glorieux, 3:58–59.

101. *De duplici logica*, ed. Glorieux, 3:59–60: "Et hoc est quod quidam non irrationabiliter dicunt quod theologia suam habet logicam et modum loquendi proprium et quod in ea nihil esse falsum de virtute sermonis debet admitti; immo dictum huiusmodi tamquam irreligiosum, impium et blasphemum a catholicis auribus reiici congruit."

102. *De duplici logica*, ed. Glorieux, 3:61: "In quibus tamen est falsitas aperta aut scandalosa juxta locutiones usitatas et secundum rhetoricam in materia tali servandam.... Propterea non imprudenter condemnatae sunt aliquando propositiones tamquam articuli erronei aut revocandi in quibus tamen erat veritas de vi vocis et logicae prioris ut ista: Ecclesia manens Ecclesia potest errare."

103. *Quae veritates*, 1:24c–d: "Falsum, blasphemum et haereticam est asserere quod sensus litteralis Sacrae Scripturae sit aliquando falsus... dicimus quod aliud est littera, aliud est sensus litteralis.... Est enim sensus litteralis vere et proprie dictus, ille quem Spiritus Sanctus principaliter intendebat et qui ex circumstantiis litterae Scripturae Sacrae trahi potest et debet, sicut expositores sacri fecerunt et docuerunt." See also Glorieux, 6:185. Cf. Wyclif, *De veritate sacrae scripturae* 6, 1:119–20.

104. *De sensu litterali sacrae scripturae*, in *Opera Omnia* 1:3a: "Sensus litteralis Sacrae Scripturae accipiendus est non secundum vim logicae, seu dialecticae, sed potius juxta tropos et figuratas locutiones, quas communis usus committit, cum consideratione circumstantiarum litterae ex precedentibus et posterius appositis. Habet enim Scriptura Sacra sicut moralis et historialis scientia suam logicam propriam, quam rhetoricam appellamus." See also Glorieux, 3:334.

105. *Propositiones de sensu litterali*, 1:3b. See also Glorieux, 3:335.

106. *De examinatione doctrinarum*, 1:13d. See also Glorieux, 9:466.

107. *Propositiones de sensu litterali*, 1:4b. See also Glorieux, 3:336–37.

108. *Octo regulae super stylo theologico*, ed. Glorieux, 10:257.

109. *Octo regulae super stylo theologico*, ed. Glorieux, 10:257–58.

110. *Octo regulae super stylo theologico*, ed. Glorieux, 10:258–59.

111. *Octo regulae super stylo theologico*, ed. Glorieux, 10:259: "Et ideo si una assertio habeat unum sensum erroneum, scandalosum aut piarum aurium offensivum, potest rationabiliter condemnari, non obstante quod de virtute sermonis grammaticalis aut ex vi vocis logicalis, ipsa habere posset aliquem sensum verum."

112. *Prosperum Iter*, ed. Glorieux, 5:476.

113. *Prosperum Iter*, ed. Glorieux, 5:476: "Hoc practicatum est in hoc concilio de multis articulis Wiclef et Joannis Hus, quorum aliqui poterant vel de vi logicae vel grammaticae defensionem aliquam recipere."

114. *Collectio Judicorum*, vol. 1, ed. D'Argentre (Paris, 1728; reprint, Brussels, 1963), 128b.

115. *Prosperum Iter*, ed. Glorieux, 5:476–77: ". . . similiter et theologia suam habet propriam logicam et sensum litteralem aliter quam speculativae scientiae. Haec directio vel lex praservavit hactenus praeclarum Universitatem Parisiensem a plurimis erroribus dum scholasticos suos semper ad certam regulam fidei loqui jussit et compulit."

116. *Prosperum Iter*, ed. Glorieux, 5:477: "Concilium generale potest et debet damnare propositiones multas vel assertiones hujusmodi quamvis non possent ex solo et nudu textu expresso Sacrae Scriptuare patenter reprobari seclusis expositionibus doctorum vel usu celebri Ecclesiae et ceteris."

117. Michael Shank, *Unless You Believe, You Shall Not Understand: Logic, University, and Society in Late Medieval Vienna* (Princeton, 1988), 182–84.

118. Zénon Kaluza, "Le Chancelier Gerson et Jérôme de Prague," *Archives d'Histoire Doctrinale et Littéraire du Moyen Age* 51 (1984): 81–126. See p. 115.

119. *De necessaria communione*, in *Johannes Gerson Opera Omnia*, 1:457b–c. See also Glorieux, 10:55.

120. *De necessaria communione*, 1:457d–458a. See also Glorieux, 10:56.

121. *De necessaria communione*, 1:458a. See also Glorieux, 10:56.

122. Cf. Wyclif, *De civili dominio*, 1:422–24.

123. *De necessaria communione*, 1:458d. See also Glorieux, 10:57.

124. *De necessaria communione*, 1:459a: "Scriptura Sacra recipit interpretationem et expositionem nedum in suis verbis originalibus, sed etiam in suis expositoribus." See also Glorieux, 10:57.

125. *De necessaria communione*, 1:459c: "Scriptura Sacra in sui receptione et expositione authentica, finaliter resolvitur in auctoritatem, receptionem et approbationem universalis Ecclesiae, praesertim primitivae, quae recepit eam et ejus intellectum immediate a Christo revelante Spiritu Sancto in die Pentecostes, et alias pluries." See also Glorieux, 10:58.

126. *De sensu litterali sacrae*, in *Johannes Gerson Opera Omnia*, 1:3a: "Sensus Scripturae litteralis judicandus est, prout Ecclesia Spiritu Sancto inspirata et gubernata determinavit, et non ad cujuslibet arbitrium vel interpretationem." See also Glorieux, 3:335.

127. *De sensu litterali sacrae*, 1:3c. See also Glorieux, 3:335.

128. *De sensu litterali sacrae*, 1:3c: "Sensus litteralis Sacrae Scripturae fuit primo per Christum et Apostolos revelatus et miraculis elucidatus, deinde fuit per

sanguinem martyrum confirmatus; postdum sacri doctores per rationes suas diligentes contra haereticos . . . postea successit determinatio sacrorum conciliorum, ut quod erat doctrinaliter discussum per doctores, fieret per Ecclesiam sententialiter definitum." See also Glorieux, 3:335.

129. *De sensu litterali sacrae,* 1:3d–4a: "Sensus litteralis Sacrae Scripturae si repiritur determinatus et decisus in decretis et decretalibus et codicibus conciliorum, judicandus est ad theologiam et Sacram Scripturam non minus pertinere quam symbolum apostolorum: propterea non est spernendus tanquam humana seu positiva constitutione fundatus. [Haeretici] dicunt omnes tales scripturas apocryphas esse vel falsas, nisi ostendatur quod sint expresse in Scriptura Sacra: et consequenter negant quatuor doctores et concilia, putantes quod ex sacra Scriptura convinci non possint." See also Glorieux, 3:336.

130. Christoph Burger, *Aedificatio, Fructus, Utilitas: Johannes Gerson als Professor der Theologie und Kanzler der Universität Paris* (Tübingen, 1986), 148.

131. *De sensu litterali sacrae,* 1:4a: "Sensus litteralis quamvis sit in multis, praesertim in his quae sunt necessaria ad salutem, satis expressus in libris Sacrae Scripturae, vel ex illis evidenter consequatur apud eruditos in eisdem libris: nihilominus expedivit tales sensus sub certis articulis compendiose in publicum tradere, quemadmodum de Symbolo Apostolorum et Athanasii factum fuisse cognovimus." See also Glorieux, 3:356.

132. Meyjes, *Jean Gerson,* 326.

133. *Contra haeresim de communione,* 1:459c–d: "Haec enim est infallibilis regula a Spiritu sancto directa, qui in his quae Fidei sunt, nec fallere potest nec falli. . . . Universalis Ecclesiae circa ea quae Fidei Sacramenta respiciunt et dispensationem ipsorum; quam autoritatem Doctoris unius particularis etiam Sancti." See also Glorieux, 10:57.

134. *De examinatione doctrinarum,* in *Johannes Gerson Opera Omnia,* 1:8a–b: "Examinator authenticus et finalis Judex doctrinarum Fidem tangentium, est generale Concilium. . . . Nam persona quaelibet singularis de Ecclesia, cujuscunque dignitatis, etiam Papalis, circumdata est infirmatate, et deviabilis est, ut fallere possit et falli." See also Glorieux, 9:460.

135. See Meyjes, *Jean Gerson,* 309–11.

136. Oakley, "Gerson as Conciliarist," 199–200.

137. Oakley, "Gerson as Conciliarist," 179–81.

138. Thomas Izbicki, "Papalist Reaction to the Council of Constance: Juan de Torquemada to the Present," *Church History* 55 (1986): 7–20.

139. Denzinger, 1375.

140. *Contra haeresim de communione,* 1:459d–460a: "Unde valde mirandum videtur apud aliquos considerativos, dum vident quod statim ut Doctor aliquis composuit unam lecturam vel unam compositionem; aut glossam super Decretalibus

aut Decretis redegit in scriptis; habetur illa glossa seu lectura in reverentia tali, quod allegatur authentice in Scholis et Judiciis: qui Doctor si viveret, non esset comparandus mille et mille qui jam sunt in vita. Et tamen si tota una Universitas, exempli gratia, quae habet Doctores in omni facultate peritissimos, declararet aut determinaret unam expositionem circa unum passum Scripturae sacrae vel Decretorum aut Decretalium, vix reputabitur aut recipietur hujusmodi testificatio; quasi vidilicet scriptura morta sit majoris autoritatis quam viva. Et si opponatur, quod in vivis pervertitur judicium propter perversionem affectus; cur non similiter potest dubitari quod in mortuis regnaverint dum viverent passiones judicii subversiva." See also Glorieux, 10:57.

Chapter 7. The Enduring Dilemma

1. See the bull *Exsecrabilis* in Denzinger, 1375.
2. For biographical information, see Wendy Scase, "Reginald Pecock," in *Dictionary of National Biography*, 43:382–86; and Scase, *Reginald Pecock* (London, 1996).
3. R. M. Ball, "The Opponents of Bishop Pecock," *Journal of Ecclesiastical History* 48 (1997): 230–61. See also Mishtooni Bose, "Reginald Pecock's Vernacular Voice," in *Wycliffites and Their Influence in Late Medieval England*, ed. Fiona Somerset, Jill Havens, and Derrick Pittard (Suffolk, 2003), 217–36.
4. *The Reule of Chrysten Religioun*, ed. William Cabell Greet, Early English Texts Society 171 (London, 1927), 461–62.
5. *The Reule*, 463–65. See p. 465: " . . . þe ruyde and symple leuyng to þi scripture and to doctouris seiyngis wiþout resoluyng of it into ferþer groundis out of whom her writings and seiyngis comen forþ, haþ holde men, and dooþ holde so ȝit, into greet derkenes and blyndnes."
6. *The Repressor of Over Much Blaming of the Clergy* 1.2, ed. Churchill Babington, 2 vols., Rolls Series 19 (London, 1860), 1:10.
7. *The Repressor* 1.3, pp. 1:13–17.
8. *The Repressor* 1.4, pp. 1:18–20.
9. *The Repressor* 1.5, p. 1:23.
10. *The Repressor* 1.17, pp. 1:93–97. See p. 1:93: "Open experience schewith that a viciose man is as kunnyng a clerk for to finde, leerne, and vndirstonde, which is the trewe and dew sentence of Holi Scripture." And p. 1:95: " . . . ȝit we mowe haue that hise ȝiftis and gracis of wit he ȝeue as plenteuoseli to a bad man as to a good man, and sumtyme more plenteuoseli to the lasse good man than to the better man."
11. *The Repressor* 1.15, pp. 1:83–84: " . . . al the feith being positijf lawe to man, which Scripture groundith or teachith, is not so worthi in it silf, neither so necessarie and profitable to man, for to serue God and deserue meede in heuen, as is the

seid doom of resoun being moral lawe of kinde; and therfore Holi Scripture as in the positijf lawis of feith to man is not so worthi in him silf, neither so profitable and necessarie to man as is the seid doom of resoun, which is the lawe of kinde."

12. Everett Emerson, "Reginald Pecock: Christian Rationalist," *Speculum* 31 (1956): 235–42.

13. Kantik Ghosh, "Bishop Pecock and the Idea of 'Lollardy,'" in *Text and Controversy from Wyclif to Bale: Essays in Honour of Anne Hudson*, ed. Helen Barr and Ann M. Hutchison (Turnhout, 2005), 251–65.

14. *Book of Faith* 1.3, ed. J. L. Morison (Glasgow, 1909), 148–49: " . . . and for it is so knowen bi sure experience, is resonable, and if resonable, thanne vertuose, and so thanne meritorie, and rewardable."

15. V. H. H. Green, *Bishop Reginald Pecock: A Study in Ecclesiastical History and Thought* (Cambridge, 1945), 125.

16. E. F. Jacob, Book review of *Bishop Reginald Pecock*, by V. H. H. Green. *Journal of Theological Studies* 47 (1946): 244–48; quote at p. 245.

17. Green, *Bishop Reginald Pecock*, 54–59. For more on the trial and its aftermath see Scase, *Reginald Pecock*, 28–42.

18. *Loci e Libro Veritatum*, ed. James Thorold Rogers (Oxford, 1881), 99–100.

19. *Loci e Libro Veritatum*, 49.

20. For biographical information, see James G. Clark, "John Bury," in *Dictionary of National Biography*, 9:61.

21. *Gladius Salamonis* 2, appendix to *The Repressor of Over Much Blaming of the Clergy*, ed. Babington, 2:576–78. See 2:578: " . . . quare sufficienter in Sacra Scriptura omnium actuum dirigibilium in Deum sufficiens fundatio reperitur."

22. *Gladius Salamonis* 42, pp. 2:611–12.

23. *Gladius Salamonis* 2, p. 2:581: "Suppono insuper quod Sacra Scriptura triplicem legem continet, scilicet, naturae, synagogae, et ecclesiae."

24. *Gladius Salamonis* 6, pp. 2:584–87. See p. 2:587: "Propterea dicimus, quod Vetus Testamentum et Sacra Scriptura prius erant quam scriptorum calamis et digitis exararentur."

25. *Gladius Salamonis* 30, pp. 2:591–92.

26. *Gladius Salamonis* 42, pp. 2:607–608.

27. *Gladius Salamonis* 36, pp. 2:596–97. Cf. Augustine, *De doctrina Christiana*, prologue, 5–6.

28. *Gladius Salamonis* 39, p. 2:600.

29. *Gladius Salamonis* 40, pp. 2:602–4. See p. 2:604: "Tolle Scripturarum certissimam constantissimamque sinceritatem, et quid de Christo habes? Quid de Deo sentis, quomodo Trisagion, aut Homoüsion tibi sonant? Quae sacramentorum remedia; quae redemptionis virtus; quae bonorum merces; quae malorum afflictio cognoscitur?"

30. Mishtooni Bose, "After Chichele: 'John Bury contra Pecock' Revisited" (unpublished paper presented at the Forty-fourth International Congress on Medieval Studies, Kalamazoo, MI, 2009).

31. See the statement on infallibility issued by the First Vatican Council in Denzinger, 3074.

32. Brian Tierney, *Foundations of the Conciliar Theory: The Contribution of the Medieval Canonists from Gratian to the Great Schism*, enl. new ed. (Leiden, 1988), 180–81. Quote at p. 181.

33. Tierney, *Foundations of the Conciliar Theory*, 184–98. Quote at p. 197.

Bibliography

PRIMARY SOURCES

General Works and Collections

Biblia latina cum glossa ordinaria. 4 vols. Edited by Karlfried Froehlich and Margaret Gibson. Strassburg, 1480; reprint, Turnhout, 1992.
Biblia Sacra iuxta Vulgatum Versionem. Edited by Robert Weber. Stuttgart, 1969.
Chartularium Universitatis Parisiensis. 4 vols. Edited by Henry Denifle. Paris, 1889–97.
Corpus Christianorum. Continuatio Medieavalis. Turnhout, 1971– .
Corpus Christianorum. Series Latina. Turnhout, 1953– .
Corpus iuris canonici. 2 vols. Edited by E. Friedberg. Leipzig, 1879; reprint, Graz, 1960.
Corpus Scriptorum Ecclesiasticorum Latinorum. Vienna, 1866– .
Decrees of the Ecumenical Councils. 2 vols. Edited by Norman Tanner. London, 1990.
Decretum Gratiani Emendatum et Annotationibus Illustratum vna cum Glossis. Paris, 1601.
Enchiridion Symbolorum. 36th ed. Edited by Henry Denzinger and Adolf Schönmetzer. Rome, 1976.
Fasciculi Zizaniorum Magistri Johannis Wyclif cum Tritico. Edited by W.W. Shirley. Rolls Series 5. London, 1858.
Miscellanea Hustica. Edited by Jan Sedlák. Prague, 1996.
Monarchia S. Romani Imperii. 3 vols. Edited by M. Goldast. Frankfurt, 1614; reprint, Graz, 1960.
Patrologia Cursus Completus. Series Graeca. Edited by J. P. Migne. Paris, 1857– .
Patrologia Latina Cursus Completus. Series Latina. Edited by J. P. Migne. Paris, 1844– .
Rerum concilii oecumenici constantiensis. 6 vols. Edited by Hermann von der Hardt. Frankfurt and Leipzig, 1697–1700.

Individual Authors

Aquinas, Thomas. *Opera Omnia*. 34 vols. Paris, 1871–80.

———. *Summa Theologiae*. 4 vols. Rome, 1950.

Auriol, Peter. *Compendium sensus litteralis totius divinae scripturae*. Edited by Philbert Seeboeck. Quaracchi, 1896.

———. *Peter Aureoli Scriptum super Primum Sententiarum*. Edited by Eligius Buytaert. St. Bonaventure, NY, 1952.

Bacon, Roger. *Rogeri Bacon Opera quaedem hactenus inedita*. Edited by J. S. Brewer. Rolls Series 15. London, 1859.

Basil of Caeserea. *De Spiritu Sancto*. Edited by Benoît Pruche. *Sources Chrétiennes*. Paris, 1968.

Bonaventure. *Opera Omnia*. 10 vols. Quaracchi, 1882–1902.

———. *Opera Omnia*. 15 vols. Paris, 1864–71.

Bury, John. *Gladius Salamonis*. In *The Repressor of Over Much Blaming of the Clergy*, edited by Churchill Babington. 2 vols. Rolls Series 19. London, 1860.

d'Ailly, Pierre. *Collectio Judicorum*. Paris, 1728; reprint, Brussels, 1963.

———. *Quaestiones magistri Petri de Ailliaco cardinalis cameracensis super libros Sententiarum*. Strassburg, 1490; reprint, Frankfurt, 1968.

———. *Tractatus et Sermones*. Strassburg, 1490; reprint, Frankfurt, 1971.

Dietrich von Niem. *Dialog über Union und Reform der Kirche 1410 (De modis uniendi et reformandi ecclesiam in concilio universali)*. Edited by Hermann Heimpel. Leipzig and Berlin, 1933.

Duns Scotus. *Opera Omnia*. Edited by P. C. Balić. Vatican City, 1950–.

———. *Opera Omnia*. 26 vols. Paris, 1891–95.

FitzRalph, Richard. *Summa Domini Armacani in questionibus Armenorum*. Edited by Johannis Sudoris. Paris, 1511.

Gascoigne, Thomas. *Loci e Libro Veritatum*. Edited by James Thorold Rogers. Oxford, 1881.

Gerson, Jean. *Johannes Gerson Opera Omnia*. 5 vols. Edited by Louis Ellies Du Pin. Antwerp, 1706; reprint, Zurich, 1987.

———. *Oeuvres Complètes de Jean Gerson*. 10 vols. Edited by P. Glorieux. Paris, 1960–73.

Grosseteste, Robert. *Roberti Grosseteste Episcopi Quondam Lincolniensis Epistolae*. Edited by H. R. Luard. London, 1861.

Henry of Ghent. *Lectura Ordinaria super sacram scriptura*. Edited by R. Macken. Leiden, 1980.

———. *Summa quaestionum ordinarium*. Paris, 1520; reprint, St. Bonaventure, NY, 1953.

Hugh of St. Victor. *Didascalicon*. Edited by C. H. Buttimer. Washington, DC, 1939.

Huguccio Pisanus. *Summa Decretorum: Distinctiones I–XX*. Edited by Oldřich Přerovský. Vatican City, 2006.

Hus, Jan. *Mistr Jan Hus*. Edited by Jan Sedlák. Prague, 1915.

———. *Magistri Iohannis Hus Tractatus de ecclesia*. Edited by S. Harrison Thomson. Cambridge, 1956.

———. *Magistri Iohannis Hus Opera Omnia-Spisy*. 25 vols. Edited by František Ryšánek, Amedeo Molnár, Jaroslav Eršil, and Anežka Vidmanová-Schmidtová. Prague, 1959– .

———. *Magistri Iohannis Hus Opera Omnia*. 3 vols. Edited by W. Flašhans and M. Komínková. 1905; reprint, Osnabrück, 1966.

———. *The Letters of Jan Hus*. Translated by Matthew Spinka. Manchester, 1972.

———. *Magistri Iohannis Hus Questiones*. CCCM 205. Edited by Jiří Kejř. Turnhout, 2004.

———. *Magistri Iohannis Hus Quodlibet*. CCCM 211. Edited by Bohumil Ryba. Turnhout, 2006.

Marsilius von Inghen. *Quaestiones super Quattuor Libros Sententiarum*. 2 vols. Edited by Manuel Santos Noya. Leiden, 2000.

Netter, Thomas. *Doctrinale Antiquitatum Fidei Catholicae Ecclesiae*. 3 vols. Edited by B. Blanciotti. Venice, 1757–59; reprint, Farnborough, 1967.

Nicholas of Lyra. *Postilla super Totam Bibliam*. 4 vols. Strassburg, 1492; reprint, Frankfurt am Main, 1971.

Olivi, Peter John. *Peter of John Olivi on the Bible*. Edited by David Flood and Gedeon Gál. St. Bonaventure, NY, 1997.

Pecock, Reginald. *The Repressor of Over Much Blaming of the Clergy*. 2 vols. Edited by Churchill Babington. Rolls Series 19. London, 1860.

———. *Book of Faith*. Edited by J. L. Morison. Glasgow, 1909.

———. *The Reule of Chrysten Religioun*. Edited by William Cabell Greet. Early English Text Society 171. London, 1927.

Peter Lombard. *Sententiae in IV libris distinctae*. 2 vols. Edited by I. Brady. Rome, 1981.

Peter of Mladoňovice. *John Hus at the Council of Constance*. Translated by Matthew Spinka. New York, 1965.

Rufinus of Bologna. *Summa Decretorum*. Edited by Heinrich Singer. Paderborn, 1963.

Summa Parisiensis. Edited by Terence McLaughlin. Toronto, 1952.

Terreni, Guido. *Guidonis Terreni Quaestio de magisterio infallibili Romani pontificis*. Edited by B. M. Xiberta. Münster, 1926.

———. *Summa de haeresibus et earum confutationibus*. Edited by Iodocus Badius Ascensius. Paris, 1528.

Totting von Oyta, Henry. *Henrici Totting de Oyta Quaestio de Sacra Scriptura et de Veritatibus Catholicis*. Edited by Albert Lang. Münster, 1953.

Woodford, William. *De causis condempnationis articulorum 18 damnatorum Joannis Wyclif* in *Fasciculus rerum expetendarum et fugiendarum prout Orthuino Gratio . . . editus est Coloniae*. A.D. MDXXXV. Edited by Edward Brown. London, 1690.

———. *Quattuor Determinaciones Fratris Willelmi Woodford de Ordine Fratrum Minorum contra Wyclyff in Materia de Religione*. Edited by M. D. Dobson. Unpublished Oxford B. Litt. thesis, 1932.

Wyclif, John. *De apostasia*. Edited by Michael Henry Dziewicki. London, 1889.

———. *De benedicta incarnacione*. Edited by Edward Harris. London, 1886.

———. *De civili dominio*. 4 vols. Edited by Reginald Lane Poole and Johann Loserth. London, 1885/1900–1904.

———. *Dialogus sive speculum ecclesie militantis*. Edited by A.W. Pollard. London, 1886.

———. *De ecclesia*. Edited by Johann Loserth. London, 1886.

———. *De logica*. Edited by Michael Henry Dziewicki. London, 1893.

———. *Opera Minora*. Edited by Johann Loserth. London, 1910.

———. *Polemical Works in Latin*. 2 vols. Edited by Rudolf Buddensieg. London, 1883.

———. *De potestate papae*. Edited by Johann Loserth. London, 1907.

———. *Sermones*. 4 vols. Edited by Johann Loserth. London, 1887–90.

———. *Trialogus cum supplemento Trialogi*. Edited by Gotthard Lechler. Oxford, 1869.

———. *De trinitate*. Edited by Allen DuPont Breck. Boulder, CO, 1962.

———. *De universalibus*. Edited by Ivan Mueller. Oxford, 1984.

———. *De veritate sacrae scripturae*. 3 vols. Edited by Rudolf Buddensieg. London, 1905–7.

SECONDARY SOURCES

Alban, Kevin. *The Teaching and Impact of the "Doctrinale" of Thomas Netter of Walden (c. 1374–1430)*. Turnhout, 2010.

Asztalos, Monika. "The Faculty of Theology." In *A History of the University in Europe*, 4 vols., edited by Hilde de Ridder-Symoens, 1:409–41. Cambridge, 1992–2011.

Ball, R. M. "The Opponents of Bishop Pecock." *Journal of Ecclesiastical History* 48 (1997): 230–61.

Bellitto, Christopher. *Nicolas de Clamanges: Spirituality, Personal Reform, and Pastoral Renewal on the Eve of the Reformations*. Washington, DC, 2001.

Benrath, Gustav. *Wyclifs Bibelkommentar*. Berlin, 1966.

Bernstein, Alan. "Magisterium and License: Corporate Autonomy against Papal Authority in the Medieval University of Paris." *Viator* 9 (1978): 291–307.

Betts, R. R. "The *Regulae Veteris et Novi Testamenti* of Matěj Z Janova." *Journal of Theological Studies* 32 (1931): 344–51.

Bierbaum, Max. *Bettelorden und Weltgeistlichkeit an der Universität Paris*. Münster, 1920.

Bose, Mishtooni. "Reginald Pecock's Vernacular Voice." In *Wycliffites and Their Influence in Late Medieval England*, edited by Fiona Somerset, Jill Havens, and Derrick Pittard, 217–36. Suffolk, 2003.

———. "After Chichele: 'John Bury contra Pecock' Revisted." Unpublished paper delivered at the Forty-fourth International Congress on Medieval Studies, Kalamazoo, MI, 2009.

Bougerol, Jacques Guy. "Une Theologie biblique de la revelation." *Antonianum* 48 (1973): 95–104.

Brandmüller, Walter. "Hus vor dem Konzil." In *Jan Hus zwischen Zeiten, Völkern, Konfessionem*, edited by Ferdinand Seibt, 235–42. Munich, 1997.

Burger, Christoph. *Aedificatio, Fructus, Utilitas: Johannes Gerson als Professor der Theologie und Kanzler der Universität Paris*. Tübingen, 1986.

Burrows, Mark. "Jean Gerson on the 'Traditioned Sense' of Scripture as an Argument for an Ecclesial Hermeneutic." In *Biblical Hermeneutics in Historical Perspective: Studies in Honor of Karlfried Froehlich for His Sixtieth Birthday*, edited by Mark Burrows and Paul Rorem, 152–72. Grand Rapids, MI, 1991.

———. *Jean Gerson and De Consolatione Theologiae*. Tübingen, 1991.

Buytaert, Eligius. "Circa Doctrinam Duns Scoti de Traditione et de Scriptura Sufficientia Adnnotationes." *Antonianum* 40 (1965): 346–62.

Cardaropoli, Gerardo. "La Sacra Scrittura nel Pensiero di G. Duns Scoto." *Antonianum* 48 (1973): 123–44.

Catto, J. I. "Wyclif and Wycliffism at Oxford: 1356–1430." In *History of the University of Oxford*, vol. 2, edited by J. I. Catto and R. Evans, 175–261. Oxford, 1992.

———. "William Woodford." In *Dictionary of National Biography*, 60 vols., edited by H. C. G. Matthew and Brian Harrison, 60:179–80. Oxford, 2004.

Cesalli, Laurent. "Le 'pan propositionnalisme' de Jean Wyclif." *Vivarium* 43 (2005): 124–55.

Chapman, D. J. "On the Decretum Gelasianum: De Libris Recipiendis et non Recipiendis." *Revue Benedictine* 30 (1913): 187–207, 315–33.

Chenu, M.-D. "'Authentica' et 'Magistralia': Deux lieux théologiques aux XII–XIII siècles." *Divus Thomas* 28 (1925): 257–85.

———. *Introduction a l'étude de Saint Thomas D'Aquin*. Paris, 1950.

Clark, James. "John Bury." In *Dictionary of National Biography*, 60 vols., edited by H. C. G. Matthew and Brian Harrison, 9:61. Oxford, 2004.

Congar, Yves. "Aspects ecclésiologiques de la querrele entre mendicants et séculars." *Archives d'Histoire Doctrinale et Littérature du Moyen Age* 28 (1961): 35–151.

———. *Tradition and Traditions.* London: 1966.

Conti, Alessandro. "Wyclif's Logic and Metaphysics." In *A Companion to John Wyclif: Late Medieval Theologian,* edited by Ian Christopher Levy, 67–125. Leiden, 2006.

Copsey, Richard. "Thomas Netter of Walden: A Biography." In *Thomas Netter of Walden: Carmelite, Diplomat, and Theologian (c. 1372–1430),* edited by Johan Bergström-Allen and Richard Copsey, 23–111. Faversham, Kent, and Rome, 2009.

Courtenay, William J. "Force of Words and Figures of Speech: The Crisis over *Virtus Sermonis* in the Fourteenth Century." *Franciscan Studies* 44 (1984): 107–28.

Dahan, Gilbert. *L'Exégèse chrétienne de le Bible en Occident médiéval XII–XIV siècle.* Paris, 1999.

David, Zdeněk. *Finding the Middle Way: The Utraquists' Liberal Challenge to Rome and Luther.* Washington, DC, 2003.

De Lubac, Henri. *Exégèse médiévale: Les quatre sens de l'écriture.* 2 vols. Paris, 1959–64.

Denifle, Henry. "Quel Livre servait de base a l'Enseignement des Maitres en Théologie dans l'Université de Paris." *Revue Thomiste* 2 (1894): 149–61.

Donneaud, Henry. "Le sens du mot *theologia* chez Bonaventure." *Revue Thomiste* 102 (2002): 271–95.

Dove, Mary. "Wyclif and the English Bible." In *A Companion to John Wyclif: Late Medieval Theologian,* edited by Ian Christopher Levy, 365–406. Leiden, 2006.

Doyle, Eric. "William Woodford's 'De dominio civili clericorum' against John Wyclif." *Archivum Franciscanum historicum* 66 (1973): 49–109.

———. "William Woodford on Scripture and Tradition." In *Studia historico-ecclesiastica: Festgabe für Luchesius G. Spätling, O.F.M.,* edited by Isaac Vazquez, 481–502. Rome, 1977.

Emerson, Everett. "Reginald Pecock: Christian Rationalist." *Speculum* 31 (1956): 235–42.

Flanagin, David Zachariah. "God's Divine Law: The Scriptural Founts of Conciliar Theory in Jean Gerson." In *The Church, the Councils, and Reform: The Legacy of the Fifteenth Century,* edited by Gerald Christianson, Thomas M. Izbicki, and Christopher M. Bellitto, 101–21. Washington, DC, 2008.

Froehlich, Karlfried. "'Always to Keep to the Literal Sense in Holy Scripture Means to Kill One's Soul': The State of Biblical Hermeneutics at the Beginning of the Fifteenth Century." In *Literary Uses of Typology from the Late Middle Ages to the Present,* edited by Earl Miner, 20–48. Princeton, 1977.

———. "Fallibility Instead of Infallibility? A Brief History of the Interpretation of Galatians 2:11–14." In *Teaching Authority and Infallibility in the Church: Lutherans and Catholics in Dialogue VI,* edited by Paul C. Empie, T. Austin Murphy, and Joseph A. Burgess, 259–69, 351–57. Minneapolis, 1980.

———. "Christian Interpretation of the Old Testament in the High Middle Ages." In *Hebrew Bible/Old Testament: The History of Its Interpretation*, vol. 1, pt. 2, edited by Magne Saebø, 496–558. Göttingen, 2000.

Fudge, Thomas. "The 'Law of God': Reform and Religious Practice in Late Medieval Bohemia." *Bohemian Reformation and Religious Practice* 1 (1996): 49–72.

———. *The Magnificent Ride: The First Reformation in Hussite Bohemia*. Aldershot, 1998.

Gabriel, Astrik. "The Ideal Master of the Mediaeval University." *Catholic Historical Review* 60 (1974): 1–40.

Ghellinck, J. de. "Pour L'Histoire du Mot 'Revelare.'" *Recherches Sciences Religeuses* 6 (1916): 149–57.

Ghosh, Kantik. *The Wycliffite Heresy*. Cambridge, 2002.

———. "Bishop Pecock and the Idea of 'Lollardy.'" In *Text and Controversy from Wyclif to Bale: Essays in Honour of Anne Hudson*, edited by Helen Barr and Ann M. Hutchison, 251–65. Turnhout, 2005.

Gradon, Pamela. "Wyclif's *Postilla* and his Sermons." In *Text and Controversy From Wyclif to Bale: Essays in Honour of Anne Hudson*, edited by Helen Barr and Ann M. Hutchison, 67–77. Turnhout, 2005.

Green, V. H. H. *Bishop Reginald Pecock: A Study in Ecclesiastical History and Thought*. Cambridge, 1945.

Gryson, Roger. "The Authority of the Teacher in the Ancient and Medieval Church." *Journal of Ecumenical Studies* 19 (1982): 176–87.

Hackett, John. "The State of the Church: A Concept of the Medieval Canonists." *Jurist* 23 (1963): 259–90.

Harvey, Margaret. "Richard Ullerston." In *Dictionary of National Biography*, 60 vols., edited by H. C. G. Matthew and Brian Harrison, 55:867–68. Oxford, 2004.

Hayes, Zachary. *The Hidden Center: Spirituality and Speculative Christology in St. Bonaventure*. New York, 1981.

Herold, Vilém. "Platonic Ideas and 'Hussite Philosophy.'" Translated by Zdeněk V. David. *Bohemian Reformation and Religious Practice* 1 (1996): 13–17.

———. "How Wycliffite was the Bohemian Reformation?" Translated by Zdeněk V. David. *Bohemian Reformation and Religious Practice* 2 (1998): 25–37.

———. "Wyclif's Ecclesiology and Its Prague Context." Translated by Zdeněk V. David. *Bohemian Reformation and Religious Practice* 4 (2002): 15–30.

———. "Jan Hus: A Heretic, a Saint, or a Reformer?" *Communio Viatorum* 45 (2003): 5–23.

———. "Štěpán of Páleč and the Archetypal World of Ideas." Translated by Zdeněk V. David. *Bohemian Reformation and Religious Practice* 5 (2004): 77–87.

Hobbins, Daniel. "The Schoolman as Public Intellectual: Jean Gerson and the Late Medieval Tract." *American Historical Review* 108 (2003): 1308–37.

Hoenen, Maarten. "Virtus Sermonis and the Trinity: Marsilius of Inghen and the Semantics of Late-Fourteenth-Century Theology." *Medieval Philosophy and Theology* 10 (2001): 157–71.

Hoffmans, J, ed. *Les Philosophes Belges.* Vol. 5. Louvain, 1932.

Hudson, Anne. "The Debate on Bible Translation, Oxford 1401." *English Historical Review* 90 (1975): 1–18.

———. *The Premature Reformation: Wycliffite Texts and Lollard History.* Oxford, 1988.

———. "From Oxford to Prague: The Writings of John Wyclif and His English Followers in Bohemia." *Slavonic and East European Review* 75 (1997): 642–57; reprinted in *Studies in the Transmission of Wyclif's Writings.* Aldershot, 2008.

———. "Thomas Netter." In *Oxford Dictionary of National Biography,* 60 vols., edited by H. C. G. Matthew and Brian Harrison, 60:444–47. Oxford, 2004.

———. "Wyclif's Works and Their Dissemination." In *Studies in the Transmission of Wyclif's Writings,* 1–16. Aldershot, 2008.

Hudson, Anne, and Anthony Kenny. "John Wyclif." In *Oxford Dictionary of National Biography,* 60 vols., edited by H. C. G. Matthew and Brian Harrison, 60:616–29. Oxford, 2004.

Hurley, Michael. "'Scriptura sola': Wyclif and His Critics." *Traditio* 16 (1960): 275–352.

———. "A Pre-Tridentine Theology of Tradition, Thomas Netter of Walden." *Heythrop Journal* 4 (1963): 348–66.

———. "Wyclif or Woodford?" *Carmelus* 49 (2002): 31–46.

Izbicki, Thomas. "La Bible et les Canonists." In *Le Moyen Age et la Bible,* edited by Pierre Riché and Guy Lobrichon, 371–84. Paris, 1984.

———. "Papalist Reaction to the Council of Constance: Juan de Torquemada to the Present." *Church History* 55 (1986): 7–20.

———. "The Authority of Peter and Paul: The Use of Biblical Authority during the Great Schism." In *The Companion to the Great Western Schism (1378–1417),* edited by Joëlle Rollo-Koster and Thomas Izbicki, 376–93. Leiden, 2009.

Jacob, E. F. Book review of *Bishop Reginald Pecock,* by V. H. H. Green. *Journal of Theological Studies* 47 (1946): 244–48.

Johnson, Mark. "Another Look at the Plurality of the Literal Sense." *Medieval Philosophy and Theology* 2 (1992): 117–41.

Jotischky, Andrew. *The Carmelites and Antiquity: Mendicants and Their Pasts in the Middle Ages.* Oxford, 2002.

Kaluza, Zénon. "Le Chancelier Gerson et Jérôme de Prague." *Archives d'Histoire Doctrinale et Littéraire du Moyen Âge* 51 (1984): 81–126.

———. "Les sciences et leurs langages." In *Filosofia e Teologia nel Trecento: Studi in ricordo Eugenio Randi,* edited by Bianchi Luca, 197–258. Louvain-la-Neuve, 1994.

Kaminsky, Howard. *The History of the Hussite Revolution.* Berkeley, 1967.

———. "John (Jan) Hus." In *Dictionary of the Middle Ages*, 13 vols., edited by Joseph Strayer, 6:364–69. New York, 1982–89.

Kempshall, M. S. *The Common Good in Late Medieval Political Thought.* Oxford, 1999.

Krmíčková, Helen. "Utraquism in 1414." Translated by Zdeněk V. David. *Bohemian Reformation and Religious Practice* 4 (2002): 99–105.

Lahey, Stephen. *John Wyclif.* Oxford, 2009.

Lang, Albert. *Heinrich Totting von Oyta.* Münster, 1937.

Larsen, Andrew. "John Wyclif, c. 1331–1384." In *A Companion to John Wyclif: Late Medieval Theologian*, edited by Ian Christopher Levy, 1–65. Leiden, 2006.

Le Bras, Gabriel. "Les Ecritures dans le Décret de Gratien." *Zeitschrift der Savigny-Stiftung für Rechtsgeschichte: Kanonistiche Abteilung* 27 (1938): 47–80.

———. "Velut splendor firmamenti: Le Docteur dans le droit de l'Église médiévale." In *Melanges offerts à Etienne Gilson*, 372–88. Toronto, 1959.

———. *Histoire du droit et des institutions de l'Eglise en Occident: L'Age classique, 1140–1378.* Paris, 1965.

Leclercq, Jean. "L'Idéal du théologien au Moyen Age." *Revue des Sciences Religieuses* 21 (1947): 121–48.

Levy, Ian Christopher. "Was John Wyclif's Theology of the Eucharist Donatistic?" *Scottish Journal of Theology* 53 (2000): 137–53.

———. "Defining the Responsibilities of the Late Medieval Theologian: The Debate between John Kynyngham and John Wyclif." *Carmelus* 49 (2002): 5–29.

———. "John Wyclif's Neoplatonic View of Scripture in Its Christological Context." *Medieval Philosophy and Theology* 11 (2003): 227–40.

———. *John Wyclif: Scriptural Logic, Real Presence, and the Parameters of Orthodoxy.* Milwaukee, WI, 2003.

———. "Texts for a Poor Church: John Wyclif and the Decretals." *Essays in Medieval Studies* 20 (2003): 94–107.

———. "Grace and Freedom in the Soteriology of John Wyclif." *Traditio* 60 (2005): 279–337.

———. "John Wyclif and the Christian Life." In *A Companion to John Wyclif: Late Medieval Theologian*, edited by Ian Christopher Levy, 292–363. Leiden, 2006.

———. "John Wyclif on Papal Election, Correction, and Deposition." *Mediaeval Studies* 69 (2007): 141–85.

———. "John Wyclif and the Primitive Papacy." *Viator* 38 (2007): 159–89.

———. "Guido Terreni: Reading Holy Scripture within the Sacred Tradition." *Carmelus* 56 (2009): 73–106.

———. "The Literal Sense of Scripture and the Search for Truth in the Late Middle Ages." *Revue d'Histoire Ecclésiastique* 104 (2009): 783–827.

———. "Thomas Netter on the Eucharist." In *Thomas Netter of Walden: Carmelite, Diplomat, and Theologian*, ed. Johan Bergström-Allen and Richard Copsey, 273–314. Faversham, Kent, and Rome, 2009.

———. "Holy Scripture and the Quest for Authority among Three Late Medieval Masters." *Journal of Ecclesiastical History* 61 (2010): 40–68.

Long, R. James. "'Utrum iurista vel theologus plus proficiat ad regimen ecclesiae': A *Quaestio disputata* of Francis Caraccioli. Edition and Study." *Mediaeval Studies* 30 (1968): 134–62.

Lytle, Guy Fitch. "Universities as Religious Authorities in the Later Middle Ages and Reformation." In *Reform and Authority in the Medieval and Reformation Church*, edited by Guy Finch Lytle, 69–97. Washington, DC, 1981.

Maccarrone, Michele. "Una questione inedita dell'Olivi sull' infallibilità del papa." *Rivista di Storia della Chiesa in Italia* 3 (1949): 309–43.

Madrigal, Santiago. "The Place of the *Doctrinale* of Thomas Netter of Walden in the History of Ecclesiology." In *Thomas Netter of Walden: Carmelite, Diplomat, and Theologian (c. 1372–1430)*, edited by Johan Bergström-Allen and Richard Copsey, 201–30. Faversham, Kent, and Rome, 2009.

McGuire, Brian Patrick. *Jean Gerson and the Last Medieval Reformation*. University Park, PA, 2005.

McLaughlin, Mary Martin. *Intellectual Freedom and Its Limitations in the University of Paris in the Thirteenth and Fourteenth Centuries*. New York, 1977.

McLoughlin, Nancy. "Gerson as a Preacher in the Conflict between the Mendicants and Secular Priests." In *A Companion to Jean Gerson*, edited by Brian Patrick McGuire, 249–92. Leiden, 2006.

Meyjes, G. H. M. Posthumus. "Quasi Stellae Fulgebunt: On the Position and Function of the Doctor of Divinity in Mediaeval Church and Society." In *In Divers Manners: A St. Mary's Miscellany to commemorate the 450th anniversary of the founding of St. Mary's College, 7th March 1539*, edited by D. W. D. Shaw, 11–28. St. Andrews, 1990.

———. *Jean Gerson: Apostle of Unity*. Leiden, 1999.

Minnis, Alastair. "'Authorial Intention' and the 'Literal Sense' in the Exegetical Theories of Richard FitzRalph and John Wyclif." *Proceedings of the Irish Academy* 75 (1975): 1–31.

———. *Medieval Theory of Authorship*. London, 1984.

———. "Tobit's Dog and the Dangers of Literalism: William Woodford O. F. M. as Critic of Wycliffite Exegesis." In *Defenders and Critics of Franciscan Life: Essays in Honor of John V. Flemming*, edited by Michael F. Cusato and G. Geltner, 41–52. Leiden, 2009.

———. *Translations of Authority in Medieval English Literature*. Cambridge, 2009.

Minnis, Alastair, and A. B. Scott. *Medieval Literary Theory and Criticism, c. 1100–1375*. Oxford, 1988.

Morrall, John. *Gerson and the Great Schism*. Manchester, 1960.

Noya, Manuel Santos. "Schrift, Tradition, und Theologie bei Marsilius von Inghen." In *Marsilius von Inghen: Werk und Wirkung*, edited by Stanisław Wielgus, 73–91. Lublin, 1993.

Oakley, Francis. "Pierre d'Ailly and Papal Infallibility." *Mediaeval Studies* 26 (1964): 353–58.

———. *The Political Thought of Pierre d'Ailly: The Voluntarist Tradition*. New Haven, 1964.

———. "Gerson as Concilarist." In *A Companion to Jean Gerson*, edited by Brian Patrick McGuire, 179–204. Leiden, 2006.

Ozment, Steven. *Homo Spiritualis: A Comparative Study of the Anthroplogy of Johannes Tauler, Jean Gerson, and Martin Luther (1509–16) in the Context of Their Theological Thought*. Leiden, 1969.

Pascoe, Louis. *Jean Gerson: Principles of Church Reform*. Leiden, 1973.

———. "Jean Gerson: The 'Ecclesia Primitiva' and Reform." *Traditio* 30 (1974): 379–409.

———. *Church and Reform: Bishops, Theologians, and Canon Lawyers in the Thought of Pierre d'Ailly: 1351–1420*. Leiden, 2005.

Pennington, Kenneth. *Popes and Bishops: The Papal Monarchy in the Twelfth and Thirteenth Centuries*. Philadelphia, 1984.

Prügl, Thomas. "Thomas Aquinas as Interpreter of Scripture." In *The Theology of Thomas Aquinas*, edited by Rik Van Nieuwenhove and Joseph Wawrykow, 386–415. Notre Dame, IN, 2005.

———. "Medieval Biblical *Principia* as Reflections on the Nature of Theology." In *What Is 'Theology' in the Middle Ages?* edited by Mikołaj Olszewski, 253–75. Münster, 2007.

Rosato, Leo. "Ioannis Duns Scoti doctrina de scriptura et traditione." In *De Scriptura et Traditione*, edited by P. C. Balić, 233–52. Rome, 1963.

Rosemann, Philipp. *The Story of a Great Book: Peter Lombard's Sentences*. Peterborough, ON, 2007.

Rosenthal, Frank. "Heinrich von Oyta and Biblical Criticism in the Fourteenth Century." *Speculum* 25 (1950): 178–83.

Scase, Wendy. *Reginald Pecock*. London, 1996.

———. "Reginald Pecock." In *Dictionary of National Biography*, 60 vols., edited by H. C. G. Matthew and Brian Harrison, 43:382–86. Oxford, 2004.

Schuessler, Hermann. "Sacred Doctrine and the Authority of Scripture." In *Reform and Authority in the Medieval and Reformation Church*, edited by Guy Fitch Lytle, 55–68. Washington, DC, 1981.

Shank, Michael. *Unless You Believe, You Shall Not Understand: Logic, University, and Society in Late Medieval Vienna*. Princeton, 1988.

Shogimen, Takashi. "William of Ockham and Guido Terreni." *History of Political Thought* 19 (1998): 517–30.

Siebel, F. X. "Die Kirche als Lehrautorität nach dem 'Doctrinale Antiquitatum Fidei Catholicae Ecclesiae' des Thomas Waldensis (um 1372–1431)." *Carmelus* 16 (1969): 3–70.

Šmahel, František. "'*Doctor evangelicus super omnes evangelistas*': Wyclif's Fortune in Hussite Bohemia." *Bulletin of the Institute of Historical Research* 43 (1970): 11–34.

Smalley, Beryl. "John Wyclif's *Postilla super Totam Bibliam*." *Bodleian Library Record* 5 (1953): 186–205.

———. "Gerard of Bologna and Henry of Ghent." *Recherches de Théologie Ancienne et Médiévale* 22 (1955): 125–29.

———. "The Bible and Eternity: John Wyclif's Dilemma." *Journal of Warburg and Courtauld Institutes* 27 (1964): 73–89.

———. "Wyclif's *Postilla* on the Old Testament and His *Principium*." In *Oxford Studies Presented to Daniel Callus*, 253–96. Oxford, 1964.

Smith, Kirk Stevan. "An English Conciliarist? Thomas Netter of Walden." In *Popes, Teachers, and Canon Law in the Middle Ages*, edited by J. R. Sweeney and Stanley Chodorow, 290–99. Ithaca, NY, 1989.

Spicq, Ceslaus. "Le canon des livres saints au XIII Siècle." *Revue des Sciences Philosophiques et Théologiques* 30 (1942): 424–31.

Spinka, Matthew. *Advocates of Reform: From Wyclif to Erasmus*. Philadelphia, 1953.

———. *John Hus' Concept of the Church*. Princeton, 1966.

Sutcliffe, E. F. "Jerome." In *The Cambridge History of the Bible*, 3 vols., edited by G. W. H. Lampe, 2:83–93. Cambridge, 1969.

Swanson, Robert. "The 'Mendicant Problem' in the Later Middle Ages." In *The Medieval Church: Universities, Heresy, and Religious Life: Essays in Honour of Gordon Leff*, edited by Peter Biller and Barrie Dobson, 217–38. Woodbridge, Suffolk, 1999.

Synave, P. "Le canon scripturaire de Saint Thomas D'Aquin." *Revue Biblique* 33 (1924): 522–33.

Taber, Douglass. "Pierre d'Ailly and the Teaching Authority of the Theologian." *Church History* 59 (1990): 163–74.

Thijssen, J. M. M. H. "Once Again the Ockhamist Statutes of 1339 and 1340: Some New Perspectives." *Vivarium* 28 (1990): 136–67.

Tierney, Brian. "Grosseteste and the Theory of Papal Sovereignty." *Journal of Ecclesiastical History* 6 (1955): 1–17.

———. *Ockham, Conciliar Theory, and the Canonists*. Philadelphia, 1971.

———. *Origins of Papal Infallibility: 1150–1350*. Leiden, 1972.

———. "A Scriptural Text in the Decretales and in St. Thomas: Canonistic Exegesis of Luke 22:32." *Studia Gratiana* 20 (1976): 363–76.

———. "'Only the Truth Has Authority': The Problem of 'Reception' in the Decretists and in Johannes de Turrecremata." In *Law, Church, and Society: Essays in Honor of Stephen Kuttner*, edited by Robert Somerville and Kenneth Pennington, 69–96. Philadelphia, 1977.

———. *Foundations of the Conciliar Theory: The Contribution of the Medieval Canonists from Gratian to the Great Schism*. Enl. new ed. Leiden, 1988.

Turley, Thomas. "*Ab Apostolorum Temporibus*: The Primitive Church in the Ecclesiology of Three Medieval Carmelites." In *Studia in Honorem Alphonsi M. Stickler*, edited by Rosalio Castillo Lara, 559–89. Rome, 1992.

Ullmann, Walter. *Medieval Papalism: The Political Theories of the Medieval Canonists*. London, 1949.

Van Engen, John. "Studying Scripture in the Early University." In *Neue Richtungen in der hoch- und spätmittelalterlichen Bibelexegese*, edited by Robert Lerner and E. Müller-Luckner, 17–38. Munich, 1996.

Verger, Jacques. "Teachers." In *A History of the University in Europe*, 4 vols., edited by Hilde de Ridder-Symoens, 1:144–68. Cambridge, 1992–2011.

Vooght, Paul de. "La décrétale Cum Marthae et son interprétation par les théologiens du XIV siècle." *Recherches de Science Religieuse* 42 (1954): 540–48.

———. *Les sources de la doctrine chrétienne*. Bruges, 1954.

———. "L'Ecclésiologie des adversaires de Huss au Concile de Constance." *Ephemerides Theologicae Lovanienses* 35 (1959): 5–24.

———. *L'Hérésie de Jean Huss*. Louvain, 1960.

Walsh, Katherine. *A Fourteenth-Century Scholar and Primate: Richard FitzRalph in Oxford, Avignon, and Armagh*. Oxford, 1981.

———. "Preaching, Pastoral Care, and Sola Scriptura in Later Medieval Ireland: Richard FitzRalph and the Use of the Bible." In *The Bible in the Medieval World: Essays in Honour of Beryl Smalley*, edited by Katherine Walsh and Diana Wood, 251–68. London, 1985.

———. "Wyclif's Legacy in Central Europe in the Late Fourteenth and Early Fifteenth Centuries." In *From Ockham to Wyclif*, edited by Anne Hudson and Michael Wilks, 397–417. Oxford, 1987.

———. "Richard FitzRalph." In *Dictionary of National Biography*, 60 vols., edited by H. C. G. Matthew and Brian Harrison, 19:917–22. Oxford, 2004.

Watt, J. A. "The Use of the Term 'Plenitudo Potestatis' by Hostiensis." In *Proceedings of the Second International Congress of Medieval Canon Law*, edited by S. Kuttner and J. Ryan, 161–87. Vatican City, 1965.

Wei, Ian P. "The Self-Image of the Masters of Theology at the University of Paris in the Late Thirteenth and Early Fourteenth Centuries." *Journal of Ecclesiastical History* 46 (1995): 398–441.

Wulf, M. de, and A. Pelzer, eds. *Les Philosophes Belges*. Vol. 2. Louvain, 1904.

Xiberta, B. M. *De scriptoribus scholasticis saeculi XIV ex ordine Carmelitarum*. Louvain, 1931.

Zamagni, Gianmaria. "Ermeneutica e metafisica: I due Prologhi della Postilla litteralis di Nicola di Lyra O. F. M." *Dianoia* 12 (2007): 57–85.

Zeleny, Rostislav. "Councils and Synods of Prague and Their Statutes." *Apollinaris* 45 (1972): 471–532, 698–740.

Index

Abel, 198, 200
Abraham, 14, 198, 229
Acts
  9:17, 99
  10, 123
  10:25–33, 6
  15, 203
Adam, 65, 229
Alban, Kevin, 264n.1
Alexander V: *Regnans in excelsis*, 209, 234
Alexander of Hales, 20
allegorical sense, 12, 14, 20, 67–68, 72
Ambrose, Saint, 124–25, 138, 146
Anacletus, 40, 111
anagogical sense, 12, 14, 20, 68
Ananias, 99
Andreae, Joannes, 233
Andrew of Brod, 179–82, 186
Anne of Bohemia, 152
Anselm of Canterbury, 173
Antichrist, 63, 88, 159, 161
apostasy, 157
apostles, the, 7, 16, 26–29, 31–32, 35, 76, 179–80, 186, 230
  Apostles' Creed, 27–28, 31, 34, 36, 38, 105, 126, 144, 167, 192, 219
  Aquinas on, 25, 28
  authority of, 9, 17, 24, 25, 26–27, 34, 38, 43, 46, 47, 74, 75, 97, 98–99, 100, 103, 105, 106, 107, 111, 115, 119–22, 125, 126–27, 130–31, 132, 134, 135, 137, 141, 143, 145, 148–49, 181–82, 225
  Gerson on, 207
  and Holy Spirit, 25, 28–29, 31, 34
  Hus on, 161
  Netter on, 121, 126–27, 130–31, 132, 134, 137, 139–40, 141, 143, 145, 146–47, 148–49
  Páleč on, 166, 167
  relationship to bishops, 40–42, 98–99, 100, 101, 139–40, 195
  Wyclif on, 83, 143
Aquinas, Thomas, Saint, 79, 91, 155, 183, 194
  on the apostles, 25, 28
  on authorial intention, 13
  on canonical scriptures, 11, 25
  on church authority, 27–28
  on the creed, 27–28
  De potentia 4.1, 68
  on faith, 25, 27–28
  on literal sense, 12–13, 20, 68

on scriptural authority, 27–28
on spiritual sense, 12–13, 68
Summa Theologiae, 12–13, 20
Aristotle
on four causes, 3
Metaphysics, 3
On Interpretation, 21
Physics, 43
Arius, 22, 71, 104, 110, 128, 137, 146, 148, 230
Armenian Christians, 172
Arnošt of Pardubice, 151
Arundel, Thomas, 92, 107
Athanasian Creed, 108, 144, 219
Athanasius: *De decretis* 5.21, 110
Augustine, Saint, 82, 104, 155, 175, 227, 230
on Arian heresy, 148
on baptism, 95
on biblical canon, 2, 25
on Christ and biblical text, 7–8
on Christian virtues, 7–8
on church authority, 6, 34, 36, 133, 166, 199
on the church from Abel, 56, 126, 198, 199
Confessions, 13
De baptismo contra Donatistas, 177
De civitate Dei, 198
De doctrina christiana, 5, 33, 62, 108–9, 113, 217
De trinitate, 105
on Donatist heresy, 85
on the Eucharist, 218
on literal sense, 13, 14
on Paul and Peter, 51
on predestination, 177
on revelation, 24
on salvation, 108–9
on sanctity of exegetes, 7–8, 80, 205

on scriptural authority, 2, 5, 6, 19, 33, 45
on the Septuagint, 19
on the Trinity, 105, 148
on truths in scripture, 62, 63, 90, 108–9, 113, 156, 161, 217
Augustinian friars, 102
Auriol, Peter, 9, 43
authorial intention, 7, 19, 62–63, 75, 171, 186, 215, 227
relationship to literal sense, 12, 13, 15, 20–21, 22–23, 67, 68–70, 71, 103, 156, 209, 211, 212, 213, 219
relationship to sanctity of exegetes, 10–11, 12
relationship to *virtus sermonis*, 22–23, 63, 67, 69–70, 71–72, 78, 156
authority of antiquity, 29, 46, 179–88, 189–90, 191, 216, 223
Gerson on, 189, 218–20
Netter on, 117–19, 121, 125–26, 130–32, 134, 135–36, 137, 139, 140–41, 143–44, 145–49
Páleč on, 166
Woodford on, 95–96, 98–99, 100–101, 115, 116

Babylonian Captivity, 224
Bacon, Roger, 11–12, 23–24
Baconthorpe, John, 118
Ball, R. M., 223
baptism, 95–96, 99, 123, 126, 164, 211, 217
Basil of Caesarea, 26–27, 102, 141, 143
Baybroke, Robert, 107
Baysio, Guido de, 196
Benedict XIII, 177
Berengar of Tours, 95
Bernard of Parma, 48
Bethlehem Chapel, 151, 157, 168
Biceps, Nicholas, 152

bishops, 45, 131, 133, 135, 208
    and priests, 40–42, 98–99, 100, 139–40
    relationship to the apostles, 40–42, 98–99, 100, 101, 139–40, 195
Blackfriars Synod, 76, 81, 112
blasphemy, 157, 162
Bohemia, reform in, 150–53, 235
Bonaventure, Saint, 115–16, 183
    on Christ and scripture, 8, 194
    on Christ and the sacraments, 28–29, 96
    on faith, 8
    on the New Testament, 28
    on papal authority, 41
    on philosophy and scripture, 24, 25
    rule of, 86
    on the saints, 24–25
    on sanctity of exegetes, 80, 205
Boniface VIII: *Unam Sanctam*, 160
Bose, Mishtooni, 231
Bourgchier, Thomas, 226
Bridget of Sweden, 223
Brutus, Peter, 113
    De victoria contra Iudaeos 1.15, 114
Burger, Christoph, 219
Burrows, Mark, 189
Bury, John, 223, 224
    on divine law, 229
    on divine revelation, 230
    Gladius Salamonis, 227–28
    on human morals, 228, 229
    on reason, 228, 230
    on scriptural authority, 225, 227–31
    on theology, 228, 229

canon, biblical, 5, 7, 25–26, 33, 34, 35, 235
    Augustine on, 2
    and church authority, 19–20, 30, 166, 172
    Duns Scotus on, 29–30
    Jerome on, 11, 19, 57, 58, 61
    Netter on, 131–33, 134, 140–41, 142
    Woodford on, 103–4, 106–7, 114
    Wyclif on, 55–63, 106, 131
    See also scriptural authority; scripture
canon law, 11, 12, 78, 166, 170, 180, 181, 190, 231
    d'Ailly on, 195, 196–97
    Gerson on, 200–204
    Hus on, 156, 161, 171, 216, 233
    and papal authority, 40–42, 45–51, 83, 97–98, 233
    and theology, 33, 37–38, 42–45, 85, 91, 200–202
    Wyclif on, 73–74, 75, 83, 85, 91, 129, 200, 233
    See also Gratian's *Decretum*
Caraccioli, Francis, 43
Carmelites, 102, 117
Catto, Jeremy, 59, 93–94
charity, 7, 8–9, 10, 68, 123, 183, 200, 204, 206
Charles University, 152
chastity, 102
1 Chronicles 22:10, 14, 69
church authority, 4–7, 18, 34–37, 38–39, 51, 179–80, 184–88, 227
    Aquinas on, 27–28
    Augustine on, 6, 34, 36, 133, 166, 199
    and biblical canon, 19–20, 30, 166, 172
    and Christ, 41
    and conscience, 174–75
    d'Ailly on, 199–200
    Duns Scotus on, 29–31, 146
    and faith, 5, 6, 27–28
    Gerson on, 189–90, 200, 203, 208–9, 218–20, 232
    Henry of Ghent on, 4–5

Hus on, 150, 157–62, 164–73, 189, 191
Netter on, 81, 118–19, 120, 121, 122–28, 129–34, 135, 136, 137, 138–40, 141, 142, 146–49, 232
Páleč on, 150, 161, 164, 165, 166–73, 232
Stanislav of Znojmo on, 165–66
Woodford on, 97–98, 108, 111–12, 115, 116, 232
Wyclif on, 54, 58, 63, 74, 81, 116, 124, 131, 133, 147–48, 165, 191, 192, 199, 200
See also general councils; papal authority
church fathers, 11, 27, 158, 166, 175, 176
authority of, 12, 15, 24, 25–26, 38, 46, 49, 55, 78, 82, 91, 95–96, 102, 105, 107, 109, 114–15, 118, 119, 120, 121, 125, 126, 129, 132, 133, 135–36, 137, 138, 141, 147, 170, 171–72, 178, 182, 190, 210, 218, 221, 223, 224, 227, 230, 231
Netter on, 121, 128, 129, 133, 134, 135–36, 137, 138, 141, 143–44, 146, 147, 148, 223
Pecock on, 223
Wyclif on, 55, 90
church hierarchy
apostle-bishop relationship, 40–42, 98–99, 100, 101, 139–40, 195
disciple-priest relationship, 40–42, 166
Gerson on, 208–9, 219, 220
Netter on, 124, 130, 139
Páleč on, 167
Stanislav of Znojmo on, 165–66
Woodford on, 98–99, 100–101
Wyclif on, 55, 78, 139–40, 208

church reform, 189, 190, 234
Hus on, 157–58, 159
Wyclif on, 54, 55, 73, 78, 84, 85, 86
civil law, 43, 74, 156, 170, 196, 200, 214
Gerson on, 201–2
Clamanges, Nicholas, 206
Clementine Decretals, 38
Clement of Rome, 100, 106
Clement VI, 14
Colossians
1:18, 199
4:16, 103
concomitance, 163, 183, 184
confession, 201
Confirmation, 28, 96, 98
Congar, Yves, 260n.6
conscience, 174–75
consubstantiality, 32, 104, 105, 110, 134, 146, 215
contextualization, 72, 100, 110, 176, 189, 212, 216–17
1 Corinthians, 185
2:6–13, 80
3:10, 143
10:2, 67
10:4, 124
11:17–29, 180
12:4–11, 208
13:11, 132
2 Corinthians
3:2, 127
3:6, 121, 210, 211
10:13, 40
Cornelius, 6, 123
Council of Basel, 221, 233
Council of Constance, 117, 135, 136, 184, 195–96, 214–15, 233
Haec sancta decree, 190, 220
John XXIII deposed by, 124, 171, 190, 208

Council of Constance (*cont.*)
    and lay communion, 178–79, 187
    trial of Hus, 152, 158, 159, 162, 164,
        173–78, 189, 215, 216–17, 234, 235
Council of Constantinople, 90
Council of Ephesus, 46, 134, 136
Council of Florence, 222
Council of Nicea, 90, 134, 138, 146
    See also Nicene Creed
Council of Pisa, 135, 177, 193
Council of Rimini, 46, 136
Council of Trent, 235
Cyprian, Saint, 180
Cyril, Saint, 134

Dahan, Gilbert, 12
d'Ailly, Pierre, 215–16, 221
    on canon law, 195, 196–97
    on church authority, 199–200
    on divine law, 195, 196–97
    on faith, 194, 195–96, 197, 199–200
    on general councils, 189, 195–96
    on heresy, 198
    on papal authority, 194–95
    Recommendatio Sacrae Scripturae, 198
    relationship with Gerson, 194, 200, 206, 214
    on scriptural authority, 45, 189, 196, 197, 198–99, 234
    on theologians, 42, 194–200
    on universal church, 199–200
    on universals, 173–74
deacons, 98–99, 100, 139
Decretum Damasi, 11
Decretum Gelasianum, 11, 45
Denifle, Henry, 42
Deuteronomy
    4:2, 44
    6:5, 13

De Vooght, Paul, 55, 93, 176, 177, 178
Dietrich of Niem
    on faith, 192–93
    on general councils, 82, 161, 193
    on papal authority, 190–93
    on universal Catholic Church
        and apostolic church, 191, 192–93
dispensation, 47–48, 74, 97, 193, 233
divorce, 97–98, 105
Dominicans, 102
Donation of Constantine, 74, 185
Donatism, 84, 85, 124, 159, 163, 164, 168–69
Dove, Mary, 59
Doyle, Eric, 93, 260n.6
Duns Scotus
    on biblical canon, 29–30
    on church authority, 29–31, 146
    Ordinatio, 29–32
    on sacraments, 31–32
    on transubstantiation, 146

Easter, 106
Ecclesiastes 12:11–12, 228
Emerson, Everett, 226
Enoch, 60, 198
Ephesians
    2:20, 125
    4:5, 125
    4:11, 139, 195
epikeia, principle of, 88, 157, 204, 210
Eucharist, the
    and Christ, 35, 178, 179, 181–82, 183–84, 186, 188
    lay communion, 151, 163, 178–88, 217, 235
    Netter on, 144–47, 148
    transubstantiation, 32, 86, 91, 95, 144–46, 163, 174, 184

Index 307

utraquism, 152, 178–88, 217, 218, 235
  Wyclif on, 78, 79–80, 91, 92, 94–95,
    144–46, 152, 174
Eumenides, 60
Extreme Unction, 28, 96
Ezra, 57

faith, 10, 19, 26, 44, 50, 84, 172, 190
  Aquinas on, 25, 27–28
  articles of, 27, 31, 32, 34, 35, 36–37,
    38, 43, 46, 47–48, 52, 74, 76, 77,
    88, 91, 110, 112, 119, 120, 126, 130,
    134, 144, 145–47, 148, 154, 167,
    168, 187, 192–93, 217
  Basil of Caesarea on, 27
  and biblical exegesis, 8, 21
  Bonaventure on, 8
  Catholic Church as object of, 127,
    130
  and church authority, 5, 6, 27–28
  d'Ailly on, 194, 195–96, 197,
    199–200
  Dietrich of Niem on, 192–93
  Henry of Ghent on, 5, 6
  justification by, 272n.34
  Netter on, 122, 125, 134, 142,
    145–47, 148
  Páleč on, 168
  Pecock on, 226
  as virtue, 8, 68, 123, 206
  Wyclif on, 58–60, 89, 90, 91, 109,
    119
  See also apostles, Apostles' Creed;
    Athanasian Creed; Nicene Creed
fasting, 102, 105
FitzRalph, Richard, 20, 60, 79, 91, 101,
    113, 114
  on literal sense, 14–18
  Summa de questionibus Armenorum,
    14–18

Florovsky, George, 27
Franciscans, 8, 41, 86
  Spiritual Franciscans, 4, 26, 28
  See also Woodford, William
fullness of power (*plenitudo potestatis*),
    48

Galatians
  2:11, 51
  2:11–14, 85, 202, 205
  3:19, 57
  4:22–24, 67
  4:24, 14, 69
  5:6, 123
  6:2, 57
Gascoigne, Thomas, 223, 224, 227, 231
general councils
  authority of, 17–18, 28, 33, 38,
    45–46, 47, 49–50, 50, 52–53,
    53, 76–77, 111–12, 115, 120,
    121, 127, 130, 132, 133, 135–38,
    146, 148, 149, 166, 172, 177–79,
    184, 187, 188, 193, 207, 219,
    220–21, 222, 232–33
  and Christ, 111, 136, 137, 138, 190
  d'Ailly on, 195–96
  Dietrich of Niem on, 82, 161, 193
  Gerson on, 111, 130, 135, 188, 189,
    190, 207, 219, 220, 222
  and Holy Spirit, 76–77, 111, 136,
    137, 138, 188, 190, 220
  Netter on, 76, 118, 120, 121, 127,
    130, 131, 132, 135–38, 146–47,
    148, 149, 232
  Páleč on, 166
  Woodford on, 76, 111–12, 115,
    232
  Wyclif on, 76–77, 136–37
  See also Council of Constance;
    Council of Nicea

Genesis, 56, 97
  1:3, 64
  17, 67–68
  17:14, 211
  21:1–14, 14
Gerard of Abbeville, 41
Gerard of Bologna, 5–7, 36, 85
Gerson, Jean, 18, 87, 200–221
  on the apostles, 207
  on authority of antiquity, 189, 218–20
  on canon law, 200–204
  on church authority, 189–90, 200, 203, 208–9, 218–20, 232
  on church hierarchy, 208–9, 219, 220
  on civil law, 201–2
  on contextualization, 217–18
  on divine law, 200, 201–4, 205, 214
  Eight Rules on Theological Style, 214
  on excommunication, 203
  on general councils, 111, 130, 135, 188, 189, 190, 207, 219, 220, 222
  on heresy, 152, 176, 203, 209–10, 212, 214–16, 217, 218–19, 221
  on Holy Spirit and the church, 220
  and Hus, 40, 45, 150, 201, 202, 204, 210, 214, 234
  on literal sense, 67, 72, 156, 209–17, 218–19
  on logic and rhetoric, 213–14, 216
  on papal authority, 40, 205, 207, 219, 220
  on predestination, 208
  Prosperum Iter, 215–16
  relationship with d'Ailly, 194, 200, 206, 214
  on sanctity of exegetes, 205–6
  on scriptural authority, 45, 189, 205–9, 211, 212, 216, 217–20, 234
  on theology, 40, 77, 200, 201, 202, 203, 204, 205–9, 213–16, 219, 221
  and Wyclif, 40, 45, 67, 72, 156, 201, 202, 203, 204, 205, 206, 207, 209, 210, 212, 213, 214, 225, 234
Ghosh, Kantik, 54–55, 59, 67, 78, 80, 94, 118, 226
Giles of Rome, 95
glosses, 23, 43, 71, 78–79, 91, 210, 220, 221
Glossa Ordinaria, 24, 46, 50–51
God
  as Father, 8, 10, 16, 22, 64, 66, 67, 70, 71, 90, 105, 110, 125, 132, 134, 154
  foreknowledge of, 29, 148
  grace of, 14, 21, 156, 158, 166–67, 168, 208, 225, 230
  revelation from, 24, 34–35, 37, 49, 121, 148, 194, 201, 205, 212, 224, 228, 230
Godfrey of Fontaines, 4, 41–42, 80, 87, 209, 221
Gospel of Bartholomew, 132
Gospel of Nicodemus, 60, 61, 62, 250n.27
Gospel of Thomas, 132
Gradon, Pamela, 249n.5
Gratian's *Decretum*, 42, 45, 63, 109, 158, 181, 182
  Audire episcopum, D. 24, c. 2, 100
  Ecclesiasticarum, D. 11, c. 5, 26, 102, 141
  Ego solis, D. 9, c. 5, 33
  Haeresis, C. 24, q. 3, c. 27, 2, 21, 63, 96, 156, 227
  In novo testamento, D. 21, c. 2, 40
  Noli frater, D. 9, c. 9, 33
  Palam est, D. 11, c. 9, 34
  Sacrosancta, D. 22, c. 2, 111
  Si ad sacras scripturas, D. 9, c. 7, 113
  Sicut sancti, D. 15, c. 2, 132

Si papa, D. 40, c. 6, 50
Sunt quidam dicentes, C. 25, q. 1, c. 6, 41, 46, 50, 75, 160
Green, Vivian, 226
Gregory the Great, 46, 132, 210
Gregory XII, 177
Grosseteste, Robert, 10, 64, 79, 86, 194
Guido de Baysio, 47

Habakkuk 2:11, 15
Hebrews
   1:1–2, 228
   1:5, 14, 69
   10:20, 140
Henry of Ghent, 41–42, 73
   on church authority, 4–5
   on faith, 5, 6
   Lectura Ordinaria super sacram scripturam, 3
   on scriptural authority, 3–5, 85
   Summa, a. 10, q. 1, 6
heresy
   d'Ailly on, 198
   defined, 2, 21, 43–44, 96–97, 157, 178–79, 186–88, 226–27, 231
   Gerson on, 152, 176, 203, 209–10, 212, 214–16, 217, 218–19, 221
   Hus on, 157, 162–63, 176
   Jerome on, 2, 63
   Netter on, 120–21, 122–23, 126, 127–28, 134, 135, 137, 141, 143–44, 145, 148, 234
   Páleč on, 152, 166, 168, 172
   papal heresy, 24, 46, 49–51, 53
   and *virtus sermonis*, 23, 71
   William of Ockham on, 43–44
   Woodford on, 95, 96–97, 98, 104, 107, 108, 120, 152, 234
   Wyclif on, 63, 73, 74, 76, 77, 84, 89, 95, 116, 118, 128, 206
   See also Arius

Herold, Vilém, 152, 159
Hilton, Walter, 223
Hobbins, Daniel, 205
Holy Spirit, 172, 205, 206, 224
   and the apostles, 25, 28–29, 31, 34
   and the church, 27, 28–29, 36, 52–53, 127, 128–29, 173, 180, 181, 182, 218, 220, 232
   and church fathers, 24
   filioque doctrine regarding, 15–16, 90, 91, 110
   and general councils, 76–77, 111, 136, 137, 138, 188, 190, 220
   at Pentecost, 98, 218
   and the sacraments, 28–29, 32
   and scripture, 2, 6, 8, 9, 10, 13, 17, 19–20, 22, 32, 61, 63, 67, 78, 96, 113, 127, 141, 146, 154, 156, 160, 161, 211, 212, 213, 217, 227
Homer, 60
homoousios, 90, 104, 110
Honorius III, 41
hope, 68, 123, 200
Hosea 14:9, 21
Hostiensis, 47, 48, 196, 197
Hudson, Anne, 93, 117
Hugh of Saint Victor, 11
Huguccio of Pisa, 46, 50
humility, 80, 124
Hurley, Michael, 55, 80, 93, 118
Hus, Jan
   on the apostles, 161
   on canon law, 156, 161, 171, 216, 233
   on Christ, 154–55, 156, 161
   on church authority, 150, 157–62, 164–73, 189, 191
   on church corruption, 150
   on church reform, 157–58, 159
   and conciliarists, 189, 191
   on conscience, 174–75

Hus, Jan (*cont.*)
  criticisms of, 1, 83, 150, 152, 156, 159, 161, 162–64, 167–73
  De ecclesia, 157–62, 176–77
  on divine law, 156–57, 170, 201, 202, 204
  on the Eucharist, 163, 164, 168, 174
  and Gerson, 40, 45, 150, 201, 202, 204, 210, 214, 234
  on heresy, 157, 162–63, 176
  on human law, 156–57, 170, 201, 202, 204
  influence of Wyclif on, 152, 153
  on literal sense, 156, 210
  on the mass, 163–64
  and Nicholas of Lyra, 156, 161
  On Simony, 157
  on papal authority, 40, 160–61, 162, 170, 177, 189, 191, 233–34
  on piety, 153, 154
  on predestination, 158–60, 171, 177
  on present righteousness, 158–60
  on reason, 154
  on salvation, 154, 155
  on scriptural authority, 45, 153–57, 158, 160, 161, 171–72, 189, 198, 216, 233
  Sermo de ecclesia, 159
  on theology, 154
  trial of, 152, 158, 159, 162, 164, 173–78, 189, 215, 216–17, 234, 235
  on the Trinity, 156
  on universal church, 171, 176–77
  on universals, 173–74
  as university master, 170, 173, 176, 223, 232, 234–35
  and Wyclif, 40, 45, 117, 152, 153, 154, 155, 156, 157–58, 162–64, 168, 174, 200, 223, 233

Ignatius of Antioch, 95
impanation, 147
Innocent III, 48
  Cum Marthae, 35, 102, 105
Innocent IV, 47, 48, 86
Izbicki, Thomas, 49

Jacobs, E. F., 226
Jakoubek of Stříbro, 181–84, 185–87
James
  1:25, 57
  5:14, 96
James, Saint, 130
Jan of Jenštejn, 151
Jeremiah and Baruch, 15
Jerome, Saint, 51, 106, 113, 155, 227
  on biblical canon, 11, 19, 57, 58, 61
  Haeresis, 2
  on heresy, 2, 63
  Prologus Galeatus, 11, 19, 58, 61
  translation of, 12, 57, 58, 114
Jerome of Prague, 153, 216
Jesus Christ, 25, 28, 34, 43, 46, 106, 119, 122, 148
  baptism of, 126, 127
  church as mystical body of, 81, 158, 172–73, 202
  and church authority, 41–42, 50, 52–53, 55, 58, 85, 101, 111, 112, 124–25, 129, 130, 131, 133, 161, 165, 172–73, 177, 181, 187, 191–92, 193–94, 200, 208, 218, 219, 220
  descent into hell, 31, 90
  divine nature of, 16, 22, 33, 65–66, 66, 70, 72
  and the Eucharist, 35, 178, 179, 181–82, 183–84, 186, 188
  and general councils, 111, 136, 137, 138, 190

on God the Father, 70, 71
as head of church, 82, 83, 158, 169, 172–73, 191, 199
human nature of, 22, 33, 65–66, 70, 72
law of, 56–57, 60, 62, 74, 83, 85, 89, 127, 132, 142–43, 156–57, 162, 170, 182, 191, 193–94, 197–98, 200, 202–3
on love, 56
in Luke 22:32, 6, 16, 32, 36, 50, 51, 52, 58, 60, 76, 125, 127, 232–33
Passion of, 85, 155, 200
on perfection, 132
and the sacraments, 28–29, 31–32, 35, 96–97, 147, 163–64, 178, 179, 181–82, 183–84, 186, 188, 225
on salvation, 217
as Savior, 65
and scripture, 4, 5, 7–9, 19–20, 21, 55, 62–66, 70, 80–81, 87, 103, 104, 107, 113, 132, 133, 142–43, 145, 147, 154–55, 197, 198–99, 211
as Son, 8, 10, 14, 64, 66, 105, 110, 134
as Truth, 184
as Word of God, 8, 10, 59, 62, 64, 65, 66, 70, 74, 80, 154, 155
Jews, 30, 57, 58, 113, 132, 211, 225
Johannes Teutonicus
Glossa Ordinaria, 24, 46, 50–51
on papal heresy, 24, 46, 50–51
John
1:1, 10
1:3–4, 64
1:45, 133
3:1–10, 60
5:39, 21
6:53–56, 178
6:56, 184
6:58, 217

7:16, 119
10:30, 22, 70, 128
10:35–36, 66
10:36, 154
13:34, 56
14:28, 22, 70, 71–72, 128
15:26, 136
16:12, 29, 31, 181–82
18:40, 110
19:26–27, 124
21:15–17, 16
21:25, 99, 103, 143
canonical status of, 106
1 John 1:18, 76
Johnson, Mark, 13
John XXII, 40, 124
John XXIII, 124, 152, 171, 190, 208, 209
Jotischky, Andrew, 117–18
Judas, 158, 179
Judges 9:8–15, 13
Judith, Book of, 11, 19–20
justice, 197, 200, 224, 229

Kaluza, Zénon, 22–23, 216
Kónrad of Vechta, 152
Kynyngham, John, 71–72, 77–78

Lateran Council, Fourth, 146
Latin Bible, corrupt text of, 11–12, 17–18, 19, 57, 58–60, 112–14
lay communion, 151, 163, 178–88, 217, 235
Lenten fast, 102, 105
Leviticus, 97
Linus, 106
literal sense, 11–23
Aquinas on, 12–13, 20, 68
Augustine on, 13, 14
duplex sensus litteralis, 14, 20, 69, 211

literal sense (*cont.*)
  FitzRalph on, 14–18
  Gerson on, 67, 72, 156, 209–17, 218–19
  Hus on, 156, 210
  Netter on, 72
  Paul of Burgos on, 20–22
  relationship to authorial intention, 12, 13, 15, 20–21, 22–23, 67, 68–70, 71, 103, 156, 209, 211, 212, 213, 219
  and spiritual sense, 12–14, 20, 24, 67–68, 69–70, 71, 109, 114, 179, 198
  as *virtus sermonis*, 22–23, 67, 69–70, 71–72, 78, 104, 156, 213
  Woodford on, 72, 103, 109, 111, 114
  Wyclif on, 67–72, 103, 104, 109, 130, 210, 212
Lombard's *Sentences*, 37, 43, 153–54, 157, 163, 207
Luke
  6:1–5, 104
  19:12, 66
  22:32, 6, 16, 32, 36, 50, 51, 52, 58, 60, 76, 125, 127, 232–33

1 Maccabees, 11
2 Maccabees, 11
  2:1, 103
  2:13, 103
  2:23, 103
Madrigal, Santiago, 118
Marcion, 120
Mark
  1:5–6, 212
  16:16, 217
marriage, 97–98, 105
Marsilius of Inghen, 37–39
Marsilius of Padua, 203, 220

Martin V, 125
mass, 163–64
Matěj of Janov
  on lay communion, 151
  Regulae Veteris et Novi Tentamenti, 151
Matthew
  5:15, 196
  5:29–30, 13
  5:48, 132
  13:52, 196
  15:32–38, 180
  16:18–19, 16, 51, 111, 124, 161, 187, 194, 198–99
  17:27, 143
  18:20, 136
  24:34, 141
  26:27, 179
  28:20, 58
Maurice of Prague, 186–87
McGuire, Brian, 205
mendicant orders
  and papal authority, 40–42, 47, 89, 234
  Woodford on, 86, 87, 92, 97, 98, 101–2, 109, 116
  Wyclif on, 86–89, 94, 101–2, 109, 110, 116, 209
  See also Franciscans
metaphor, 22, 69–70
Meyjes, Posthumus, 203, 219
Milíč, Jan, 151
Minnis, Alastair, 54–55, 59, 67, 80, 93, 252n.41
miracles, 115, 185, 219
Monophysitism, 252n.41
moral sense. *See* tropological sense
Moslems, 58, 60
mystical sense. *See* spiritual sense and literal sense

natural law, 7, 199, 201, 204, 225, 226, 228–30
Nestorius, 134
Netter, Thomas, 55, 68, 95, 167, 199, 221
  on the apostles, 121, 126–27, 130–31, 132, 134, 137, 139–40, 141, 143, 145, 146–47, 148–49
  on authority of antiquity, 117–19, 121, 125–26, 130–32, 134, 135–36, 137, 139, 140–41, 143–44, 145–49
  on baptism, 123
  on biblical canon, 131–33, 134, 140–41, 142
  as Carmelite, 117, 121, 264n.1
  on Christ and councils, 137
  on Christ and the church, 129, 133, 143
  on Christ's earthly ministry, 126, 127
  on church authority, 81, 118–19, 120, 121, 122–28, 129–34, 135, 136, 137, 138–40, 141, 142, 146–49, 232
  on church fathers, 121, 128, 129, 133, 134, 135–36, 137, 138, 141, 143–44, 146, 147, 148, 223
  on church hierarchy, 124, 130, 139
  on divine revelation, 121
  on doctrinal development, 118–19, 131–32, 144–49
  Doctrinale Antiquitatum Fidei Catholicae Ecclesiae, 117–49, 142
  on the Eucharist, 144–47, 148
  on extra-scriptural traditions, 140–44
  on faith, 122, 125, 134, 142, 145–47, 148
  on general councils, 76, 118, 120, 121, 127, 130, 131, 132, 135–38, 146–47, 148, 149, 232
  on heresy, 120–21, 122–23, 126, 127–28, 134, 135, 137, 141, 143–44, 145, 148, 152, 234
  on literal sense, 72
  on papal authority, 118, 120, 124–25, 130, 135, 137, 138, 146, 149, 232
  on Peter, 124–25, 127, 138, 140
  on predestination, 122
  relationship with Woodford, 117, 234
  on religious orders, 138, 140
  on sacraments, 142, 144
  on scriptural authority, 118, 119–20, 120, 121, 127, 129–30, 133–34, 137, 140–44, 145, 147–48
  on universal and apostolic church, 125–28, 129–31, 133, 134, 135, 136, 149
Nicene Creed, 108, 120, 122, 129, 130, 137, 142, 144, 186, 219
  filioque clause in, 15–16, 90, 91, 110
  homoousios in, 90, 104, 110
Nicholas de Tudeschis, 49
Nicholas of Dresden, 184
Nicholas of Lyra, 20, 113, 183
  and Hus, 156, 161
  on literal sense, 13–14
  on reason, 9–10
  and Wyclif, 9, 67, 68, 69, 73, 79, 91
Nicholas III, 255n.88
Nicodemus, 60, 61, 62

Oakley, Frances, 220
obedience, 102
Oberman, Heiko, 27
Olivi, Peter John, 8–9, 25, 51
Origen, 30
Oxford University, 92, 93, 117, 152, 153, 162–63, 194
  Wyclif at, 18, 71, 77, 78, 122

Páleč, Stephen, 153, 154, 163, 223, 234, 235
  on the apostles, 166, 167
  on authority of antiquity, 166
  on church authority, 150, 161, 164, 165, 166–73, 232
  on extra-scriptural authority, 171–72
  on faith, 168
  on general councils, 166
  on heresy, 152, 166, 168, 172
  on papal authority, 166, 167, 169, 170–71
  on predestination, 166–67, 168, 169
  on scriptural authority, 171, 172
  at trial of Hus, 174, 176–77
Panormitanus, 49
papal authority, 33, 34, 46–53, 220–21
  Bonaventure on, 41
  and canon law, 40–42, 45–51, 83, 97–98, 233
  d'Ailly on, 194–95
  Dietrich of Niem on, 190–93
  dispensation, 47–48, 74, 97, 193, 233
  Gerson on, 40, 205, 207, 219, 220
  Hus on, 160–61, 162, 170, 177, 189, 191, 233–34
  and mendicant orders, 40–42, 47, 89, 234
  Netter on, 118, 120, 124–25, 130, 135, 137, 138, 146, 149, 232
  Páleč on, 166, 167, 169, 170–71
  papal decrees and decretals, 12, 35, 38, 46, 49, 52, 63, 74–75, 78, 102, 146, 156, 160–61, 162, 170, 171, 180, 205
  papal infallibility, 49, 51–53, 76, 125, 130, 232–33
  and papal schism, 38, 49, 82, 124, 161, 171, 173, 192, 194, 195, 208, 232, 234
  and primacy of Peter, 16, 36, 47, 101, 124–25, 127, 140, 161, 166, 167, 191–92, 193–94, 198
  Stanislav of Znojmo on, 165–66
  Woodford on, 101, 107, 112, 232
  Wyclif on, 55, 57, 63, 74–76, 82–83, 85–86, 89, 102–9, 112, 120, 124, 191, 192, 194, 209, 233
papal heresy, 24, 46, 49–51, 53
papal sanctity, 190, 191–92
parabolic sense, 14, 20, 68
Paris statute of 1340, 22–23, 69, 70
Pascoe, Louis, 189, 194, 195
Paul, Saint, 14, 35, 40–41, 60, 74, 119, 138, 140, 141, 158, 185, 205
  and Ananias, 99
  on Christ, 16, 65, 69, 197
  on Genesis 17, 67–68
  Peter resisted by, 51, 85
  on traditions, 103, 143
Paul of Burgos
  Additiones ad Postillas Nicolai Lyrani, 20–22
  on authorial intention, 20–21, 22
  on literal sense, 20–22
Pecock, Reginald, 178, 222–31
  on church fathers, 223
  on doctrinal development, 224
  on faith, 226
  on moral principles, 224–26, 228, 229, 230–31
  on reason, 223, 224, 225, 226–27, 230–31
  Repressor of Over Much Blaming of the Clergy, 224, 227
  Reule of Chrysten Religioun, 224
  on sacraments, 225, 226
  on salvation, 226
  on scripture, 224–26, 227, 228, 229
Pelagius, 120

Peter, Saint, 34, 76, 111, 130, 202
  as Bishop of Rome, 34, 105, 106
  and Cornelius, 6
  faith of, 32, 50, 52, 58, 124–25, 138
  Netter on, 124–25, 127, 138, 140
  primacy of, 16, 36, 47, 101, 124–25, 127, 140, 161, 166, 167, 191–92, 193–94, 198
  resisted by Paul, 51, 85
1 Peter 3:15, 76
Peter of Mladoňovice, 173
Petit, Jean, 210
Philip and Nathaniel, 133
Philippians 2:7–8, 65
Philip VI, 40
Pius II, 222
  Exsecrabilis, 221
poverty, 8, 102, 124
Prague, 175, 194, 221, 234
  Wyclif's influence in, 54, 143, 150, 152–53, 162–63
predestination
  Augustine on, 177
  Gerson on, 208
  Hus on, 158–60, 171, 177
  Netter on, 122
  Páleč on, 166–67, 168, 169
  Wyclif on, 81–85, 118, 122–24, 199, 265n.30
presbyters, 98, 100, 101
priests, 45, 110, 186, 208
  and bishops, 40–42, 98–99, 100, 139–40
  moral character of, 49, 84–85, 123–24, 151, 163–64, 168, 169, 174
  priest-disciple relationship, 40–42, 166
prophets, 103, 124, 133, 139, 140, 201, 213
  authority of, 9, 17, 19, 25, 29, 41, 43, 46, 130–31, 230

Proverbs
  9:1, 198
  30:6, 44
Prügl, Thomas, 42
Psalms
  44:10, 9
  118:53, 147
Pseudo-Dionysius, 98–99, 100, 207, 209, 223
  De ecclesiastica hierarchia, 41

Quidort, John, 147

reason, 16, 21, 30, 37, 115, 200, 201, 217
  Bury on, 228, 230
  Hus on, 154
  limitations of, 7, 9–10, 25, 194, 205
  Pecock on, 223, 224, 225, 226–27, 230–31
Revelation, 56, 106
  3:12, 140
  21:18–19, 4, 37
  22:18, 44, 187
reverent exposition (*exponere reverenter*), 24
Richard II, 107, 152
Rolle, Richard, 223
Roman council of 382, 11
Romans
  6:15, 57
  9:5, 16
  10:4, 197
  16:16, 199
Rosemann, Philipp, 38
Rufinus of Bologna, 46, 49

sabbath, 105
Sabellius, 128, 230

316   Index

sacraments
  administration by priests, 84–85, 90, 123–24, 151, 163–64, 168, 169, 174
  and Christ, 28–29, 31–32, 35, 96–97, 147, 163–64, 178, 179, 181–82, 183–84, 186, 188, 225
  Duns Scotus on, 31–32
  Netter on, 142, 144
  Pecock on, 225, 226
  Woodford on, 94–99
  See also baptism; confession; Eucharist, the
saints, the
  authority of, 23–24, 33, 46, 66, 73, 80, 85, 90, 114–15, 119, 132, 133–34, 160, 172, 227
  communion of, 158, 181, 193
  See also church fathers
salvation
  Augustine on, 108–9
  Christ on, 217
  Hus on, 154, 155
  Pecock on, 226
  truths necessary for, 25, 29, 30–31, 33, 34, 35–37, 46, 47–48, 88–89, 93, 99, 105, 107, 108–16, 126, 127, 144, 154, 155, 156, 184, 187, 201, 206, 218, 260n6
  Woodford on, 93, 108–9, 114
  Wyclif on, 65–66, 142
Sancta Romana, 45
sanctity of exegetes, 21, 80–81, 122, 225
  Augustine on, 7–8, 80, 205
  Bonaventure on, 80, 205
  Gerson on, 205–6
  relationship to authorial intention, 10–11, 12

scriptural authority, 1–11, 12, 23, 25–28, 29, 40, 42–45, 46, 49–53, 72–77, 97, 118, 133–34, 190, 193, 223, 224–25, 227–31
  Aquinas on, 27–28
  Augustine on, 2, 5, 6, 19, 33, 45
  Bury on, 227–31
  d'Ailly on, 45, 189, 196, 197, 198–99, 234
  Gerson on, 45, 189, 205–9, 211, 212, 216, 217–20, 234
  Henry of Ghent on, 3–5, 85
  Hus on, 45, 153–57, 158, 160, 161, 171–72, 189, 198, 216, 233
  Netter on, 118, 120, 121, 137, 145
  Páleč on, 171, 172
  William of Ockham on, 43–45
  Woodford on, 89, 101, 102, 114–15, 116, 120, 207
  Wyclif on, 3, 18, 45, 54–66, 69, 74–75, 78–79, 86–91, 93–94, 96, 101, 102–9, 113, 115, 119, 120, 128, 130, 142–43, 147–48, 171, 197, 198, 199, 212, 216, 229, 231, 233
scripture
  as Book of Life, 9–10, 59, 61–62, 64, 65, 66, 107, 113, 114, 115, 123, 154, 229
  and Christ, 4, 5, 7–9, 19–20, 21, 55, 62–66, 70, 80–81, 87, 103, 104, 107, 113, 132, 133, 142–43, 145, 147, 154–55, 197, 198–99, 211
  Divine Author of, 2–4, 5, 7, 8, 10–11, 12, 13, 17, 18–22, 29, 44, 63, 67, 70, 74, 75, 89, 91, 103, 146, 154, 156, 186, 209, 211, 212, 213, 217, 219
  explicit and implicit truths in, 30–31, 33, 34, 35, 36–37, 61, 87–88, 90–91, 103, 108–11, 140, 145–46, 155, 156, 160, 161–62, 201

and *filioque* doctrine, 15–16, 90, 91, 110
and Holy Spirit, 2, 6, 8, 9, 10, 13, 17, 19–20, 22, 32, 61, 63, 67, 78, 96, 113, 127, 141, 146, 154, 156, 160, 161, 211, 212, 213, 217, 227
and human traditions, 26–39, 74, 87, 94, 102, 103, 105–6, 110, 115, 143, 171–72, 207, 214, 217, 234
interpretation of, 7–9, 10–11, 12, 32, 49, 52, 53, 54, 55, 63, 65–72, 75, 78–81, 94, 96–97, 104, 108, 111, 115, 118, 119–20, 121, 128–29, 130, 135–36, 140, 141, 146, 149, 161, 166, 171, 182, 186, 188, 205, 207, 217–18, 223–24
New Testament, 14, 15, 21, 28, 31–32, 35, 45, 46, 49, 51, 56, 57, 58, 63, 67, 76, 106–7, 196, 197, 225, 228, 230
Old Testament, 14, 17, 19–20, 21, 45, 46, 49, 56, 57, 58, 60, 61, 63, 66, 67, 69, 106, 113, 132, 139, 196, 197, 228, 229, 230
truth in, 2, 3, 4, 5, 7–8, 9–10, 12, 13, 14, 17, 17–18, 21–23, 26, 27–28, 29, 30–31, 32–34, 35–36, 37–38, 45, 52, 53, 54, 58–62, 63, 64–65, 70, 71, 72–73, 80–81, 89–91, 93, 99–100, 107–9, 113, 114–15, 118, 120, 122, 133, 141, 145, 146, 154–55, 160, 161–62, 171, 194, 197–98, 201, 211, 212, 217, 223, 225, 228–30
and university masters, 42–45, 195, 196, 205, 207
See also literal sense; sanctity of exegetes; spiritual sense and literal sense; textual corruption
sense experience, 115

Septuagint, 19, 126
Siebel, F. X., 118
simony, 151, 157, 182, 185, 190, 192
Sirach, 11, 19–20
  24:32, 9
Šmahel, František, 152, 153
Smalley, Beryl, 55
Smith, Kirk, 135
Spiritual Franciscans, 4, 26, 28
spiritual sense and literal sense, 12–14, 20, 24, 67–68, 69–70, 71, 109, 114, 179, 198
Stanislav of Znojmo, 150, 152
  on church authority, 165–66
  on papal authority, 165–66
  on scripture, 166
state of the church (*status ecclesiae*), 48, 89, 182, 209
Stokes, John, 162–63
Summa Parisiensis, 47
Sylvester, 185

Taborites, 143
Tancred, 47
Ten Commandments, 47–48
Terreni, Guido, 118
  on church fathers, 25–26
  on heresy, 2, 26
  on papal infallibility, 52–53, 76, 125, 130, 232–33
textual corruption, 11–12, 17–18, 19, 57, 58–60, 112–14
theology, 37–45
  Bury on, 228, 229
  and canon law, 33, 37–38, 42–45, 85, 91, 200–202
  d'Ailly on, 42, 194–200
  Gerson on, 40, 77, 200, 201, 202, 203, 204, 205–9, 213–16, 219, 221
  Hus on, 154, 156

318   Index

theology (*cont.*)
   William of Ockham on, 43–45, 195
   Wyclif on, 54, 73–74, 75–76, 77–78, 79, 80–81, 91, 199
   See also university masters
2 Thessalonians 2:15, 103, 143
Thomson, S. Harrison, 158
Tierney, Brian, 50, 233
2 Timothy 1:11, 197
Titus, 98
   1:12, 60
   2:10, 142
Tobias, 110, 207
Tobit, Book of, 11, 19–20
Torquemada, Juan de, 49, 220
Totting de Oyta, Henry, 38, 212
   on biblical canon, 18–19
   on extra-scriptural truths, 35–37, 102, 108
   and Wyclif, 57, 60, 67, 114
transubstantiation, 32, 86, 91, 95, 144–46, 163, 174, 184
Trinity, the, 25, 130
   Augustine on, 105, 148
   and consubstantiality, 32, 104, 105, 110, 134, 146, 215
   filioque doctrine, 15–16, 90, 91, 110
   Hus on, 156
   Woodford on, 110
   See also God; Holy Spirit; Jesus Christ
tropological sense, 12, 20, 68, 72
Turley, Thomas, 118
Tyconius, 82

Ullerston, Richard, 193–94
University of Paris, 4, 24, 39–40, 42, 89, 194, 205, 206, 209, 216, 232
   statute of 1340, 22–23, 69, 70

university masters, 3, 4, 17, 33, 71, 112, 175, 190, 205–9, 210, 213–14, 223–24
   authority of, 23–25, 39–45, 51, 54, 73–74, 75–76, 77–78, 79, 80–81, 91, 194–97, 199, 205, 221, 232–35
   Hus as, 170, 173, 176, 223, 234–35
   Wyclif as, 54, 55, 72–78, 80–81, 91, 121–22, 221, 223, 231, 232
   See also theology
Urban I, 102
utraquism, 152, 178–88, 217, 218, 235

Veronica, Saint, 106
Virgil, 60, 62, 139
Virgin Mary, 85, 124, 140–41, 179, 200
Vulgate. *See* Latin Bible, corrupt text of

Waldensians, 208
Waldhauser, Konrad, 151
Wei, Ian, 42
William of Ockham, 111, 199, 200, 203
   Dialogus, 32–35
   as Franciscan, 86, 108, 115–16
   on heresy, 43–44
   on scriptural authority, 43–45
   on theology, 43–45, 195
   on truth, 32–36
William of Saint-Amour, 40
William of St. Thierry, 140
Winterton, Thomas, 72, 86
Wisdom of Solomon
   1:7, 10
   7:26, 3, 9, 10, 73, 91
Woodford, William, 55, 68, 167
   on authority of antiquity, 95–96, 98–99, 100–101, 115, 116
   on baptism, 95–96
   on biblical canon, 103–4, 106–7, 114

on church authority, 97–98, 108,
    111–12, 115, 116, 232
on church hierarchy, 98–99,
    100–101
on creeds, 112
De causis condempnationis, 94–109,
    110
De dominio civili clericorum, 101
on divorce based on consanguinity,
    97–98
on extra-scriptural truths, 28, 93–94,
    99–100, 102, 103–16, 139, 141
as Franciscan, 29, 98, 101–2, 115–16
on general councils, 76, 111–12, 115,
    232
on heresy, 95, 96–97, 98, 104, 107,
    108, 120, 234
on literal sense, 72, 103, 109, 111, 114
on mendicant orders, 86, 87, 92, 97,
    98, 101–2, 109, 116
on papal authority, 101, 107, 112, 232
Quattuor Determinaciones, 109–16
relationship with Netter, 117, 234
on sacraments, 94–99
on the saints, 114–15
on salvation, 93, 108–9, 114
on scriptural authority, 89, 101, 102,
    114–15, 116, 120, 207
on textual corruption, 112–14
on the Trinity, 110
on truths of faith, 93–94, 99–100, 109
on Wyclif's conception of scripture,
    89, 93–94
on Wyclif's exegetical program, 92
on Wyclif's motives, 95
on Wyclif's views of the Eucharist,
    94–95
Wyclif, John
    on the apostles, 83, 143
    on authorial intention, 68–70, 71, 103

on baptism, 95
on biblical canon, 55–63, 106, 131
on canon law, 73–74, 75, 83, 85, 91,
    129, 200, 233
on Christ, 55, 56–57, 58, 59, 62–66,
    69–70, 74, 76, 80, 82, 83, 85, 89,
    142–43, 154, 155, 197
on Christian freedom, 57
on church authority, 54, 58, 63, 74,
    81, 92, 116, 124, 131, 133, 147–48,
    165, 191, 192, 199, 200
on church fathers, 55, 90
on church hierarchy, 55, 78, 139–40,
    208
on church reform, 54, 55, 73, 78, 84,
    85, 86
on civil dominion, 80, 86
on creation, 64, 72–73
on creeds, 103
criticisms of, 1, 29, 54–55, 59–60,
    67, 68, 70–72, 77–81, 83, 84, 86,
    87, 89, 91, 92–116, 117–49, 152,
    153, 162–64
De apostasia, 86
De civili dominio III, 86
De ecclesia, 81, 157–58
De ideis, 153
De religione, 86, 93, 109
De trinitate, 90, 162
De universalibus, 153
De veritate sacrae scripturae, 57, 212
Dialogus, 153
on divine law, 87–89, 195, 197, 200,
    201, 202, 204
on divorce based on consanguinity,
    97–98
on doctrinal development, 86, 90,
    131–32, 149
on the Eucharist, 78, 79–80, 91, 92,
    94–95, 144–46, 152, 174

Wyclif, John (*cont.*)
   on evangelical law (*lex evangelica*), 56–57, 59–60
   on excommunication, 203
   exegetical methodology of, 1, 9, 54–55, 65–72, 78–81, 85, 92, 130, 143, 205
   on faith, 58–60, 89, 90, 91, 109, 119
   on *filioque* clause, 110
   on general councils, 76–77, 136–37
   and Gerson, 40, 45, 67, 72, 156, 201, 202, 203, 204, 205, 206, 207, 209, 210, 212, 213, 214, 225, 234
   on heresy, 63, 73, 74, 76, 77, 84, 89, 95, 116, 118, 128, 206
   on human law, 87–88, 195, 200, 201, 204
   and Hus, 40, 45, 117, 152, 153, 154, 155, 156, 157–58, 162–64, 168, 174, 200, 223, 233
   on the Incarnation, 65–66
   influence in Prague, 54, 143, 150, 152–53, 162–63
   on law of love (*lex amoris*), 56–57
   on literal sense, 67–72, 103, 104, 109, 130, 210, 212
   on marriage, 97–98
   on mendicant orders, 86–89, 94, 101–2, 109, 110, 116, 209
   on moral status of clergy, 83
   and Nicholas of Lyra, 9, 67, 68, 69, 73, 79, 91
   on obedience to God, 85–86
   at Oxford, 18, 71, 77, 78, 122
   pan-propositionalism of, 64
   on papal authority, 40, 55, 57, 63, 74–76, 82–83, 85–86, 89, 102–9, 112, 120, 124, 191, 192, 194, 209, 233
   Postilla super totam bibliam, 56, 69, 249n.5
   on predestination, 81–85, 118, 122–24, 199, 265n.30
   on remanence, 95, 163, 174
   on salvation, 65–66, 142
   on scriptural authority, 3, 18, 45, 54–66, 69, 74–75, 78–79, 86–91, 93–94, 96, 101, 102–9, 113, 115, 119, 120, 128, 130, 142–43, 147–48, 171, 197, 198, 199, 212, 216, 229, 231, 233
   on senses of scripture, 67–72
   on theology, 54, 73–74, 75–76, 77–78, 79, 80–81, 91, 199
   and Totting, 57, 60, 67, 114
   Trialogus, 92, 93, 95–97, 153
   on truth in scripture, 18, 58–62, 63, 64–65, 72–73, 80–81, 89–91, 103–4, 107, 109, 113, 115, 120, 197
   on unity of the scriptures, 56
   on universals, 65
   as university master, 54, 55, 72–78, 80–81, 91, 121–22, 221, 223, 231, 232

Zbyněk Zajíc of Házmburk, 151–52

Ian Christopher Levy
is associate professor of theology at Providence College, Providence, Rhode Island.